HISTORY OF ESOTERIC AND ANAGOGIC DOCTRINES

CIHANGIR GENER

BALBOA.PRESS
A DIVISION OF HAY HOUSE

Translated to English by ARTUN ALYAN

Cover Design by ECE GENER DOGAN

Balboa Press books may be ordered through booksellers or by contacting:

Balboa Press
A Division of Hay House
1663 Liberty Drive
Bloomington, IN 47403
www.balboapress.com
1 (877) 407-4847

ISBN: 978-1-9822-4648-8 (sc)
ISBN: 978-1-9822-4649-5 (e)

Print information available on the last page.

Balboa Press rev. date: 04/20/2020

CONTENTS

ABOUT THE AUTHOR

Cihangir Gener

Was born in Ankara in 1957. He graduated from TED Ankara College (high school) in 1975 and from the Faculty of Communication, Gazi University, in 1979. Between 1978 and 1980, he worked as a reporter in charge of domestic news at Anka Agency. In 1980, started working as international news reporter at Anadolu News Agency, where he worked between the years 1980 and 1985. Establishing Avalon Exports Imports and Trading Co. Ltd. in 1986, he stepped into the private sector. Having gained experience in imports, retailing and free trade, he returned to the Media Sector in 1990. From 1990 to 1992, he worked at the Economic Bulletin Agency (EBA); in 1993, he started working at the Radio and Television Supreme Council (RTUK), as an expert in the Department of Monitoring and Evaluation. Following this post, he was appointed as Head of Local and Regional Broadcasting Department. Between the years 2002 and 2004, worked as the Executive Editor of RTUK Communication Magazine. After completing his 25 years in the Press sector, Gener was granted the Permanent Press Card. In 2006, he retired from his post in RTUK. Gener, who later worked in various magazines and newspapers as editor and columnist, as well as foreign relations advisor for several private companies from 2006 to 2010, is a member of the Association of Journalists and the GLFAAM of Turkey.

Cihangir Gener's first book, titled the History of Esoteric and Anagogic Doctrines was printed in 1993. The second volume of this book was printed in 2000. Later, in 2000, the two volumes were combined and re-printed. This work has already been printed 17 times, and is being used as supplementary course book in some universities. Owing to Gener's intensive efforts, this work has evolved into an encyclopedia. Comprising 4 volumes, this encyclopedia, named as "Encyclopedia of Esoterical Teachings" is published this year (2019).

Gener's second book, titled "Hiram Abiff", based on the life of the legendary patriarch of the Free Masonry, was printed in 2002. This book was re-printed for the fourth time in 2019. His third book, explaining the unknown aspects of Jesus' life, "Son of the Light" was published in 2010, followed by its second edition in 2014.

Another book of Gener, titled "Quantum, Scientific Proof of Esoterism", was published in 2013, and re-printed in 2014 and in 2019, with the addition of its second volume. This book has the intent to unite the latest scientific foundings on Quantum Physics with thousands of years old Esoterical Doctrine. Gener's another work "God, I am coming back to you" (a study on Pantheistic Philisophy), which was published in 2013 and re-printed in 2014, proceeded. His latest book, "Illuminati, The Supreme Mind" was published in 2018. Gener is currently working on his new book: "Tarot - The Atlantis Initiation System" concurrently.

Cihangir Gener, who has a good command of English, is married with three daughters.

PREFACE

When I first took Brother Cihangir Gener's book in hand, I honestly did not think that I would come across such an alluring and informative piece of work. However, as I turned over the pages, I promptly came to realize that his works would enlighten our cultural history, so I could not put the book aside.

Ever since man has become aware of his existence, he started looking for the answers to two questions: The former being "how" he came to exist, and the latter "why" he exists. Man gave the answer to the first question in various ways, but always through the existence of a super power to always order or at least permit man's existence, and when man was troubled in answering why such a superpower wanted such an existence, he reached the conclusion that there was no way other than "believing" in certain causes but follow this belief; as a result, man came to accept that existence could not be limited to the mortal life on Earth, and that the soul was an independent existence of the body at another level, that the soul continued life either by living in another human's body, or reaching immortality in a place called Eternity. When that was the case, it was then considered that the limited period which the soul spent with the body was accepted as a period of examination leading to eternal torture and misery, or conversely the infinite welfare and prosperity of the soul.

However, expressing the answer as such not only led man to think of death throughout his lifetime, to reject world's blessings so as to gain and deserve eternal life, but also caused to sow seeds of dispute among people. Those who belong to different religions but are believers of one sole God, have spent their lives dissimilating their temples, holy books, festivity days, even their holidays and attire, as well as labelling cemeteries and even 'life to come' such as "your temple – my temple", "your cemetery" – "my cemetery", and tried to divide up that sole God's heaven (or hell) by naming it as "my heaven" – "your heaven".

Hence, the esoteric way of thinking has gone beyond all that, interpreting a school of thought where the holy books are not expressed by their words but by their essence, and representing a movement that "faith" could not contradict "wisdom", that people could not be forced to believe in some actions and orders that they could not prove by their intelligence. However, this movement has always been rejected by those who could only understand the form of a religion, rather than its essence, and the supporters of this current have always been accused everywhere of denying their religions. Dante, who never hesitated to reflect the esoteric philosophy, even in the scholastic dark ages, said the following, in the section related to "Heaven" in the "Divina Commeida – Divine Comedy":

> "Listen, they always call for Christ,
> They always cry out for Christ,
> In eternal life will they
> Be no closer to Christ
> Than those who do not recognize Christ!"

It is not sufficient to belong to whatever religion or to go to the Synagogue, the Church or the Mosque to be able to enter Heaven. Despite not having fulfiled any of those mentioned, a person who is honest, kind, merciful and generous will be closer to Christ and still go to Heaven with respect to those who have done nothing but call out his name all their lives.

As a matter of fact, against all odds, quarrels on religion that continue even today among the peoples who have accepted and declared that they are the creatures of the sole God, and that they are brothers, the Esoteric way of thinking becomes all the more important. It is owing to this way of thinking that people can grasp the real religion, the REAL COMMANDS that lead them to happiness, peace, and sinlessness, and could reach the virtue of living, as God wished. Starting with Cabala and continuing with the Templars and finding its sublime voice in the Islamic mysticism, this line will continue to exist, despite all kinds of restraint from different directions, for as long as there is the 'thinking human being'.

As well expressed by Brother Namik Kemal, "Work, remove the cognizance from humanity, if at all possible". However, as the removal of this cognizance is not possible, these restraints will always be diverted by mankind.

I congratulate my Brother Cihangir Gener for this work in which he expresses all these issues, and I wholeheartedly recommend it to all luminaries.

Prof. Dr. Sahir ERMAN

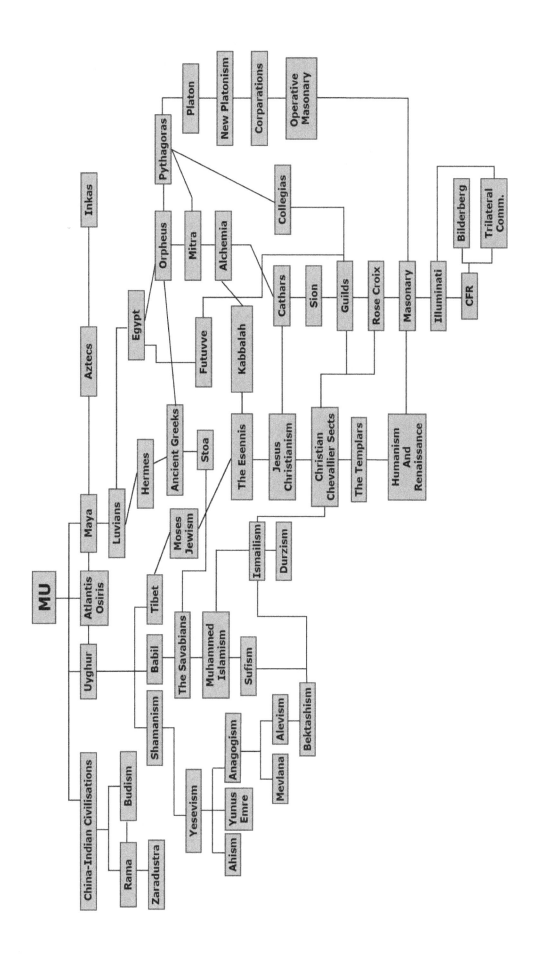

GETTING STARTED...

The reason why I have decided to write this book is to show the discrepancies and similarities between the basic trend, as old as or even older than the human history known by which it has been shaped and Freemasonry, the prominent supporter of this trend today along with other organizations still existing or those embedded in time. This trend, which is known as "esoteric" and "anagogic", is a trend which defends the main principles that can only be perceived with love and can only be revealed by radical thinking, and which solely aims at Man evolving into perfect human beings, and thus allowing them to conjoin with God. Esoteric Doctrines, known as "pantheism" in the world of philosophy, has taken the name "Sufism" in the Moslem World, showing its biggest effect in the modern world through Freemasonry, and has played an important role in the formation of the western culture.

For thousands of years, a great deal has been said and written on Esoteric Doctrines. However, these teachings and their institutions have never been taken into account in a chronological order. None of the information that I wrote down here is new. As the elderly have put it: "there is no word unvoiced in the Sun". My aim is to detect the traces of this trend, which served as the key factor in the naissance of numerous religions besides many other philosophical movements, starting from the dark phases of history, and to bring it to the present day in a chronological order. In doing this, I have diligently tried to follow a historic route and show how a society with esoteric beliefs has affected the others.

I consider myself lucky as I was born in Turkiye (Turkey), at the perfect geographical point of the world, where this book could be written. It is at this geography that all civilizations meet. (This geography is the meeting point of all civilizations). Who knows, perhaps there is a reason for my existence at this place, at this time. It is not possible to abstract esoteric doctrines from human history. This land, which has been the birthplace of many philosophical trends, as well as several monotheistic religions, has given me the opportunity to study them on-site.

While writing this book, in order not to distract my readers, I have intentionally avoided writing footnotes and indicating references. Instead, works and references cited have been given at the end of each chapter.

I am deeply grateful to Professor Sahir Erman, Mr. Can Arpaç, Mr. Kaya Güvenç, and Proffessor Bozkurt Güvenç, who have not hesitated to contribute in evolving my book. I dedicate this book to my wife Seda and my daughters Aysim, Burcu and Ece, who have beautified my working environment.

I hope that my book succeeds in enlightening the current esoteric teachings and the light of Almighty enlightens those working along this route.

Cihangir Gener Ankara, October 10th, 1993

A NOTE FOR THE CONSOLIDATED AND EXPANDED PRINT

In 1993, when I started writing the History of Esoteric and Anagogic Doctrines, resources related to the subject matter were scarce and the theories put forward on the issue were respectively limited in Turkey, when compared to references available today. The number of publications made available in the market in the past 9 years, the richness of their contents almost try to prove that the current millennium is the period of illumination. This heavy flow of rich information pushed me to review my work and urged me to add new sections and chapters.

In time, these additions became so much that the content of the book doubled, compared to earlier issues. Thus the second volume of the History of Esoteric and Anagogic Doctrines got published separately. However, the issues were so interlaced and the steps followed each other so closely that, separation of some of the issues in the second volume was accompanied by some break-offs and constraints in the subjects associated with some unforeseen difficulties. Hence, the decision of combining the two volumes in one and having an enlarged version for the ninth issue with consecutive écoles was under strong influence. Additionally, for every edition to come, the plan was to place further additions so that in time, these studies would evolve into an encyclopedia.

In each enlarged issue, the readers will find the step by step rise of each esoteric and anagogic école within the time scale, and they will find that they are less affected by the historic brake-offs. All the positive feedback I have received from the readers over the years is also an indication that there really is a major lack of information in the contemporary Turkish philosophical world.

Additionally, seeing that my work is being referenced to in many studies carried out in this field, has been giving me a tremendous pleasure.

My master and respected peer, Prof. Dr. Sahir Erman, who had kindly written the foreword for the first edition of this book, rendered us great sorrow by passing away unexpectedly. My only consolidation is, I am sure that this perfect human being is now resting at a level well deserved. I hereby take this opportunity to comemorate him with my deepest respect.

I also feel that I am indebted to Honourable Master Teoman Güre, the Khalif Father, who has been a mentor to me on the "Bektashism" section of the enlarged issue, and has helped me to convey more detailed information.

Mor Efrem, an Assyrian clergy, who lived in the 4th century A.D., had said: "A thirsty person becomes happy when he drinks water. However, he never feels unhappy because he could not dry out the spring from which he drank water. The spring quenches his thirst, but does not dispose of source of thirst. If you have managed to quench your thirst without destroying the spring, you can drink from the same spring again, each time you feel thirsty. If you destroy the source when you quench your thirst, winning against the source can be to your disadvantage in the future. Be grateful for what you could take, but never complain about what is left behind. What you can take will be your share; however, whatever is left behind can still be your legacy". I know that this work of mine has got quite a distance to cover to quench the thirst of people. I am constantly trying to quench my thirst and am grateful for what I could get so far. For and on behalf of those who are in need of quenching their thirst, I consider myself obliged to offer them one more gulp and I present this enlarged issue to the discredition of my readers.

Cihangir Gener
Ankara 2003

CHAPTER I

ESOTERIC AND ANAGOGIC DOCTRINES

From the day he was born and with the tiniest sign of intelligence, mankind had started questioning where he came from and where he was going, and the moment he thought that he found the holy answer, he fought with the others who believed in other holy answers, without hesitating to kill them. Whilst the masses got fanatically committed to these answers, in other words religions, within the frame of the rules put down, the priests, who kept the real understanding of the esoteric teachings to themselves, thinking that ordinary people would not be able to understand the philosophy of the answers with their lack of knowledge, formed a system of secrets.

Teaching of the esoteric-anagogic secrets only to a certain group of people who are qualified to learn them, encompasses both the weak and the strong side of this doctrine which has played an important role in establishing today's civilization. As the teachings had exposed the secrets only to people who attained a certain level of education and personal development, this caused the teachings to remain as doctrines isolated from the masses of people. On the other hand, the fact that the secrets had been utterly well kept within the context of the language of symbols, which at every age were assigned different meanings parallel to the development of civilization, made the formation of brotherhood organizations possible by keeping these secrets throughout human history and bringing them to this day.

What are these secrets? What is the content of this doctrine that has had a great impact on the formation of current civilization and has helped the current era to be a period of secular rationalism?

Esoteric and Anagogic doctrines is expressed as Pantheism in the field of philosophy. Whereas the monotheistic religions have the dilemma of a creator and the created, in Pantheism, there is no such dilemma. Everything which exists has emanated from God and they are all identical with/to Him.

The Cosmos and God are one. God is not the creator, but the one who is present and represents the whole of the universe. God, who is eternal, exists both in the Macro and Micro Cosmos. The Spirit, which is a component of the Divine Light, never perishes, and its ultimate aim is to return to the main source where it came from, that is to God. The only way of achieving this is through evolution, which is a universal law code, i.e., perfection. The most important issue here is the spirit and the perfection of the spirit. For the spirit, matter is just something to be used and disposed of, a tool to move to the next level, an expression of existence in time. In the path of life, which starts with a divine emanation and can only be terminated by returning to God, man is the expression of divine existence at its highest known level. Man, comprising the trio of spirit-life-body, is the Micro cosmos. A Micro cosmos is identical to Macro cosmos, which consists of the father-mother and the son, or the ore and life, which is to God.

Perfection is nothing other than conversion of hidden potentials to active powers.[1] The universal law that enables the evolution of the spirit, in other words, the law which lets the spirit return to the main source is the law of renaissance. The chain of renaissance that enables the formation of spirit in

1

non-living things, which are the expressions for existence in the lowest form, to the perfect human being at the highest level, can only be broken when the spirit reaches perfection and returns to God.

In fact, all matter is alive, and its smallest particles are the essentials of life. There is no spirit without any matter, and no matter without any spirit. Matter continues to exist in the universe in seven states or strata. In the physical universe, the first sub stratum consists of simple atoms. The second is a simple combination of these atoms, or electromagnetic form of the physical matter. The third sub stratum is the light, or the energy form of matter. The fourth is its fire form. The fifth is the form called as gas by the chemists, or is the Air, esoterically. The sixth stratum of matter is the liquid, or the Water. Finally, the seventh stratum is the solid form, which is the Earth.[2]

For the spirit, the physical world is a school to be visited to learn and to gain experience. In this school, everyone experiences the enlightment sparks that show why they have to accept this examination or the other. The law of incarnation pushes the soul to find a body. As a result of this body finding, the world seems like a place where the spiritual energies are renewed. In other words, every incarned spirit will experiment a new aspect of life and will evolve this.[3]

Through lives ending one after the other, man gains more experience and these experiences form his real personality and capabilities. The differences seen between man's abilities, are proportionate to their experiences gained in previous lives and their level of personality development. Each soul starts a new life with the capabilities and personalities gained in his/her previous lives. Each new life, unless otherwise required in previous lives, starts from the top level of the previous life.

Thus, the development of consciousness and the evolution of the soul are achieved. For example, patience is one of the most difficult virtues to be achieved, and is very valuable in that sense for the development of personality.[4]

Besides returning to Earth in different countries and different time scales, the soul will experiment both male and female characteristics. Each soul lives in numerous countries and periods, testing its powers by learning different cultures and communities. It explores the divinity and creativity that lay within. The soul is not alone in approaching the divine target. It is together with other souls and learns to love them. True love relations continue infinitely. In that sense, it is possible to talk of dual or multiple incarnations of the soul, rather than an isolated one.[5]

Only the spiritually well-developed human beings remember their previous lives. Only for the "wisdom students" are many secrets, including some of their secrets from previous lives not behind a veil. Very rarely are their previous lives unveiled. It is only when the soul passes through the physical border of the Earth is this curtain unveiled; that is after death. Otherwise, prematurely learned past experiments and lives may even cause the evolution to cease.[6]

Normally, an easy and light combination is a difficult examination. It is difficult for a human being in affluence to make a breakthrough on the path to evolution, and to rise to the next level. The reason behind seeing sorrow and illness around, rather than well-being and happiness, is that eventually, the evolution of the soul is targeted. The summit to be reached is not within the life being lived. The intent is for the soul to evolve to reach the peak of the general evolvement plan; that is, to reach God. In other words, whether a person lived comfortably or not has no significance. The only foresight of the general evolution law is the soul to advance another step in the path of evolution.

It would be wrong for a person to curse his faith because of the misfortunate experiences that he has had to undergo and claim that justice does not exist. Because, what he had to live through is not only the outcome of his wrongdoings in his previous lives, but also it is aimed that these experiences will be overcome successfully for the soul to evolve. True evolution can only be built on wisdom and beauty.[7]

Since the universe is identical to God and that there is no existence other than God, both concepts related to 'good' and 'bad' are expressions of God. However, what matters is the love, the good. The highest known expression of the divine emanation, the human being, is the field where the good and the bad fight against each other. Nonetheless, what matters is love and benevolence and that the universe has been created on love, so only the soul of a good human being can turn into a perfect human being and can unite with God. Those who have been good all their lives, are incarnated at a level higher than their existing one. A bad person on the other hand, due to the law of incarnation, goes back to the previous step of evolvement/evolution.

What is the law of evolvement/evolution and how does it work? As a result of the divine eruption or of the "Big Bang" in scientific words, material world was formed. Within the physical rules of the universe, the solar systems were formed and the conditions required for the formation of life gathered at least in one planet, our planet the Earth. This does not necessarily mean that there is no life in other planets. Moreover, to claim that the only aim of the divine emanation was to form the human being only, would be a sign of human egoism. Today, the scientists accept, at least in theory, that there is life in millions of other planets, besides the Earth. However, the current technology is not advanced enough to justify this theory. Thus, we cannot know whether the last stop for the soul to reach Divine Light is the Perfect Human (Kamil Man), or are there well-qualified creatures, who are closer to God elsewhere in the universe. However, if such creatures do exist, it is only natural for the Perfect Human to be re-born as one of them.

Anyhow, the rest remains to be that creature's issue. For this reason, our book will be confined to the evolution of the Perfect Human (Kamil Man).

Scientific research has shown that, the chemical elements accepted as non-living organisms, provided that the environmental conditions are appropriate, turn into "RNA" and "DNA" molecules, which are the foundations of life. The molecules have formed the single cellular living organisms which in the course of time have formed other more complicated ones. The last stages of this evolution law, which was scientifically clarified for the first time by Darwin, involves mammals, types of apes and lastly mankind.

So, what is the aim of God to enforce the law of evolution? This question is answered differently by monotheistic religions and by esoteric doctrines. Monotheistic religions claim that God who knows everything and is the sole creator, has created the universe for the need of being worshipped to. However, there is no logical answer for the question why should God who does not need anything, be in need of being worshipped to, and even if he did need to be worshipped, why has He created all the universe, instead of creating only the servants to worship him?

On the other hand, esoteric doctrines claim that God only wanted to get to know himself better. Through the existence and living experiences of innumerous creatures within his constitution, God becomes more aware of his characteristics and thus reach a higher level of consciousness. God's primary resource in getting to know Himself better is the Perfect Human being, representing the human beings with his profound experience and thinking capacity. At this stage, it would be wise to state that Man, being a divine creation is thus an expression of God. For this reason, it would be true to say that Man is God or "I am God". However, God is not a human being. Because God is all the creatures and whole of the universe. It would be wrong to say that God is a human being, while it is true to say Man is God.

According to esoteric doctrines, due to the fact that the primary tool in increasing the divine consciousness is the Perfect Human being, the only aim should be to raise Kamil Men. Bringing up Kamil Men can only be possible by educating exquisite people who have the capacity of understanding this high level of teaching. That is why, in order to raise such Perfect Human beings, various organizations have been founded and a system of secret codes has been formed since thousands of years ago.

The language used in these teachings has been the "Language of Symbols" by whose symbolic verbalism mankind has benefited. This language of symbols has been well preserved for thousands of years nearly in each tribe and community and transferred from generation to generation through initiated people.

The word "initiation" roots from the Latin word "initiato", which means "starting to learn the secrets". The initiated on the other hand, is the person accepted into the Teaching of Secrets with a ceremony. In fact, in Greek, "initiatia" means "concluding". However, when Cicero translated this concept into Latin, he used "initiatio" which means "starting". As death and birth are experienced together in an initiation ceremony, in other words, as the beginning and the end are the same, it is not possible to speak of a paradox. [8]

The very first organization of brotherhood we could trace, whose teachings with symbols were passed from generation to generation through initiated people, is the "Nacaal Brotherhood". This organization, the cradle of the first great civilization ever known, buried in the water about 12 thousand years ago, is the organization of ruling priests in "Mu" continent in the Pacific, [9]

References

1 Stulginsky, Stepan- *The Cosmic Myths of the East*, (Doğunun Kozmik Efsaneleri), Im Trio Publications, Istanbul 2003, p. 45
2 Stulginsky, Stepan, r.w., p. 46
3 Stulginsky, Stepan, r.w., p. 112
4 Stulginsky, Stepan, r.w., p. 121
5 Stulginsky, Stepan, r.w., p. 114
6 Stulginsky, Stepan, r.w., p. 124
7 Stulginsky, Stepan, r.w., p. 134
8 Freke, Timothy & Gandy, Peter- *The Secrets of Jesus*, (İsa'nın Gizemleri), Ayna Publications- Istanbul 2005, p. 341
9 Churchward James,- *The Children of MU*, (Mu'nun Çocukları), London 1931.

CHAPTER II

MU CIVILISATION AND THE NACAALS

Most of the information we have on the Mu Continent and the Mu civilization is obtained from the explorations of the 19th century British explorer James Churchward. Churchward, who was a colonel in the British Army, was first informed on Mu when he was working in India and Tibet in the 1880's. He continued his efforts in Central America after he retired, and wrote five books on this wracked civilization.

Churchward's sources were the "Nacaal Tablets" given to him in a temple in Tibet, by the arch bishop of that temple, and the tablets found by the American geologist William Niven in Mexico, between 1921 and 1923.[1]

Orthodox* scientists have been skeptical on both the Mu civilization unveiled by Churchward, and the existence of Atlantis, another sunken continent.

However, the science world approves that, prior to when these two continents had sunk 12 thousand years ago, a major geological event had taken place. Furthermore, the myths of a

* Orthodox: Conservative

great flood occurring in almost every tribe and every nation in the world justify that there had been a great disaster, and whether this fact is accepted by the orthodox scientists or not, numerous works, whose origins cannot be traced, such as the Egyptian and Mayan ruins, and the statues in Easter Island, can be logically explained owing to the sunken continent civilizations.

According to the theory of evolution and the overall findings, 200 to 500 thousand years ago, "Homo Erectus" which could stand on his two feet, was replaced by "Homo Sapiens", the thinking human being. Even if we accept the fact that the Homo Sapiens have existed for the past 200 thousand years, it would be great selfishness to presume that mankind have merely created contemporary civilization since then. What had happened was that the Homo Sapiens, who had existed for the last 200 thousand years, and whose brain weight and thinking capacity assumed to have been the same as the present-day human being, had decided, after having waiting for 194 thousand years, to take giant steps in the last 6 thousand years. How could this have happened? As a matter of fact, the scientists today claim that the wheel and scripture were invented around 4 thousand B.C. However, although only very few documents and findings have remained due to the floods and disasters the world underwent, these documents and other findings suggest that mankind had created at least one other great civilization besides the contemporary one, and that the foundations of the present-day civilization had been laid during that ancient civilization.

In 1883, James Churchward unveiled the most important ones of those documents, in a temple in Western Tibet.

Churchward, was on duty in Tibet. While visiting old temples in Tibet, in line with his research on the roots of old religions, Churchward came across this temple in Western Tibet. Rishi, one of the prominent members of the "Great Ecclesiastic Brotherhood", and the archbishop of that temple, showed Churchward the "Nacaal Tablets", inscribed 15 thousand years before the present day.[2]

It is not clear why Rishi had shown Churchward the tablets that had been kept secret for thousands of years. However, it is assumed that Rishi, who was an initiated person himself, felt close to Churchward, who was a member of Freemasonry, another form of brotherhood that kept the esoteric doctrine alive, and thus must have decided that it was time that some of the secrets were revealed to the western world. Bearing the same perspective, the priests in Tibet had given the secrets of Nacall to Jesus, two thousand years ago.

Governed by these thoughts, Rishi mastered Churchward for two years, and taught him the extinct language the Nacaal tablets had been inscribed in.[3] Having learned the Naacal language and inspected the tablets, Churchward started his explorations, which lasted 50 years, with the hope of finding the sunken continent and the civilizsation of Mu.

Inspecting almost all the islands in the Pacific, Siberia, Central Asia, Australia, and Egypt, a new source of light shone on Churchward in Mexico. American geologist William Niven found around 2 thousand 600 tablets during his diggings in Mexico from 1921 to 1923, which were determined to have been inscribed between 11 thousand 500 and 12 thousand years ago.[4] The inscriptions on these tablets could be read neither by Niven, nor by Dr. Morley, a specialist from Carnegie Institute, who also inspected the tablets. Hearing of the presence of the tablets, Churchward went to Mexico and managed to read the tablets in Nacaal language, which he had learned in Tibet. Having completed the missing information in Tibet tablets with the information on the tablets found in Mexico, Churchward wrote his sensational books on the sunken civilization of Mu.[5]

Findings of Churchward and Niven revealed that the continent of Mu covered majority of the present-day Pacific Ocean and that the islands of Hawaii, Haiti, Fidji, Easter and Poloneisa were remainders of this sunken continent. On the other hand, Danish researcher and writer Erich von Daniken underlines the fascinating similarities in the cultures of these islands thousands of kilometers apart from one another.[6]

According to Churchward, the continent of Mu was a giant continent stretching 5 thousand kilometers from East to West, 8 thousand kilometers from North to South. Nacaal Tablets propose that this continent is the cradle of civilization. Having a civilization history of almost 70 thousand years, Mu had formed, over time, several colonies and empires all over the world.[7]

The two most important states were Atlantis and Uygur Empires, which were initially colonized and later made autonomous by the Mu civilization.[8] In addition, what we acknowledge as Ancient Egypt, China, India and Maya civilizations also originated from the Mu civilization.

It is not known when the Mu civilization started. Nacaal tablets and the ones found in Mexico could not shed light to this issue. Nevertheless, the tablets depict that Mu started colonization and spreading its religion which formed the foundation of its civilization 70 thousand years ago.

Nacaal tablets, which have been determined to be around 15 thousand years old, encompass detailed predictions about the beginning of the universe and its emergence. According to these tablets, there was merely the spirit in the beginning of the universe. Then, from this spirit emerged a chaos-governed space. In time, this chaos subsided and gave way to order, and the shapeless and scattered gases gathered. These gases became solid in order to form the solar systems and the planets. During the solidification, first the air, then the water was formed. The water covered the Earth. The sun rays heated the air and the water. These rays and the fire under the earth raised the land covered with water and this land became exposed soil. The sun rays formed the cosmic eggs (RNAs and DNAs) in the water and in the mud. The first form of life rose from the water and spread out around the Earth.

It cannot be a coincidence to have such a close match to currently valid theories on formation of the universe and of the life. Anyhow, it would be nonsense to expect something different from a civilization at least 70 thousand years old. It is also possible to trace the level achieved by the Mu Civilisation from other sources. In the Mahabharata, written in India at least 3 thousand years ago, a weapon used by the human beings in the distant past is described: "A bullet that had the brightness of a smokeless fire, scattering flames was shot. Suddenly, everywhere became dark. Later, there was a light with blinding brightness and a deafening noise. With the immense heat that followed, all the waters evaporated. Elephants, horses and human beings were instantly burned. Trees were completely parched. When everything was brightened again, all that was left over from a huge army was a handful of ashes..."

In the Indian Samsaptakabadha inscriptions, planes travelling with celestial forces and a gun with a blasting force equal to that of ten thousand suns are mentioned.

In Mausola Purva, written in Sanskrit language, a steel lightning turning a whole tribe into ashes is mentioned. Hair and nails of few survivors had dropped, the corpses had burned beyond recognition, the birds had become completely white and the food had become completely inedible.

These myths and narratives show that, despite the level of civilisation that our ancestors had achieved, their world, just as the world we live in today, had not benefited much from peace, either. Like the vanishing of Sodom and Gaomora, from Indian myths and sagas, various other myths seem to support one of the theories on the sinking of the Atlantis and Mu continents. However, as we are going to deal with this subject later, let us now have a look at the regime in the Mu civilisation and its tool, the very first monotheistic religion, the religion of the Mu.

Mu civilisation was an empire and the title of the emperor was "Ra Mu", meaning the Son of the Sun. The other name of the Mu empire was the "Sun Empire." In Mu language, "Ra" meant sun. In Egypt, the colony of Mu, the sun god was also named "Ra." In Japan, the roots of which are assumed to go back to the Mu civilisation, the title of the empire is the "Son of the Sun." Besides these, the kings in the ancient Maya and Inka civilisations used the same titles.

Under the emperor, there were the Nacaals, who were both scientists and priests, forming the governing class.[9] The "Mu Religion", disseminated all over the world by the Nacaals, who were members of the "Sacred Secrets Brotherhood", was probably the first monotheistic religion that mankind had met. When Nacaals were relating this religion to ordinary people in the main land and in the colonies, they preferred to use the language of the symbols, which was easier to understand. Esoteric meanings of these symbols were only known by the initiated brethren and the emperor Ra-Mu.

Naacal symbols mostly consisted of geometrical symbols. Nacaal teaching predicted that the most important task in the emergence of the universe was that geometry and architecture were God's attributes. According to Mu religion, God was so a holy being that, its name could not be directly spoken of. In Nacaal tablets, the creator is defined as: "The creator is not something that can be perceived by ordinary people. He cannot be picturized, nor can he be named. He is the one without any name." If God was not defined by a symbol, he could not be cognized by ordinary people. Therefore, the symbol for this Mighty Creation was the Celestial Father, the Sun, or "Ra".[10] The main conception that underlies all distorted claims that God is the Sun, or beliefs named as the Sun Cult, is this phenomenon.

Worshipping the "Celestial Father" is common concept in many religions. In the Indian Vedas, name of the Celestial Father is "Dyaus Pitar", in ancient Greek, it is "Zue Pater", later converted to "Zeus", in Rome, "Jupitar" has the same meaning.[11] In Nacaal Tablets, God is mentioned as "Our Father in the Sky". In fact, Jesus, who had disseminated his teachings based on this archaic religion, mentioned of God as "Our Father in the Sky". Churchward states that the teaching of Jesus is identical to that of Osiris, and that they both benefited from the holy scripts of Mu. As these subjects are going to be mentioned later, let us continue analyzing the Nacaal teaching.

In Nacaal teaching, the Sun was not explicitly God himself, but just a symbol to be better understood by masses that he was just the one and only. Another purpose of using the symbols was to prevent certain expression styles to become stereotyped and to relieve religion of dogmas and bigotry, by giving new meanings to symbols.

However, over time, when civilisation collapsed and the main source vanished, each of these symbols were idolized and caused the polytheistic religions to emerge.

The head priest of the religion teaching how to worship a Single God through the use of symbols, also the head of the holy brotherhood organization, was Ra Mu himself. However, the emperor had no Divine personality but was bearing the title of the 'Sun's Son', merely on account of his status quo.

The temples where the Nacaal Brethren disseminated their teachings and initiated the new members were scattered all over the continent and the colonies. These temples made of giant stone blocks, had no roof and they were called the "transparent temples". The temples used to be built without roofs, so that the rising sun could shine directly on the initiated. This was also a kind of symbol and esoterically it meant there could be no obstacles between God and the human being. In present-day Freemasonry, the same symbol is used and all Masonic Temples' ceilings are built symbolizing the sky, as though they have no roof.

The prominent symbol of Mu religion is the "Mu Cosmic Diagram."[12]

Mu Cosmic Dyagram

In this diagram, the circle bang in the middle is the collective symbol of "Ra", or the Single God. The circle in the triangle symbolizes that God is always watching the human beings. The two concentric triangles symbolize that the good and the evil exist together.

The triangle pointing upwards symbolizes the good, and thus reaching God, whereas the one pointing downwards represents resurrection according to the law of reincarnation. The star with six points in the form of two concentric triangles, is the symbol of Divine Justice.

Additionally, each point of this star represents a virtue, and the human being can reach God, only after achieving all of these virtues. The circle outside the six-pointed star represents that there are other worlds other than the earth, and the 12 loops surrounding the outer circle represent the 12 evil tendencies from which man must keep away. It is obligatory that the human soul be purged from these 12 worldly evil tendencies, prior to transferring to other macrocosms.

The eight lane road pointing downward is the representation of the stages the soul has to ascend, in order to reach God. The soul has to reach perfection; that is the Perfect Human being status, starting from the very bottom, the non-living thing status.

In Naacal temples, the moon is situated as a symbol, next to the Sun. The masculine symbol of God, who is the father, is the Sun, whereas its feminine (mother) symbol is the Moon. As can be seen in the cosmic diagram, in Nacaal teaching, the triangle and the number three are of vital importance. This importance given to the figure of three, roots from the Mu continent itself. Mu continent is a group of islands that consists of three main parts, separated by narrow straits.[13] That is why, the triangle represents both the continent of Mu, and the masculine and feminine aspects of the God, and the Divine Remark emanated from it, which is the universe. The eye inside the triangle represents that the main source, in other words God is always felt to be among humans, that He somewhat watches the human being. The watch is the duty of the Nacaals, who are the guardians of the God's teachings. This symbol had been used in Atlantis through Osiris, Egypt by Hermes, Greece by Pythagoras, and finally, the Freemasonry, in modern times.

Like most symbols, the initiation ceremonies, where members of the Esoteric Secrets Teachings are accepted, root from Mu Nacaal School. In this initiation ceremony that has reached the present day through different types of organizations, following a long and tedious preparation and investigation period, the candidate, if found appropriate, would be accepted to the brotherhood. There is no further information on this issue apart from the fact that the members were accepted into Nacaal brotherhood through an initiation ceremony. However, there is no reason to think that the initiation ceremony in the Hermetic Brotherhood of Egypt which is accepted as the last stop of Nacaal Brotherhood is any different from the ceremony used by the Nacaals. As the details of this ceremony will be seen while discussing the Egyptian Civilisation, let us return to other concepts of Nacaal teaching:

Mu religion has four basic concepts:

1. God is unique. Everything has been created from Him and they will all return to Him.
2. The spirit and the body are separate from one another. The body dies and the spirit remains alive during partition.
3. The spirit is reincarnated in different bodies, in order to reach perfection.
4. The spirit that has reached perfection returns to God and unites with Him.[14]

According to Nacaal training, God is the love itself, and created the whole universe based on love. Only the spirits that are capable of understanding this universal love will be able to return. To be a human being equipped with these qualities can only be possible by becoming a Naacal Brother and by assimilating these teachings properly and gradually. Naacals admit that only the master priests will be able to achieve this level.

Another basic foundation of Naacal teaching is the theory that the four basic powers emerged from the Divine Light transformed the universe from chaos to order. These four basic powers, accepted to be among the fundamental characteristics of God, are known as "the four great builders", "the four great architects", or "the four great geometry masters". These four basic elements are fire, air, water and earth.[15] The scientists today accept that immediately after the Big Bang, these four powers became active and the universe was transformed from chaos to order.

With the birth of Abrahamic religions, these four basic elements were named as the "four head angels". Nacaals have symbolised these four basic powers with a swastika, crooked cross. From the crooked crosses observed on the tablets found by geologist Niven, we notice that four arms of equal length represents that these four essential powers are equal, and that the arms of the crosses being bent towards left represents the good, whereas those bent towards right the evil. It is not a coincidence that Hitler, who had investigated these issues in depth, had chosen a cross with arms bent to right for his empire. The cross symbol, used in the teachings of Jesus, had also rooted from the same source, Mu.

Brahman priests said that they founded their religion based on holy tablets called "Neferits", and that the "Hanferit" language that these tablets were written in was the oldest language in the world. In his work on the Indian history, written in 1794, British researcher W. Robertson claimed that Brahmans learned this language and the religion from the Nagas.[16] It has been noted by Churchward that Nagas were the Indian branch of the Mu Empire. Through India, the Nacaal teachings had reached upper Egypt and Mesopotamia. Founders of both of these civilisations are the Nagas.

Some of the symbols unveiled by Niven, symbolizing the four basic powers.

According to Churchward, the stone tablets of Moses were copies of Naga scripts, inscribed in Mu language and Mu alphabet. With respect to Moses' teachings, Churchward explains the following: "There is no doubt that Moses based his religious laws on the pure Osiris religion, as taught by Toth. In the temple of Osiris, where the spirit is questioned, with respect to its physical life, there is a figure of God symbolizing 42 questions asked. Moses turned these 42 questions into 10 commandments, understandable to ordinary people. The biggest difference of Moses was that these commandments were to be applied not to the dead, but to people alive. The contents of the ten commandments are present also in the holy scripts of Mu. The only difference is that they are in question form."[17] In fact, Moses is an Osiris priest and is fully aware of all details of the religion rooting from Mu. Naga teachings and Osiris religion are based on the same root. As a result of the unification of Egypt, both religions intermingled and evolved into a single teaching. Moses' scripts are written partly in Naga, partly in Egyptian language.

During his exile in Babylon, Ezra learned the Naga language used in Babylon. However, as he could not really grasp the real meanings of the holy hieroglyphics of Egypt, there had been many mistakes in writing the Old Testament. These issues will be dealt with in detail, in the following chapters.

References

1   Science Research Group (Bilim Araştırma Grubu)- *MU, Prehistoric Universal Civilization (MU, Tarih Öncesi Evrensel Uygarlık,* Bilim Araştırma Merkezi Pub., Istanbul 1978, p. 15

2   Santesson Hans Stephan,- *Sunken Country MU Civilization (Batık Ülke MU Uygarlığı),* RM Pub., Istanbul 1989, p. 2

3   Santesson H.P., r.w., p. 15

4   *Science Research Group (Bilim Araştırma Grubu),* r.w., p.15

5   Churchward James,- *The Sacred Symbols of MU (MU'nun Kutsal Sembolleri),* London 1933, p. 225.

6   Von Daniken Erich,- *Aussaat und Kosmos (Kozmos ve Ötesi),* Amsterdam 1978

7   Santesson H.P., r.w., p. 87

8   Santesson H.P., r.w., p. 95-99

9   Santesson H.P., r.w., p. 19

10   *Science Research Group (Bilim Araştırma Grubu),* r.w., p. 52

11   Churchward J., r.w., p. 29

12   Santesson H.P., r.w., p. 70

13   *Science Research Group (Bilim Araştırma Grubu),* r.w., p. 12

14   Santesson H.P., r.w., p. 125

15   Santesson H.P., r.w., p. 142

16   Churchward J., r.w., p. 33

17   Churchward J., r.w., p. 96

CHAPTER III

ATLANTIS AND OSIRIS

Another continent civilization that had tremendous effect on human history was the civilization of Atlantis. Among the Berber tribes in North Africa, there was a myth of a country of Attalon, that had submerged in the Ocean and would rise again soon. The Celts believed that their ancestors came from a country known as Avalon in the west. The Basques believed that they had arrived from a country called Atlantica and that they were the great grandchildren of the Atlantis.[1] In a book written by Ignatius Donnelly and published in 1882, named "The World Before the Great Flood", he had drawn attention to the fact that the Basque people had no similarities with other Europeans, neither in terms of language, nor physical terms.[2] According to Donnelly, the Basque people had migrated into Iberia from Atlantis after the flood. Basque language was a language totally specific to itself, and was identical to the language of the Paten tribe, living in South America. In Hebrew and Arabic myths, a country named "Ad" was mentioned.

It is also worth considering that the name Adam, the name of the first human being that is believed to exist on earth, had derived from Ad-Ami, which means originating from Ad community. According to Qoran, this country was punished by God, because of the sins of its people. Aztecs had always expressed that they had originated from a great island in the ocean in the East, named Aztlan. In the Scandinavian countries, people talk of a blond, blue eyed race, which lived in a country called Atland, as their ancestors.[3]

Atlantis, the country claimed to have existed in the Atlantic Ocean, was announced to humanity hundreds of years before James Churchward, by the Egyptian priests, through the Greek philosopher Plato. Obviously, Atlantis was not the first civilization cradle on Earth, without any doubt. It was a colony of Mu, and in time, it had become autonomous and had turned into an empire. Allright, but why did the Egyptian priests give this secret to Plato for no reson at all? Because Plato was initiated in Egypt, and he was a brother too.[4]

Plato has described Atlantis through the story of Timaeus and Critias. According to the conversation between these two philosophers, Solon, who visited the city of Sais during the pharaoh Amosis period (570-525 B.C.), was informed by a master priest about Atlantis. Egyptian priest Suchis had told Solon that there used to be a great big continent beyond the strait of Gibraltar, and that anyone who set out from Egypt, upon reaching the sea, could reach another continent across the ocean, passing from one island to the other. According to the priest, 9 thousand years ago (12 thousand years ago from today), due to a great flood and an earthquake, that continent submerged in the water and since then because there was no further connection with its colony Egypt, the civilization in Egypt regressed.[5]

Although he was in close contact with the ruling priests in Egypt for about 10 years, there is no information on whether Solon was initiated to their brotherhood or not. However, it is quite possible that he, as many of the Greek philosophers, was initiated to the temple of Osiris and was given the secrets. On the other hand, another initiated person, the Greek historian Herodotus, during his visit to Egypt, also talked to the priests, and the priests told him that their organization had existed for the past 11 thousand years.

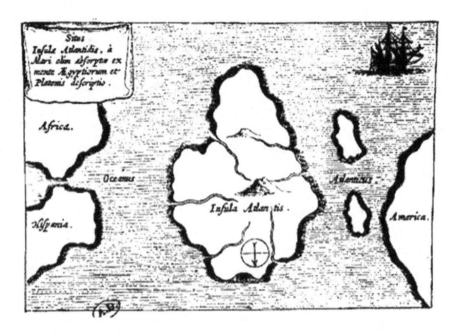

Atlantis was on Atlantic Ocean...

According to Plato's tellings, the Egyptian priest Suchis, told Solon the following:

"Those days (before the great flood) people used to have voyages in the ocean. Out in front of the strait that you call the Pillars of Herculese, there used to be an island. The size of that island was bigger than Asia Minor (Anatolia) and Libya put together. Sailing past that island, it was possible to reach the continent across surrounding the main ocean, as the sea surrounding the island was a narrow pass, whereas the other one was the main sea. And the land surrounded by it was big enough to be called a continent.

Nothing has been conveyed to you from old traditions and time-worn scientific knowledge. The great flood happened 9 thousand years ago. It seems like a legend now, but in reality, the objects turning around the world and in the skies deviated from the Earth. Severe earthquakes and floods occurred. The island of Atlantis submerged in the sea. When the gods gave the great flood disaster to earth, the shepherds in the mountains survived, whereas the people that lived in the cities were swept away by the waters. In those regions, the sea is still inaccessible, due to the routes having been covered in low mud, as the island sank in water. However in this country, neither then, nor now, the level of water has never arisen above the fields. Thus, we may claim that everything which exists here, is the most ancient. Whatever important incident took place in the past was noted and kept in our temples. According to our divine records, our city (Sais) had been established 8 thousand years ago.

There was a temple in Atlantis, dedicated to Poseidon. Its exterior was of silver, towers were of gold, and its roof was of ivory. The laws given to the people of Atlantis by Poseidon, were inscribed on Orichalcum columns and were erected inside the temple."[6]

The Greek philosopher claimed that the Egyptian settlements by the banks of the Nile started 23 thousand years ago. Plato recites that Suchis told Solon, prior to the great flood, that the armies of Atlantis had invaded the countries along the Mediterranean shores, but were eventually driven back by the Athenians and were chased after all the way back to their island. However, with the great flood happening in those days, both Atlantis and the Athenian army had disappeared.

Plato states that these conversations between Solon and Suchis are said to have been transferred to him by his Egyptian teacher Priest Seknuphis. Greek historian Heredotus states that there was 15 thousand years between the Egyptians and the times of Osiris. Aristo, on the other hand, believed that some of the monuments, and hence the pyramids in Egypt were 10 thousand years old.[7]

The fact that the Athenians had beaten the Atlantis army and chased them all the way to their island, concludes that both armies were technologically of same capacity. Considering that all Asian and European territories belonged to the Uyghur Empire, an ally of the Mu Empire, it is highly probable that the Athenians had beaten them with the support of this powerful Empire. This battle was like a part of a war going on between Mu and Atlantis, and on account of the occurrence of the great flood at the final stages of the war, it can be assumed that Atlantis forces, concerned about being invaded by Mu, as a final solution, had tried using the most powerful arms, and this might have caused Mu empire to reciprocate with similar weapons, which in turn caused such a disaster.[8] According to ocean scientists, 11 thousand years ago, the level of the seas surrounding the Earth was 90 meters lower than that of today. For example, the eastern coast of America was 150 km. further out into the ocean than it is today. However, with the sudden melting of the glaciers, all shallow coast lines in the world were covered in water.[9]

Churchward says that Atlantis existed between Africa and America. Although some other researchers are looking elsewhere for this sunken island, affinities between the name Atlantis and the name of the ocean where the continent sank, strengthen the arguments that Atlantis was in the Atlantic ocean.[10]

In 1898, when the technicians were laying telegram lines underwater, just off-shore from the Azores, they came across some glass-like remainders of lava. Only the contact of lava with air could have caused such glass-like structure. The fact that the sea water could decompose lava layers in 15 thousand years, brought out the reality that the area was on the surface before 15 thousand years.[11]

During an ocean bed study by the USA in 1949, occasional shore sand was detected 600 kilometers off-shore. These types of sand, which is said to be formed only along shallow shores indicated that they had remained there since 20 to 10 thousand years ago. Similarly, several types of corals were found in deep areas, which were impossible to develop in regions deeper than 15 meters.[12]

The bottom of the Atlantic Ocean has been swept by numerous ships so far. An elevated mass extending from South of England to Cape Orange in South America, and stretching towards southeast to East Africa was identified. This mass is 2 thousand 500 meters higher compared to the ocean base around it. This mass, called the Dolphin Ridge, is one thousand 600 kilometers in width, and its highest point goes above the ocean level at the Azores. On the surface of the mass, there are mountains and valleys, impossible to rise above the ocean level. These uneven surface is also a proof that the mass at one stage in history, was above the sea level.[13]

200 million years ago, all continents on Earth composed of a single land mass, known as the Pangaea. With the movements of the Earth's crust, the continents separated and parted from each other. When the drawings of the lands on either side of the Atlantic overlap, it can be observed that South America matches perfectly with Africa, whereas North America and Europe do not match at all.

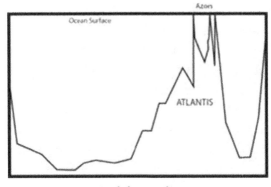

Dolphin Ridge

There is a hole between North-West Africa, Europe and North America. This hole shows that, some time ago, there was a piece of land there, which probably had sunk. By replacing Dolphin Ridge in to this hole, the continents match perfectly well.[14]

The map drawn by Piri Reis in 1513, matches perfectly well to the trigonometric principles used in map-drawing today. In this map, the shores of America are precisely drawn. When viewed on a flat surface, it is thought that the coasts are not shown properly; however, when the map is posed on a sphere, the match is perfect. It is obvious that, whoever drew this map, knew that the Earth had a spherical shape. Both on this map, and on the Oronteus Fienus map, drawn in 1531, the shores of the Antarctic, currently covered in glaciers, are depicted in detail.[15]

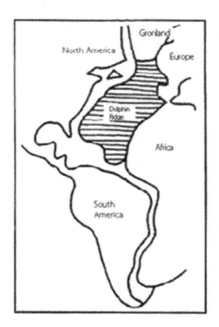

Unification of Continents

Scientists today have confirmed, using present-day techno-logy, that these old drawings were very accurate, the bays and estuaries under the glaciers were located correctly. In the Ibni Ben Zara map published in 1487, it can be seen that Northern Europe was covered in glaciers. It is believed that these maps are copies of a map that was in the Alexandria Library, 2 thousand years ago, and that they were drawn when Europe was covered in glaciers and the Antarctic was totally free of glaciers, by a civilization that could view the world from above and knew how to apply global map drawing technique.

During excavations at the Maya Ruins by an American team, in 1927, a skull was found, carved out of all in one piece quartz crystal. As carbon aging techniques cannot be applied to quartz material, the age of this carving could not be determined. However, the experts stated that carving of that crystal was not possible even with present-day technology, to such perfection, and that it was possible that the carving had been made by a civilization, far more developed than ours. When the skull, which is currently at display at the British Museum, was microscopically examined, as a result of which it was stated that no metal tool was used in carving the quartz crystal.[16]

In 1882, a British commercial vessel found an island 200 miles south of the Azores, which had recently arisen above the water level. On this island, covered in volcanic ashes, without any vegetation, some remains of walls were observed. Near the walls, inside a stone sarcophagus, a mummified human body, bronze swords, animal figures, human head reliefs, rings and hammers were found. No sooner had the island risen above water than it re-submerged, never to be seen again. On the other hand, what happened to the findings taken to Britain, is not known.[17] Since then, numerous reports from different regions of the Atlantic on findings of buildings, walls and roads have been received. Pilots flying over the Atlantic claimed to have seen ruins of cities, roads, even a pyramid under the water.[18] An underwater exploration executed by the Soviets in 1947, confirmed these findings. Exploring the region where the island was reported to have emerged and then disappeared, traces were observed, reminiscent of human life and activities 3,000 meters below the sea level. A mark of five ladder steps was found on a wall 75 cm wide and 1,5 meters long, showing clearly that the wall was built by human beings and was photographed. In the region, the mountains occasionally peaked at 400 meters.[19]

American paleontologist and geologist Manson Valantine, during his explorations in 1968, on the Bahama Shelf, observed huge man-made stones. Remnants of various structures and stone roads, these stones were either put on top parallel with each other or intercepted at right angles and laid straight as a line. Continuing his explorations, Valentine found precision cut building blocks and a statue of a cat's head weighing around 100 kilos.[20] It was also noted that each of the building blocks weighed around 25 tons. Again, in Mexico, Cuba, Florida and Venezuela, walls were found underwater, some of which extended for hundreds of kilometers.[21]

American writer Charles Berlitz said that, on the Bahama shores, the fishermen and pilots had seen underwater pyramids on the ocean base. In an investigation executed in the region in 1978, a pyramid was found, based on 200 meter below the sea level, with its tip reaching 50 meters. Ari Marshall, organizer of the exploration said that a green light radiated from the bottom of the pyramid, possibly due to gas or energy crystals.[22]

British explorer Churchward expressed that Atlantis was given a specific importance in Naacal Tablets and that having previously developed as a colony of Mu, Atlantis, over time had become autonomous and had set its own empire. The tablets indicate that while Atlantis was the colony of Mu, there were schools teaching the Mu Cosmic religion, but after gaining autonomy, they had alienated from the principal religion. According to Nacaal tablets, the priests in Atlantis preferred to corrupt the principal religion to their benefit, in order to increase their influence on the society.

This religious corruption in Atlantis continued until the rise of Osiris. Two of the Nacall tablets were reserved for this great man, who was born 22 thousand years ago, in Atlantis.[23] According to the tablets, at a very young age, Osiris left his birthplace and went to Mu, where he attended one of the

"Wisdom Schools". Staying in the continent of Mu until he received the titles of "master priest and divine brother", Osiris returned to his own country, to instigate a religious reform. In the hieroglyphs in two temples, one being in Himalayas, and the other in the city of TEB, it was inscribed that Osiris was born in Atlantis, studied religion and science of opinion in a Nacaal school in Mu, and returned to his country, upon receiving the title Teacher.[24]

Having declared war against the corrupted Atlantis religion and the clergy, and owing to his strong character, Osiris got the support of the people and purged the temples, which had lost their dignity, from corrupted priests. Until his death, Osiris remained as the spiritual (religious) leader of his country, and declined the title of emperor offered to him. After his death, his followers and priest brethren gave the name "Osiris Religion", to the religion he had been disseminating.

The name Osiris was also mentioned among Egyptian Gods. It is believed that this religion was brought to Egypt by Hermes (Toth), but in time, this pure religion was corrupted and Osiris was turned into a god, taking his place in the Pantheon. In the Pantheon of the Egyptian gods, Isis, always mentioned alongside with Osiris, was the female expression of God, and their son, Horus was the expression of the divine word. Just as was the case with Osiris and Isis, after a certain period, Hermes was also converted to a god, given the name of Toth.[25]

According to American writer Shirley Andrews, in Atlantis, people believed in immortality of the soul, in reincarnation, and that the soul matured through different experiences in different lives, and united with the God after completing its evolution. The Circle symbolized the Mighty God, who was the source of everything. For that reason, people of Atlantis built their temples and houses in a circular shape. The New Year ceremonies were held in open air, in Poseidon Temple, on June 21st. The people who gathered in the temple as the sun rose into the New Year for the first time, saluted the rays of the sun, facing the east. When the sun reached at its peak, the head priest would point the crystal in his hand to the sun, and would let the rays shine on all the participants. After the sunset, the priests would talk of the value of the sun, and evil of the darkness, and with the head priest's call, "Let There Be Light", the temple would be lighted with magnificent sources of light.

Atlantis Cosmic Dyagram

The people of Atlantis looked upon the Sun as the source of life, and the symbol of the Almighty God. They also believed in the existence of secondary degree gods that acted in line with the rules of the Almighty God.[26]

Priesthood was a profession that lasted a lifetime and needed continuous meditation. The first stage was physical cleanliness and the second stage was mental purity. The priests first got to know their inner world, then they would open their minds to universal knowledge.

With different rituals, they passed an examination where they experienced partial death, and thus would completely become relieved from the fear of leaving this world. It was accepted that, as a result of this examination, they were re-born, having attained different powers.[27] Color of the outfits of the priests at the highest level was white.

Even today, in the current Shaman ritual, first the body is cleaned, then a mental cleaning is done; the person is left in a totally dark environment, hungry and thirsty for days, experimenting deep trance. It is believed that the soul leaves the body and reaches higher levels and matures during this trance.

In his book, "Occult Sciences in Atlantis", American author Lewis Spence claims that the priests underwent three stages: Initiation, Mastership and Magnus. The person to be initiated used to be put in an underground labyrinth, then tested by earth, air, water and fire, and later would be transfered into the reincarnation stage. The candidate who survived this stage, would be passed through a very dense beam of light, and was born again.

Those who passed all the tests would be admitted into Poseidon Temple and his training would start. People who received training in varied fields of science, during a period of 20 years first became a Master, and following another 20 years of meditation, if found appropriate, they would receive the rank of Magnus, which was the highest level in priesthood. Spence wrote that the Magnus had the ability to desert their bodies and unite with the universe, whenever they wished to do so.[28]

American psychic Edgar Cayce claims that the people in Atlantis knew about electricity and atom, and that they could control solar power. According to Cayce, the energy source in Atlantis were the huge reflecting crystals that they called as fire stones. These crystals, located in Poseidon's Temple of the Sun, were used for all kinds of energy requirement, and the protection of the environment was realized through them. However, the great flood was caused by misuse of these crystals.[29] Another psychic Gareth Knight has declared that Atlantis was ruled by a king and this king was only responsible to head priest of the sun. Sun religion was the secular religion of the people. Towards the final days of the civilization, the priests' cast corrupted, polytheistic religions, grew stronger, and the priests started using their powers for their own benefits. However, "The Priests of the Light" did not divert from the real path of the teaching and continued their real teachings behind a veil of secrets. Just like the teachings of these priests, technological knowledge of the artisans were also hidden from the masses, as secrets.[30] American author Murry Hope also supported this view and said that the main source of energy was sonic, but this was kept as secret, only known by the 'Masonic' wing of the priests, who were scientists. From this explanation by Hope, it seems possible to reach a conclusion that the word 'Mason' in Atlantis was being used for the Scientist Priests.[31]

As was the case in final years of the civilization, corrupted polytheistic religions became effective. The minority group of priests called as the 'Priests of the Light' by Knight, and as 'Scientist Priests' by Hope, as a result of pressure put forth by corrupted polytheistic religions, were but those priests of the monotheistic Osiris religion who were pushed to go underground to continue their activities in secrecy. The 'Mason' was a word developed by these priests, in order to define themselves, in line with Esoteric teaching, containing the male and female virtues of God, as well as representing the divine word.

The letter *"M"* present in the word Mason, symbolizes Mu Continent, where the main source of the teaching came from, and is male in that sense. The letter *"A"* indicates Atlantis, where the teaching was raised again and disseminated to all colonies, and is female in that sense. The letter *"S"* represents the divine word which is formed by the combination of the two letters M and A, and *"SON"* was used in its literal meaning, as well as our physical "SUN". This word is still used in contemporary western countries, meaning the Son and the Sun, with some minor changes. Together with the letter *"O"*, representing "Osiris", the meanings of "Son-Osiris" and "Divine Word-Osiris come about. The last letter *"N"* reverts to Nacaals, the first group of teachers of Mu. In other words, the MASONS of Atlantis acted just like the Nacaals in Mu; they are the Osiris priests who have lead and continued their trainings, being the All Seing Eyes of the god who could see everything. In the latest periods of the civilization, believers of the polytheistic religions have owned "MA" as "Maia" the daughter of the mighty God Atlas, or as the Mother Goddess; in other words, this belief continued its existence in other colonies of Atlantis, even after the great flood.

As there are hardly any remains of either Mu, or Atlantis civilizations to the date, some Orthodox scientists take this as if none of these civilizations ever existed. However, considering that more than 10 thousand years have gone by, and that following a war, a great flood was experienced resulting in total destruction, it is quite normal that only a few rocks or stones have survived to the present day. Although granite is one of the hardest materials on earth, not affected easily by the conditions of the nature, there will be nothing left from our civilization today, 10 thousand years later. Only a few stones will remain for the people of the future to understand us, 10 thousand years from now.

MAYAS

Maya Version of All Seeing Eye

Apart from Atlantis, the other two most important colonies of Mu civilization, were Maya and Uyghur civilizations.[32] Among these, Maya Colony in the Continent of America is important, from the point of view that it contains most of the findings on the existence of Mu and Atlantis. It is not a coincidence that in Mayas, who are believed to be one of the first colonies of Mu, and their descendants Aztecs and Inkas, the emperors are named the "Son of the Sun" and they worship a Sun Cult.

Additionally, resemblance of Egyptian and Maya pyramids, which were used for ceremonies, as well as likeness depicted in their mummifying of the dead, which is a corrupted form of believing in reincarnation, all prove that these two civilizations originate from the same root. In Peru, the Sun is called "Raymi", whose resemblance with Ra-Mu is very obvious. Aztecs had expressed that their name originated from "Aztlan." In Aztec, "Az" means water, and "Tlan" means land, and the two together speak of an island. From this explanation, it can be derived that, the people of Maya empire are mostly of Mu origin, whereas Aztecs are the Atlantis people who have arrived at this continent after the great flood.[33]

In "Codex Troanus", a Maya inscription currently displayed in the British Museum, it is stated that Mu civilization disappeared into the sea, one thousand 60 years before the book of Maya civilization was written, on the 13th day of the month of Zac, with a population of 64 million inhabitants. From this expression, it can be understood that Codex was written in circa 2 thousand B.C., and this fact has been proven scientifically. In Codex, Mu is mentioned as the "mainland". In Maya language, "Ma" means "country or land". In an old Hawaiian saga, it reads: "Our mainland and our kings lay under the ocean." In Maya's holy book Popul Vuh (A bouquet of leaves), it is expressed that during the great flood, "sticky substances, fire, and ashes have fallen off the skies, the waters rose and the lands sank in the water".[34] In another inscription of Popul Vuh, the great disaster experience is defined as follows: "A great fire, poison and rocks have fallen off the skies. Winds hotter than fire destroyed the people. First, their nails have dropped, then their skins peeled, they got blind, their flesh decayed and decomposed. The deadly wind reached everywhere. Even the hunters at the furthest corners of the towns had big wounds in their bodies.[35]

American archeologist and writer Augustus Le Plongeon claimed that the inscriptions on the walls of Xochicalho Pyramid belonging to Maya civilization described the sinking of Atlantis.

However, as Le Plongeon was not aware of the Mu continent in the Pacific during his research in the 19th century, he had interpreted the name of the sunken continent incorrectly. According to Le Plongeon, this continent was called "Mu" by the Mayas and "Atlantis" by the Greeks. Descriptions given in this inscription, the translations of which were done by Le Plongeon, complied with the information transferred by Plato. The natives call these inscriptions as Akabdzip (Black Inscriptions). According to these inscriptions, the great flood happened on Chuen (Friday), 13th of Zac, and 64 million inhabitants in Atlantis disappeared in the water overnight; the waters rose and reached as high as the highest mountains. From this description, one can conclude that both continents sank on the same day. According to Le Plongeon, prior to the great flood, although a decimal system was being used in Maya, after the sinking of the Mu continent, mathematical system was changed to a system based on 13. Additionally, at the bottom of the unlucky Friday the 13th lies the great flood.[36]

For Mayas, the only visible representative of God Almighty is the Sun, which is a perfect circle, and gives life to everything. They only worship the Sun. The Sun is the visible manifestation of the Holy Spirit. The Holy Spirit that created everything was named as "Ku" by the Mayas. He is "Lahun", which means a Whole in One, and One that contains everything. Everything was created with Uol, with the great will of Ku, and this creation was represented by a cosmic egg, in the form of a perfect circle. To create the visible universe, Uol started with replicating himself inside an egg. This egg developed and came into being, known as Meneh, and was symbolized by a snake, holding its tail in its mouth, and hence forming a perfect circle.

This symbol can be seen on the façade of a temple in Chicken. On top of the entrance of this temple named "Kana", which means the House of God, the cosmic egg of the Creator, Meneh was symbolized. Another name given to the Egyptian Creator God Ptah was Meneh. Ptah, who had come out of his father Kneph's mouth as an egg, was defined as the Great Architect by the Egyptians.

According to Indian Brahma teaching, the Holy Spirit created the universe from a cosmic egg. In the book Manava-Dhra-ma-Sastra, the following is written: "The Holy Spirit conceived the revelation of the universe from its material core substance/matter, first by creating the waters where it sowed a fertile seed. This seed became an egg, shining like a star of one thousand lights. The Holy Creation was replicated in this egg in Brahma form." According to the Brahmanist belief, all creatures have been created as a result of the unification of Brahma and Maya, being the personalization of nature's feminine powers. The Sun prey of the Brahmans goes as follows: "He, the ultimate power of the gods covers the skies and the Earth with its shining net. He is the soul of everything. You are the one created from within yourself. You are the most perfect beam. Please grant me with your light." From these verses, it can be understood that the origin of this religion lies on the belief in the Sun, which is the symbol of the Mighty Creation.[37]

Uxmal temple, which is also known as the "Temple of Holy Secrets", located in Yucatan, shows that this place was also used for initiation ceremonies, just like the ones in Egypt. Presence of a fire chamber in the temple, where candidates were examined, shows that this temple, built after the great flood, is the place where primitive forms of the Mu religious practices are continued.

According to the research done by Churchward, initiation ceremony applied to Maya Priests consists of seven stages.[38] At the first stage, candidates of initiation to the holy secrets had to pass two rivers, one of blood, and the other of mud. Only after crossing these dangerous rivers would they be able to reach the guiding priests awaiting them. From this point on, the candidates were guided by the priests, travelling through four different paths colored in red, green, black and white, and reached a council consisting of 12 master priests who were waiting for them. There, the candidates were asked to sit down. However, if the candidate did sit down, he would immediately regret having done that. Because, the rock that he was asked to sit on would be previously heated, and, therefore, the candidate would be dismissed from the ceremony, for not showing the required respect to the council.

Those who refused to sit down would be sent to a room where no light entered, and they would spend a night there. Here, the candidates were given a torch and were supposed to keep the torchlight going until daylight. Otherwise, they would be dismissed from the ceremony.

At the next test, the candidate was given a valuable plant and was asked to protect this exquisite plant from warriors armed with spears. At the fourth stage, the candidate would be left in a very cold place known as the ice-house, and had to spend a night there. At the next stage, the candidates had to combat wild animals, and if they survived this stage, they would then spend one more night in an environment as hot as an oven, known as the fire house. Those who managed to pass all these tests would then spend a night in the Bat God's house, filled with dangerous weapons. If the candidates did not keep vigil continuously, they could be beheaded by one of these weapons.

Mayas regarded the obelisks and their developed versions, the pyramids, as the symbols of laws of the invisible Gods. For the triangular vaults used in their buildings, the same holy principles also applied. In Maya belief, a triangle symbolized both the male and female virtues of God and the universe created from the combination of the two. They accepted the Circle of Horizon as the emblem of the infinite universe, and they symbolized the concept of Almighty God as flawless, simple equilateral triangles placed in a circle. The triangle pointing up represented the fire, and the triangle pointing downwards represented water. With the unification of these two, all beings in nature were created. Two concentric triangles placed in opposite direction were another representation of the Creator God. As it can be seen in the symbol used in the beginning of this chapter, the All Seeing Eye of the God, located in the center of the two concentric triangles, is the Mu-Nacaal symbol, adopted by the Mayas. As seen in the symbol below, sometimes the Sun, representing the Divine

Word, or the Replicate of the God were placed in the triangles, instead of the eye. Aztecs used the same symbol and this symbol became famous as the Maya/Aztec Calendar. The symbol of God placed inside two concentric triangles has been replaced by the letter "G" inside the Square-Compass, used by Freemasonry today.

Maya-Aztec Celendar is the root of Masonic Symbol, Square and Compass

Chaldeans had also described the creator in the form of an equilateral triangle. The All Seeing Eye inside an Equilateral Triangle radiating light, had formed the cosmic diagram of the Chaldeans. In Maya language, Chalti means surrounded by a fence. It is likely that the word Chaldea originated from the fact that the residential areas of the people migrated from Atlantis to Middle East were surrounded by fences or walls.[39]

Maya priests would hide the secrets concerning their teachings in secret places within their temples and entrusted these secrets only to their sons or distinguished princes. Same procedure can also be observed in Egypt and in Babylon. The Head Mayan Priest's title was Manek Maya or Hakmak, both having the meaning of Perfect Human Being (Kamil Man). The etymology of the word Babylon is based on the combination of "Ba" and "Bel". In ancient Mayan language, these words mean Way and Ancestor, the combination of which can be defined as the "City of our Ancestors who have arrived from a distant place". The title of Chaldean head priests was "Rabmak". This word, just like Hakmak of the Mayas, also means the Kamil Man.[40] The words "Hak" and "Rab" continue their existence in Abrahamic religions.

We had explained before that the priests of the Osiris religion in Atlantis were called the Masons. After the great flood, the first known usage of the word Mason was in 7 thousand B.C. in Western Anatolia. As it was written on clay tablets in a symbolic language different from the Hittite language, the very first settlers of the west Anatolian coast, who lived 9 thousand years ago, called the "Luvi", reached us to this day through the Hittites who had founded a powerful empire in Anatolia in 2 thousand B.C. The word "Luvi" meant, "The Children of the Light" in their language. The likeness between the pictures and the symbols of Miken inscriptions and Luvi inscriptions could be observed.

Luvi language comes from the Indian-European language family. The name of the Mother Goddess that the Luvi people worshipped was "Ma", whereas Ma was also the name of the oldest known Mother Goddess in Anatolia.[41]

In his book named "The Children of Mu", James Churchward states that a branch of the people that disseminated to all corners of the earth, starting from Mu, went to the East, and there, they first founded the Maya civilization, then the Maya Empire. From there, they moved to Atlantis,

25

and traveling past Atlantis, they reached all the way the shores of the Mediterranean. Maya-Atlantis colonizers that settled down in the Aegean islands, carried their affection to their main land, to other side of the ocean, and made Maia (Ma), the daughter of Atlas and the mother of all Gods, especially of Apollon and Hermes, the Mother Goddess. Goddess Maia lasted for many years, and the month of May was named after her in many Western calendars. May festivals which are currently celebrated in the Christian world, and which were attributed to Virgin Mary originated from the Mayan belief.[42]

The Miken civilization was founded based on the teachings by Atlantis colonizers. While a branch of these people founded the lower Nile colony, another branch founded the Miken colony in the island of Crete and settled down in the Western coast of Anatolia. Luvis, thus, are the Maya-Atlantis people that settled down in western Anatolia coastline. Thus the Luvi were people of Maya. Another branch of these peoples were the Phoenicians, who named themselves as the "People of Carou". It is thought that the name Phoenician has been derived from the word "phoiniks", which means red in Greek, and that this name was given due to the color of their skin. Phoenicians had red skins. Phoenicians from Sur, Sidon, Babylon and Ugarit, worshipped El, the Father God El, and his wife Balat or Astarte (Venus), as well as their son Baal. Although El, represented by the Sun, loved his dear wife infinitely, his biggest pleasure was to get female human beings pregnant.

El used to introduce himself as a stranger to those passing by. For that reason, in order to satisfy his desire, it was the duty of all Phoenician women to offer themselves to complete strangers in certain periods of the year, in temples dedicated to Goddess Balat or Astarte. These periods coincided with the autumnal and vernal (spring) equinoxes. The women used to sell themselves to strangers throughout the day, and with the money raised, they used to buy sacrifices to offer to Balat. Only outsider men were allowed to enter these places where sexual intercourses took place. These whores of the temple were called the Hirodules, which meant "Holy Servants".[43]

As explained before, in Maya language, the word "Ma" is a reference to the first country it originated from. The settlers who arrived in Egypt from the west, named the region along the Nile as "Maui". In Egyptian, the word "Ma" means the "West" and the "Place".[44] The Mother Goddess "Ma" represents the Mu Continent (M) sunken in the Pacific and the Atlantis (A) continent sunken in the Atlantic.

In Luvi language, "Mara" meant the sea, the names Marmara and Marmaris, which are currently used in Turkey, meant the "sea of the Mother Goddess Ma". Luvis, as if to point at the civilization from where they arrived, called the highest mountain in the region where they settled, as "Mount Maya", which is also the name currently used. Their most important male god is Apollo. Apollo is the son of Ma. Originally an Anatolian God, Apollo was later accepted to the Greek Pantheon of Gods. He is also known as the "God of the Light", and is symbolized by the Sun.

The old copper coins found in Pitane, one of the oldest settlements in Anatolia, have a star with five edges with a dot in the middle.[45] The same symbol is being used in today's Masonry.

In Luvis, who believed in reincarnation, the most advanced profession was construction work. The oldest wall building technique known belonged to them. They were very famous with their bricks floating on water. They were the first to use the stone roof technique in the region, which later evolved to archways. They were also the first to build surrounding walls around the settled areas.

They were again the first to build holy houses that belonged to the Mother God. In ancient Egyptian language, "Bethes" meant a house. The city of Thebes, in which there was a great big temple devoted to God Amon. The word "The" is generally used as God in Egyptian. Bes is short for Bethes and their usage together meant the "House of the God". The same word, which originated from Mu language, was used as Tao in Chinese and as Teo in ancient Turkish civilizations. Teo-Man means God-Man, which means the "Kamil Man" in Turkish. The same word has also been used in Hebrew and Greek as "Tau" and is the last letter of the Hebrew and Greek Alphabets. The symbol of this letter that indicates eternity, which will later be used by the Christians, is the renowned cross. The word theology, which means the science of god, has also originated from the same root.

In Luvis, Beth is also used for the meaning of a house. Ma Beth is the House of the Mother Goddess Ma and has been transformed into Turkish as "Mabet", the holy place of God. Turkish Masons calls their temples as "Mabet". Another name given to the Holy Kabe of Muslims is Beytullah, which means the House of Allah.[46]

The word Ma has been transformed to Western languages as "matter-mother". The other name "Son", as mentioned earlier, is also still being used in the same languages. The name given to stone builders who built temples for Ma and Ma priests was "Mason", just as it was in Atlantis. Masons are the Sons of Ma, that is the children of the Mother Goddess. The first Mason is Ma's son Apollo, the Sun God. His followers are equally called the Masons. As Ma represented the two main continents where the teaching had initiated from, and her son being the Sun, it would be quite right to call the Masons as "The Sons of Atlantis and Mu"; in other words, the "Sons of the Sun and Light".

Currently, the term "Sons of the Light" is an expression used by modern day Masons for defining themselves. The very first known source of another expression used by the Masons to define themselves as the "Children of the Widow", was also the Luvis. When Attis, the husband of mother goddess Ma, had an affair with a mortal woman, She and her husband had a raging quarrel. In order to free himself from his wife's jealousy attack, Attis cut-off his male organ and died of hemorrhage. The children of Ma, the Masons, were then the children of the widow.

Attis, later, was buried by a river and a big pine tree grew on the point where he was intered. This tree had been regarded as the symbol of reincarnation. Each year, the priests of Ma would cut-off the newly accepted priests' sexual organs, and they were all made eunuchs. They would hang their organs as a vow to Attis on the branches of the holy pine tree, and would purify themselves by bathing in the river. Hence, it can be seen that circumcision and baptism ceremonies also date back to the Luvis.[47] The origin of Christmas Tree tradition also dates back to Luvis. Luvis moved to the southeastern parts of Anatolia around 2 thousand BC, where they met the Saabians. Abraham, the separatist leader of Saabians, ordered his followers to continue the Luvi tradition of cutting sexual organs, but instead of having them cut off from the bottom, he decided to have only the tips cut off and hung on the tree.

Another 2 thousand years passed and Christianity came to these lands. Jesus was against circumcision. So his followers continued the tradition by hanging other kinds of gifts or vows onto the branches of the holy pine tree on Christmas Eve.

During the initiation ceremony of the Luvis, priest candidates were placed in a hole, which were their graves to be. While the candidates were in the hole, the priests would bring a bull and cut its throat. With the blood of the bull pouring onto them, the initiated were purged, and they were taken as reborn. The initiated, then were regarded as gods' equals and were invited to a holy feast, where they were served nectar. The ceremony continued with a mystical unification with the Goddess. The candidates, each one of whom had now become Attis, after touching the male organ of the sacrificed bull joined a symbolic wedding ceremony. In the evening, the initiated would have intercourse with nuns who represented the goddess for just one last time, before becoming eunuchs.

The same practise was later adopted by the Kybele cult, another Anatolian mother goddess.[48]

Heredotus wrote that, another son of Mother Goddess Ma, Hermes, was initially the god of nomadic Pelasgs, who later settled down in the vicinity of Athens, and who were experts on mining and metallurgy, where the fire element was overwhelming, were known as "Oven Masters".[49] According to Heredotus, Hermes' motherland was Arcadia. Pelasgs arrived at the Morea peninsula from north of the Aegean in 3 thousand B.C, and were a branch of the Luvis in Anatolia.

Luvis were the founders of the Troy civilization. Hery Schileman, the famous archeologist who explored Troy, noted that he believed Troy was founded by people from Atlantis. Letters Hery Schileman left to his grandson, Dr. Paul Schileman, were published by The New York American magazine, in 1912. These letters announced findings that proved the fact that Troy was founded by the Luvis, who migrated to Anatolia from Atlantis.

Following declarations were made in these letters, by Schileman himself:

"While digging in the ruins of Troy in 1873, in Hisarlık, I found the treasures of King Piram of Troy. Among them, was quite a large brass vase. Inside, there were some objects, which I could not understand the material they were made of. I also found some coins made from the same material. On the vase, "Kronus, the King of Atlantis" was inscribed. I had the material analyzed in a laboratory. It was composed of platinum, aluminum, copper, as well as some other materials, inexplicable by the scientists. Our current technical knowledge is not sufficient for making this alloy."[50]

Paul Schlieman explained the contents in the vase left to him by his grandfather, as follows: "There were two rectangular plates made of a strange material that looked like white silver. On it, there was an inscription that I had not seen before. At the back of the plates, it said in hieroglyph characters: 'From the Temple with Transparent Walls'.

Temples with Transparent Walls was a name given to open roof temples, both in Mu and in Atlantis.[51]

UYGHURS

The biggest colony of Mu, as Churchward has expressed it, the biggest civilization established by Man after Mu, was the Uyghur Empire. The Empire covered almost all Europe and Asia. It extended from the Pacific in the east to the Atlantic in the west, and included Iran, Mesopotamia and India in the south. While Churchward claimed that all roots of Ari races went back to the Uyghurs, French researcher and author Edouard Schure wrote that 5 thousand years ago, the continent of Europe was an ancient Scythian land.[52]

Despite spreading over such a vast land, the center of the Uyghur Empire was the plains of Central Asia. All eastern sagas claim that Central Asia, which are steps and desert today, was covered with fertile land and forests. This land that was good enough to be the center of a strong empire remained under water after the great flood and became a desert. The availability of a huge amount of fresh water right underneath the Gobi desert is an indication how fertile this land once was. Churward wrote that the Uyghurs had white skins, colored eyes and blond or black hair.[53] According to Naacal archives, Uyghur colony was the first colony founded by Mu, 70 thousand years ago. The tablets indicate that Mu religion was dominant throughout the land and Nacaal Brotherhood priests remained as the ruling class, even after the empire became independent.

The British researcher wrote that, during the great flood which caused Mu and Atlantis to sink, most of the Uyghur land remained underwater and the empire ended. Churward pointed out that only Nacaal Brethren living in the plateaus of Tibet and the Brethren in Babylon had survived the great flood, as they were far away from both of the oceans and thus could overcome the great flood with minimum possible damage. Ara Avedisyan, in his book "The Great Secret in the Universe", which he wrote in 1973, indicated that Uyghurs were the heirs of Mu.[54] Among the organizations left behind after the great flood was one in Tibet from which the information reached us unblemished to this day, and this was made possible owing to the Tibet Naacals getting hold of Uyghur archives and concealing them after the flood waters had receded. The tablets which priest Rishi showed Churchward were a part of those archives. On the other hand, although the Brotherhood of Babylon had corrupted the original teaching to a certain extent, together with Hermes Brotherhood of Atlantis in Egypt, they had played an important role in disseminating the esoteric teaching all over the world again, and affecting the present day civilization.

Uyghur Empire had left numerous marks on other empires established after the great flood, in terms of its symbols, religious structure, beliefs and their life style. Not only in Asia and Europe, but also throughout the world had the Uyghur symbols made a mark, among which the single or double headed eagle ranked first and was thought to be utilized as the emblem of the empire.

Double Headed Uyghur Eagle

Many researchers claim that the double headed eagle, known as the Uyghur Eagle, was first used in Lagas city of the Sumerians that dated back to 5 thousands B.C. However, one can come across this symbol in some graves in Central Asia and in North America, and archeologists say that those graves date back to 8 thousands B.C. Again in Egypt, in some graves which belong to periods hundreds of years before Egypt was ruled by the pharaohs, double headed eagle decorations can be seen carved on some stones. Egyptologists claim that those graves are graves belonging to at least 7 thousands B.C.

Shamans in central Asia and in Europe accept this symbol as sacred, just as did the Shamans in North and South America. Starting from Japan, all peoples in Asia, Europe and the Americas have accepted this symbol either as a symbol of the highest level of administration, as the totem of their tribe, or as the emblem of their empire. It has been used for thousands of years, and is still being used today.

Let's start our research with the Sumerians, introduced to us by the contemporary science as the oldest civilization of Man. Archeologists state that the founding of Sumerians date back to 5-6 thousands B.C. However, let us not forget that one hundred years ago, Sumerians were not recognized and history was said to have started from a respectively younger period, from Egypt, in 3 thousand 500 B.C. However, Sumerians themselves refute the thesis that history starts with them. Clay tablets inscribed in cuneiform, frequently depicted that there had been a great flood and only a few people had managed to survive the disaster. In the "Sumerian Royal List", one of the most important tablets, it was noted that at least 10 kings had lived and they had ruled at least between 110 thousand and 60 thousand years. The list ends with the following phrases:

"After the great flood, the kingdom has been sent down from high above."

From this, it can be understood that the level of civilization was far more advanced before the great flood, and a new start was given following the great flood. During the post-flood era, Scythians, a branch of the Uyghurs, separated from the central administration and settling in Mesopotamia, established the Sumerian State.

Because the double headed eagle was observed in all Asia, Europe, and even in America, for thousands of years, it is highly probable that it had been the emblem of the Uyghur Empire. It can be seen that one head of the eagle is directed toward east, that is, the Mu Empire in the Pacific, while the other is turned toward west, the Atlantis Empire in the Atlantic.

The center of the Uyghur Empire is Central Asia; in other words, the motherland of the Turkic Tribes. In Mu language, "Hun" means "Single" and "One", and is a sacred word,[55] always referring to God. The very first word the Turks have described themselves with was this word. Double headed eagle was the symbol of Volga and Tuna Huns. Besides the Huns, the double headed eagle had been the symbol of Yakuts - the Siberian Turks, Kutluks - the Second Gokturk Empire, Mongols, Scythians, Cumans, the Uz, Patzinaks, Hungarians, Bulgarians, in short, many Turkish clans, in a region extending from the Adriatic to Kamchatka. In more recent times, the Oghuzs and the Seljuks used this symbol as the heraldic emblem of the state.

Arms of the Seljuk Empire

In Sumerians, regarded as a clan of the Scythians, as well as in Hittites who had arrived at Anatolia from the North, the same emblem was being used as the symbol of representatives of Gods on Earth. The personal emissaries of Turkish God Ulgen, Greek God Zeus, and Sumerian God Samas had always been the eagle. Just like being the personal emissary of the Horus, or the Divine Word.

Arthur Parker, an American researcher, stated that the Turcs in Central Asia had used either single or double headed eagle since 4 thousand B.C. and that the double headed eagle symbol was named as "Hamca" in Turkish. On the Great Hun Emperor Atilla's flag, there was an eagle named "Tugrul". Gokturks had used an eagle with horns and long ears as their emblem to represent power. Ears of the owl was added on to the eagle's sharp vision thus making it capable of hearing at night. Amidst the famous Gokturk Emperor Gultekin's helmet, displayed in Ural Batur museum, there is an emblem of a single headed eagle. It is also known that the Bulgars and the Patzinaks had used the eagle as their emblem in the 7th century. The title of the Arpads, known as the 2nd dynasty of the Hungarians, is the eagle clan. Merkit clan of the Altai Turks is symbolized by a black eagle, whereas the symbols of Yurtas clan and Yakuts are the white eagle and the "father eagle", respectively.

In Central Asian Turks, the single headed eagle was the symbol of the khan, solely, whereas, the double headed eagle represented that women also had the say in ruling the state. While one of the heads represents the male, the other represents female, together symbolizing power and continuance for generations. Remaining from the Uyghurs, a double headed eagle figure found in a Budhist temple in Eastern Turkistan, dates back to 8th century A.D. It is also interesting for a Turkish clan to establish an empire bearing the same name as a pre-flood empire thousands of years after the great flood.

These practises of the double headed eagle in Turkish states and clans, as well as other Eurasian civilizations, indicate that this symbol originated from a single source; that is the pre-flood Uyghur Empire that encroached upon the continent.

As the religious and philosophical meaning of the double headed eagle among Turks will be dealt with later on in the book, let us now examine the single and double headed eagle symbols, in terms of historical chronology, in Sumerian and Hittite civilizations.

According to Sumerian cuneiform tablets, it was owing to God Ningersu that mankind had not been totally swept because of the great flood. Gods got angry with man because of their efforts in trying to be like the Gods, so they covered the whole world with water. However, God Ningersu managed to convince the gods before all human beings had perished, and had the waters to recede. This is nothing other than the phenomenon of the great flood, as narrated by Sumerians.

Ningersu is also known as the founder God of Lagas city. The symbol of Ningersu is the lion headed eagle, named as Imgig. On a silver vase that is left from 2 850 B.C., displayed in the Louvre museum, there are four lion headed eagles. Again, on a cylindrical Babylonian seal that belonged to a priest of Ningersu, a double headed eagle of Imgig was inscribed. On this seal, also a young man's naked figure was inscribed, who was believed to have been offered to goddess Bau, the wife of god Ningersu by a priest or a nun. This scene represents the initiation ceremony when becoming a priest. Right behind the Godess is a double headed eagle, one of whose heads represent Ningersu and the other Bau. Another sculpture of a god, and some tool symbols surrounding Guda, found in Lagas date back to 4 thousands B.C.

The protecting God of Lagas city was Ninutra, symbolized by a giant eagle with its wings wide open. The task of this God, who was also known as the thunder bird, was twofold. One was to provide rain, providing abundance and wealth, and the other was to lead the armies with thunder and lightning to encourage the warriors.

An eagle can spot its prey from miles away. It is monogamous. It takes good care of its babies, and does not hesitate to fight for them, if necessary. The eagle is the symbol of power, strength and supremacy, king of all creatures in the sky, and the only ruler there. Because it can fly closest to the Sun and is the only creature that can look at the Sun without blinking an eye, it is also the symbol of the Sun. Just as the eagle can fly to the sun, the supreme human beings will also fly towards the reality and will unite with God.

Being the "Son of the Light", the eagle represents the mighty king. It is also the guardian of the seventh floor of the sky. Carrying the super souls under its wings, the eagle takes them to God. It is ascension towards the Light. It is the symbol of spiritual and social ascent. The double headed eagle has a vision of 360 degrees. One of the heads is turned towards the Earth, whereas the other head is turned towards the other realm. The eagle is the messenger between the two worlds. As well as being the symbol of God, in Sumerians, an eagle is also a messenger between the God and human beings, due to its speed and power. In some eagles in Sumerians, in order to reinforce its power, the head of the eagle has been replaced by a lion's head, thus the lion headed eagle was formed. The Eagle is the fastest creature that can fly to the highest point. The life-span of an eagle is long. With such capabilities, the eagle can fly among humans, as well as Gods' levels.

As has been expressed before, the eagle is the personal emissary of Samas, the god of the Sun. Another eagle motif frequently used in Sumerian tablets is the sun disk with wings. This disk is an expression of the oneness of the eagle and the Sun.

According to a saga, animated during the New Year ceremonies in Babylon, accepted as the successor of the Sumerians, the Fate Tablet of the Chief God Marduk with the word "Power" inscribed on it, was stolen by the Underground God Zu. Having lost its power, Marduk died and was buried. Marduk's wife, Mother Goddess Istar and their son God Nabu tried to save Marduk, but could not succeed. Drought and poverty set in Babylon. Help was requested from the Sun god Samas and Moon goddess Sin through the double headed eagle. As a result of collaboration, the tablet was rescued from Zu, and Marduk returned to Earth from underground. Re-birth or renaissance was realized. Drought and poverty disappeared, and wealth and prosperity returned to Babylon.

Among the holy animal figures on the façade of the Goddess Sin temple in Horsabat city of Assyria, there is also an eagle figure. On an Assyrian-Babylonian cylinder displayed in France, there is an eagle figure between Chief God Marduk and Mother Goddess Istar. Marduk's son Nabu is frequently depicted wearing an apron, and holding a square. In Kalde cult, the symbol of the Moon Goddess Sin was an eagle, which was from here that it was adopted by the ancient Greeks, and so the eagle became the symbol of Goddess Diana. The double headed black and white eagle represented the angel of death and eternity in Babylon, Greece and Rome.

In Hittite language, the eagle is pronounced as "Hara". As the symbol of the Moon Goddess Sin is an eagle, the city where the goddess Sin's temple was located was also named as Harran. Haranian means, like an eagle. As a cult center named Marren Nasr (Master Eagle) was established in Hatra campus near Harran, it is understood that eagle was accepted as a holy bird by Haranians.

The following expressions were found in a Hittite purification ritual:

"I am going to release the eagle. Go and tell the Sun God and the Thunder God that if they are eternal, then the king and the queen should be eternal, too...."

As it can be seen here, the eagle is a messenger among the priests, the royalty and the Gods.

Some of the entrance gates to Imbelt city situated by the shores of the Euphrates, belonging to the Hittites that came to Anatolia in 2 thousands B.C., were carved in the shape of an eagle's head. In Hittites, Ittinu meant chief building master, and was derived from the word "Tin" in Sumerian, which meant the same thing. The title of the sculpture makers or the stone carvers was Esi or Eru. The secrets of this art, described as the Royal Art (as in Masonry), were hidden in the teachings which were passed on from the masters to the apprentices. Among the many carvings and sculptures made by the Esis, there were also double headed eagles. These were respectively, in their production order, Kultepe and Bogazkoy double headed eagles, Alachoyuk double headed eagle and Yazilikaya double headed eagle. In Hittites, the name of the double headed eagle was "Tesup".

The first double headed Hittite eagle dates back to 1900's B.C. It was first observed on seals used in commercial centers, but then was seen on the entrance gates of the cities as a symbol of sovereignty and protection/protectiveness.

Kanes Karum (known as Kultepe today), was one of the important Hittite commercial centers between 1900 and 1700 B.C. At the excavations at Kültepe, many double headed eagle figures were observed to have been inscribed on the cylindrical shaped clay seals. Similar seals and stamps were also found in Bogazkoy Karum.

On a similar seal found in Tarsus, the eagle was carved, carrying a god on its back. Other eagle symbols found on cylinders here were the sun disks with wings attached on them, like the ones used by the Sumerians.

The double headed eagle carving found in Alacahoyuk has been the oldest Hittitean double headed eagle carving found so far. It is believed that it was made between 1400 and 1200 B.C., when relations between the Hittites and the Egyptians were at a peak. The Egyptian influence can clearly be seen in the eagles' carving style. The double headed eagle was carved in the inner side of one of the gates. Wings and the tail was formed of seven symmetrically carved feathers. The heads, body and the legs were deeply carved. The eagle grasped two hares with its two claws. Alacahoyuk double headed eagle is currently being utilized as the emblem of the Turkish Historical Society.

Hattusas (Bogazkoy in today's name) was the capital of the Hittites for 450 years, from 1650 to 1200 B.C. Situated 2 kilometers away from Bogazkoy, there is the Yazilikaya Open Air Temple. Total length of this temple, which has two separate sections, is almost 50 meters. On its walls, 63 god, goddess and holy animal figures were carved, using the relief technique. The carvings on the east wall belonged to the gods, whereas the ones on the west wall were of the goddesses. They had been depicted from the profile, and as if they were walking as a group. Height of the carvings ranges from 80 cm to 2.5 meters. Compared to the Alacahöyük double headed eagle, the Yazılıkaya double headed eagle, inscribed between the two feet of the Mother God, is rather dainty. Its wings are similar to that of the Sumerian sun disk. Feathers of the tails are not detailed.

The double headed eagle is the messenger bird of the Hittite God Family. The eagle can commute freely between the human world and the world of Gods, and establish communication. It was even believed that the task of carrying the soul of the dead to the Gods' level was the eagle's duty, as well. Another duty of the eagle was to always keep vigil and warn the human beings, as well as the Gods in time against the evil and the dangers.[56]

We shall discuss this widely-used symbol of the Uyghur Empire by others in the world, primarily by Turkish Civilizations, in the following chapters.

Another impact of the Uyghur Civilization to this day was the Rama discipline, which was the main source of Zoroastrianism, Brahmanism and Buddhism.[57] After the great flood, Scythians, who were a branch of the Uyghurs, had parted from the central authority and formed an ever degenerating state in Europe. They united with Celtics, who had run away from Atlantis. The ruling class was the clergy in this state. However, these priests, named as the "Druids" had corrupted the religion to such an extent that, they instigated to sacrifice human lives, which had been the most valuable thing in ancient civilizations. Similar corruptions were also observed in Mesopotamia and in Central American states.

Druids would teach very few elite people from beginning to end. From this point of view, it was a form of teaching initiative secrets. Druid meant "Very Knowledgeable" in Celt language. As in all other initiative organizations, Druids too believed in immortality of the soul and that life continued in another body after death.[58] The most famous of the Druid doctrines known by mankind is the Book of the Feryllt. It is reported that the Feryllts were the monotheist bishops of Atlantis and having survived the great flood, these priests of the Sun had managed to come ashore on the west coast of Wales. Another point where the Celtic people arrived in Europe from Atlantis is the Iberian Peninsula. The word Portuguese has been derived from the combination of 'Porto' and 'Gallis', which means the gate of the Celts.[59]

The religion of the Druids roots from this legendary Atlantis Brotherhood. However, as was the case in many sun cults, Feryllt Brotherhood also got distorted in the course of thousands of years, moving from Monotheistic Osiris religion towards a polytheistic structure.[60]

Druids were the Celtic priests. Although the Celts were matricentric socially, their religion was patriarchally structured. It has been understood that the Scythians had adopted this system of the Atlantis priests in a period of thousands of years. The word Druid meant "Oak Men." Witchcraft was predominant. Druids called themselves as "The Mystical Clan". Druid tradition required that the disciplines be given orally and never permitted anything to be written. For that reason, all information obtained on the Druids were through Roman historians. Ammianus, a Roman historian, had written that Druids defended immortality of the soul, and shared the beliefs of Pythagoras. While Ammanaus Marcellinus had written that Druids believed that they would be re-born into another region in a different place and time, Julius Caesar had mentioned, Druids' immortal gods, and their methods for calculating the connection between the movements of stars and human lives.

Caesar had written that the Druids specifically would choose their students from among the Celtic noblemen's children, trained them in isolated places and that the training lasted around 20 years. The Romans had pointed out that there were plenty of similarities between the Greek Orfeic philosophy and the Celtic Druid philosophy, and that exchange of disciples and preceptors between the Greek and Egyptian academies and the Druids' academies were of.[61]

In the Druids' system, the apprentices used to wear green gowns. Admittance into apprenticeship began with an initiation ceremony. There is absolutely no written documentation on this ceremony, which is known to be a theatrical act. Throughout the apprenticeship, they were taught law, astronomy, poetry, and music. During poetry, which was second in level, they wore blue gowns. Their task was to travel in the country and to carry messages, convey what they have learned to the apprentices, and to gain mastery in different levels of administration. Each raise in level was celebrated with a ceremony. It was compulsory to complete the training to learn the astrological and mystical relations of symbols within a period of several years. At the third level, being accepted as the most respected status, Druids wore white gowns, which was the color representing purity, knowledge and spiritual integrity. They used to summon the people to worship the Sun every seventh day. This is where the word Sunday arose from. They would gather once every four months and act as judges between the clans and people. Homicide was absolutely forbidden. For that reason, Druids never took part in any war. Telling lies and exposing the secrets of the profession were good enough to be dismissed from being a Druid. Druid priests were not allowed to get married, either.[62]

From the time when the Druids were all over Europe and Northern Asia, practicing their polytheistic religion, to approximately 5 thousand years before today, Rama, a student of Naacal School, who presumably had survived up till then, re-appeared. Rama, whose name had understandably derived from Mu emperors Ra-Mu, started fighting against the Druids in order to make the monotheistic religion rule again. However, he could not succeed, and he, along with his supporters, was forced to migrate east. Edouard Schure states that Rama and his supporters, who had migrated to Afghanistan and Iran, where they united forces with other clans of the Scythians and the Uraltaics who had mixed with the yellow race, invaded India. Nevertheless, even after Rama's death, over time, corrupted versions of the Monotheistic religion in the form of Brahmanism, Shamanizm, Zoroastrianism and finally Buddhism arose.

The people that defeated the first settlers of India, the Nagas and took control of the country were the Druids, whose name is indicative of their origin of Northern territories. In the Brahma composite teaching, which at first was formed with the religious beliefs of the Nagas and the Druids combined, and attained its final version after the Arian invasion in 1600's B.C., it was believed that those who did a good job would be re-born in better conditions, and conversely, those who did badly would be born into worse circumstances. There is merely one supreme truth, and that is Brahma. He is the one who is present everywhere. The whole universe is nothing other than Brahma. It is Brahma who keeps all the gods, all worlds and all creatures united. Maya is the material reflection of Brahma on Earth; that is, the name of Earth. Maya, who came out of Brahma, resembles the heat coming out of a fire. There is no heat where there is no fire, but the heat is not the fire. The true immortal spirit is Brahma. The ultimate aim is to unite with this eternal and immortal, infinite spirit.

Brahma is "Trimutri", which means three gods in one. Brahma is the creator, Visnu is the protector, and Shiva is the destroyer. Spirit is immortal and strives to return to the source, through re-births.

In Brahmanism, the society was divided by a cast system. The Cast system consists of: 1) Brahman: Monks (Gurus), the clergy 2) Kshatriya: Kings, warriors, nobles; 3) Vaishya: Tradesmen and professionals, 4) Shudra: Peasants, workers, servants 5) Untouchables and slaves. Generally, Brahmans were Arians with fair complexion; Kshatriya were generally Arians and few dark skinned nobles. Conversion of individual spirits to cosmic spirits; in other words, the path to salvation/ redemption, was accesible only to the Brahman cast. The sole intention of those who were born into other Casts, was to strive to be re-born in this upper cast. Women, however, could only hope for being re-born as a man in their future lives.

Brahmanists believed that the human body disintegrated with death, and that the plants absorbed parts of these bodies; as a result, the animals that ate these plants were believed to have incepted part of the human beings. That is why cattle (including cows) are regarded as sacred.

In Brahmanism, it is believed that the holy books, Vedas were brought down from the Gods' level. There are four Vedas: Rig Veda; Yacur Veda; Sama Veda and Atarva Veda. In Brahma religion, the only way to benefit from the gods was to offer them sacrifices. It was compulsory that the acceptance ceremony of the sacrifices be performed exactly as defined in Vedas. The only ecole that could perform this ceremony were the Brahman priests. As a result of this privilege given through an initiation ceremony, the priests were given the right to have the gods do whatever they wished for. Consequently, this drew the conclusion of their being more powerful than the gods.

Brahma religion resulted from the combination of Arians' beliefs and the pre-Arian Hindu philosophy. Another source accepted as much holy as the Vedas was the Upanishads. Being the products of the pre-Arian Indian religious thinking, Upanishads claimed that the universe was not created, but came into being of its own accord due to compulsory reasons within. Mighty Father was God Pracapati. Pracapati had divided himself into innumerous pieces, but without losing its wholeness, had formed the universe from his own core/nature/entity/ substance. Although every creation displayed different images, they shared the essence/core which was unique and unchanged. The fact that the universe, in its unity and wholeness, seemed as being prosperous and diverse was but a result of an illusion. Together with Vedas, Pracapati left his place to Brahman.

According to Upanishads, Atman is the name given to pieces of Brahma in human beings. As well as being Brahma himself, Atman was the universal consciousness and power of mind. One who knows himself, knows his god.

In the Indian Mahavira inscriptions, the following expressions take place: "The secrets of the holy science are only known to the initiated people. For thousands of years, the saints, Brahma and the others have won victories with these arms. Krichacva has disclosed the secrets of Mantrashs (the Mu Supreme Priests)'".[63] Meaning of Upanishad is "Secret Discipline". Upanishad principles were taught to those tested, through a "coming of age" ceremony. The secrets of existence could not be taught through ordinary methods. This training, which could only be given together with a Guru guide, is called Yoga. Meaning getting to know himself through meditation and unity, Yoga had remained from pre-Arian civilization. In order to reach salvation (moshka) and free oneself from the turmoil of being born again, Yoga training was compulsory. Through Yoga, it was possible to reach salvation (Nirvana), even when one was still alive. Those who reach Nirvana while alive, were called Civanmukti (Kamil Man). In Upanishads, men and women were equal.

Buddha, was born in 563 B.C., lived for 80 years, and died in 483 B.C. His real name was Sidharta Gotoma. Buddha was his title, meaning enlightened person. It roots from the word "Budh" meaning "One Who Knows" in Sanskrit language.[64] Buddha was influenced by the Upanishads. Hence, the Buddha discipline can be regarded as a continuation of Brahmanism. Because Brahmanism was not established in Panjab and Ganja region when Buddha was alive, it could not stand up against this new wave strongly enough.

Buddha opposed sacrifice ceremonies. The ban of eating meat was only restricted to the meat of sacrificed animals.

Buddha made the discipline given through initiation in Brahmanism accessible to everyone. Just like Christianity, this view has helped Buddhism to spread worldwide. Dissemination of the discipline was considered a religious duty. According to the legend, Buddha was not conceived in his mother's womb through sexual intercourse. In her dream, Buddha's mother had seen a white elephant with whose trunk she got pregnant.

Buddha had forbidden all kinds of miracles, thinking that they would not be any use in the dissemination of the discipline in any way. A person should not search for the light elsewhere but within himself. Therefore, only those who can see the light within, can reach Nirvana. In order to find the light, one should not allow himself to get lost among earthly possessions, nor should he be completely insusceptible to them, or should torment himself by suffering. The mid way is the only way to reach Nirvana. A person who searches for his identity, without binding himself on the possessions, but without suffering either, will reach Nirvana and will break the vicious cycle of re-birth. What causes the desire for re-birth is the stubborn energy that keeps human passion and thought. By reducing such desires that yield to re-birth as much as possible, the chain of soul migration can be broken. The soul is a transient illusion.

The mid way that reaches Nirvana has 8 steps. These steps are: full vision, full comprehension, veracity, perfect behavior, decent way of living, full effort, full practise, full consciousness, and full awareness. The most important hurdle facing Nirvana is suffering. The source of suffering is the desires and passions that move the human being from one birth to the other. As long as the desires and passions are reduced, man can free himself of his sufferings. There are Four Mighty Truths: In life is suffering. There is a reason for suffering. If the reason is eliminated, then suffering will be removed as well. There is always a method that can eliminate the cause.

There is no privilege arising from Cast or ancestry, nor is there a place for the gods. Brahma, seated on the throne of the gods, is responsible for the destiny of neither the world, nor of the humans. Each human being should attend to his own destiny.

Arians that invaded India were of the same origin with the Persians. The great god of Arian belief was Mazdek. In time, the name Mazdek turned to Ahura Mazda, meaning "Master of Life". Ahura Mazda was life itself that puts soul into creatures, thus spreading everywhere. He is the master of the universe, god of the truth, the entity that makes the law of nature, and the father of every creation. There are many points in common between Indian Vedas and the Persians' holy book Avesta. The legendary motherland of the Arians was the very first piece of land Mazda had created.

In the Iranian Panteon of gods, Mitra represents the sun. He is the judge that awaits the souls beyond death to reach a verdict. However, the sacredness attributed to Mitra and to fire which was his symbol dates back to ancient times, way up to Babylonian civilization. It is a well-known fact that people who believed in Mitra had formed a cultural center in Babylon and the clergy in the temples kept the Holy Fire going incessantly.[65] In Babylon, the king that believed in Mitra was regarded as the brother of the sun and the moon. In his personality, the king represented three titles: The chief priest, combatant commander and the head architect. He used to carry symbols of these titles, depending on the task he was executing at the time. The symbol of ruling was a coat embroidered with stars.[66]

In Iran, Mitra is believed to have evolved into dualist Ahura Mazda belief, together with Zarathustra. Zarathustra's religious teaching is based on the reformation of Mitra religious belief. Arians' god Mazda and Mitra are identical.

Instead of Mitraism that had turned into a polytheist system, Zarathustra announced that he was the prophet of Mighty God Ahura Mazda, to whom he had also given the title of "Creator". However, some of the people in the region did not accept this reform movement and carried on with their old beliefs. While the Mitra belief encroached in all corners of the world during the Roman period, Ahura Mazda belief also spread among its supporters.[67]

According to Ahura Mazda belief, the world was created from the body of the Sun god Ahura Mazda, the sky was created from his skull, and the water was created from his tears, plants from his hair, living creatures from his hands and the fire from his spirit. It was believed that the world created was the creator himself. According to Zarathustra belief, Ahura Mazda is the one and only mighty god. Ahura Mazda said: "I have created the universe, the world and man from within myself. Man is a part of the god. Man is a miniscule replica of the universe and the world. From his own self, Mazda first created the soul, then the matter. When in the state of a soul, the human being is pure. Ahura Mazda's divine light is present in the human being's immortal soul. However, upon unification with the matter, the evil has entered it. It is also believed that, besides Ahura Mazda, there is another god which governs the evil. Ahura Mazda is the creator of the good, whereas the creator of the evil is Angre Manyu. Angre Manyu is the counterpart of Satan in divine religions.

The world is founded on the battle between the good and the evil. In the end, the god of good will win. The souls will face Ahura Mazda; according to their actions on Earth, the good ones will be sent to heaven, whereas the bad ones will be sent to hell. For this reason, one has to aim to be good in his thinking, saying and in his actions. The human being, accepted as the unification of the two sides, has the capability of distinguishing between the good and the evil, using his wisdom.

If the human being is good throughout his life using his power of taking decisions and his free will, he will return to god. In partition with death, while the body is returned to earth, the good soul reaches heaven with its accumulation of goods, thus reaches Ahura Mazda. Otherwise, the soul becomes the slave of Angre Manyu in hell. The soul is immortal. The body will return to earth, whereas eternal soul will raise to the sky. The three basic principles of the doctrine are to think good, to speak good, and to do good. Whatever human beings sow in their lives will be what they reap in the other world. In Yasna, which is accepted as the last speech of Zarathustra, it is said that a world of happiness awaits afterlife for those who have been good in the world and those who have been bad will face the evil. This temporary world is where Ahura Mazda examines the human beings.[68]

According to Zarathustra belief, while she was a virgin, at the age of 15, Zarathustra's mother became pregnant through a cluster of light, sent by Ahura Mazda. Being born of a virgin is a common characteristic of many beliefs, and was latest seen in Christianity. Zarathustra's mother's ancestry is dated back to the holy Manu family.

The real name of Zarathustra, who lived around 600 B.C., was Spitama. He was given the name Zarathustra after he declared that he was a prophet, meaning "the son of golden light". When he became a prophet, a golden star started shining on his forehead, representing the Divine Light. This Golden Star thus became the name of the prophet.

When Zarathustra was 30 years old, meditating in a cave, Ahura Mazda showed himself up in a ball of fire, and gave the holy book, Avesta to him. The fire gave no harm to Zarathustra. Thus, the fire was accepted as the sacred symbol of Ahura Mazda belief. The holy fire said: "Hear me Zarathustra, I am Ahura Mazda, the one who created and selected you. From now on, my voice will speak to you." Zarathustra was trembling. He was now the prophet of Ahura Mazda.

Ahura Mazda continued: "Wind (air) was created out of fire, water out of wind, earth of water, and everything on earth was created out of earth. The most important thing in life is for one to develop and to go beyond himself." Ahura Mazda had set the final goal, which was to develop and to be a good human being. A good man need not have fear of fire. Even if they pass through the fire, the fire will not harm the good men. According to Avesta, the fire is either the soul or the son of Ahura Mazda. Fire is sacred and dirtying the fire is a crime that requires a death sentence. That is why the dry wood logs that will feed the fire are handled by priests wearing white gloves. The fire distinguishes between sinful and innocent people. A person claimed to have committed a crime is put in the fire. If he burns, he is then guilty; he is innocent if he can manage to come out of the fire unburned. People passing through fire without getting burned, is a common characteristic of many religions. The best known implementation is Prophet Abraham being put in the fire and Abraham's coming out without getting harmed.[69]

Since fire is accepted as sacred, it constantly gets going in the temples of Ahura Mazda. The sacred fire temple in Shiz, named as the Throne of Salomon, is a place where people pay a visit for pilgrimage. Dawn in the morning, mid-day sun and dusk are the best times for worship. Besides the fire, the earth and water are also sacred. That is why dead bodies are never burned, or buried underground; nor are they thrown in the water in order to keep these sacred places clean. Instead, dead bodies are placed on high rise towers, known as the towers of silence, where they decompose and be eaten by birds.

Having declared his prophethood, Zarathustra disowned the old gods. He refused the bloody sacrifice ceremonies, especially those performed for Mitra. He said that it was a sin to slaughter animals.

Matraist clergymen, community leaders and governors who realized that Zarathustra was going to overthrow them, started a campaign against Zarathustra. Zarathustra left the country with a few followers and went to Khorasan, where he disseminated his belief. Later, he returned to Urmiye, his birth place, and here he became more effective in disseminating his religion.

According to Zarathustra, Ahura Mazda was surrounded by 7 holy angels, appointed to rule the universe, each one of whom were assigned with specific tasks.

It is seen here that Zarathustra had converted the 7 gods accepted by the locals to angels and presented them as second level/degree holy creatures. Zarathustra followed the route of Orpheus and many other recent religion leaders, trying to disseminate his own belief by compromising Mitra belief to a certain extent. All heavenly religions, especially Christianity, used the same method, and regarded the local gods as saints or angels.

Again, as in Mitra belief, in societies committed to Zarathustra belief, the king was the political leader and the highest priest. The state was governed by Zaotars, clergy of the highest degree, besides the king. The name of the fire priests' class is Athravan. When Zarathustra became a prophet, he was wearing a white shirt. For that reason, as with most other priests, the outfits of Ahura Mazda priests are white.

As in Mitra belief, Ahura Mazda priests also uses an initiation system of 7 degrees. These degrees were stated by a Christian priest Hiyeronymus, in Latin, as follows: 1- Corox (Recognition); 2-Eryphius (Secret); 3-Miles (Battle); 4-Leo (Lion); 5-Perses (Farsis/Persians); 6-Heliodromus (Sun); 7-Pater (Father).

Of these, the first three degrees were preperation stages, and the pupils in these three degrees were not admitted to Athravan meetings. Third degree represented the symbolism of death and resurrection. The four main elements in the ceremony of this degree were Fire, Water, Air and Earth. Passing to the fourth degree was done by another ceremony. In this ceremony, reunion of the soul and the body was symbolized. Those who passed to the fourth degree with this ceremony were admitted to Athravan group. In Zarathustra's Gathas, the 4th degree was recalled with the name "Urvata". The priest in the fifth degree was the bearer of the people's spirit and he could have direct contact with the spiritual creatures. The priest in the sixth degree experienced mystical death. The priest in this degree could see the sun in the middle of the night, the sun becoming the bearer of his soul, and was recalled as the hero of the sun. The highest rank priests were those in the seventh degree, and they were recalled as "Father". "Father" was a priest who had deserved to be with Ahura Mazda. He would reach God after death. All of the Zoatars, who were the ruling class, were 7th degree Fathers.[70]

According to Zarathustra belief, a re-birth was in question, before reaching heaven. In Yasht 19.11, this matter is handled as follows: "When the deads become alive, the ones who are alive come without getting old. Lives are arranged according to individuals' wishes." All children born, after a re-birth (Navjote) ceremony, were accepted as a member of Zarathustra religion. They wore a holy shirt, a holy belt and a holy hat.

In Zarathustra belief, men and women are equal. Ahura Mazda had created the first human couple (Meshnave /Meshnayak). While they were living in heaven, God was not pleased with their behavior, so they were dismissed from heaven. These people increased in number on Earth. As what they did on Earth was sinful, Ahura Mazda had the majority killed by a great flood, while he permitted a small number of them to survive.

This and many other similar sagas have been included in many heavenly religions, which are considered to be a continuation of Zoroastrianism. While the Jews were kept in Babylon, many of the Zoroastrianist beliefs were taken into Torah. Again, it is known that Pythagoras, Plato and other Pythagoreans went to Babylon to learn about Zoroastrianism. In short, Zoroastrianism was a source of inspiration for philosophical movements as well as other heavenly religions that followed.

As we will refer to Shamanism and Shanman practises, the two Mu and Uyghur based disciplines at a later stage, let us now analyze the ancient Egyptian civilization stage.

References

1   Hope Murry,- *Atlantis, Legend or Reality?, (Atlantis, Efsane mi Gerçek mi?),* AD Pub., Istanbul 1994, p. 19.

2   Avedisyan Ara,- *The Biggest Secret in the Universe (Evrende En Büyük Sır),* Sümer Pub., Istanbul 1973, p. 242

3   Andrews Shirley,- Atlantis, *Llewellyn P.,* USA, 1997, p. 299

4   Schure Edouard,- *Big Initiates (Büyük İnisiyeler),* RM Pub., Istabul, 1989, p. 541

5   *Science Research Group (Bilim Araştırma Grubu),- MU; Prehistoric Universal Civilization (MU; Tarih Öncesi Evrensel Uygarlık),* Bilim Araştırma Merkezi Pub., Istanbul 1978, p. 58.

6   Andrews P., r.w., p. 96.

7   Santesson Hans Stephan,- *MU, The Sunken Country Civilization (Batık Ülke Mu Uygarlığı),* RM Yayınları, Istanbul 1989, p. 93

8   Hope M, r.w., p. 24-25

9   Hope M, r.w., p. 58

10 Churchward James,- *The Children of Mu,(Mu'nun Çocukları),* London, 1931

11 Cayce Edgar, *Atlantis before the Flood (Tufan Öncesi Atlantis),* RM Pub., Istanbul, 1989, p. 15

12 Andrews P., r.w., p. 36

13 Hope M., r.w., p. 61

14 Hope M., r.w., p. 66.

15 Hope M., r.w., p. 194

16 Hope M., r.w., p. 196

17 Hope M., r.w., p. 70

18 Andrews P., r.w., p. 136

19 Hope M., r.w., p. 73

20 Hope M., r.w., p. 173

21 Andrews P., r.w., p. 227

22 Hope M., r.w., p. 196

23 Churchward James,- *The Sacred Symbols of MU (MU'nun Kutsal Sembolleri),* Eng., 1935, p. 240.

24 Avedisyan A., r.w., p.128

25 Churchward J., r.w., p. 238

26 Andrews P., r.w., p. 74

27 Andrews P., r.w.,p. 114

28 Spence Lewis,- *Occult Sciences in Atlantis (Atlantis'de Okült Bilimler),* Sannel Weiser Inc., 1978, p. 119

29 Hope M., r.w., p. 209

30 Hope M., r.w., p. 214

31 Hope M., r.w., p. 222

32 Santesson HP., r.w., p.95

33 Hope M., r.w., p. 19

34 Hope M., r.w., p. 54

35 Avedisyan A., r.w., p.64

36 August Le Plonge,- *Origin of Egyptians (Mısırlıların Kökeni),* Ege Meta Pub, Istanbul, p. 72

37 August L.P., r.w., p. 180

38 Churchward J., *Children of Mu,* London, 1931

39 August L.P., r.w., p. 91

40 August L.P., r.w., p. 58

41 Umar Bilge,- *Historical Names in Turkey (Türkiye'deki Tarihsel Adlar),* Inkılap Pub., Istanbul 1999, p. 530

42 August L.P., r.w., p. 85

43 Knight, *Christopher;* Lomas, Robert,- *The Book of Hiram (Hiramın Kitabı),* Bilge Karınca Pub., Istanbul 2008, p. 114

44 August L.P., r.w., p. 147

45 Taşkın Sefa,- *Light People of Mysia (Mysia'nın Işık İnsanları),* Sel Pub., Istanbul,1997, p. 72

46   Bobaroğlu Metin,- *Anagogic Tradition (Batıni Gelenek),* Ayna Pub., Istanbul 2002, p. 23

47   Taşkın P., r.w., p. 91

48   Signier, Jean Francois/Thomazo, Renaud- *Secret Organizations (Gizli Örgütler),* Larousse, Oğlak Güzel Kitapları, Istanbul 2006, p. 25

49   Sibel Özbudun,- *Transformation Dynamics of a Religious Tradition from Hermes to Idris (Hermes'ten İdris'e Bir Dinsel Geleneğin Dönüşüm Dinamikleri),* Ütopya Pub., Feb. 2004 Ankara, p. 55

50   Avedisyan, A., r.w., p.101

51   Avedisyan, A., r.w., p.104

52   Schure E., r.w., p. 53

53   Churcward James- *Lost Continent of Mu,* London 1931, p. 123

54   Avedisyan, A., r.w., p.107

55   Ada, Ural,- *Cultural Origin of Turks (Türklerin Kültür Kökeni),* HKEMBL Pub.

56   Ayan Tamer,- *Double Headed Eagle (Çift Başlı Kartal),* İtidal Olgunlaşma Pub., Istanbul 1998, p. 131

57   Schure E., r.w., p. 78

58   Signier, Jean Francois/Thomazo, Renaud,- *Secret Organizations (Gizli Örgütler),* Larousse Oğlak Güzel Pub., Istanbul 2006, p.31

59   Avedisyan, A., r.w., p.155

60   Monroe, Douglas- Merlyn, New Age Pub., Istanbul 2004, p. 17

61   Monroe, Douglas, r.w., p. 30

62   Monroe, Douglas, r.w., p. 40

63   Avedisyan, A., r.w., p. 138

64   Freke, Timothy&Gandy, Peter- *Mysteries of Jesus (İsa'nın Gizemleri)* Ayna Pub., Istanbul, 2005, p. 401

65   Xemgin, Ethem, - *Mazda Belief in the Origin of Alevism and Zoroastrian Doctrine (Aleviliğin Kökenindeki Mazda İnancı ve Zerdüşt Öğretisi),* Berfin Pub.- Istanbul 1995, p. 46

66   Xemgin, Ethem, r.w., p. 44

67   Xemgin, Ethem, r.w., p.62

68   Xemgin, Ethem, r.w., p. 120

69   Xemgin, Ethem, r.w., p.116

70   Xemgin, Ethem, r.w., p. 247

CHAPTER IV

EGYPT AND THE SCHOOL OF HERMES

Egyptian civilization, the occurrence of which cannot be explained by the scientists today, has been referred to by Ernest Renan as follows:

"Egypt has never lived its youth. In the very beginning, it was mature and old. This civilization has had no childhood."[1]

In Egypt, the language seems to have perfected itself long before the Pharaoh Menes (5 thousand B.C.). In the old inscriptions, the dates of which could not have been determined for certain, the language has been used in a correct format. This language is not related any of the African or Asian languages, either. Just like the Egyptian civilization, Egyptian language does not have any early or development stage. Same letter characters can be given different meanings. The hieroglyphs that are understood by ordinary people, also have hidden meanings that can only be understood by the initiated people. The scripts can be read in three different formats, ideographically, symbolically and alphabetically. It is also observed in Egypt that Teb dialect in Upper Egypt has been used together with Menfis or the Lower Egypt dialect. Among these, the lower Egypt dialect seems to have appeared at the peak of its development.[2]

In Turin Papyrus that gives the names of the kings that ruled Egypt, there is a list of 10 gods. After that list, then there are the names of nine families. Of the papyrus, the large numbers of pages of which have been worn out beyond recognition, last two letters read as follows:

"Rulers until Shemsu-Hor (has been translated as the comrades of Horus): 23 thousand 200 years. The elders of Shemsu-Hor: 13 thousand 420 years.[3] Here, the similarity of the names "Shems" and Samas, the sun god of Sumerians, is quite intriguing.

These numbers add up to 36 thousand 720 years. Considering that Egypt was a colony of Atlantis before the great flood, it can be concluded that the kings given here were also the kings of the Atlantis. As two different periods were defined, and Horus was the son of Osiris, the determination was made between before and after the implementation of Osiris religion, and in a way, Osiris has been accepted as the year zero.

On the tablets of the Egyptian Edfu temple, it is inscribed that the people who built the temple have arrived from an island known as "the Country of the Elderly". They have fled that island, as is it was under the danger of sinking. This group of people also known as the "Masters of the Light", were later named as "Architect Gods." These gods were not immortal, and were replaced by children that they brought up.[4] While the Roman historian Diodorus Sicilus, who lived in the 1st century A.D., has expressed: "Egyptians were strangers who settled by the shores of the Nile, having brought civilization, calligraphy and a different language from their country, in the ancient times. They had come from the land where the sun set." His colleague, Ammianus, who lived in the 3rd century, has claimed that these people who were experts in old secrets foresaw the great flood and built underground dens and secret passes for preserving the archaic knowledge and implementing ceremonies.[5]

It has been observed that some of the skulls and bones found in graves belonging to pre-families' period was bigger compared to those of the locals. The people in these graves located in the Northern part of Egypt were traditionally called "Comrades of Horus" and were the leaders of their communities in their period.[6] Toth, who brought calligraphy to Egypt, was also a Horus Comrade. In the legends of the Phoenicians, the name "Taut" is mentioned as the inventor of writing. Egyptian Priest Manehto has expressed that Toth (Hermes Trimagistus) has written all information on tablets, using holy inscriptions.

Egyptian civilization was formed by unification of two colonies set up by Mu and Atlantis, after the great flood. In both of these colonies, while the monotheistic and esoteric teaching was valid initially, Mu colony got degenerated afterwards and started implementing polytheism. Atlantis colony on the other hand, was founded by Hermes (Toth) and was implementing Osiris religion.[7] In the letters left to his grandchildren, Henry Schileman, the explorer of Troy, following lines were found: "On the lions gate among the ruins of Miken, the following lines were inscribed: 'Misor is the son of Toth.' Toth is a hierophant married to the daughter of Kronus, the king of Atlantis, and founded the very first colony in Egypt. The temple in Sais was built by Toth. Toth is regarded as a god by ancient Egyptians.[8] The word Hierophant meant the Head Priest and dated back to Atlantis.

Hermes, one of the followers of Osiris, who lived 6 thousand years after him, 16 thousand years before today, went to Nile delta from Atlantis and founded a colony there and started disseminating Osiris religion there. It was observed that there was not an independent kingdom in Southern Egypt. Hermes, who built a temple in Sais for Osiris, the following description is made in the famous "Book of the Dead": "Master of the devine word and the owner of the holy secrets." Northern Egypt was ruled by the Hermetic priests from Hermes period to Pharaoh Menes period (5 thousand B.C.). Later, Hermes, who has been referred to as prophet Enoch and also prophet Idris, in the holy books of the monotheistic Abrahamic religions, has been named by the Ehyptians, then by the Greeks, as "Trimaggistus", meaning three times big, since he was a king, a head priest and a religion founder.

Manetho of Egypt, a priest that lived in the 4th century B.C., is the person who has ensured that Hermes Trimagistus' expressions and inscriptions have reached the present day. According to Manehto, the Gods' rule that lasted for 13 thousand and 420 years, ended with the Old men of Horus, and left the rule to human kings, starting with Menes. Manetho, the protector of Akashi records, has said that Toth, Egypt's god of calligraphy and the master of his time, wrote 36 thousand 525 books that contained archaic information.[9] It is not possible for all those books to be written by one man. It is quite possible that these were the Akashi records of the Atlantis. Akashi is the name given to the core of the matter, which the universe is believed to float in. As all events since the very beginning have been recorded on this liquid, Akashi in the meantime, is a universal memory. It is also believed that having reached sufficient maturity, people can rise to the same frequency level and receive the necessary information from there.

On Sothis, one of the rare papyrus documents that has managed to reach today, in genuine words of Manetho, it is written as follows: "I am the chief priest of the holy temples in Egypt and writer Manetho, sir. I hereby present my greetings to Ptolome. Our ancestor, the books written by three times great Hermes by holy letters will show you what will happen to the world."[10] From this, it can be deducted that Pharaoh Ptolome has asked Manetho whether he could see the future.

It says in the Corpus of Hermetica that, in the legendary Emerald Plates of Hermes Trimagistus, the following has been stated: "It is true, correct and certain that, the one at the bottom, is like the one at the top, and that is to realize the miracle of just one thing. As everything present is one and has come out of one, everything, through adaptation, everything has been born out of one." Hermetica consists of proverbs imputed to Hermes, and has reached the present day through the Academy of Plato, which has received it from the ancient Greek.[11] According to Hermetism, Hermes has written the seven archaic information on this emerald tablet.

In the holy book of Stobeaus imputed to Hermes, contains the following expressions: "Among you, there will be fair kings, philosophers, statesmen, law makers, real soothsayers, real healers, real prophets of the gods, expert musicians and competent astronomers, staying on the edge of a more holy universe."

In Primarder, the oldest philosophical work in Egypt, the following expressions are present, with respect to creation:

"Out of the chaos, a pure and illuminous fire rose and dispersed in the air. The water, the core of which is cringed in the fire, has occupied the middle zone. The water and the fire were so intervened that there was no sign of the earth covered by water."

French author and researcher Francois Lenorment, says in his work titled "Antique History" that the following expression were found on another Egyptian papyrus:

"He is the only creator of the sky and the earth. He was not created, nor he was born. He is the one who has created everything, but he was not created. He is the only god, who has created him from himself."[12]

In section 64, which is regarded as one of the oldest sections of the Egyptian Book of the Dead, it is stated in an article on an Egyptian papyrus dating back to 3 thousand 370 B.C., that the following were inscribed on an iron block by engraving lapis lazuli on the block: "I am yesterday, today and tomorrow. I am capable of being born again."[13] According to a drawing in the papyrus, there was a symbol consisting of a triangle in a circle inscribed on an edge of the same block. On another papyrus dating back to 4 thousand 260 B.C., it is stated that during Pharaoh Menkara period, the King's chief architect found the above mentioned iron block in a very old temple, under the feet of God Toth, on an altar.

Toth, in the Egyptian pantheon of Gods, is the God of the Moon, just like Sin of Babylon.[14] He is the founder of the stately order and the initiator of the holy worshipping. In Egyptian sources, he is referred to as "the one who established the two Egypt by his commands". It was possible to unite the two parts of Egypt and to establish a central administration, through his foresights. He is the oldest lawmaker, the one who has brought the law to people, or in other words, "The Master of Law". Toth is the creator of the divine word, the science, writing, books and is the one who has established the religious order, the ceremonies, and the temples.

In the archives of Denderahand Philae temple, Toth is defined with various titles, such as the master of magical and secret science, master of construction of the temples, the god of eloquence and fine art, master of physicians, and the god of the crafts.[15] Toth, according to Memphis theology, is the remark who has created himself, through pleasant singing. Toth is the one who has emerged from a word. Together with Horus, he is the first of the emanations that have appeared from Ptah. Together with Horus, he is the one who creates by remarks, the one who organized and managed chaos, and is the master of holy remarks. He is the mediator god who has united the Upper and Lower Egypt. In the Book of the Death, in Toth's words, the following is said: "I have ended the fight of two comrades, and wiped away their sorrows."

Initially, Egypt was established as two kingdoms, as upper and lower Egypt. Along with the suggestions made by Toth, in 5 thousand B.C., when Pharaoh Menes invaded lower Egypt, the two were converted into a single kingdom. When the two kingdom united, their gods were also united in the same pantheon. The name of the creator god was Aton in lower Egypt, and Amon in the upper kingdom.[16]

Here is a poem written for Amon-Ra, which is one of the best examples for the belief in Amon being the creator:

> God is one and only, there is no one else.
> He is one. He is the one who created everyone.
> God is a spirit, and unseen spirit. The spirit of the spirits. The might spirit of Egypt.
> The divine Spirit.
> He was present in the very beginning.
> He is the very first creature. He was there when there was nothing else.
> He created everything, after he was born.
> Creator of the initiators.
> He is infinite, from the very beginning until the very end of the time.
> His existence that has continued from pre-eternity will continue until the eternity.
> God is secret. No one has ever seen him.
> No one has even seen anyone similar.
> He always remains secrets for those he created.
> God is the truth. He lives with the truth. He is the true Pharaoh.
> God is life, people can only live with him.
> He is the one who fills the lungs with air.
> He is the mother and the father. Father of the fathers, and mother of the mothers.
> God creates, but has never been created. Gives birth, but has never been born.
> He gives birth to himself, creates himself.
> He makes, but is never made.
> He is the creator of his own existence, he is the purifier of existence.
> He is the creator of the earth, sky, deep seas and the huge mountains.
> He extends to heaven, goes to the depths of the earth.
> Whatever dawns in his heart, it is realized.
> Whatever he says, happens, reaches eternity.
> He is the father of all gods and all divine creatures.
> He is merciful to those who are scared of him, hears their cries.
> Protects the weak, against the strong.
> He recognizes the ones that recognize him.
> He extends his hand to help, to those who serve. Protects his followers.[17]

Egyptian priest and historian Manetho has stated that people were monotheists during the 1st dynasty, and the symbols of gods were regarded as different qualifications of God. During the 2nd dynasty on the other hand, through a decision taken by the board of priests, instead of worshipping the creator, along with the beliefs of the ruling upper Egyptian family, people have started worshipping holy symbols, and in time, the symbols have become gods, themselves. As a result of this decision taken, Egyptian civilization became polytheist. Within the frame of the new belief system, the pharaoh was God Horus, and ex-pharaoh was God Osiris.

The main source of information on the rituals, after death of a pharaoh is the inscriptions inside the five pyramids in Sakara, known as the "Pyramid Texts". The pyramid texts show that the ritual for a new pharaoh contains a ceremony of baptizing, before the birth of a new Horus. From Egypt to present day, throughout the history, there have always been water tanks in initiation halls or temples. Rituals have been different from sprinkling holy water on to the candidate to dipping him completely in water.[18] The most important of the Pyramid Texts is the one in the pyramid belonging to King Unas. This pyramid is the youngest of the five. Some Egyptologists estimate the age this pyramid, where ritualistic ceremony was held, as 4 thousand 300 years. On the other hand, the age of the written ritual was given as 5 thousand 300 years. As can be understood from this discrepancy, there is no certainty on the age of the pyramids.[19]

In the Corpus of Hermetica, written in 2nd century A.D. in Greek, and gathered in Alexandria, containing the teachings of Hermes, Aton has been referred to as the creator of everything, god of pure kindness and of pure love.[20] Aton, is the source of the light that has created everything after him and the first cause of everything. Some of the remarks given in Hermetica, written in a poem format, are as follows:

"Philosophy is a spiritual effort, to reach the knowledge of truth of the only god Aton, through continuous meditation. One who learns philosophy, searches for the information dedicated to Aton. It is that information which discloses the secrets of the universe, arranged with the power of the figures. I, three times mighty Hermes, have inscribed the secrets of the gods on stone tablets, through divine symbols and hieroglyphs, for you to attain to that information. I have reached the truth through meditation. I write all these lines herein with such realization.

I got free of my body, and flew to my thoughts. An extensive and infinitesimal creature addressed me: "Hermes, what are you looking for?" I am the thoughts of the single god Aton. I am with you, anytime, and anywhere. All of a sudden the truth has been exposed. I have had the endless vision. All melted in the light, united with love.

Remarks of Aton are the creative ideas. He is the one that feeds everything that is created through him, is a mighty endless power. He is the almighty and the absolute truth. He is present everywhere. He is the source of everything. Aton is full, like the figure one. Even if he divides or multiplies, he remains as he is. The universe is one. The sun, the moon and the earth, are all one. Do you think there are several gods? God is only one. Don't think that there is anything more visible than Aton. He has created everything. You can see him through all those. Meditate on the cosmos, as his ancient body. He is the secret one, clearly visible in all his works.

Think of how you were formed in your mother's womb. Think of that masterful workmanship and start searching for the artist. Aton is the one who shapes a beautiful god-like creature. He is the first of everything. The second, is the Cosmos, created on the appearance of Aton. He is impossible to die. Nothing is present in Cosmos, as lifeless or dead. Aton is light, is the source of energy that will last until eternity. Endless distributor of life itself. Our soles are fed with the light of Aton. Ra is nothing like Aton, that can only be known through meditation. Ra is present in time and in the space, and we can see it with our eyes. Sun is a representation of the Mighty Creator, and the human being is of the sun.

The mighty father, the life and the light, gave birth to humanity, with his own identity. In the beginning, immortal was the man. However, Aton saw that he could not add his labor to earth, without an envelope. A mortal body was needed for the human being, besides an immortal soul. Aton is one. Cosmos is one, and so is the human being. Just like the Cosmos, he is also one that consists of many different pieces. Master created the man, in the order of the Cosmos. His piece that is called appearance of Aton, is spiritual and eternal. The other piece consists of four materialistic elements, and is mortal. Aton, Cosmos, and the human being; Cosmos is the son of Aton, human being is the grandson. All spirits are a part of the spirit of the Cosmos. Birth is not the beginning of life. Death, on the other hand, is not the end. Death is disintegration of a tired body. Only a good spirit gets to know Aton. Now, a spirit as such has completed its marathon. After leaving its physical form, then becomes a creature with a body of light.

Understand that you are immortal. See in your mind that everything is present together. Then, you will get to know Aton. Some become like a god, through the power of the mind. This is what Osiris taught. Gods are immortal human beings, and the human beings are mortal gods. The spirit is fed by fire and air. The body on the other hand, by water and earth. Mind is the fifth part. It has rooted from the light, and has only been given to human beings. The word alone, can never convey the truth. However, the power of mind is great. When the words direct him, can find the truth and the peace.

Aton is a musician, who has composed the order of the cosmos and has conveyed to the human being, the rhythm of his music. When the music loses its rhythm, do not blame the composer. Perhaps a wire has got loose on his lyre, which gives an unpleasant tune, destroying the unmatched beauty of the melody. When an artist gets in contact with an honorable theme, a wonderful piece of music is heard, astonishing anyone who listens to. Aton's power will make your music perfect, too.

I am on earth and in the sky, in the water and in the air. I am the one who is present everywhere, I am the existence. I can see your mind with mine. I know the One. I see a fountain bubbling with life. I am the mind. Now, as you have learned these secrets, promise that you will remain silent. These teachings have been recorded specifically to be read only by those, whom Aton has wanted to."

According Hermetica, Aton is the first source of light. He has created the universe from himself, and is identical. Ra, is the name of our sun, which is the physical symbol of this divine light. Aton gives life to universe, and Ra gives life to earth. Thus, the pharaoh, who is the symbol of the divine power on earth, has also been named as Ra. Ra is the name of the visible physical light. Aton on the other hand, is a spiritual source of light, totally invisible by the eye. In other words, Ra is the representative of Aton on the physical plane. As Aton has enlightened the universe, Ra enlightens our world.

Hermes is the founder of Lower Egypt, established as a colony of Atlantis. For that reason, Aton is of Atlantis origin and an expression of monotheism in Osiris religion. Amon on the other hand, is the name of God in the Upper Egypt, established as a colony of Mu. Ra, in both states, is the name of our sun, representing the heavenly power. When Lower Egypt was invaded by Upper Egypt, Egypt became a single state, while the conquerors' god Amon comes up front, the losers' god Aton remained behind. In other words, both Amon and Aton are the names of the creator god. This oldest creator god is symbolized by a sun disc. The sun god was identified with "Ra" and the duo was named as Amon-Ra and was symbolized by a flacon headed with a sun disc on his head.

The name Aton is seen in the records taken during Queen- Pharaoh Hachepsut's time. Hachepsut, who was the widow of Pharaoh Thotmoses II (1492–1479 B.C.) became a regent after the Pharaoh's younger son from a secondary wife was crowned as Thotmoses III. In the 7th year of her regency, she declared herself as the Queen-Pharaoh. It can be seen that the following have been inscribed in the Temple of Karnak by the Queen Hachepsut:

"I am Aton, the one who created the living things, gave power to earth and completed the creation of the world…"

It is known that during Queen Hatchepsut's era, Yemeni Shebas that worshipped the sun, have visited the pyramid in the plateau of Giza, for pilgrimage. According to Shebas, the pyramids that they helped to be built, have been devoted to the stars and the planets and their great grandfather and great leader Sab, son of Hermes, who gave the tribe his name, have been buried under the big pyramid. In other words, the roots of the Saabis go back to Sab, the son of Hermes.

As it will be seen later, the Saabis in Harran have a Hermetic belief. The Shebas in Yemen, who are a branch of the Harran Saabis, also believed in Hermes. The most important god of all these tribes is the Sun. It is quite possible that Queen Hachepsut, who was in contact with the queen of the Shebas at the time, was impressed with the beliefs of the Shebas and put Aton in forecourt. However, in this period, Aton was no longer a single God, was an important God in the Egyptian Panteon of Gods.[21]

The very first brotherhood organization found in the written records of Egypt was founded by Pharaoh Thotmoses III, in the 15th century B.C. The name of this organization was "the Great White Brotherhood." Its aim was to protect the information and disciplines remained after the great flood, and to disseminate them to the world. Center of the organization was the Temple of Karnak. Thotmoses means the son of Toth (Hermes).[22]

In Egypt, the Law of Maat was valid. Maat philosophy, based on righteousness, justice and the truth ruling in all sectors of life, was not a religion. A concept of justice which was not based on any religion, was so rare to be seen and implemented. The concept of justice which is not based on any religious belief has formed the way of thinking in several esoteric and anagogic principles, based on the Maat philosophy of Egypt.

Initially representing order and philosophy, Maat in time got perceived as a goddess and took her place in the pantheon of gods. The word that can be translated as the gods of Egypt is "Neter". Neters represents several nature of a single existence covering everything. "Gods" is different visuals or faces of a single god.[23] According to the Pantheon of Gods, the brother of goddess Maat is Toth, the moon god. He is symbolized as an ibis carrying a baton of wisdom in his hand, with a moon sphere on his head. He was the teacher of the art of construction and of religion, the master of divine word and the owner of the divine secrets, and he was the one who taught writing and reading, and the science of medicine to humanity. Another old Egyptian god is Ptah. The names of this god, other than Ptah, meaning initiator, are the "Divine Artist and Divine Constructor". His symbol is a square with two open sides. This god in Upper Egypt belief is believed to correspond to four basic elements in Mu religion, that brought order from caos.[24]

Egyptian religious beliefs, immortality of the soul and the re-birth philosophy have been clearly written in "Anana Papyrus", named after the chief clerk Anana, who wrote the papyrus in 1320 B.C., in Pharaoh Seti II period:

"Witness the contents of all written in this bunch. Read it, those who will find it in unborn days, if the gods have given you the ability to read. Read it the children of the future, read the secrets of your both too far yet to near past.

Human beings do not get born for once and leave this earth forever, after they die. They live many times in numerous different places. They don't all need to happen on this world, either. There is a dark curtain between each of these lives. Finally, all doors will open and all the rooms that have been entered to will be displayed in front of our eyes.

Our religion teaches us that we have lived since pre-eternity. Now, since there is no ending in the eternity, there can never be a beginning, either. It is a circle. Thus, if we are going to live until the eternity, we have also lived since pre-eternity.

In the people's eyes, god takes different faces and each person can swear that he has seen the real image of God.

However, they are all mistaken, because they are all correct.

Our "Ka"s, in other words our spiritual bodies show themselves up to us in different ways. Contacting with the infinitesimal well of wisdom, a desire that is hidden inside everyone, helps us to have a look at the truth, and gives us, the one who have come here by specific orders, the power to manage wonderful things. A soul should not be judged by the body, nor should a god be judged by his house.

Skarabe insect of the Egyptians is not a god. It is the symbol of the creator. Because by rolling a piece of mud between its legs, it lays his eggs just there. Just like the Creator rolling the earth between its legs and thus creating life there.

All gods send their love to earth, otherwise the world cannot survive without them. My belief, perhaps a little moreclear than yours, teaches me that the life does not end with death and for that reason love, which is the soul of life will continue, for as long as the life does.

The power of unseen connections will continue bringing together two different spirits, long after the world dies. It is possible that the spirits present together in an existence, will be present again in another one, and without getting to know the reason, they can be brought together. A human being is born several times. But, they never know their previous lives. Every now and then, a short day dream or a sudden thought may take him to a scene from a previous life. Although the scene looks too familiar, the mind can never justify when and where that scene was experienced. Nonetheless, finally all previous lives will reveal themselves.[25]

In the book of dead, it is written that any soul will fly towards the sky and will melt in the universal soul, located in the sun, the heat of which has given life to bodies of the living things.[26] Universal Soul is the source of all other souls, is the origin of all creatures and all other gods were created from the universal soul. These gods are only the identical copies of the Universal Soul. The symbol of the universal soul is the eye of Horus. In a pray after the death of someone, the following has been said:

"Here, the dead. I am putting the eye of Horus in your eye, opened by an Osiris priest." The soul of the dead, which has taken the shape of a bird will melt in the Eye of Horus, combine with a creating light and he himself will also be a drop of the source of life.

Eye of Horus

In the Egyptian language, Hermes means "The Enlightened Person" or the perfect human being. Ra, that exists in the same words, when spelt as He Ra-Smus, Ra points at the Sun god, or the source of light. The same word is used in Hebrew as "Hiram" and in Turkish as "Ermish" (Kamil One). It is believed that the words Rahim (Creator) and Rahman (Created) in Arabic are of the same root.

The eagle symbol that we investigated earlier, is seen in Egyptian civilization, too. In Ancient Egypt, the symbol of the letter "A" or as better known in Greek, "Alpha", in other words the symbol of no precedent is a single headed eagle. In Hermeticism, the white eagle is the symbol of everything related to the sky, but especially of the soul of the perfect people, also is the re-birth symbol of the soul that has got close to divine Kingdom. In Hermeticism, there are 33 esoteric raising degrees following the initiation, details of which we are going to handle later. The top degree, which is the 33rd degree can only be held by 3 people, the pharaoh, the vizier and the chief priest.

At this point, we need to give a break to Hermes and the development of brotherhood organization in Egypt and the Egyptian beliefs, and go back to the great disaster, the great flood that caused an era to finish and another one to start.

The concept of the great flood has been etched in everyone's brain around the globe, not be wiped off easily. The great flood was not limited to Mesopotamia and the Middle East, as claimed by some historians. On the contrary, one of the least affected parts of the world is the Middle East. There are almost no nation or tribe that does not mention of two giant continents sinking, in myths and religious sagas, due to a massive flood. Scandinavians, Indians, Greeks, Jews, Turks, Red Indians, Polynesians, in short, all tribes from all corners of the world mention of the great flood in full details. Besides, it is a well-known fact that the glaciers in the north pole melted last 12 thousand years ago. Everywhere, except for the areas too far from the oceans and places too high up, were covered in water by massive waves and water by the melting glaciers.

The oldest documents found with respect to the great flood are some clay tablets of the Sumerian period, written in 6 thousand B.C. In the most important one of these tablets, the Sumerian Royal List, it is expressed that at least 10 kingdom reigned before the great flood and each lasted between 10 thousand and 60 thousand years. The list is ended as follows: "After the great flood, the kingdom was sent from the mighty places."

From this, it can be understood that the level of civilization was far too high before the great flood, and a new start was given after the flood. Again, in so many Sumerian tablets it is given in great detail how the flood has started. Babylonian civilization is continuation of the Sumerians. Babylonian historian Berrossus, who has clearly received the information from Sumerian tablets, has written in the 13th century B.C., that Khasisatra ruled for 64 thousand and 800 years, and the great flood occurred at the end of that period.[27] It is very likely that this date shows the existence period of Uyghur Empire. God Kronos has shown himself up to someone called Kisturos and explained that all humanity would drown in a flood and asked him to build a boat and take all his loved ones and pairs of animal types on this boat. The rest of the story is the Babylonian version of the Noah legend that we know so well from the holy books. It is clear that the holy books have conveyed this story from Sumerian documents. Berrossushas also written that civilization was brought to Mesopotamia by 6 people. These people have taught the locals how to read and write, the art of building cities, all sciences and the science of the sky, and institutionalized the religious system.

Chinese and Eskimo legends claim that the world was heavily sub-sided during the great flood. Chinese legends say that after the world has shaken, the sky went down towards the North, the directions of the Sun, the Moon and the planets have changed.[27] In the tomb of Senmouth, the architect of Egypt's female Pharaoh Hachepnut, there were two different map of stars. The stars were located completely different in the two, which shows that the world's axis has changed in the past.[28] In Oera Linda, the holy book of the ancient Scandinavians, it is expressed that during the great flood, the earth shook as though it was dying, the mountains had opened up and started blowing fire, while some mountains sank, others arose in other places. The sun remained behind the clouds for a long time after the flood, the climate had changed and humidity remained hanging in the air.[29]

From all these definitions, it is possible to conclude that there was a deviation of the earth's orbit, the poles exchanged places after the great flood, and the eclipse, which was perpendicular before, became distorted, and the distance of the Earth to the sun has increased. Additionally, areas covered in glaciers melted and due the poles changing places, new glaciers came up in other places. On the old maps, specifically on the map of Piri Reis, the shores of the Antarctic have been shown free of glaciers. Again, due to the flood, Gobi and Sahara, which used to be very fertile lands, turned into deserts. It is highly probable that the sudden change in the climate caused the mammoths to disappear. Before the flood, due to the perpendicular eclipse, there used to be no seasonal changes in the weather, and the weather kept the same throughout the year. As the elevation of the eclipse had changed, seasons have started.

Archaic information shows us that the Earth was closer to the Sun before the great flood. In the inscriptions from Egyptian, Kalde, Indian, Maya, Inca and Chinese origin, 12 months are mentioned, each of 30 days long. A solar year has always been given as 360 days, symbolizing circular perfection. It is understood that, when the orbit changed after the flood, the distance to the Sun also changed, and a complete tour around the Sun became 365 days, increasing by 5 days.[30] During the flood, thousands of tons' dust spread into the atmosphere and that caused glaciers to occur in certain places of the earth, and the world was confronted by a wet and cold climate. The cold and damp period lasted until 6 thousand years ago. Civilization under such conditions went backwards and could only start pulling itself together with positive changes in weather conditions.

There are three theories put forward for this disaster which almost brought humanity to end:

One of these is that a giant meteor has hit Mu, at such a great speed to cause the orbit of the Earth to change. According to this theory, that is why there is hole in the Pacific and there are only a few reminders of the Mu continent. However, while this theory claims that Atlantis also sank due deviation of the axis of rotation, it does not explain why the other continents did not get affected at all. Furthermore, in none of the ancient legends stated above, an object arriving from the sky is mentioned of. In addition, as a meteor that struck the earth 65 million years ago that made the dinosaurs extinct, and caused considerable increase in the amountof rare metals, no such change has been observed after the great flood, 12 thousand years ago. Investigations carried out in the Atlantic hole revealed findings pointing at a massive nuclear blast, rather than a meteor strike.[31]

Second theory is the one put forward by Churchward, sinking of the continents due to geologic reasons.[32] Churchward has claimed that masses of gas under the Atlantis and Mu continents caused the continents to raise above the sea level, and as some of those gasses have surfaced in time, the parts on top of these pockets created due to loss of gases filled by water, those pockets and hence the continents sank. However, the British explorer could not explain how the disappearance of the two continents has coincided, so closely. And with today's technology, we know that giant masses of gas do not cause the continents to rise.

The third theory is that Mu and Atlantis, who have achieved a lot in civilization and in technology, have entered a war and thus prepared the end of one another. When we consider the technological achievements we have made, to use atomic power in many ways, only 12 thousand years after the great flood and 6 thousand years after the period that we accept as the beginning of our own civilization, it may be possible to imagine the level of technology and weapons those civilizations have achieved in 70 thousand years that they lived. There is no reason to believe that the human being was then less ambitious, than that they are now. It would be absurd to think that only today, two super powers would compete to gain control all over the world.

In the Book of Dead, that contains wall inscriptions taken from temples and pyramids, the wars in the air before the collapse of the world and "Universe Breaking Tyrans" are mentioned of. In one of the most important prays of the book, the following expressions are present:

"I am the God of the times and of the places. No one ever has given birth to me. I have created the hierarchy in the sky and the self-creating matter. I am Aton. When there was nothing in the cosmic universe, I was here. I am the beginning and the end of the universe. I am Aton and I know that in Osiris, the dead are eternal. After the great massacre and after the pieces of Osiris was scattered here and there, and after the worlds have collapsed, I set up the order in the skies, again. I returned their brightness and I saw the light, birth of Ra, which is my light."[33]

In these expressions, it is clear that what is symbolized by Osiris is the Atlantis. After the great flood, God brought order to Earth, again.

In some ancient Tibet, Maya and Indian documents, as well as some monotheistic religions books such as the old testament and the Qoran, some information with respect to the weapons used in this battle has reached the present day, as mixed in some legends. The use of some nuclear weapons and more powerful weapons that our technology is not yet aware of, caused both continents to sink at the same time, the orbit of the earth to change, and a heat wave that was too hot, melt the glaciers and caused giant waves. While the giant waves covered the world, only very high locations and some inner parts of the Mediterranean, Black Sea and the Red Sea, that were respectively protected and of equal distance to both continents, were relatively less affected from the flood. Nonetheless, as can be seen in Noah type legends, some people have managed to survive this great disaster, just by sailing on some small wooden boats.

However, after the great flood, the deterioration in civilization was inevitable. As the flood was respectively ineffective in places like Tibet, Maya, Egypt and Mesopotamia, the level of civilization in such places remained reasonably high, whereas in rest of the world, there was a serious deterioration.

These people, even if they survived the flood somehow, returned to stone age, effected by the weather conditions, as well. This is the story behind the stone age period, which is claimed by the contemporary scientists that took place 5-6 thousand years ago.

On the other hand, just like cooling of the planets that have broken off the main light source, all brotherhood organizations that have remained alive have gone into a similar deterioration and corrupted in time. Centers such as Tibet, Maya, Egypt and Babylon that could reduce the corruption to a certain extent, have become the centers of today's civilization.

In Torana and Cortesianus Codex, which are rare hand written documents that have reached the present day, the sinking of Mu is described.[34] Additionally, in Torana Codex, Prince Coh, his sister and wife Moo, who lived in Can dynasty, are mentioned of. There, it is explained how Prince Coh's brother Aac has killed him to take over the throne. This legend seems to have been transferred to Egypt as the trio of Isis-Osiris and Seth. Pharaoh Osiris has been killed by Seth, who wanted to take over the royalty, and his body was disintegrated to thousands of pieces and have been scattered all over the world. Osiris' wife Isis got those pieces together and had sex with him. After this sexual relation, while Osiris died again and returned among the Gods, Isis has given birth to his son, Horus. Horus fought with his uncle Seth and winning his fight against his uncle, forcing Seth to get back to underground. From then on, any Pharaoh who has died was named Osiris, and the successor was called as Horus.

In the Torana Codex, translated by Henry Schliman, the following expressions can be noted, with respect to sinking of Mu and Atlantis together: "On the 9th Akbal date of Kayab month of the 3rd Sat year, the earth started shaking tremendously. The disaster continued until the 22nd Manik. Finally, the lands of Limon, Mu and Atlantis sank in one night."[35] In an inscription called "The Star of Baal", which is kept in Cairo museum today, a transparent walled temple is mentioned of: "When the Star of Baal fell, seven cities and the temple with golden dome and transparent walls shook vigorously. Ra-Mu, the mighty saint of Mu has said to the people: "You have been warned of the disaster". His words were muted by fire and smoke. Cities have disappeared with their people."[36] The Star of Baal mentioned here seems to be a weapon, rather than a comet, or a meteor. It was this weapon that destroyed the two civilizations, because of feelings of vengeance between the parties.[37]

In his book titled "The Origin of Egyptians", American explorer Augustus Le Plongeon, states that after the death of his husband and the throne was overtaken by Aac, Queen Moo went to Egypt, with her loyal followers, and met with the Maya people, who have gone there before. Moo was declared as the queen of this country under a new name of Isis, and became a god in time. Other names of Isis in Egyptian are "Mut" and "Tmau". The symbol of Osiris, as the king of the land of Amenti, where the souls migrate to, is a leopard keeling on his feet, or the Sphinx. As the queen of Amenti, the symbol of Isis is also a leopard keeling on his feet. As can be understood in these expressions, Sphinx was built when the Lower Egypt was a colony of Atlantis. How about the pyramids?

Majority of the Egyptologists today give 3 thousand B.C. as the date for building of pyramids in Giza, Cheops, Chephren and Mycerinus. However, these dates are not certain and some historians accept that these pyramids could have been built long before these dates.[38]

It has not been understood how the ancient Egyptians built these hypogeums and how they have provided light to work on such intricate art works inside them. There are no signs of soot on the walls or on the ceiling to suggest that oil lamps were used. It is not possible to use mirrors for such depths either, because the reflected power of the light would have diminished after travelling for so far. There is a very interesting drawing on a wall in Dendera temple in Egypt. Investigator and author Charles Berlitz defines this absurd drawing as follows:

"1.5 m long light bulbs, connected to a transformer, having a snake like wire inside, through high voltage isolators and coil wires …"[39]

Interesting drawing on the wall of the Temple of Dendera

2 million 600 thousand giant blocks have been used in building Cheops pyramid, alone. These blocks were quarried from hundreds of miles away, their surfaces were roughed down until almost smooth, carried to the construction site and located on top on each other, to perfection.[40] It has been calculated that if 10 blocks were cut a day, it would have taken 694 years to cut the 2.6 million blocks used in the construction of Cheops pyramid.[41] How did they manage to complete this impossible construction? Experts calculate that even using today's technology, construction of such a building would have taken at least a hundred years.

According to an Arabic legend with respect to building of the pyramids, the blocks lost all their weight when a priest hit the ground with his stick, would then move freely in the air like a feather, and were located on their places.[42] What is mentioned here, is the implementation of sonic energy science, not achieved by the contemporary technology yet, in buildings. There are also some signs in Babylonian tablets too that sound was used in lifting of Stones.

Arabic philosopher and scientist Ibn-ı Batuta, has written that the pyramids were built to protect the art and the science. In a Copt papyrus, it is written that the "walls of the pyramids were inscribed with useful information and secrets on science, astronomy, geometry and physics." Copt historian Mesudi has claimed that the Cheops Pyramid was built 300 years before the great flood by Pharaoh Surid, in order to protect the archaic information. However, the coverings that the archaic information written on had disappeared in time and the information were lost.[43] French author Gerard De Nerval, in "The Queen of Sheba" legend that he has relayed from a Turkish narrator, has claimed the same. In the story, Tubal Cain, Adam's grandson and Cain's son, has said that during the great flood he was alive and could survive this disaster by hiding in the pyramids, built for protecting the archaic information. Tubal Cain has also said their race has built the great pyramid that would remain intact as long as the earth continued to exist, and that pyramid was in Giza plane. Tubal Cain has also said: "This pyramid had a narrow door opening outside. On the last day of the old world, which was the day of the flood, I covered that entrance, building a wall." These archaic information coming all the way from his old ancestor Enoch (Hermes), were inscribed on two columns, one out of stone and the other one of metal, and the information were entrusted in the next civilization to come.[44]

Pyramid shaped building is wide-spread throughout the world. It is possible to come across pyramids in Maya Civilization, in China, in Bosnia and elsewhere of the World. In the Polynesian island, believed to be a part of Mu, there are the ruins of a temple. There is a pyramid in Penope island, too.[45] The big pyramids in Egypt were built by Hermes priests, using pre-flood technology and they were not just tombs for the Pharaohs, as thought of today. Besides some of them being tombs, they were mainly temples where the archaic information was kept and initiation ceremonies took place. Pyramids built after the great flood are small and simple, almost childish, compared to original ones, and their only function was being a tomb of the pharaohs.

Greek historian Heredotus has confirmed that the first pyramids, as well as many mysterious works like the sphinx, were built before the great flood.[46] Egyptian priests have told Heredotus that the pyramids were built before the great flood, during Pharaoh Surid's time, who then ruled Egypt, in order to keep the "Secrets of Mastership", and 341 generations have gone by, since. With a rough calculation made based on the information given by the priests, we can say that the pyramids were built 12-13 thousand years before today. Egyptian priests mentioned another Greek philosopher, Plato, of another flat roofed pyramid in Atlantis. Priests also mentioned that a copy of this pyramid was also built in Egypt, and a Sphinx was locted on top. The sphinx represented the motherland, Atlantis. It was an expression of a man that reached the divine soul. And the holy temple that it was located on was devoted to Holy Light. Holy Light was the light scattered by single god Ra.[47] 3400 years ago, Pharaoh Thutmes had the following written on a plate placed between the front legs of the Sphinx: "Since the very beginning of the earth, the biggest secret is hidden inside the Sphinx.[48]

Findings with respect to the first pyramids, especially the one of the Cheops pyramid, are very intriguing in the sense that these findings clearly display that it is a very special building. Measurements used in the construction of this pyramid clearly highlights that it is the work of great architects, who has been using mathematics and geometry for thousands of years.

If the height of Cheops pyramid, which is claimed to have been built specifically for initiation ceremonies by Edouard Schure, is multiplied by 1 million, gives the value of 149 million kilometers, which is the distance between the Earth and the Sun. The meridian that crosses the tip of the pyramid divides the lands and the water of the World into two equal parts. In the meantime, Cheops is on the 30th parallel, which means that its location coincides very nicely with other interesting places on Earth. A straight line drawn east, passing through the tip of the pyramid reaches Lhasa, the capital of Tibet. If you turn 180 degrees from this point, you reach Atlantic Ocean, or the sunken continent. Again, if you turn by another 60 degrees, you reach Maya pyramids in Yucatan.[49] Total perimeter of Cheops' base is 931 meters and 22 cm. The height is 148 meters and 28 cm. If you divide perimeter by twice the height of the pyramid, you get 3.1413, which is the constant Pi.[50]

Numerous chambers inside Cheops Pyramid, which clearly has been constructed by Hermes priests, are clearly used for ceremonies as fire and death rooms.

Do you wander who have passed through the mysterious temple in Cheops Pyramid? Orpheus, Pythagoras, Plato, Moses, and many others…

Egypt, ruled by Hermes and following him the chief priests, has been the shelter and school of the esoteric doctrine. In Egypt, where the ruling Pharaohs were initiated, just as in Atlantis and the organization of the priests were the symbolic leaders, esoteric secrets were easily kept, due to such strong organization. In the book of dead, it is said that there are some secrets, only available to the initiated people and the ancient Egyptians were initiated to secrets of existence, long before building of the pyramids. All priests used to swear not to disclose secrets and to stop teaching from getting corrupted. In order to have the oath kept, the punishment for disclosing even the least important of the secrets was death. Heredotus, who is understood to have passed the initiation, while giving some information on a ceremony in the temple of Sais, has said: "Just like the Demeter ceremonies Tesmofories, let us keep our silence on Egyptian ceremonies, too. I know the secrets too well, and I refrain from disclosing them. Just as I will refrain from disclosing the ones related to the institute in Ceres. I can only tell as far as my religion allows me to do so.[51]

Hermes, the protector of all initiated information, has said the following to the initiated people:

"Outside of an article is the same as its inside. Small, is like the big one. There is just one law and it is only One that is active. That is why in the celestial order, there is nothing small, and there is nothing big, either. The second key is this: Human beings are mortal gods. Gods are immortal human beings. Happy is he who can understand these. Because, understanding these means having the key for everything. Never forget that the secrecy law contains the mighty truth and the full information will only be given to those who have passed from the tests we have had. It is compulsory that the truth is explained relevant to the level of intelligence. For that, never forget to keep the Truth from those who are so weak that they can loose their way or from those who can only grasp a part of and use them for their foul purposes. Bury the truth in your heart. Let the truth be only seen and talk in your Works. Let science be your power, faith be your weapon, and silence be your indestructible armor..."

Egyptian Priest Suchis has explained to Solon that there are the priests cast and a group of artisans implementing their art individually and these never got mixed with the others. Besides these, there was also warriors, hunters and animal breeders.[52] Artisan organizations, thought to have started in Atlantis and Mu initially, specifically the construction guilds have taken active role in building pyramids and other temples. Role of the Jewish guilds, which were continuation of the Egyptian guilds, are better known for their contributions in building the Temple of Solomon.

Egyptian traders and artisans have developed within the frame of temple based guilds system, operating for producing and exchanging services for the temples.[53] As Hermes/Toth is present both in the books of magic and in the books of the priests, the priests themselves were astrologists, magicians, fortune tellers and alchemists.

This class of priests, traders and artisans were the most enlightened people of their era, as they were in contact with people of different cultures. This made it for them possible to keep away from the pressures of the official ideologies and of the politicians.

It is expressed that Toth is also the first implementer of alchemy. Like the hieroglyphics, the roots of alchemy implementations are also unknown. But, it is expressed that a pure copper cylinder was found dating back to 4 thousand B.C., iron tools were found inside Cheops Pyramid, and their dates could not have been determined for sure, and goods made of white gold, mercury, lead and glass have been found in some Egyptian tobs, dating back to 1600's B.C or more. All these show that the history of metallurgy goes back to ancient times in Egypt.[54]

On a couple of papyrus documents written in Greek, which express that they are copies of the older originals, there are a lot of instructions on melting of metals, their separation, preservation of their purities and of their imitations. On the papyrus documents, it is also stated that the instructions given were for competent workers. In one of these papyruses called Leyden Papyruses, it is also saying: "Plants and other things have been named as such that, those who do not know about it follow a wrong path and waste their efforts. Only those who know the hidden meaning of the information and those who can interpret them correctly can use." This shows that the language used is an allegoric one, and chemical applications have been kept as a professional secret.

As it is explained in the Book of Dead[55], a priest candidate who awaits initiation, used to be blind folded and brought in front of a temple gate, where there was a sculpture of Isis, the female expression of Osiris, with its face covered. Here, the candidate was informed that no un-initiated person had ever seen the face of Isis and was advised to return, while he still had the opportunity. The candidate was informed that if he had arrived by coincidence or by expecting some personal benefits, he would only find himself getting crazy or would die. At the entrance of the temple, there were two pillars, one red and one black. The red pillar represented the opportunity of reaching Osiris' light and the black pillar represented death.

If the candidate insisted on entering the temple, his guide used to take him to outer yard and handed him over to other officials, after opening his eyes. The candidate who stayed here for about a week implemented some purgatorial procedures.

On the evening of the examination, the candidate was accompanied by two apprentice priests and was taken through a dull corridor filled with sculptures, mummies and skeletons. Apprentice priests said to the candidate that he still had the opportunity to return, and if the candidate insisted on proceeding, then they pushed him through a very narrow opening through a wall. This pass that was just big enough for one person to pass, was in fact the entrance to the Temple of Osiris, in other words the Great Pyramid. Anyone who entered this entrance, could never return. He either had to succeed, otherwise would get destroyed.

As the candidate moved forward in that pass with difficulty, a voice from the depths was giving warnings, saying: "those idiots who have an eye on the science and power will get destroyed here." The pass slowly rose to a steep hill. At the end of the pass, the candidate found himself on top of a deep pit.

The candidate's only way out of here was a steep ladder that was hardly visible, right on top of his head. Candidates that did not fell into the pit or were left incapable of doing anything, climbed the ladders and found themselves in a large hall giant sculptures.

Here, the candidate was met by an officer called the "Chaperon of Holy Symbols" and he would congratulate the candidate for being successful so far. In this hall, under 22 giant statues, there were 22 figures and letters, representing the 22 basic secrets. Starting by explaining that of these, 1 and A represented the God, and the human being, his highest expression on earth, the candidate was then given the other secrets, in order.

After learning all the secrets in this hall, was later ushered to the central chamber of fire. Having seen giant flames in this chamber, the candidate's hesitancy was dissolved by the guide saying that he once had to pass through the same chamber as well. Having walked into the flames, the candidate would see that the flames were not real, they were just illusions. The test of fire used to be followed by a test of water, the candidate used to try to pass through a very dark pool of water, with deep holes inside, shivering and trying hard not to drown.

The candidate who has passed this stage as well, would be met by two priests and they would take him to a room with a comfortable bed. There, the candidate used to pass out, helped by a tranquil music as well. When he woke up, the candidate would meet a beautiful nude woman.

The woman would serve the candidate a drink and would tell the candidate that she was a present offered to successful candidates. If the candidate fell for the trap and had an intercourse with the woman, he would then fell asleep with the help of the sleeping substance in his drink and would find himself alone, upon waking up. It was also recorded by Ara Avedisyan that the candidate was tested by a woman.[56] Shortly after, "Hyorofan", chief priest of the temple, would enter the cell and tell the candidate that although he has been successful in all the previous tests, could not manage to beat himself, and anyone who give in to his desires would also give in to his feelings and such people deserved to live in darkness and solitude. These candidates would live as prisoners in these small rooms, until they died.

However, if the candidate refused the drink and the woman, 12 priests would enter the room with torches in their hand and take the candidate to the Temple of Osiris with a chequered floor, where Hyorofan and the officers waited him. There, Hyorofan was accompanied by numerous "Prophets", meaning priests with master degrees. The "Chaperon of Holy Symbols", who organized the initiation ceremonies, was also a Prophet. In the meantime, Moses, whose task was the "Secretary of Secrets", was also a Prophet. This title later was converted to a figure of a person, receiving revelations form God, first in Judaism, then in other celestial religions followed it. The apprentice priests given tasks at lower levels were called the "Servants of God".[57]

In the temple, there was a statue representing Osiris, and a statue of Isis, accepted as his wife, with their son Horus in her arms. Hyorofan used to get the candidate to take an oath that he would keep all the secrets that he would learn there, even if that cost him his life, and declared him as a brother priest. Thus the candidate got the title of apprentice priest. But, he had a very long path of learning.

The apprenticeship period varied from person to person. An apprentice would only be allowed to a higher degree, if his guide Prophet decided so. In this period that could last for years, the apprentice continuously received lessons from his master priest and meditated in his room. In this long waiting period, the apprentice's job was not to know, but to learn. The apprentice kept under surveillance all the time, and obeyed the strict rules in full discipline, slowly found himself changing. Observing the change in the apprentice, the guide would decide that it was the time and would give him the good news that soon the truth would be disclosed.

Hyorofan used to tell the candidate that in order to reach the light of the truth, the candidate had to die and get born again, otherwise no one could join the divine council of Osiris. If the candidate answered as "I am ready to sacrifice myself", he would then be taken to the "chamber of re-birth" by the officers, where a tomb was placed in a corner.

Here, saying that death was for everyone, but every living would be born again, Hyorofan used to place the candidate in the marble tomb and close the lid. Being in absolute darkness and by himself alone, candidate lost the concept of time and although he only spent an evening in the tomb, he would feel as though he were there much longer. Candidate would only realize by the sun rise that he had a small opening on top of his head. This opening shaped as a star with five edges, was arranged as such that when the morning came, the light of "Sotis", the Morning Star hit that hole and caused it to shine. This star seemed to the candidate as the proof of the God's existence and the Light of the Truth.

As the light started to decrease slowly, the lid used to be opened and Hyorofan gave apprentice the good news:

"Last night you died, and after seeing the light of Osiris, you were born again. You are now an initiated brother who has deserved to learn the big secrets."

After this explanation, the new master priest was then taken to a large hall called "Grand Orient", where all prophets were ready, and the ceremony continued here. The door was short enough to get everyone to bend their heads. In the east, just above the Hyorofan's desk, there was a very powerful light, the source of which totally unknown, pouring out of an eye in the middle of an equilateral triangle. This symbol was called "The Eye of Osiris" that saw everything.[58]

The Eye of God Osiris that sees everything

At this stage, Hyorofan, continued as follows:

Having succeeded incoming so far, you have now arrived at the doorsteps of great secrets. Until now, you have been given the minor secrets, in other words, the secrets of Isis. Now, you will be given the major secrets, the secrets of Osiris."

God Osiris is a trio which consists of himself, his wife Isis and their son Horus. Osiris represents the holy father, from whom the life was born, Isis represents his female and productive side, and Horus represents the divine word, the materialistic world. God is complete and one. This division into three people is not a sign of weakness, but an expression of perfection.

People born of this mighty creature are mortal people. On the other hand, prefect people that have a little left to reach the almighty are immortal human beings. In the celestial order, nothing is small, yet there is nothing big. Happy is he who can understand these. Because, understanding these means owning the mighty secrets. Bury the truth in your heart and disclose the truth be only in your Works."

After this speech, new Prophet was made to wear his special master outfit and took an oath. If the new master was an Egyptian, he would work in the temple as an administrating priest. If he was a foreigner, would then be sent to his hometown, either to form a religion, or to accomplish another duty. But, these initiated people would be asked to take an oath again, not to disclose the secrets of the temple to those who are not initiated. They were also reminded that death waited for the otherwise, no matter where they were.

In the teaching of Moses[59], who was an initiated Osiris Prophet himself, this oath was the reason why he could not disclose the absolute truth and could only disclose the doctrine behind three layers of secrecy. Obviously, Moses did not behave this way because he was scared of being killed, but he was acting so, believing that it would not be an honorable thing to do, as a Perfect Master under oath.[60] Besides, Moses was fully aware of the fact that he would not be able to explain his teaching fully openly. No matter how close they were to esoteric teachings, he knew that he had to simplify all speeches in order to be able to teach a new religion to his followers, who were relatively unenlightened on such issues.[61]

References

1   Hope Murry, - *Atlantis, Legend or Truth (Atlantis, Efsane mi Gerçek mi?)*, AD Pub., Istanbul 1994, p. 156
2   August Le Plonge, - *Origin of Egyptians (Mısırlıların Kökeni)*, Ege Meta Pub., Istanbul, p. 153
3   Hope M., r.w., p. 161
4   Knight, Christopher; Lomas, Robert - *Book of Hiram (Hiramın Kitabı)*, Bilge Karınca Pub., Istanbul 2008, p. 130
5   Hope M., r.w., p. 44
6   Hope M., r.w., p. 44
7   Santesson Hans Stephan, - *Sunken Country Mu Civilization (Batık Ülke Mu Uygarlığı)*, RM Pub, Istanbul 1989, p. 91
8   Avedisyan Ara, - *The Biggest Secret in the Universe (Evrende En Büyük Sır)*, Sümer Pub., Istanbul, 1973, p. 102
9   Hope M., r.w., p. 237
10 Hope M., r.w., p. 183
11 Hope M., r.w., p. 160
12 Hope M., r.w., p. 163
13 Gener Cihangir, - *Hiram Abif*, Nokta Pub., Istanbul 2009, p. 138
14 Özbudun Sibel, - *Transformation Dynamics of a Religious Tradition from Hermes to Idris (Hermes'ten İdris'e Bir Dinsel Geleneğin Dönüşüm Dinamikleri)*, Ütopya Pub., Ankara 2004, p. 128.
15 Özbudun P., r.w., p. 130
16 Gener C., r.w., p. 147
17 Yurdakök, Murat. - *Traces of Old Beliefs (Eski İnançlardaki İzler)*, Ankara 1994, p. 12
18 Freke, Timothy & Gandy, Peter - *Mysteries of Jesus (İsa'nın Gizemleri)* Ayna Pub., Istanbul 2005, p. 51
19 Gener C., r.w., p. 126
20 Freke Timothy/Gandy Peter, - *Hermetic (Hermetika)*, Ege Meta Pub., Istanbul 1997, p. 26-159
21 Gener C., r.w., p. 148
22 Tecimer, Ömer - *Rose and Cross (Gül ve Haç)* Plan B Pub., Istanbul 2004, p. 17
23 Freke, Timothy&Gandy, Peter - *Mysteries of Jesus (İsa'nın Gizemleri)* p. 107
24 Schwarz Fernand, - Maat, Yeni Yüksektepe Pub., Ank. 2001, p. 74
25 Gener C., r.w., p. 139
26 Champdor Albert, - *Egypt's Book of the Dead (Mısır'ın Ölüler Kitabı)*, RM Pub., Istanbul 1984, p. 78
27 Hope M., r.w., p. 167
28 Hope M., r.w., p. 87
29 Hope M., r.w., p. 90
30 Hope M., r.w., p. 84
31 Hope M., r.w., p. 116
32 Hope M., r.w., p. 187
33 Churchward James, - Lost Continent of Mu, England 1931, p. 257
34 Champdor A., r.w., p. 56
35 August L.P., r.w., p. 101
36 Avedisyan A., r.w., p. 57
37 Avedisyan A., r.w., p. 107
38 Avedisyan A., r.w., p. 86
39 Schure Edouard, *Great Initiatives (Büyük İnisiyeler)*, RM Pub, Istanbul 1989, p. 172
40 Hope M., r.w., p. 167
41 Scognamillo Giovanni, - *The Secret Owners of Our World (Dünyamızın Gizli Sahipleri)*, Koza Pub., Istanbul 1973, p. 38
42 Avedisyan A., r.w., p. 167
43 Hope M., r.w., p. 182
44 Hope M., r.w., p. 185-186

45   De Nerval Gerard, - *Travel to the East (Doğuya Seyahat)*, Kültür Bakanlığı Pub., Ankara 1984, p. 171

46   Avedisyan A., r.w., p. 244

47   Von Daniken Erich, - *Chariots of the Gods (Tanrıların Arabaları)*, Milliyet Pub., Istanbul 1973, p. 147

48   Avedisyan A., r.w., p. 164

49   Avedisyan A., r.w., p. 158

50   Schure E., r.w., p. 178

51   Avedisyan A., r.w., p. 171

52   Von Daniken E., r.w., p. 133

53   August L.P., r.w., p. 198

54   Hope M., r.w., p. 25

55   Özbudun P., r.w., p. 123

56   Özbudun P., r.w., p. 177

57   Avedisyan A., r.w., p. 189

58   Schure E., r.w., p. 180

59   Signier, Jean Francois/Thomazo, Renaud - *Secret Organizations (Gizli Örgütler)* Larousse Oğlak Güzel Kitaplar, Istanbul 2006, p. 14

60   Santesson H.P., r.w., p. 117

61   Bilim Araştırma Grubu, - *Mu, Prehistoric Universal Civilization (Mu, Tarih Öncesi Evrensel Uygarlık)*, Bilim Araştırma Merkezi Pub., Istanbul 1978, p. 61

CHAPTER V

MOSES AND JEWISH ESOTERIZM

According to American explorer Augustus Le Plongeon, there were two different religions in Egypt. The first one of these was for the initiated priests and was completely monotheistic. In this religion, there were no images and idols of the polytheistic religions. Plongeon claims that the strongest proof of this is non-existence of such items in the old pyramids. This religion defined by Plongeon is the ancient Osiris religion. The other religion, which is Amon-Ra religion, was degenerated, polytheistic, pompous, and was for occupying the eyes and brains of the people through different ceremonies[1]. The Single God teaching was implemented in Egypt behind a curtain of secrecy, was never attributed to the masses, kept only for the initiated priests. While this was partly because of the principles of the teaching, more so it was forced to be kept secret because of historical events.

About 4 thousand B.C., in almost everywhere in the world, religions have been corrupted and polytheism has started in many places, and all the old symbols have been idolized.

As well as Babylon, the leading education center of the Uyghur Empire, Egypt could not have been preserved from this corruption.

It was natural for Babylon to get back, because the main source of light, Mu, has long gone, and the priests, in order to increase their influence on the people, have given ground for religious corruption. However, the situation was different in Egypt. The school in Lower Egypt was not tied to Mu, but to Atlantis and the teaching to this colony was brought by Hermes, one of the followers of Osiris religion, which was so new, compared to Nacaals. What has happened then? Why has this trend gone backwards in Egypt, where monotheistic principles and Hermes priests ruled? The answer to this question needs to be searched in the war between Mu and Atlantis.

Long before the flood, when Atlantis established a colony in Nile delta, Nagas, the Indian branch of Mu, setup another colony in Southern Egypt, in order to prevent this strategically important country to go completely under the control of Atlantis. Before the great flood, fighting between these two colonies continued for years, without a definite advantage of either side. Perhaps due to the fact that the region was not affected so much by the great flood, battles between the two colonies continued until Pharaoh Menes period. Finally, the war was won by the kingdom in the South, where corruption was bigger[2]. South Egypt religion that believed in god Amon, god Ptah, and many other secondary degree gods, was accepted as the official religion of the country. Hermes priests went underground and took the decision to continue their teachings in secrecy.

Besides all, the people in Northern Egypt did not forget the trio of Osiris, Iris and Horus, as well as Hermes. In time, each one of these has taken its place among the gods in the Egyptian Pantheon. Until they lost the war, the administrating Pharaoh was given the title of Horus, the son of Osiris, as a symbol only. After this period, all Egyptian pharaohs have started believing that they had divine powers and they were gods.

Only one pharaoh, Amonhotep IV (1353-1335 B.C.), who was most likely initiated by the secret Osiris priests, rejected this. He tried to get rid of the polytheistic religion and establish a new monotheist religion that he called the "Aton religion"[3]. As explained earlier in this book, Osiris was the founder of Mu monotheist religion in Atlantis, 22 thousand years before today. In Mu, the name of the Almighty was known as Amun (Amon), referring to Mu Continent, and in Atlantis, it was known as Aton, referring to the name of the continent. When the Upper Egypt, the colony of Mu invaded Lower Egypt, which was a colony of Atlantis, the title given to pharaohs, which was then Aton-Ra, was changed to Amon-Ra.

Thousands of years after unification of these two countries, Pharaoh Amonhotep tried to return to a monotheistic Aton religion, but could not succeed due to a resistance shown by the organization of polytheistic religion's priests, and ignorance of the masses. Along with the religious belief that Amonhotep was trying to impose on people, he changed his name too, to Akheneton, meaning the "Light of Aton"[4]. He evaluated himself as the prophet of Aton. "Ank em Maat", "Living in Maat (truth, righteousness and justice)" was the main principle of Akheneton. He has done his best in order to destroy Amon belief and to get rid of its priests, throughout his life. However, he could not manage to get rid of the powerful priests of Amon religion. Thinking their religious beliefs were going to be dissolved, people have resisted with vigor. Among the ordinary people, Akheneton was referred as "Misbelieving King." Immediately after his death, his son Smankare took the throne, but the fanatical priests operated on Smankare, blaming that his brain was invaded with genies. They took Smankare's cerebellum off, and consequently, he very shortly died. Many of the Osiris priests that surfaced during Ankhenaton's period were also killed by Aton Priests. Ankheneton's second son who took the throne was very young and due to the pressure applied by Amon priests, changed his name to Tutankhamoon from Tutankhaton. People turned back to polytheistic religion. With suspicious death of Tutankhamoon at a very young age, Aton belief joined the dusty pages of history.

Remaining Osiris priests gave up using Aton's name and pretended as priests of the polytheistic religion. On the surface, they were Amon priests, but deep inside, they were supporters of archaic monotheistic religion. With Babylon and Persia invading Egypt, they were forced to continue the brotherhood activates under great secrecy.

Now Moses was an initiated member of the brotherhood, believing in monotheism[5]. With Moses, who was an Osiris priest, the long run of the celestial religions started. With Moses reviving the ancient monotheistic belief, and with Christianity and Islam getting inspired from his religion, Judaism, although their descriptions were more complex and their aims were slightly different, the world has become a place again, where most of the people believed in monotheistic religions.

The biggest difference in the teaching of Moses was, instead of introducing the idea of God through symbols, Moses tried to explain God directly to masses. Having seen that the symbols were distorted by uneducated people and expedient priests, and that they were iconized, Moses wanted to try a different approach. In order to get people to believe in an intangible concept like God, Moses had to get them scared. Saying that those who believe in single creator would be rewarded and the non-believers would be punished, Moses did not hesitate in applying the God's punishment by his own hands. Moses and his followers slaughtered the Hebrews that tried to come back to worshipping God through a symbol, as they have been used to[6]. Before having a look at Moses' personality and his teaching, let us have a look at where the tribe which has accepted Moses' religion, The Hebrews came from and how they have come across Moses[7].

Hebrews were living in Mesopotamia, especially in Harran plain. Hebrews, who were organized as mobile kingdoms, were controlled by the Assyrians, and they belonged to Saabi religion. This religion, which was a corrupt version of a monotheistic belief, was nothing other than the street version of Babylonian teaching. Abram, who lived in Ur between 2000 and 1800 B.C., went North, to Harran, where he expected a better life. It is considered that when Abram refused to accept the rule of atheist invaders that came from the North, he had decided to leave Ur[8]. Some sources claim that Abram left Ur in a later period, between 1700 and 1600 B.C. It is very likely that Ur is today's province of Urfa.

It is known that people worshipped the Sun, the Moon, Jupiter, Mercury, Saturn and Mars, before Christianity[9] in Urfa.

According to the First Testament, after Abram settled in Harran, God has shown up to him and told him to leave that area and go to Kennan land. God would create generations and would make him the father of nations. For that reason, his name was also changed from Abram to Abraham. In Hebrew, Abraham meant "Father of the Nation"[10]. According to Quran, Abraham is the prophet of monotheist Khanif religion and invited everyone to this monotheist religion. However, majority of the people around him, including his father, who worshipped the Sun, the Stars and the idols, rejected his invitation. Abraham goes through a series of problems. King Nimrod puts him into fire to destroy him, but he did not get burnt as he was protected by his god. Due to all problems he has faced, Abraham went to Kennan land, accompanied by his wife and some close relatives.

Some researchers believe that Abraham was a Saabi priest[11]. He has rejected all other gods in the Saabi religion and went back to its original form, worshipping only the Sun. Another assumption, along with archeological findings is that, due to a great drought in Harran and its vicinity, some Saabis went to Kennan, lead by Abraham, and from there they went further, as far as Egypt. Archeological findings which show that there was a great drought in 2000 B.C. and the invasion of Egypt by Hyksos in this period, support this assumption.[12] In Egyptian, Hyksos means "Prince of the Dessert" and points at tribes who have migrated to Egypt from North. From 2000 to 1800 B.C., Egypt was ruled by the Northern tribes.[13]

If we go back to religious books, god called to Abraham going to Kennan and the land was promised to his nation. From then on, Kennan land was the "Promised Land" for the Hebrews. According to the First Testament, due to shortage of food, they also left Kennan and went to Egypt. In Egypt, the Pharaoh gave him a slave woman and this woman, named Hacer, gave birth to Ismail. Little later, his wife gave birth to Isaac. It is claimed that Abraham has named his sons Ismail and Isaac, dedicated to goddess Isis, in order to be sympathetic to the rulers of this new land. According to Hebrew traditions, the tribe would be lead by the first son, after the death of the leader. However, Ismail was not born from a free woman, but from a slave. In order to guarantee his son Isaac's rule in the future, Sarah asked Hacer and her son to be removed from the tribe. Abraham took Hacer and Ismail to Hejaz. Settling here, Ismail would become the source for Islam hundreds of years later. When the Hyksos rule in Egypt ended, Saabis returned to Kennan land lead by Isaac's son Jacob. In Kennan land, the ladder where Jacob was claimed to have talked to God was nothing other than referral to the famous gardens of Babylon and the temple called "Ziggurat". This is also a proof that the Hebrew are of Assyrian origin[14].

Another claim with respect to the growth of Aton religion is the Saabi belief of Egyptian Vizier Joseph[15]. According to this claim, Abraham left Ur between 1700 and 1600 B.C. According to this calculation, if it is considered that 300 years had gone by, Joseph was the Vizier during the 18th dynasty (1550–1307 B.C.)

This calculation seems to be correct for the birth of the monotheistic Aton religion in Egypt. Joseph is an important member of the Prophets Family, starting with Abraham, who is accepted as the great ancestor of all the three celestial religions. Joseph is the son of Jacob, who is the son of Isaac, who is the son of Abraham, is the 4th generation. It was Joseph, who brought the Saabis back to Egypt, and saved them from getting extinct due to a great drought. Saabis, who were named as Haribu by the Egyptians, later were known as the Hebrews[16]. Migrating Hebrews, after they settled down in civilized Egypt, changed their way of living and their cultures, although they kept their religion. They were mainly involved in construction and arms making professions. This interaction would play a major role in establishment of Jewish States.

According to this claim, rising to the level of being the vizier of the pharaohs by his personal efforts, Joseph was the one who founded monotheistic "Aton" religion in Egypt. His belief in monotheism has impressed Akhenaton so much, and according to some, the first monotheistic religion, "Aton" was founded. It is believed that Moses had combined his monotheistic belief with Saabi based beliefs and founded Judaism. If Joseph had not lived in Egypt, it can be argued that Moses and the monotheistic belief would surface and the divine religions would arise.

After having a quick look at this information, let's return to Moses to refer to Saabi beliefs later.

Moses, who is claimed to be the son of a Jewish mother in the Old Testament, in fact was the nephew of Ramses[17]. Moses was a master who has received esoteric training and monotheistic learning from Osiris priests. Having seen with unsuccessful attempt of Akheneton that he would not be able to get the people in Egypt to accept the idea of monotheism,

Moses turned to another source, relatives of Joseph, living in Egypt. Hebrews engaged in brick laying and stone masonry at the time. Although some had started believing in polytheism, majority of them continued believing in their ancestors' monotheist religion. After arriving in Egypt, they had worked in constructing various temples and other buildings, and become majority in Egyptian guilds sheltering stone masons. Hebrews carried this guild system to other countries they migrated to, as well. They were very effective in disseminating this system in the Middle East.

His education and characteristics that can be accepted by Osiris priests is a proof that Moses came from a powerful aristocratic family. It is assumed that Osiris priests initiated the pharaoh's nephew Moses, in order to become strong in administering Egypt. Nevertheless, since he was so close to Pharaoh, in a short period, Moses was given the post of Holy Inscriptions Secretary of Osiris Temple[18].

This post assigned to Moses, has helped him to reach the secrets that were only available to chief priests. Building strong relations with the Hebrews, while executing his tasks at his post, got the pharaoh worried. Having the presumption that he was going to form an army of the Hebrews, and would claim the throne, Ramses II sent his army after them, after Moses had set off to retrieve to Sinai. But, what had pushed Moses and his followers to fled Egypt was not to claim the throne, but a totally different reason, he called his army back.

Protecting Hebrews under any circumstance against the Egyptians to his best, having seen that an Egyptian officer was beating up a Hebrew, Moses interfered with the situation and accidentaly had killed the officer during the struggle[19]. Isis Law was very clear. No matter who and how, anyone who killed a person was to be expelled from the temple and would be judged.

Seeing no future left for him in Egypt, Moses retrieved to Sinai, together with his Hebrew supporters. Here, joining the principles of Saabi "Elohim" belief and Osiris religion, Moses established the basis of his teaching under "Ten Commandments." But, the Ten Commandments Moses wrote was in Hieroglyphics, as he had learned in the Temple, since he did not know Hebrew.

On the other hand, majority of the people did not know the language Moses used. This is where the handicap started in Jewish religion. Although Egyptian Hieroglyph is very advantageous in the sense that it is possible to write in short form, its real meaning could only be understood by initiated people and the number of such people was very rare among Moses' followers. This form of writing meant nothing to ordinary people. For example, the name given to God by Jewish people is "Jehovah", and is based on letters "J", "H" and "V". This is a unified version of God's male form in Esoteric doctrine, "Jod" and the female form "Eve", in other words a mixture of Osiris and Isis[20]. As the symbolic meanings of the Hieroglyphics were not known at the time, this resulted in the Jewish religion changing shape and a lot of myths creeping in the religion.

Due to the education he has received, it was not possible for Moses to write otherwise. Only the initiated people could have understood this language. Initiated ones, the very small minority among Moses' followers, followed a different route from the others and they were separated from other Jewish groups after working on Kabbalah, the esoteric interpretation of the Old Testament.

On the other hand, during Solomon's reign, Genesis translated to Phoenician language had converted tremendously from its original meaning. During their captured period by the Babylonians, the old treatment organized in Aramaic, got closer to the original meaning, however several myths from different beliefs have been placed for the parts that could not have been understood. Re-organization of the Old Testament became compulsory, after some Jewish priests were initiated in an old Babylonian Esoteric School, and those priests developed realistic views on Moses' real teaching.

However, Jewish reverends did not know at all the language Moses used. Jewish chief of Priests Ezra, who wrote the Old Testament again, 800 years after Moses, even misinterpreted the existence and defined God as not as emanating from itself, but supported the idea that God was the creator of the universe from nothing and had that written in the Old Testament as such. Following this solidarity had disappeared; the religion was based on a dual system, where there was a creator and the created ones. Monotheistic belief that had supported God's unity was changed all together, and the aim was changed from the people trying to reach the God, to going to heaven as a prize for worshipping well, being a created servant. A similar misinterpretation was made with respect to the gender of God. Ezra had found it appropriate picture God as a male, who has been both male and female until then. As a result of this, both in Judaism, in Christianity and Islamism following it, women have always been pushed to the second class. Like many other myths added into the book later, creation of Eve from the ribs of Adam, in the myth on Adam and Eve, got people to think that the women were not created directly, but created from a man who was originally created from mud, by God, and thus were pushed to second class and have been ruled by men.

As the superstitions in the myths have penetrated into the Monotheistic religions due to lack of knowledge, they caused creation of dogmas, later got more radical and finally moved away from rationalism. From that day on, clashes started between the people who knew the real meaning of monotheistic religion and defended esoteric teaching and unedujated Ortodox masses. These clashes ended up with Jews declaring Kabbalah supporters, Catholic Church declaring the Chevaliers with Esoteric beliefs and Sunni Muslims declaring the Sufis and anagogic analyzers as erratic. This behavior caused the Jews to see Kabbalah as deviant, Papacy to eliminate the Knights Templar and to excommunicate masonry, Sunni Muslims to de-skin Hallac-I Mansur who have said "Enel Hak";

"I am God", and to pressurize groups such as Ismailis and Babais, who believed in Esoterizm. As they will be dealt with in following chapters, let's now continue investigating the Jews.

After Moses, Jews could only form a strong Kingdom under David's rule. The event known as David and Goliath in mythology, David beating the giant called Goliath, refers to Jews led by David, winning wars against enemies outnumbering them, and forming a Kingdom on the Promised Land. Knowing so well that as well as the Kingdom, it was their monotheistic religion that kept their tribe together, David ordered a magnificent temple to be built for this God[21].

While constructing this temple, the Jews used their art of brick laying and stone masonry, which they have accumulated during their 400 years of living in Egypt. They have made the organization necessary for constructing such a massive building, by copying the profession guilds in Egypt. While preparations continued for construction of the temple, David died and was replaced by his son, Solomon. According to Masonic information, Solomon chose a holy place near Jerusalem for construction. When the workers cleared the ground, they found ruins of an ancient temple. They found out that it was the Temple of Hanok. After the workers cleared all the knocked over columns and other ruins, they noticed a secret pass on the floor. In a chamber at the end of this pass, they found a delta inscribed in an onyx vat, with a mysterious name carved on, and a column on which information on the world's arts and science have been carved on. These treasures were placed in the new temple by Solomon's orders. These treasures and the remnants of Judaism, as well as other treasures of Solomon have disappeared, after the temple was knocked down. Masonic myths claim that some of these treasures were recovered by the Knights Templar. However, these treasures have disappeared again at a later date[22].

Just like the treasures of Solomon and the relics, another work of art that had disappeared from the surface of the earth was Hanok's Book, which was accepted as sacred by the Jews. Hanok's Book, which was accepted as to have been written by the Egyptian luminary Hermes Trimagistus, was known very well by the high ranked Jewish religion, until the first century, by which time Christianity had started. In the 1st century A.D., Hanok's Book had disappeared and remained lost until the 18th century, till it was found by James Bruce, who was a mason himself. It was confirmed that the copy of this book, a copy of which was found in Ethiopia by Bruce, from which Hanok has learned the basic principles of astrology, was authentic, after inspecting the copy of a few pages of the Dead Sea parchments[23].

In Hebrew, Hanok means education and knowledge. Hanok's book is written in Aramaic. This book was kept in Ethiopia in Abyssinian and so some missing parts have been found among the Dead Sea parchments. As the book contained a lot of mystique events and esoteric descriptions, holy book protectors in 2nd century B.C., have taken the decision to keep Hanok's book out of sight and ensured that the book was excluded from Judaism'.[24]

According to some calculations made by Jewish historians, Hanok was born in 3382 B.C. It is also rumored that he lived for 365 years and in 3017 B.C., while he was still alive, he was taken to heaven by the angels. According to the Old Testament, Hanok is the great grandfather of Noah. Writers of the Old Testament inform that the great flood happened in around 2400 B.C. According to this, Hanok lived before the flood. Meaning of Hanok is "Made a Member". That means that he has had to undergo a special ceremony where he was given some secret information[25].

Hanok's ascent to 10th floor of the sky and acceptance to the floor of the holy of the holies is explained as follows: "I was 365 years old and alone at home. Two giant men appeared in front of me.

Hanok, they said, the Eternal One has sent us to ascend you to the sky. Those two men put me on top of their wings and took me to the first floor of the sky, made me sit on top of the clouds. There I saw an ocean far bigger than the world. They showed me two hundred angels who were responsible of the stars and celestial creatures. Then I was taken to the second floor. There were some people waiting for their final punishment, in complete darkness. We went to the third floor, and there I saw the heaven. Bang in the middle of the garden of Eden, there was a tree of life. The eternal one said: 'Hanok, this garden was prepared for people who have suffered a lifetime and have never diverted their path from the truth.' Then, the angels took me to the North of that place, where it was dark and full of torture. From there, we passed onto the fourth floor, where the rays of the Sun and the Moon shone on me. There, I saw the West side of the heaven, where there were six doors. Then, we went to the fifth floor, There, I saw innumerable armies. Those were the inspectors. They looked like human beings, but they were even bigger than the giants. Following this, we went to the sixth floor. There, there were angels grouped in different ways. On the seventh floor, I saw a blinding light and the deputies of the chief angels. Following this, we went up to the eight floor, named as Muzalot, meaning changing of seasons in Hebrew. On the ninth floor, I saw the houses of the twelve Zodiacs. Finally, the chief angel Michael took me to the tenth floor, called Avarot in Hebrew. There, I saw the Eternal One. I prostrated in front of this divine magnificence. The Eternal One and Michael started changing my outfits and blessing me with holy oil. Oil shone like the rays of the Sun. When I looked at it, I saw myself like one of the divine creatures. The Eternal One called one of his chief angels, known as Vrervoil. That angel brought me a pen and empty pages to write on. Vrervoil taught me everything in thirty days and thirty nights, and I wrote everything down.[26]

As it is explained in the book, the Eternal One spoke to Hanok: "Before the start of everything, there was nothing created, and I created everything from nothing. I created the visible from the invisibles. Listen to me very carefully Hanok. Notice that I don't share my secrets with the angels. I did not even tell them their basics and their eternity, neither have I explained them my inexplicable nature. I have created all living things and I understand them all. Today, I am going to explain to you all. Never forget that I am only one. Before all materialistic things were present, I was at the invisibles. Many of the things were not yet created. For that, I decided to crate something that a visible world would come out of. On the sixth day, I ordered the man, one of the seven elements of the universe, to be created. First, his flesh came out of the earth. Second, his blood was formed from the dew and the sun. Then, his eyes were formed from the depths of the oceans. Fourth, his bones were formed from the rocks. Then, his mind was formed from the movements of the angels and of the clouds. Sixth, his hair and his blood vessels were formed of grass. Finally, his soul was created from the wind and my own self. I created him as the second angel of the Earth. I named him after the four directions; A of Anatole (East), D of Dusme (West), A of Arktos (North) and M of Mesembria (South), ADAM.[27]

Creation of Adam and his first and second wives, Lilith and Eve, is explained in another Esoteric Jewish source, Zohar, as follows: "There was a mighty soul called Lilith, which was created simultaneously with Adam. God first created Adam from himself, and then ordered as follows: 'It is not good for man to be alone' then created the woman, to be together with Adam. Like Adam, the woman was created from the earth as well. God named her Lilith. She was going to be the perfect wife of Adam. In Hebrew, Lilith means the night. She was a creature of the night. Adam wanted Lilith to lay under him for a sexual intercourse. She resisted and demanded Adam to lay under her. She also shouted: 'I am not going to lay under you, because we are equal.' Adam answered: 'I want to be on top, because my position must be superior to yours.' Then, Lilith shouted as "YAHVE", the non-pronounced name of God and disappeared rising to the sky. Adam complained that the woman had escaped. Adam was put to sleep and Eve was created from his ribs. Giving up being a partner to Adam, Lilith decided to harass Eve's children, and to kill them. Then on, she was a demon. In the mean time, she started to pester young men and stole their sperms at nights. It is mentioned in Talmut that she stole Adam's sperms as well, after he was expelled from heaven, and he was the father of many demons.[28]

If we return to building of the Temple, Solomon was looking for a talented man to put in charge of the building. He found the very man he was looking for, in the City of Sur: "Hiram"[29].

In ancient Sami languages, "Hi" meant "God or Living". This word was adapted to Arabic as "Hu". Again, in the same languages, "Ram" meant "High, Exalted". When these two words are used together, it means 'God manifested in exalted or high man' (Perfect Human Being/Kamil Man). In fact, this expression is very suitable for esoteric doctrine supporting that God-Universe-Human Being are all identical.

Hiram was a very capable person in organizing and was a genius in bronze workmanship. There were thousands of people working in building the temple. Guilds of different professions were organized in three degrees, as apprentices, fellow crafts and masters, and the responsibilities were divided among the masters. Each worker was paid according to his degree. It was impossible to memorize among thousands of men, who was receiving a wage at which degree.

According to then current guild system, apprentices could only become fellow crafts after they were trained for certain periods, and only the very talented could become masters. Hiram developed this system further, and in order ease wage distribution, and gave a password to each degree, to be protected like the secrets of the profession, by death, if necessary. Although this system helped speeding the procedures, it also started the end for Hiram. People, who have pretended to be masters and got undeserved higher wages before, were blocked. A group of fellow crafts who were accustomed to receive undeserved wages, decided to pester and force Hiram to give them the password of the masters. However, many of them got scared of taking action against Hiram and only three of them, determined to get the password cornered Hiram in the Temple. They tried to get the password from him by force. When Hiram refused to give the password, they killed him.

Although the works were hindered for a while, Solomon found another person, and the construction of the Temple was completed. Structure of the Temple showed that it was very similar to the ones in Egypt[30]. Presence of two columns at the entrance, existence of symbols containing an eye in a triangle, a Sun, and a Moon, black and white checkered floor, and the presence of an altar show that the temple was built, impressed by the ones in Egypt. These similarities have caused claims that Hiram did not come from Sur, but from Egypt, and was specially appointed by the Pharaoh of the period for the job.[31]

Not involved so much in religion and the temple, Solomon forgot after a while whether he believed in monotheism or in polytheism, and continued living riotously. Jewish state got weaker and weaker, and finally, after Solomon's death, in 587 B.C., invaded by Nabukadnezar, the King of Babylon. Majority of the people were taken to Babylon by the invaders, to be used as slave workers. The Temple was also knocked down by the invaders[32].

Jews lived in Babylon for 50 years. In Babylon, Esoteric beliefs of the Sumerian period continued in its corrupted form. Monotheistic religion had given way to polytheism, old symbolic teachings had become myths. The School of Babylon continued producing "Caldi" priests for the polytheist religion, through initiation. Jewish priests were not strangers to initiation system. New guild system was also based on initiation system. For that reason, neither the Jewish Administrators, nor the Jewish Priests saw any problem with following the school. Consequently, no matter how corrupt it was, Jewish reverends understood Esoterism and what Moses meant in his Esoteric teachings, better. However, with their new interpretation of the Old Testament, they caused a lot of myths enter the teaching.

Jewish people's slavery by the Babylonians ended with Persian King Kyros invading Babylon (530 B.C.). Kyros permitted the Jews to return to their country and to re-construct their temple. It is argued in some sources that the Persian King was well aware of the initiation system, which was so popular then, and interpretation of Esoterism in Zoroastrianizm, and thus he allowed the Jews to re-build their temples.

Having returned to Jerusalem, although not as magnificent as the previous one, the Jews started building their temple, with the financial support of Kyros. While the temple was built, the priests have concluded that all holy scripts and the ten commandments of Moses should be written, otherwise, in case of another slavery, the religion would disappear. Hence, Ezra and his friends started writing the Old Testament, as explained before. A little group opposed including a lot of myths learned in Babylon in the holy book, but they could not get themselves heard well. This group explained that Moses wrote the commandments under three layers of secrecy, in hieroglyphics and explained its secrets to 70 people whom he had chosen and initiated. This little group known as "Kabbalah Supporters" and their followers were later isolated completely from the Jewish community and were declared as perverts. Well, who were these Kabbalah Supporters and what were the real principles of Moses?[33]

Being initiated in Osiris Temple, Moses built the new religion on Osiris Religion, and used Saabi beliefs to some extent. However, as the real secrets of Osiris religion were only known by the initiated people who have undergone some form of an education, Moses had relatively simplified his principles, in order to be able to teach them to his followers, and also used symbols for the principles he could not teach. Those were the symbols Ezra could not understand and caused the religion to have a totally different identity. Moses used an old system for his principles not to be corrupted and the real meanings of the symbols not to be changed. He chose 70 suitable people among his followers and initiated them. He completed their education in time and taught them the real meanings of the symbols. So he called them "Kabbalah Supporters", meaning the Accepted Ones.[34]

This group, the members of which have followed Kabbalah principles, and remained in Jahuda desert for political reasons, was called the Essenis. But, as we are going to return to them later, let us continue with Kabbalah principles.

Disseminating real principles of Moses among his followers through initiation system for a long time, after the land that they lived on was invaded by Ismailis after Islam, Kabbalah supporters saw that they could behave more freely. In an era when Muslim Sufi orders started to pop up, Kabbalah supporters got their principles printed, taking advantage of the air of freedom. Two most important titles of Kabbalah supporters, "Zohar" and "Seferitsire" were written in Spain, in 1200 A.D., in Moslem Andalusia. Some researchers claim that the reasons behind Islamic Sufism and Kabbalah Principles were the same, however, Islamic Sufism is based on Egyptian Hermetic beliefs, Greek Esoteric philosophy, as well as Kabbalah principles.

The ceremony of getting initiated to learn Kabbala principles is called Tiferet.[35] Symbolically, Tiferet is a ceremony of death and curbing one's desires. With this ceremony, selfishness within a person is eliminated and it is accepted that a re-birth is performed in a new dimension [34].

According to Seferitsire, the leading book of Kabbalah, the universe has appeared from the Mighty Existence, through various elements. First of these elements is fire, the illumination existence of God. Second element is the soul that has come out of this Mighty Light, which is the Air. Third element is the Water. Coming from air, water is a combination of hydrogen and oxygen. Esoteric meaning of this symbol is that the water contains life within itself. Fourth element on the other hand is the earth, solid derivative of the fire. Seferitsire also mentions of six powers, besides the four basic elements. These are the four directions, i.e. the North, East, West and the South, as well as up and down, which are the two poles.

The universe has emanated from the Mighty Existence, and is currently floating in it, and sooner or later, everything will return to it. That is why, everything is the same and all human beings are siblings. Kabbalah supporters have used the term "En Soph" for God, meaning beyond the apprehension of men. It is believed that this Egyptian based word was used to express that God has no beginning and has no end, and is believed to come from the same root as the word "Sophus" in Greek.

In another important book of Kabbalah supporters, Zohar, the same explanations have been given in more sophisticated form. According to Zohar, the aim of the whole system, which the life is built on, is for the soul, which is a part of the God, is to complete its evolution process and to return to God. It is only possible for the Perfect Human Being, or "Adam Khamun" to reach God. In every period, there has always been one or more Adam Khamuns.

Being an Adam Khamun, depends on the lifestyle of the individuals. Strongest law in the universe is the law of evolution. However, there is also another law, which is the law of creatures acting on their free will. For that, being an Adam Khamun, depends on the individual itself. But, no one can be a perfect being in a single life frame. Eternal spirit passes from body to body and searches for perfection. He can only find Perfection, in other words the Divine Secret, if he deserves it.

Following sections present in Zohar, explains the quality of the principles:[36]

"Rabbi Siemon said this: 'Torah (the Old Testament) contains divine realities and mighty secrets in its each word. But, the stories in Torah are only the outfits. Shame on those who see these outfits as the Torah itself. Because, any such person will be deprived of his share in the other world.'

And, David said the following: 'You have opened my eyes. With your laws, I have seen some wonderful things, I mean the things underneath.'

The most visible part of a person is his outfits at the top. Those who have no power of comprehension, can only see the outfits, when they look at a person. In fact, what makes the outfits look good, is the person's body itself. It is the soul that makes the body beautiful. This is the same for Torah, too. The stories in the Torah form the outfits of the body. The body is composed of the principles of Torah. People without the power of comprehension can only see the stories, which are the outfits. But in fact, those who serve the High King, and those who live on the Sinai mountain penetrate everywhere with soul, and they also penetrate Torah, which is the main principle of everything. All the same, these will be made available in the future, for Torah's spirit to have effect on the full spirit. When all these combine, Adam Khamun, or the celestial divine person who is the soul of the spirit, comes by.

God said "let there be light" and the light shone. This was the basic light created by God, this was the light to the eye. Then, he opened the door of the East, where the light flowed into, and the source of all the lights shone. In Constitution, God shined the light on the Earth, but later, he took it back, in order to keep his sinful people in darkness, and kept it for the good. As it was written, "light was for the just".

The light at the bottom is harmful, due to its nature. It destroys anything that comes near. But the light at the top is white. It neither finishes nor destroys, nor does it change. Light is the divine self, is the secret of wisdom.

God's divine name Y H V H, represents the four stages in holy existence, which increases non-stop. From the source of the holy sea, first Yod came out. Then a deep basin was formed and this basin was divided to seven channels. These channels were Greatness, Power, Fame, Victory, Kingdom, Salvation, and Sovereignty. Source, sea, flow and seven channels formed number ten. The reason for the reasons known as Sefirot, brought about the 10 sides of its existence and this crown was named as Source. This source is the never ending fountain of the Source, of the light. He appointed the source as En Soph, in another word, infinity. It has neither a shape, nor a visual, nor there is a tool that can detect it, nor there is a cup that can hold it. In itself, it is both wisdom, and comprehension. One who is wise, cannot put forward his title of wisdom through comprehension. He needs to fill this in by his own self.

Names and the titles of a man's spirit are three: Nefs (Vital Spirit), Ruah (Spirit), Neshemah (Deepest High Spirit). The three are One and they represent a unification surrounded by mysterious connections. The spirit was called Jonah (hurt). Because when a spirit goes into partnership with the body, it is open to all kinds of upsets. Nefs is the bottom most animator that gives life to body. The spirit and the body are always in close relation. Ruah supports the body and in a way, feeds it. The body rising with the support of Ruah, when reaches the correct level, becomes a throne under the spirit where the spirit can rest. When both the body and the spirit mature completely, Ruah deserves to be a Neshamah, superior spirit over the body. When it is lit completely, a perfect light comes out. This is valid for people who have reached perfection and become a saint. Knowing the characteristics of the spirit can only be possible by having high knowledge. It is a duty for the spirit to turn to God full heartedly and to pray from the bottom of his heart. When a person becomes perfect, he can only then be called as "single". When God created the human being and surrounded him with a great honor, he made it compulsory for the human being to love him. Consequently, the human being would join God with a clean hearted bond of belief, with a single aim.

When Abraham came to the country, God gave him Nefs. When Abraham travelled to South, he owned Ruah. Finally, when he reached the highest point of connection to God, he reached the level of Neshemah, which is impossible to be explained by words. Abraham had reached the highest point of wisdom and had connected to God. Abraham had given all he had to Isaac. With this, his outstanding wisdom is meant, because he has had the knowledge God's divine name. Solomon's wisdom was greater than all other children in the East, as this was descended to him from Abraham.

When the time comes for a person the leave the word, the spirit leaves the body, with a big deterioration. Adam's spirit, after leaving the body, comes to the garden of Eden. There, if it is found acceptable, enters the garden. There, four pillars await its arrival. A three colored pillar called the seating place of Mount Zion appears. With this pillar, the spirit rises to the gate of honesty of Jerusalem. The spirit found to have deserved to go higher, unites with the King's body. If this spirit is asked to rise higher, the King's magnificence is shown to it. The palace known as the Palace of Love is located on a very secret part of the sky. Any spirit loved by the Divine Person enters this palace.

Kabbalah supporters influenced anagogic Islam on one side and the esoteric principles in the Christian world on the other side. Kabbalah belief among the European Jews surfaced with Haddisims. It is possible to see Kabbalah principles brought down to people, in religion books and can be observed freely among Pantheist beliefs.

To discuss the affects of Kabbala on Chritian Esoteric doctrines, let us now have a look at another branch of Esoteric Doctrines, the form of belifs in Ancient Greek.

Four Main Powers

References

1   August Le Plonge, - *Origin of Egyptians (Mısırlıların Kökeni),* Ege Meta Pub., Istanbul, p. 198

2   Santesson Hans Stephan, - *Sunken Country Mu Civilization (Batık Ülke Mu Uygarlığı),* RM Pub., Istanbul 1989, p. 92

3   İnan Afet, - *History of Ancient Egypt (Eski Mısır Tarihi),* Istanbul, 1956, p. 108

4   Gener Cihangir, - *Different Perspectives on Hiram (Hiram Menkıbesine Farklı Bakışlar),* Barış Pub.., Ankara 2001, p. 152

5   Schure Edouard, - *Great Initiatives (Büyük İnisiyeler),* RM Pub, Istanbul 1989, p. 221

6   Örs Hayrullah, - *Moses and Judaism (Musa ve Yahudilik),* Remzi Pub., Istanbul 1966

7   Hooke Samuel Henry, - *Middle East Mythology (Ortadoğu Mitolojisi),* İmge Pub., Ankara 1991, p. 122

8   Gener Cihangir, - *Hiram Abif,* Nokta Pub., Istanbul 2009, p. 113

9   Gener C., r.w., p. 113

10   Gener C., r.w., p. 114

11   Gener C, r.w., p. 115

12   Erentay İbrahim, - *Hiram* Abif, Irmak Pub., İst. 2000, p. 145

13   Erentay İ., r.w., p. 143

14   Gener C, Rr.w., p. 113

15   Gener C, r.w., p. 143

16   Erentay L, r.w., p. 141

17   Schure E., r.w., p. 229

18   Schure E., r.w., p. 233

19   Schure E., r.w., p. 235

20   Schure E., r.w., p. 246

21   *Major Religions and Sects (Büyük Dinler ve Mezhepler),* Istanbul 1964, p. 172

22   Knight, Christopher; Lomas, *Robert- The Hiram Book (Hiramın Kitabı),* Bilge Karınca Pub., Istanbul 2008, p. 102

23   Knight, Christopher; Lomas, Robert r.w., p. 45

24   Hanson, Kenneth - *Secrets of the Lost Bible (Kayıp İncilin Sırları)*- Kozmik Pub. Istanbul, 2006, p. 73

25   Knight, Christopher; Lomas, Robert r.w., p. 60

26   Hanson, Kenneth r.w., p. 92

27   Hanson, Kenneth r.w., p. 95

28   Hanson, Kenneth r.w., p. 113

29   De Nerval Gerard, - *Travel to the East (Doğuya Seyahat),* Kültür Bakanlığı Pub., Ankara 1984, p. 97

30   Örs Hayrullah, r.w., p. 232

31   Jacq Christian, - *Master Hiram, Prophet Solomon (Hiram Usta, Süleyman Peygamber),* Arion Pub., Istanbul 2000

32   Örs Hayrullah, r.w., p. 265

33   Örs Hayrullah, r.w., p. 338

34   Baigent Michael/Leigh Richard, - *Holy Grail, Holy Blood (Kutsal Kâse, Kutsal Kan),* Emre Pub., Istanbul 1996, p. 301

35   Turkish Masonic Magazine (Türk Mason Dergisi), #21, Istanbul 1956, p. 1095

36   Scholem Gershom, - Zohar; *The Book of Glory (İhtişamın Kitabı),* Drahma Pub., Istanbul 1994

CHAPTER VI

ANCIENT GREEK ESOTERISM: ORFEUS-PYTHAGORAS-PLATO

An interaction had occurred between the Egyptian and Greek civilizations, within a long process, which were in fact the very two main bases of our present civilization. This interaction had always been one-sided; such as the new from the old, the student from the teacher, Greece from Egypt had been affected by one another.

Greek civilization co-founder Orfeus and very important philosophers, the milestones of civilization such as, Euclides, Chicero, Heredot, Pythagoras and Plato, and philosophy school and religion founders had all been initiated at the famous Egyptian 'Osiris Temple'. Even though Pythagoras and Plato have been extremely effective on today's civilization, because the Orfeik faith forms the bases of the Pythagoras and Plato schools, we shall not be able to proceed without mentioning these two famous Greek initiates.

It was believed that the father of Orfeus' was the king of Thrace, Oiagros. He had learned to play musical instruments from Apollo. The instrument he played was the seven-string lyre given to him by Apollo, which he had taken from Hermes. It was said that he had thought the Eleusis mysteries and rituals to King Midas. However, he had been killed at a Bacchus ritual for worshipping God Apollo. Orfeus was the reformist leader of the Apollo religion and founder of the Dionysius cult.[1]

Orfeus, being the first facilitator of the Hermetic belief in Greece, was the first Greek student of the Osiris priests.

Mankind, experiencing a great decline after the flood, and having been forced to start all over, underwent the era of the primitive tribes had lived once again. The era was of a matriarchal one, and thus the domination of the tribes was in the hands of the women. The 'Moon' symbolizing the feminine side of God in the Mu religion, was promoted to the 'Head Goddess' title.[2] As a result of religious corruption, while humans were being sacrificed to the Sun God, time humans were beginning to be sacrificed to the Moon Goddess.

Apollo, as previously seen, was the Sun God of the Luvis who had established the first civilization in Anatolia. In Greece, there was a constant conflict between the Bacchus religion, where worshipping the Moon Goddess was prevailing, and the Apollo religious supporters of Anatolia, who preached the temple of the Sun God. In fact, the actual reason behind the war was the question of whether the order was matriarchal or patriarchal.

The word Apollon in Phoenician language, is derived from the word 'Ap O Len' meaning 'Universal Father'.[3] It will be remembered that the Phoenicians and the Luvis were related, and that Apollon had appeared for the first time on Anatolian soil, was a sign of his connection to the ancient Atlantis culture.[4] Additionally, the implementation of this kind of initiation ceremony being held at the Delf Temple, dedicated to Apollo, was yet another proof of this relation.

According to a common belief, Orfeus is the son of a virgin nun of the Delf Temple consecrated to Apollo. The necessity of nuns attending at this temple to be virgins, had brought up the claim of the said nun to be pregnant by God Apollo, and that the same claim had found reflections in several other religious beliefs. The basis of Jesus having been born from a virgin arose from this myth.

In 700s B.C. in Greece, the Apollo believers were a minority. They were about to be destroyed by supporters of Bacchus. And just in such an environment, Orfeus fled to Greece and then to Egypt so to take shelter from Osiris priests. Initiated there and having spent twenty years among the Osiris priests, attaining the secrets of the teachings, he was sent back to his country with the mission to revive and re-face the Apollo religion.

Orfeus, gaining many supporters around him in a short time with his wisdom and strong personality just as Osiris had done in Atlantis, managed to defeat the supporters of the Bacchus religion. However, while teaching his religion, Orfeus used the method of the Egyptian priests, basing his teachings on existing beliefs, and in the meantime forming it on the Bacchus religion, as a result of which, the polytheistic religion of Zeus and the Dionysius Cult emerged.

As believed by Orfeic belief, soul was trapped within the body as if in a grave. Man's task was to purify and to liberate the soul. The soul could only be purified in both in this world and the other through ritualistic practice. The soul, while leaving the body at the moment of death, would drink water from the spring of oblivion before rebirth took place in another body. Only by admittance to the discipline of Orfeus could transmigration of the soul be ended. To prevent rebirth, the initiates were given a golden plate to be buried with, on which the hidden secrets were written.[5] After death, if the soul had lived a proper life, it was to be sent to heaven, otherwise to hell. Following the praise or the punishment stage, the soul was reborn in a new body. However, a soul having lived a proper life three times might break the rebirth cycle and become free. Accompanied by the music of a seven-string lyre, the soul would pass through the seven spheres of the skies and reach the stratum of God Almighty. As maintained by Orfeustic teachings, Zeus, being the mightiest of all Gods, was the God where the entire universe was existed from him. Dionysius was his son, in other words, he was the manifestation of The Divine Word. Another name of his was, Horus. Humans were parts of Dionysius. Initiates were the Hermeses of the human beings, meaning they were the secondary Gods. Orfeus said, 'Gods die and are re-born within us'. Orfeus, believing in rebirth, stated that true God was unique, but the secondary gods were of great variety and infinite in number. In the opinion of Orfeus, half gods were divine souls who had attained Sage Man status after being freed of the rebirth cycle.[6]

Orfeus, had applied what he had learned at Memphis and by selecting the appropriate ones from his adherents and initiating them, he had established his own school.[7] In Orfeustic faith, that the idea of 'Almighty God' was clearly put forward had caused Orfeus to be known as the first to switch from Polytheistic to Monotheistic also belief after the Flood and had been depicted as an icon in various Christian mosaics. Just as Apollo, the belief of being born from a virgin mother was also yet another reason why Orfeus was adopted by the Christianity. However, during the purge of the believers of the Mithra faith from the Christian world, it seemed that the Orpheus cult was abandoned and building of mausoleums were discontinued.

The word 'Evohe' had become the password/motto for the Orfeustic initiates. We had mentioned the usage of this word by Moses previously, pronounced as 'Yod-He Vau He' in Egypt. Let's just be content with reminding that Yod represented Osiris and that He Vau He represented Isis. The same holy word had also been used by Pythagoras as a password.

In the meantime, during the same period, just as the Orfeustic faith, trade organizations had entered Greece through Egypt. These organizations named 'Hetairies',[8] attributed to Hermes, used to accept members through initiation procedures. The supporters of these organizations, accepting Hermes as their patriarch, and just as the Egyptians, granting him the title 'Trimejit', meaning three times divine, used to call themselves as 'The Workers of Dionysius'. It was owing to this fraternity organization that Toth, the master of the state system and religion, the divine word, the script, the technical and esoteric sciences, the ascendant and of the death had been identified with Hermes of the same characteristics, and of Egyptian theology being reconciled with Greek theology. Today, the very much admired Antique Greek works and Ionian columns carry the signatures of these masters.

Members of these organizations being called The Workers of Dionysos is a sign of their Orfeus beliefs. Dionysius Workers, having benefited from the use of secret words and signs to recognize each other, had been given a lot of privileges to ease their jobs through the Solon Laws. The Dionysius Cult welcomed all segments of society including women and slaves. Anyone who passed the moral examination and paid for the right to enter, and who was able to risk the maturation rituals that would last for years, was entitled to enter the Brotherhood of Dionysius. The Dionysius Cult had spread rapidly in Greece in 6-5 B.C. and over the centuries had caused a religious awakening. Dionysius had died as a god who had become a man and had destroyed the solid wall between the God of the Olympic religion and the mortal man. With Dionysius referred to as 'The God of People', democracy had been established in Athens. Herodotus explained that the religion of Osiris was found in the origins of Dionysius rituals.

Philosopher Diotorus, confirming this, stated 'Osiris Rituals' were converted into Dionysius rituals, and that Isis rituals were converted into Demeter rituals. The only difference was only the names. All these were brought about by Orpheus'.[9] Dionysius was referred to as 'Light of Zeus'. Escaping death at the initiation ceremony, Dionysius was greeted as 'Hail New Light'. And before him, the god Attis, the Mother Goddess Ma's husband, was likewise hailed as 'New Light'.[10]

With Solon's law, this form of organization had been given great freedom. Solon Laws had been applied the law of 'Members of the same Frat, unless there was otherwise a formal decree of prohibition, may be in any providence' all along Greece'.[11] In 4 B.C. even some tax exemptions were applied to members of this organization. However, the actual task of these fraternity organizations was to create a sense of membership/belonging through secret rituals and teachings, and by creating an inner solidarity between artisans to strengthen the society. Traveling miners, sailors, lumberjacks, stone craftsmen and other Dionysius brothers had attained the status of 'half-sanctified' thanks to trade secrets that were secretly hidden among the brothers and never given to those who did not know the special descriptive signs. Even the mysteries of trade and of magic were thought to be the same thing. Fratrie members were free. They were solely responsible for contracts against the Kingdom and with Solon Laws, they were granted liberty of movement by all means.

The organization of Dionysius had in time transformed into the Corporations of Rome and the Collegians.[12] These artisan Corporations and Collegians, gathered in their private premises (Schola), enjoyed all sorts of freedom and travel rights, just like their predecessors, owing to their mysterious trade secrets. This tradition of privileged recognition, which descended from Ancient Greece, Egypt, Babylon, perhaps Atlantis and Mu, continued in Christian Europe in the middle ages and allowed Masonry to continue its existence.

In relation to the Dionysius-Eluisis cult, Hermes was the son of Zeus, the chief god of Olympos, and Maia of Arkadian, the daughter of Atlas.[13] Also the Sun God Apollo's brother. According to Homeros' statement, it was not possible for his mother to be regarded as the immortal god of

Olympos, because of her being a nymph, and the first request of Hermes upon birth, was that he was accepted to 'the ritual of Apollo'. In order to attain this desire, he made a lyre and with the music he played, he deceived Apollo's herds of cows and even stole some. And by burning these herds that he stole, he sacrificed them to the immortal gods.

Having learned what had happened, Apollo complained Hermes to Zeus. Hermes found salvation in his music and softened his brother's heart by singing with his own lyre. Providing he taught the knowledge of music to him, Apollo would give Hermes immortality, supreme wisdom, and the transmission of information between the gods and the world of the dead. Thus, Hermes became the teacher of the hidden symbols, the divine word, rhetoric, music, and the god of all the secret sciences.[14] The task of communication between Zeus and other gods was also dictated to Hermes. Thus, he had become the god that ended hostilities by negotiations, conventions, and therefore had become the God of Peace. Hermes taught him to talk, when mankind was created. The only weapon that he possessed was his music and his persuasion ability. Hermes was the god of Olympic Games too, which regulated political relations between Greek city states. Over time, these duties included written agreements, and thus, script, alchemy, astrology and eventually the virtue of being the god of reason and wisdom. In the Strasbourg Cosmogonian from Hermoupolis, dating back to the 4th century, it was described as to how Hermes with the help of his father Zeus, had created order out of chaos and had created the Cosmos and how he had established the first city on Earth (Hermoupolis) in Egypt.[15]

Dionysius of Orfeus was no one but Apollo himself. Apollo, the Sun God, was the Divine Light. At the door of the Delf Temple, which was dedicated to Apollo, there stands the quote 'Know Thy Self'. The Delf Temple, consisting of a triangular roof over the four Doric pillars, houses the foundations of the esoteric teachings.

The four pillars, on which the temple was built, were the four major creative powers of the Mu religion, the four basic elements of Egyptian and Kabbalah esoterism. These four columns at the same time represent the physical environment in which the human being exists, the world and the Micro Cosmos. The triangular ceiling above the four pillars, facing upwards, that is, toward God, is the symbol of God, the Macro Cosmos, which man strives to reach. The triangle of the roof, refers to the Divine Trinity, masculine and feminine principles, the Divine Word, that is the Son. At the center of the Hermetic Eluisis mysteries is a God-Human myth that dies and is re-born. The most important ceremonies of the Eluisis cult, for the Mother Goddess and Dionysius was the 'Rebirth Celebration Ceremonies'. Eluisis city, 20 Km to Athens was dedicated to Demeter, the God of Fertility. The mysteries of Eluisis were open to every man and woman, providing they did not commit any crime. Even slaves could be initiated to the mysteries. All initiates were sworn to secretly keep the initiation ceremonies in which re-birth faith was staged. At the end of the ceremony, the hall would be illuminated with a powerful light and the birth of a child was declared. The candidate who was reborn was enlightened by this light. Plato, in his book 'Fedon', states, 'While those who die without initiation go directly to Hades, those who have been initiated will be promoted next to the gods.'[16]

About 30 thousand pilgrims (hadjis) attended this celebration every spring equinox. Sacred Eluisis temple was being walked to barefooted for 30 kilometers, fasted throughout the stroll, sacrifices were offered to the gods. Those who were to be initiated were harassed by the previously initiated wearing masks along the sacred path, and sometimes were struck with sticks. The intent of this practice was to test the patience of the new initiatives and to accustom them to modesty and frugality. At the beginning of the regiment, a sculpture of Dionysius was carried to guide the initiates and the pilgrims. After the naked bathing and other purification ceremonies at sea, the Telestorion hall was reached where the initiation ceremony was to be held place. Only the old initiates and candidates could enter this hall.

Cicero makes the following statement for the Eluisis mysteries; 'In the mystery ceremonies called initiation, we not only have gained the first principles of life, a happy life, but also the understanding of dying with hope.' Plato says the following for the initiation ceremony: 'we have been initiated to the blessed mystery and saw endless dreams shining in pure light.' Dionysius, the disciple of the same path, has said, 'it is a difficult path to follow. It's dark and full of glooms. But if an initiate is guiding you on the way, the initiation becomes even brighter than the brightness of the Sun.'[17]

Behind closed doors, what inspiring ceremony was being performed that so deeply had affected the greatest philosophers, artists, statesmen and scientists of the ancient world? All initiates were being sworn in on Hermes and Dionysius to keep the secret given to them. Because of the fact that all participants of the ceremony stayed loyal to their vows, there were no written documents. However, from several implications and hints, we know that they witnessed a supreme theatrical ceremony.

Although the Eluisis initiation ceremonies had been carried out for more than 1100 years, there were no satisfactory written documents as to what had happened during the ceremonies. The information at hand is based on evidence obtained indirectly. It is thought that it was Orpheus who first initiated the death of Dionysius into the ceremonies. The newly initiates were named as 'Mystea'. It means 'eyes shut' in Greek. Such words as Mystery and Mysticism are believed to have originated from this word. And for high ranking initiates the word 'Epopthae' was being used which means 'the one who has seen'.[18]

The initiates were entering along with powerful music and their eyes used to dazzle because of the lights. They would bathe in a giant ball of fire and would shiver with a gong's sound deafening their ears. The name of the head priest guiding the ceremony, just as their predecessors in Egpty was Hyorofan. Hyorofan would dress just like the main character Dionysius and would personify his death and re-birth. The main aim of this divine drama, where life was eventually being victorious over death, and that the birth of joy after every suffering was being depicted, was the idea for every initiate to share the predestination of Dionysius. At Eluisis, while the initiates were witnessing the inspiring tragedy of Dionysius, they were sharing his pain, death and re-birth, and thus experiencing a spiritual purification.

The initiates would symbolically live the death and re-birth of Dionysius and a different state of awareness was experienced through the spiritual purification ceremony called 'Katarsis'. Aristo explains the situation as 'the initiates don't have to learn anything but are required to reach a certain level of state of mind'.[19] The word Cathar is believed to come from Katarsis. People initiated to mysteries, were asked to admit their flaws and sins in front of people and thus purify themselves in this way. The priest would ask the initiate to admit his worst sin. The first request for the confession of a sin or flaw from an initiate was seen in the Egyptian 'Book of The Dead'. In all Pagan mystery ceremonies, a dinner of love called Agape would take place. The initiates were called 'Adelphoi' which meant 'to be a brother'. The members were Philadelphians, in the sense of bearing brotherly love for each other. The believers of Jupiter, called their members as 'Fratres Carrissimi' meaning 'the most loving brother'.[20] There were 3 degrees/ranks in Greek initiations. They were, Catharmos (Purification); Paradosis (Passing on Esoteric Teaching), and Epoptheta (Reaching Truth).[21]

In the basis of Hermetic Dionysius philosophy, there lies an understanding as 'All is One'. The mysteries carry the purpose of arousing the feeling of a Supreme Unity within the initiate. Diogenes states the following for initiation using the same 'Sun' definition like Plato; 'Every initiation is aimed to unite with the world and with God. This is a difficult path to follow. However, if a Master guides you, the initiation becomes even brighter than the brightness of the Sun'.

In the ancient Greek Hermetic doctrine, the objective of initiation was not something to be learned by the participants, but to provide them with experimenting a different state of awareness. Aristotle, states this experiment as: 'The initiates should try not to learn something, but rather accomplish a certain state of mind. The initiates are to experience themselves as immortal souls imprisoned within a physical body. By sharing the death of Dionysius, they are reborn as souls and experience their own immortal Godly selves. Life and death are not just one time specified events causing endless rewards or punishments, but are parts of a repeating cyclic process. Every soul, through this rebirth, has a chance to complete the path returning to God'.

Two grave inscriptions found in Crete and Cappadocia, are an indication as to how much the Hermes cult had been glorified within the Greek civilization. On the grave inscription found in Crete, dated back to second century A.D., the expression of 'The All Absolute' for Hermes and at a concurrent time on a Cappadocia inscription, the expression of 'Lord and Christ' is seen to have been encrypted.[22]

After the death of Orfeus, the supporters of the ancient Bakus religion, having successfully managed to hide themselves, re-appeared and did all in their power to ensure the abolition of Orfeic beliefs. The systematic work of the Orfeus opponents bore their fruits as so much that, after a while even the name 'Orfeus' became the name of a mythical being. Even present day researchers of ancient Greek are not in agreement as to whether Orfeus has ever existed or not.

In the wake of this systematic destruction attempt, Dionysius Temple was largely worsening, while the Delf Temple of Apollo, which was already present before Orfeus, managed to survive. Dionysius Priests clothed themselves as Apollo priests and identified themselves as priests of the polytheistic system, while continuing to secretly attend Orfeik initiations.

In this environment, two centuries after Orfeus, Pythagoras was born in 570 B.C.[23] After being initiated at the Delf Temple, he entered the world of esoteric doctrines. Despite having learned the Orfeik doctrine thoroughly, he was not content and thus he decided to learn the secret teaching from its source just as Orfeus had done. It was easy for Pythagoras who had gone to Menfis, to be admitted to the Osiris Fellowship at an early age, for the Egyptian priests had already acknowledged his existing knowledge of the esoteric doctrine.[24]

Living there for 22 years and learning the most hidden secrets of the Osiris religion, it was particularly the esoteric usage of the numbers that intrigued him most. Pythagoras decided to use this method for his students to better understand the system he was to introduce in the future.

The interpretation of the name Pythagoras captures his personality and the mission he has undertaken. The name Pithagoras as it is written in Greek is made up of the combination of three words. The first word being Pi represents the Sun God, the circle symbolizing the light, a constant number representing the ratio of the diameter to the circumference. The name of the Creator God of Egypt Pytha arises as Tha in the second part of the word. The word Tha refers to the first regulatory principle. The last part of the word Goras, indicates the one who has united with Ra, and has lightened from darkness, when considered as a whole, the word represents Sage Man (The

Kamil One.) Pythagoras, in Egypt, as an initiate of the Osiris cult, had attained the golden disk of Atum-Ra. And thus, all doors to the secret knowledge of Egypt had been made accessible to him.

After the invasion of Egypt by Kambiz, the Babylon King, Pythagoras was taken to Babylon among all Memphis Priests. These priests, though brought captive, gave incentive for the Babylon School, which, despite being corrupted, persisted to exist for many centuries. Pythagoras, after being accepted to Babylon school along with other priests, found the chance to look into not only the differentiated teachings of this school but also the Zarathustra religion accepted as state religion during the Persian invasion of Babylon. During his stay in Babylon, traveling once to India and to Jerusalem, Pythagoras made contact with 'Gimno-Sophists' who advocated the ancient 'Rama' religion in India, and the Cabalists in Jerusalem. Pythagoras, examining the interpretation of mystical number technique of Cabala, remained there for twelve years. Demodes, an initiated friend from the Babylon School and also personal doctor of the king helped Pythagoras to obtain his freedom. He returned to Greece, after 34 years being expat.

During his training in the East, Pythagoras gained a lot of talents and developed hand skills considered to be miraculous in the eyes of a westerner. He would heal the sick with his hands just like Jesus, who was to show same miracles in the forthcoming centuries. Again, just as Jesus had done, he too stopped the waves of the rivers and the sea, and could be seen at two different places at the same time. It is said that he spoke both in Metapontum in Italy and Tauromenium in Sicily concurrently. The distance between these two points is far above the distance that can be traveled in a day in those days.[25]

Pythagoras, first thing to be done upon his return to Greece, visited Delf Temple, where he had left Greece for Egypt. Pythagoras, trying to present a synthesis of his learnings in Egypt and Babylon to the Delf priests and to Apollo priests, who only recognized the Egyptian school of the esoteric doctrine, found it hard to make his interpretations accepted; as a result, he moved to Italy after a year where he established his own school in Cratone, a colony of Greece.[26]

Pythagoras' goal was not to teach esoteric doctrine to those who were selected only by the method of initiation, but to use this doctrine to establish the first nucleus and institute to carry out a new political organization. Pythagoras reached this goal in a short time. All the brothers who were initiated in the institute that he founded were not limited to only esoteric doctrine; they also learned all the mathematics, psychic, religious and political sciences of the period. This type of education was the first step towards the beginning of the age of science, and centuries later it ensured the birth of Renaissance in Italy.

Pythagoras, after long and sometimes years of surveillance of the candidates who would like to enter the institute, admitted merely those worthy of entering. At the entrance of the institute, there was a statue of Hermes and it wrote 'Unbeliever, keep distance'. Ones believed worthy to enter the institute were subject to some examinations. Although these exams seemed to resemble the ones in Egypt, they were much more softened versions.[27] For instance, the candidates were left alone in a cave to spend the night alone, ones refusing or escaping from the cave were not admitted to the institute.

In the next test, a Pythagoras symbol, which the candidate had never seen before, was shown and asked to comment on it. 'What does the triangle inside a circle tell you' or 'what is the meaning of the number...?' The candidate was given 12 hours to prepare the answer to these questions, while being left hungry and thirsty.

The third and toughest one was to test the pride and personality of the candidate by apprentices of the institute. This test was to ridicule the candidate, and make him angry. The candidate would have to manage and control himself. For the candidate to behave otherwise, become angry or cry or respond rudely, would mean for him to be fired by Pythagoras watching him from a distance.

Although this method had brought in highly qualified and positive people to the school, it was also the reason for the collapse of the institute. Candidates humiliated and not admitted to the school had become hostile towards Pythagoras and his disciples. Simon was one of these people who started the events that led to the demolition of the Institute and the killing of hundreds of his supporters and Pythagoras himself. To return to this subject later, let us now examine the four-degree system of fraternity that the school was based upon.

The candidate having passed the examinations and accepted to the brotherhood, was called 'Novice' meaning apprentice or recruit. The novice period, depending on the person's abilities, was limited to minimum 2 to maximum 5 years. The novices were expected never to talk, ask questions and argue, they were just to listen to the lessons in peace. The aim was to improve the learner's intuition ability. Pythagoras, stating the idea of an invisible abstract world above the visible world could only be perceived with intuition, wanted his apprentices to first sense the presence of God and then love him. Stating that the whole universe was based on love, Pythagoras taught that the first step of learning about love began in the family with the love of parents, and that the father was the masculine, and that the mother was the female expression of God. According to Pythagoras, the person born of these two was the representative of God on Earth. In addition, Pythagoras also wanted the Novices to form groups of two and to know each other really well and become friends. The Novices, having learned that unconditional love is one the most perfect expressions, would be taught such esoteric interpretations that can be summarized as: 'You are a friend and you are indeed one'. The Novices were expected to show eternal obedience and commitment, disciplined behavior to their masters, show adherence to health rules, and to all-time cleanliness.

The Pythagorean disciples, purposing for spiritual purifi-cation, believed that the body, together with the soul, should be clean, and thus sometimes would be cleaned several times a day. The outfits of the disciples, like their bodies, were also immaculate and white in color, the symbol of purity. Not only the outfits of the Ismaili sectarian disciples who assumed their esoteric beliefs from Pythagoreanism but also those of the Templier Knights of their continuation in the Christian world were white as the Pythagoreans. The Pythagorean disciples had to marry. The school, accepting the existence of God's masculine and feminine duality, regarded the marriage institution and the family as holy as its extension. In the same view, both men and women could be initiated at the institute. The only rule the disciples were expected to obey about marriage was to marry an initiate like themselves. Otherwise, it would be very difficult to find virtue in the non-initiated. Pythagoreans were renowned for paying respect and giving freedom to their women. Pythagorean ancient texts emphasize the equality of women with men. The first teacher of Pythagoras was Themis-Toclea, a nun of the Delf Temple.

Pythagoras in his letter to Croton women, wrote: "Women are more inclined to religiousness as gender." Pythagoras had entrusted all his writings to his daughter Damo. The writer of the book Dionysos Rites is a writer named Arignote, also a disciple of Pythagoras.[28]

The last thing taught to Novices, was to treat all the Gods as one. Having learned that all religions were to be tolerated, thanks to the important teaching of toleration in the studies, the Novices would see that all Gods were one and only, and that all regions were there to reach God.

The title of "Nomoteth" was given to the second degree devotees, and to these initiates the 'Science of the Numbers' was taught. A special ceremony was held for the transition to the second degree, and as Pythagoras expressed, the teaching of the facts would begin with this ceremony.

There was a temple called the "Muses Temple", forbidden to Novices, where only the Nomoteths, also called the mathematicians, and the ones in higher degrees could enter. In this rounded temple, there were the statues of the nine Muses and of the guardian of the divine principle, Vesta. Every single Muse was the protector of each science. Of these, the most important three were the guardian of Astronomy and Astrology, Urania; the guardian of the world beyond, Poymnia; and the guardian of life and death, and of the science of Rebirth, Melpomen. Vesta standing in the middle, had fire in one hand, and showing the skies with the other, was explaining the beginning of all came from the fire of the skies. The teachings in this Temple would begin with the explanation that all what Muses and Vista symbolize were in fact existent in the human structure. Pythagoras would continue training the Nomoteths stating that the entire meaning of the universe exists within the numerical symbolism.

Pythagoras, stating that 'Numbers rule the Universe' and with this quote he would say God has specifically pointed out the numbers as a series of prototype symbols and thus for this reason each and every number was a symbol with a character. Pythagoras did not identify the numbers as one, two, three but rather with their own characters, Monad, Diad, Triad.

According to Pythagoras, the number 1 was Monad, meaning singular. It would symbolize the singularity, eternal life, and the masculine fire out of which all life began and thus symbolize God himself. The symbol was a dot and besides the Supreme Being, it also symbolized wisdom meaning the Divine Intelligence. Pythagoras had said 'God is one, and as some of you might think, he is not out of this world, but he is inside. He is the inspector of all ages, the first of all, the father of all, the Intelligence of the Universe, and life-giving spirit.'[29] Monad, with his wit, giving something out of him, but never changing at the same time, was a symbol of God, and with God, he was the manifestation of men on Earth. In other words, Monad contained both the Macrocosmos and the Microcosmos. Pythagoras claiming that the only goal of the microcosm was to unite with the Macrocosmos, said 'It is possible only through initiative training, if one is able to mature himself; however, one lifetime would not be enough for this. No matter how long it takes for the soul to achieve its goal, then it will be re-incarnated as much needed.'

Number two, coming after one, 'Diad', was representing the duality present in the universe. The indivisible self and the divisible ore; passive feminine principle that provided the formation of life with the active masculine principle that granted life: Osiris and Isis. 'Diad' was the idea born out of wisdom, was fertile and thus with this quality, feminine. Water contained life itself and it was the feminine version of God.

'Triad' meaning number three, emerged from the combination of Monad and Diad, was the creation of thought of wisdom. It was Horus, the son of Osiris and Isis. His symbol was a triangle and the key to all the laws of the life scale, especially the Re-Birth Law. Triad was the Divine Word, the cosmos itself and the living ore of earth. Did man not also come from Fire, Water, and Soil? In all the God's manifestations, there were the soul, life and body trilogy. Soul was made of Fire, Life of Water and Body of Soil.

The number four, 'Tetrad' was the symbol of eternity and immortality. Tetrad, symbolized by the square, was considered to be the expression of the four basic powers that transformed the cosmic from chaos to order. The four basic powers we mentioned before, fire, water, earth and air, were named as the four angels or the horsemen of the 'Judgement Day' (Armageddon) in the equestrian religions. Each corner of the five-pointed star that had been used since the time of the Naacals (Mu) and passed through the Egyptians to the Pythagoras School represented the Fire, Water, Soil, Air and the Earth as the combination of all. Pentad, seen as the total of Diad and Triad, was considered to be the earthly love and the symbol of marriage. The number six was symbolizing the six directions of the cosmos, north, south, east, west, above and below. This number being represented with a six corner star, was at the same time the symbol of Divine Justice. Today, known as the Prophet Solomon's six corner star, is considered to be representing Solomon's Justice. The number seven had a great importance for Pythagoreans. Since it originated from the sacred Triad and Tetrad, the creator of order, was the symbol of evolution, and its symbol was a pyramid of triangles on a square.

Since the sacred Triad and the formative Tetrad had come to fruition, it was the symbol of the law of rebellion, and its symbol was a pyramid of triangles. In this way, Pythagoras was also putting forward a reasoning for the construction of the pyramids: the symbols of 'Divine Evolution'. In addition, the science of music which proved that everything in cosmos was in harmony was also made up of seven notes. Just as the combination of the seven colors of light was bringing about the color white, creating purity, the playing of the notes in rhyme was composing the perfect purity and harmony of music.

The Pythagoreans, believing in spiritual tuning and harmony of the soul, just as in the Orfeus and Dionysos ceremonies, used music in all of their ceremonies. This belief had enabled the development of rhythm and harmony knowledge and harmonic music in the classical sense.

The number nine was represented with a pentagram. Pentagram was a figure consisting of three intertwined triangles, and according to Pythagoras, it symbolized the Golden Ratio, which was the representation of beauty and balance found in nature. And it had become the symbol or recognition among the Pythagorean disciples after the school was destroyed.[30]

Apart from these numbers, number 10 was the most important one. Number 10 called the 'Sacred Tetraktis' was symbolized with its four-part triangle, and was made up of the sum of Monad, Diyad, Triad and Tetrad. The Holy Tetraktis, due to its characteristics, was a symbol of perfection, and the unity of the Sage (the wise/kamil one) with God. 10 was also the numerical symbol of the harmonious manifestation of macro cosmos. He depicted that all beings would come together again in great harmony in the Macro cosmos. The number 10, just as for the Pythagoreans, represented the first letter of the Creator's name for the Kabbalists. According to Kabbalah, Jehovah comprised of the letters J and H, and according to Aebced calculation Y=10 and H=5, meaning from the perfect creator 10, the universe meaning 5 had emerged. The word Jehovah emphasized the singularity of God and the Universe. The other numbers are transmissions of divine intelligence.

The Holy Tetraktis

Having fully learned the science of these numbers at Sacred Tetraksis, the disciple was then granted one more step towards the spiritual evolution and was raised to the third degree. The disciple, who was aware of the numbers and the initiative secrets, was now ready to learn these carefully kept dangerous secrets. The third degree ceremony was only held in the 'Properzin' Hall of the 'Seres' Temple, where only the disciples of this degree were allowed to enter. At this point, the disciples were informed about the structure of the universe, the human being's existence on Earth, the state of death, and life after death, the world beyond, the semi-divine transformation of The Sage Men to half God, and the final stop of the life scale which was to unite with God. As stated by Pythagoras, there was fire in the center of the universe, and the Sun, was just a small reflection of the giant fire. The earth was round and together with the other planets; they were emanated from the sun. These planets and the Earth revolved around the Sun. Pythagoras was the first western philosopher to state the fact about the world being round. Plato followed him and used the same expression in his work 'Phadeo'. Again Pythagoras said that the world was not in the center of the universe, that there was a fire in the center, and that the world was a planet circling around it in circular motions.[31] The stars were other solar systems that were subject to the same laws that governed our solar system. Like all beings in the universe, planets and suns were parts of the universal soul. Each planet was a different expression of God's thought, and each had a special function. Like all beings, these planets were also grateful for four elements: the solid state of the earth, the water that is liquid, the air that is gaseous, and the fire that is not measurable.

Pythagoras, also at this stage, would tell his brothers about the emergence of life on Earth. As claimed by him, the flora and fauna appeared almost concurrently on Earth. Pythagoras stated that the evolution of the animals was not only dependent on the law of natural selection, but that, in addition to this basic law, there was a second law, called the 'Shock Law' which was in force. According to Pythagoras, superior beings were living in different parts on Earth, and when the time came, they changed the characteristics of some animal species in accordance with universal laws and created new types of species.

And human beings, emerged as a result of such practices on the species of ape by these superior beings. In terms of global evolution, human being was the final stop of the spirits of the world with the 'Sage Man' model. Pythagoras believed that the beings that created the people of the world were very high spirits, given the name of celestial beings.

Pythagoras learned a great deal about the changes of the sphere from the Egyptian priests, who knew about the previous civilizations of Atlantis and Mu. Prior to this, according to Pythagoras, who claimed that the world was shaken six times by catastrophic events, in every flood period, humanity managed to establish great civilizations and today's civilization would end with the same fate. Pythagoras argued that the events in the world did not affect the quality of God, just as the Supreme Being resembled a sea and the fluctuations in the sea did not change the quality of the sea.

He said that the Supreme Being was constantly watching all the realms and all beings, and that only the Sage Men who had developed their spirits to the highest level would realize this. Pythagoras' greatest rule was, 'Know yourself and thus in this way, you will know the world of God'. According to Pythagoras, the soul ascended from the very bottom of the life scale, starting from lifeless beings. Providing its life was sufficient enough to pass to an upper level, the soul would come to the world as a superior being in the next life, and if not, it would return to a lower level on the life scale. Man was entitled to be human by going through their entire life scales. But the vast majority was not aware of it, and therefore was sentenced to return. Pythagoras would say that the only being whose spirit rose to the skies when dead and return to Earth when born was the human being. Just like Hermes and Orfeus, Pythagoras would say to his disciples: 'you can only reach God through your own efforts'.[31]

Pythagoras, had said that all life is limited between birth and death, and that the body was means of the immortal soul. To his students, he said 'You shall be immortal. Death shall be forever distant from you. You shall be an untouchable.' Pythagoras stated that, in one of his previous lives, he had been the son of Hermes.

At the moment of death, he argued that the spirit left the body and went to a temporary world called Araf in Islam, Horeb in Judaism and Purgatory in Christianity where the decision was made whether the soul would go up or down depending on his behavior in life.

At this point, another universal law came into being, which was a law that reflected the lives on one another. To give an example, it was natural that a person who lived a previous life in the presence of an animal showed certain behavior patterns of that animal in his own life. If the individual corrected these patterns, he might become a superior person in his next life, and if he did not correct, he could return into the animal body. Pythagoras said, 'Every life is the praise or the punishment of the previous one.'

Pythagoras had another claim: 'Just as animals are relatives of people, so are people relatives of the gods' he said. Passing through numerous stages such as from the plant kingdom to the animal kingdom, and then to the human kingdom, it was the transition to the kingdom of Gods that man was awaiting. In the distant future, Plato, a follower of Pythagoras who hoped that people would achieve the most mature level of humanity by applying the law of spiritual selectivity in all marriages, had said 'In the distant future the gods will reside in the temples of people'.

According to Pythagoras, the Sage, or the wise one was the one who had broken this vicious cycle, and would no longer be reincarnated. The souls of such people were fully purified and had reached the Divine Light. In general, the wise ones would reach God for the last time after their deaths. Sometimes, however, there were people who lived in the Divine Light. Such people were semi-gods who had been sent back to the world for very specific missions. These semi-gods scattered the light of the beauty and truth to the world.

The third degree brothers, who had reached the summit of initiation together with Pythagoras, were entrusted as disciples and masters, which were the fourth and last degree. The duty of the masters who had no more to learn about the initiation was to go down to the depths of their inner being, to see the Divine Light, to accrue reality in intelligence, Virtue in spirit and cleanliness in the body. Secondary duties of the masters were to supervise and guide the lower grade brothers and to carry out the administrative duties.

The title of the masters who were supposed to transfer the level they attained to all life was 'Intellectual' which signified the enlightened person. Pythagoras believed that all people should be directed by the Intellectual, and this idea was first applied in the city of Crotona where the institute was located, and then in all of southern Italy.

Living in Crotona for 30 years, Pythagoras had undertaken many reforms in this aristocratic city. The city was ruled by the Parliament of Thousands, where only aristocrats could become members. Pythagoras formed a Parliament of the Three Hundreds, which was above the Parliament of Thousands where only the Intellectuals could enter. The Trilateral Council, which strictly adhered to the oath of confidentiality on the issues discussed inside, also formed out the government that undertook the city administration. Crotona soon became the capital of Southern Italy. Thus Pythagoras became the president of this state. The Pythagoreans ensured that the masses would voluntarily accept their system, wherever they went, to bring together justice and harmony.

Pythagoras, aware of the secrets of the world attracting the public's curiosity, and the fact that these secrets led to the birth of many rumors against him, tried to confront them with great patience and tolerance. But he was 80 years old and tired. There was great disconnection between the elite of the institute and the people. The people were convinced that the institutes were superior to themselves. In the meantime, a group of demagogues, who resorted to joining the school but were rejected for various reasons, constantly propagated against the institute. Silon, who was at the head of this group, evaluated the opinion of the public very well and set up an opposition club.

In addition to the demagogues, Silon, who invited people's leaders in his club, accused Pythagoras in short, of dictatorship, restricting the free will of people and managing the state as he wished. Silon said, 'It is not possible for the Crotonians to be free unless the institute is abolished.'

These intense propagandists of Silon and his supporters' actions gave their fruit in a short time, and one night, a very crowded mass led by Silon, attacked the school. The institute was set on fire. Hundreds of people, including Pythagoras were burned to death. The same madness took place repeatedly throughout southern Italy, and the majority of the Pythagoreans were destroyed. Few, who managed to survive, took refuge in Sicily.

Although some of them returned to Italy after calm was restored, they failed to revive the institute. These Pythagoreans, for the first time in their existence in Italy, joined the mason guilds, 'Collegias' founded in the 700s.[32] The Collegiale, which were the continuation of the 'Hetairies' organization in Greece, performed the same things as the Greek masons did in Italy and laid their signature under the famous Roman architecture. With the involvement of the pilgrims in this association, the Collegiales were much stronger in the doctrine, and they formed an intellectual core for the Renaissance to emerge in the future. It is now necessary to go back to Greece and examine Plato, another great name influenced by Pythagoras; therefore, the Collegiales' role on Roman and later Christian civilizations will be discussed later.

Plato, was born in Athens in 427 BC.[33] At that time, Greece was struggling with wars between Sparta and Athens. Plato's first teacher was Socrates. The search for good, beautiful, and especially of the truth, led Socrates to the same search becoming the most prominent element in Plato's life. When Socrates learned that the honor of commissioning the famous Delphic Temple was offered to him on account of his philosophy that can be summarized as seeking the truth and concealing no truth from the people, but that he would be granted this honor providing he would be obliged to take an oath of confidentiality, he rejected it.

Socrates had gone so far in search for truth that he had even begun to question the society's spiritual and religious values and as he did not give up its stance, he was sentenced to death. The unfair murder of Socrates hurt Plato deeply, and he abandoned Greece, saying, 'Now I have understood his incapability to express his truth'.

Plato, unlike his tutor, was aware of the fact that reality was not be found only by reasoning and logic. For this reason, while Socrates was still alive, he accepted to be initiated in Delf Temple, and after his death he had gone to Egypt to obtain the truth from the source. Like Pythagoras, Plato too did not have any difficulty in accepting Osiris. Plato, however, did not reach the highest ranks like Pythagorean, because he had not spent enough time at the temple. Plato, who stayed in Egypt for a short time, could only rise to the third degree. The Greek philosopher who passed from Egypt to Italy met with the Pythagoreans, who still were persisting their existence. Knowing that Pythagoras was the highest of Greek wisdom, Plato learned his teachings from his disciples. However, he was not a Pythagorean, and for this reason, it was impossible for all the secrets to be given to him.

Plato, learning from the Osiris priests and the Pythagorians that truth was only to be grasped through intuition, despite this, was still influenced by Socrates, who argued that the only way to find the truth was logic. The contribution of Plato's esoteric teachings was to place rationality on a more solid ground within the doctrine. The esoteric doctrine, in the language of the symbols used, was already able to stay away from all kinds of dogmatism. With Plato, however, concepts such as logical approach to events and the rationality of all truths had become more powerful.

Plato, who returned to Athens after Italy and founded 'Academia', began to spread his philosophy. Plato wrote, 'Dialogues' in Athens, which was a subdued and softened version of esoteric teachings. He had to behave in this way because he was also bound to his vows. Plato, who was very successful at telling concepts like truth, beauty and good to the public, had said that these three qualities were divine qualities, and that the soul of one, in search of the good, the right and the truth, would be purified and immortal. Plato, with his relatively easy to understand and freed from secrets and symbols "Dialogs and Ideas Theory, largely influenced generations after him. Plato led the ancient Alexandrian school to accept the philosophy called 'New Platonism' and for the most philosophers of the period to gather under his thoughts. Platon had great influence on Christian theosophists and Islamic Sufis.

Founded in Egypt, Alexandria in 305 BC by the most prominent representatives such as Plotinos, Porphyry and Jamblik, the Alexandria School was greatly influenced by Plato's and Pythagoras's ideas.[34] Moreover, for the birth of the Alexandrian school, the old school in Egypt, the Osiris temple, was not to be forgotten. The Osiris Temple was destroyed by the Roman commander Teodosius in 385 BC. When the temple was being destroyed, the mechanical instruments used during the initiation ceremonies and the rooms where the tests were conducted, had created great sensations in the world in those days. The destruction of the Temple had a great impact on the disciples of Osiris, and the initiations had become impossible. Nevertheless, the Osiris priests continued their existence in the Alexandria School which they founded. In other Esoteric schools in the region such as Harran, Baghdad and Basra, the teachings and the acceptance of the doctrine of the esoteric-battle as the official religion in the Ismailles, the Fatimis and other states, provided the ideas preserved by the Osiris priests.

The school of Alexandria was founded by Plolemel Soter (Ptolemyus), Pharaoh of Egypt of Greek origin. In this school, all branches of science, astronomy, cosmogony, mathematics, natural history, geography and medicine were taught, and famous scholars from all over the world, including Euclides and Archimed were teaching there. 700.000 works were collected within the school of Potolemi. 400.000 of them were kept in a section called the museum, and 300.000 of them were hidden in Serapis Temple. During the conquest of Alexandria in 47 BC by Julius Caesar, the museum and its 400,000 artifacts were burned as a result of an accident.[35]

After Christianity reached these lands, in 408 AD, the Alexandrian Patriarch Teophilus ordered the closure of the temples of Pagan gods, who were still present. All the temples were destroyed and all believers of Polytheistic Egyptian religions were murdered.[36] The use of the ancient hieroglyphic writing was forbidden. In 416 AD, Bishop Cyril ordered the burning of the Serapis Temple and its contents and a large portion of the remaining 300.000 books were burned as a result of the fire. Nevertheless, a secret group maintained the old teachings and continued to read and write in the ancient form. A few thousand books that had been saved from the fire were burned during the Muslim invasion in 642 by the order of Khalif Umar.

After this invasion and the fire, the last group to retain the old teachings dispersed, and the caste text was buried in the dusty pages of history as much as it was re-revealed and deciphered in the 19th century. Some anagogic circles claim that a few hundred works recovered from this fire are still hidden in a secret place. Whatever happened to the Alexandria Library also happened to the Mayan libraries and their books. During the Spanish invasion of South America in 1565 AD, Bishop Diggo De Landa ordered that all Mayan writings be destroyed.[37]

After the destruction of the Serapis Temple, a group of Egyptian alchemists went to Jerusalem. There, joining the Jewish Essene sect, the science of alchemy was introduced to the Cabalistic too.

Upon the occupation of Jerusalem by Saladin Ayyubi in 1188 AD, the cults of the alchemist members living in the city moved to Europe along with the Christian Knight sects and were then referred to as 'The Knights of the Orient.'[38] It is believed that, later, as other Christian Knight sects, they had joined Masonry.

References

1   Tülek Füsun, - Orpheus' Sorcery (Efsuncu Orpheus), Arkeoloji ve Sanat Pub., Istanbul 1998, p. 8

2   Schure Edouard, - *Great Initiatives (Büyük İnisiyeler)*, RM Pub, Istanbul 1989, p. 301

3   Schure E., r.w., p. 349

4   Eyüboğlu İsmet Zeki, - *Sufism, Cults, History of Sects (Tasavvuf, Tarikatlar, Mezhepler Tarihi)*, Der Pub., Istanbul 1990, p. 45

5   Signier, Jean Francois/Thomazo, Renaud - *Secret Organizations (Gizli Örgütler)*, Larousse Oğlak Güzel Kitaplar, Istanbul 2006, p. 17

6   Tülek F., r.w., p. 9

7   *Fisherman of Halicarnassus (Halikarnas Balıkçısı)*, - *Gods of Anatolia (Anadolu Tanrıları)*, Yeditepe Pub., Istanbul 1975, p. 21

8   Boucher Jules, Noudon Paul, Masonry, - *This Unknown Masonry (Masonluk, Bu Meçhul)*, Okat Pub., Istanbul 1966, p. 9

9   Özbudun P., - *Transformation Dynamics of a Religious Tradition from Hermes to Idris (Hermes'ten İdris'e Bir Dinsel Geleneğin Dönüşüm Dinamikleri)*, Ütopya Pub., Ankara 2004, p. 91

10   Freke, Timothy&Gandy, Peter - *The Secrets of Jesus (İsa'nın Gizemleri)* Ayna Pub., Istanbul 2005, p. 247

11   Freke, Timothy& Gandy, Peter r.w., p. 251

12   Özbudun P., r.w., p. 123

13   Özbudun P., r.w., p. 49

14   Özbudun P., r.w., p. 53

15   Özbudun P., r.w., p. 173

16   Signier, Jean Francois / Thomazo, Renaud r.w., p. 21

17   Freke, Timothy& Gandy, Peter - r.w., p. 29

18   Freke, Timothy& Gandy, Peter - r.w., p. 345

19   Freke, Timothy& Gandy, Peter - r.w., p. 33

20   Freke, Timothy& Gandy, Peter - r.w., p. 92

21   Freke, Timothy& Gandy, Peter - r.w., p. 401

22   Özbudun P., r.w., p. 174

23   Eyüboğlu İ.Z., r.w., p. 53

24   Schure E., r.w., p. 376

25   Freke, Timothy & Gandy, Peter- r.w., p. 354

26   Schure E., r.w., p. 411

27   Schure E., r.w., p. 415

28   Freke, Timothy& Gandy, Peter r.w., p. 142

29   Freke, Timothy& Gandy, Peter r.w., p. 106

30   Signier, Jean Francois / Thomazo, Renaud r.w., p. 84

31   Freke, Timothy & Gandy, Peter - r.w., p. 340

32   Naudon Paul, - *Freemasonry in History and Today (Tarihte ve Günümüzde Masonluk)*, Varlık Pub., Istanbul 1968, p. 24

33   Schure E., r.w., p. 525.

34   Eyüboğlu İ.Z., r.w., p. 75

35   Akin Asım, - *Freemasonry Throughout History (Tarih Boyunca Masonluk)*, Hacettepe Pub., Ankara 1998, p. 72

36   August Le Plonge, - *Origin of Egyptians (Mısırlıların Kökeni)*, Ege Meta Pub., Istanbul, p. 132

37   August L.P., r.w., p. 55

38   Ülke Faruk/Yazıcıoğlu A. Semih, - *Freemasonry in the world and Turkey (Dünyada ve Türkiye'de Masonluk)*, Başak Pub., Istanbul 1965

CHAPTER VII

A DISTINCT INITIATE, JESUS

The day Jesus was born, a large part of the known world was under Roman rule. Religiously, Romans who adopted a polytheistic belief, providing that tolerance was shown to their Gods, were not in interference with the beliefs of the people of the territories they occupied. This system was extremely useful to accommodate many different beliefs within the imperial structure. Tribes left free in their beliefs, were not coursing any significant issues for the rule. Except for one: The Jews.

The Jews were very strict. According to them, there was just a single God and to mention any other god was the greatest sin. This attitude was seen as a humiliation of their gods by the Romans and gave birth to great reactions. Such that, the Roman rulers accused the Jews of impiety, and thus Emperor Septim Severus banned impiety, namely Judaism. The Roman legions were sent off to Jewish people. Pressure was dense. Like Judaism, in later years, the Christian faith standing up for a singular god, itself could also not avoid the same charges. It was until the period when the Byzantine Emperor Constantine accepted Christianity as state religion just to avoid any chaos and separation.

Jesus was born to such an environment. The Jewish people, frustrated with the Roman oppression, looking for a miracle of salvation and looking forward to the Messiah supposedly said to arrive as stated in their Torah. Jesus was a descendent of King David by both his mother's and father's side. Such a noble blood line was enabling him claims over royalty by birth. Already the expectations of the people were such that a Messiah from Davidian blood would come to salvage them and it seemed as if Jesus was the one to meet this expectation. Jesus received the esoteric aspects of Moses' teachings from the Esenne, who had been harboring it for centuries. Already the Esenne were keeping this noble family under constant eye, and providing distinct education to boys born to this family. To stay away from religious degeneracy and political contention, the Esenne had retreated to Kumran in Yehuda desert. That Jesus was an Essene was of fact by the presumed date of his birth, December 25th. This date was the day for a sacred sacrament in the name of Elohim.[1] The manuscripts found on copper plates discovered in Kumran in 1947, constituted most of the source of what is known today about this mysterious cult. Esenne was the plural for Isiye. It meant reticent in Hebrew. While members of the sect defined themselves just as the Luvis did, as 'Children of Light'. all outsiders including Jews, were portrayed as 'Children of Dark'. Because of their opposition for war, they did not possess any war means or items to use in a war. To them, all people were manifestations of God and thus they were against slavery for they believed it was a rebellion to God. Their philosophy was based on morality, virtue and divinity. The sacrifice of animals being other manifestations of God was the biggest sin. Their reason of existence was to help people. They rushed to all in need. They definitely did not possess property, and shared their wealth with the community. Their houses welcomed all sects. They did not take along any belongings while traveling. There were officials of the organization in every Jewish town, and their duty was to fulfill the needs of their visiting brothers. To swear in the name of God, to them, was an insult to God.[2]

The Essenes sect, dominated by a rigid hierarchy, had an outer ring made of practises obliged to work for the community. True initiates, as well as their meditation, were Theoreticians who lived by practicing the art of medicine. The Theoreticians vowed to keep in secret all the truth they learned from the mysteries. At the head of the community, there was the magnificent "Lord Justice" the holder of the true mysteries. Twelve selected people as executive committee surrounded him.[3] Ones wishing to join the sect, whether born into the community or an outsider, were put on hold for a year to see how well an adaption they would display. The outsider was presented with a white cotton dress and was invited to live among them as a disciple. The outsider proving adequacy attained the candidate status, and wait for another two years. Providing the outsider received good ratings by the end of these two years, he then was accepted to the cult with an esoterical ceremony. After taking an oath to serve God, to fight for justice, do no evil to anyone, to not hide anything from cult members and not to share any secrets of the cult to any outsider even under death threats, he then was joined in as an 'apprentice'. The initiation was of three degrees, and to rise to the third degree named as 'Son of Light', the virtue of merit, was of extreme importance. There was belief in the immortality of the soul, resurrection of the body to evolve, and that only the sect members, who became Wise could reach God. The sect was governed by a board. The administrative board was headed by three people consisting of twelve people in total. Inspectors with a given name Mevakrim, within the regular organization, were represented in all Jewish settlements. The philosophy and the organizational structure of the cult were as the continuation of that Egyptian Esoteric teachings.[4]

The influence of Egypt was guarded as a secret. The secrets that Essene vowed not to expose to the outside were the 'Secrets of Hanock (Hermes)' that were kept for centuries. The Hanock cult, although it disappeared in Palestine during the 1st century A.D., this secret tradition through outstanding people and priests, continued its presence in Europe and spread among the Jews all over the world. From the Enoch Judaism tradition, the Kabbalah faith surfaced almost at the same dates.[5]

The name of the founder of the Christian religion, Jesus itself, was somewhat of a proof of his being a member of the Esenni. The name Jesus seemed as if it has been named after the Isiye cult name. Jesus is pronaunced as "Isa" in Sami languages. Before Jesus' appearance as Messiah in his thirties, he had been an active traveler as a preacher. Not much about his life was known before his chaplaincy. A large part of the men of the holy family, were trained in 'carpentry and stone carving' as a continuation of Masonic tradition ongoing since King Solomon period. Already hundreds of priests were trained as stone carvers as well in the process of rebuilding the Temple initiated by King Herod in 19 B.C. Among them was Yusouf, father of Jesus. The nickname of Yusouf was 'Tekton', meaning 'builder'. In other words, Yusouf was trained as carver of both stone and wood. And he too had taught his son the same professions.[6]

John the Baptist, who was to announce the coming of Jesus, was also an Esenne. Baptism by water was an application of this sect. Thanks to his intelligence, Jesus had risen to the highest degree of the sect at a very young age, and not being content with it, he had been educated in India and Tibet where powerful esoteric studies were practiced at the time. Jesus, after declaring his religion had been excluded by the Esenne, for he had announced the secrets of the sect to non-members. Today, according to Nasarians who claim to be the descendents of the Esenne, Jesus himself was a Nasarian, however, he was a deviant who had betrayed the secrets entrusted to him.[7]

Well, had the true doctrine of Jesus been accurately transferred by official Christian sources? Or whatever happened to Judaism also applied to Christianity as well? How well was the esoteric dimension of his doctrine transposed?

In 1958, in a monastery near Jerusalem, a document was found to be lost sections of one the four official Bibles known as the Marcus Bible. In this document, it was stated by Clement of Alexandria, one of 2nd century philosophers, that some sections of the Bible had not been published. In a letter understood to have been written to another initiated priest by Clement that some details had been deliberately removed under the veil of secrecy. The Bible said to have been stored in the Alexandria Library, beyond any Christian discourse, was to contain Gnostic knowledge.[8] The following statements took place within the letter:

"Marcus, during the period when Petrus was living in Rome, wrote what Christ (Jesus) had done. Nonetheless, he didn't publish the whole thing, nor did he present any clues. Marcus joined Alexandria by bringing along his own notes. He had copied Peter's notes to his previous book. He transferred information worthy of progress towards knowledge to his book. Therefore, he brought together a more spiritual Bible to be used by those on the way to become 'Sage' (Kamil One). Nevertheless, he did not yet disclose things not be told. Nor did he write hyero-mortal teachings of God. These knowledges were good for ingenuity. Marcos, with the usage of this knowledge, had compiled a perfect bible with a predominant aspect of anagogic side. He added new ones to already written stories. He made such statements that, by doing so he knew that the interpretations would direct the listeners towards the very inner cell of the hidden truth. However, Marcos did not mention the ones needy of being disclosed. He also did not mention the magical teachings of the Lord. Like the others, he wrote down whatever was already written down. As a person to whom religious secrets were unveiled, and as a teacher, he left the words known to him to the messengers in the far inner circle of the temple, where the truth was veiled in seven secrets. He left the compilation inside the church in Alexandria. Only the ones who wanted to become acquainted with the big secrets were allowed in. They are being very carefully maintained, and are only read to people initiated to big secrets. The sacred secrets are only delivered to priests of higher order and to their heirs expected to rise to higher orders. The advice of God's wisdom of mind is the teaching of where the Light of the Truth is to be kept from the mentally blind. We are the children of the Light. We have been initiated by the sun of the Spirit of the God Almighty. There is freedom where there is Spirit of the God. Because all is the purest of the pure."[9]

In another letter written by Clement, in the said secret Bible, it is written that Jesus had by lifting a tomb stone, held a youth's hand and lifted him from the grave, and that he had taught him the mysterious Kingdom of God and what he had to do. From these statements, it can be understood that the person in the grave was alive and a ritualistic practice was administered, which was also indicative of a practice of a common esoterical death and rebirth ritual of the period in the Middle East. It has not been possible to possess the said Gnostic Bible, for the Alexandria library had been burned down by bigoted Christians. However, in 1945, in Upper Egypt in Hamada, examples of Gnostic Bibles were uncovered. On the covers of most of the Nag Hamada books, there were the 'ankh' hieroglyphs known as Divine Life. Among the findings, in addition to the biblical text attributed to Gnostic Bibles and Hermes, there were also works of Pythagorean Sextus and sections of Plato's Republic.[10] The Nag Hamada manuscripts, being a collection of the Gospels written by 10 Gnostic characters, include such manuscripts as the Thomas Gospel, the Gospel of Rightness and Gospel of the Egyptians. These works were translated into English in 1977. Scientists today are in agreement that these Gospels dating back to the 4th century A.D., were in fact manuscript copies of the originals and that they were not written after 150 A.D... Indeed, the Thomas Gospel is believed to have been written by Apostle Thomas himself or drafted by a friend who knew him. These documents, for having survived the Roman censorship and having no rectification on them, reveal the true teachings of Jesus.[11]

Gnostic Christians regarded these Gospels not as historical records, but as allegoric literature encrypting eternal truths. They were expected to interpret the myths and the teachings in their own style.[12] The most interesting aspects of the Hamada findings were that along with Gnostic Bibles, numerous Hermetic documents were also found in the same place. Upon examination of these documents, it has been possible to more easily understand the (Hermetic Corpus) attributed to Corpus Hermeticum written in the 2nd century A.D., said to be sourced on Egyptian documents older than five thousand years. The identification process of Toth and Hermes, gained pace thanks to the Potolemius dynasty established in Egypt during and after the conquests of Alexander the Great. Both in the Egyptian and Greek civilizations, because of their functions, the vocational guilds were the ones with the most extensive contact with the ruling class, and this situation had also not changed in the Ptolemius era. Thus, the Hermetic Corpus attributed to Hermes, had emerged as a result of merchants and artisan guilds who had preserved the temple traditions as well as worldly relations.[13]

The Hermetic Corpus is a continuation of religious views referencing a supreme being and the divine system. The Serapis cult, a mixture of Osiris, Apis, Zeus, Helios, Mithras and Aesculapius created by the Potole-Apis, is a result of a seeking compromise between the ruling Greco-Macedonian elements and Egyptian religious institutions. In a letter send to Philadelphius, the second Pharaoh of the Potolemies by an Egyptian historian priest Menetho, which read 'I shall inform you of the future from the holy books written by Hermes-Toth in sacred hieroglyphics before the great flood and later translated to Greek after the great flood. I shall submit you, your anchestor Hermes Trimegistus's writings on to the Egyptian temples and I shall present you the holy books I have learned.' This expression is believed to indicate the first manuscripts of the guild, later to be known as the Hermetica Corpus.[14]

This Hermetic literature believed to have been written in Egypt between the 1st century BC and the 3rd century A.D., was a form of a source for occult sciences such as encyclopedia of ancient knowledge, alchemy and astrology. It was based on the ancient book of Cyranides, said to have been written by Hermes. There is a remarkable resemblance between this word read as 'Kuranides' and the holy book of Islam, the Kor'an. It is said that the 'Kuranides' is an expression of revelations to the public and written in a form of dialogues by a Sage enlightened by divine revelations from the Divine Mind.[15]

The Hermetic Corpus, consisting of a total of 17 Greek philosophical treatises, is referred to as 'Corpus Hermeticum'. In this Corpus, which contains theological discourses mostly on divine, humanistic and material origin, nature and moral characteristics, there are expressions such as 'it is God himself who created Man he loved as his own child, with all the crafts. Art and knowledge are the manifestations of Man's Divine light. However, just as energies of divine light affect the Cosmos and Man, likewise Man affect nature through art and knowledge. God being one and only, is blessed with fertility of both the sexes, and whenever he wishes to reproduce, he does so'.

Christian philosopher Clemens of Alexandria, in 2nd century A.D. stated that there were 42 holy Hermes books in the hands of the priests continuing on the ancient Egyptian religious rites, on which their rituals were based. The first of these were the hymns to the gods, and the second was the book describing how the life of a pharaoh should be. Apart from these, there were 4 books about the sun, moon and the stars, 10 volumes on materials used in temple construction, 10 volumes on education, 10 volumes on clerical training and another 6 volumes on skin diseases and drugs. Among these books, the Asclepius book was an astrological book in a form that dealt with the correlation between man and the universe, meaning the micro and macro-cosmos.[16]

Corpus Hermeticum, although written down in Greek, was totally a result of 'Egyptian' work. 'Egyptianism' is proudly mentioned in several sections of Corpus Hermeticum. The sections in the Asclepius Prophesy book shall reveal this fact:[17]

"While trying to translate our language to their language, the Greeks shall create serious distortions and uncertainty. This discourse expressed in our mother tongue retains the clear meanings of the words. Per se the nature of the speech and the sound of the Egyptian, contain the very energy of the objects they talk about. Therefore, my King, for as long as you can force, do not allow the interpretation of this speech so that, such a great mystery won't get in the hands of the Greeks. So that extravagant, loose and dandy Greek phrases won't attenuate something as pompous and concise as tradition energetic Egyptian phrases. For the Greeks speak hallow, o my king, they are only energetic of what they show, and the Greek philosophy is an empty hype of silly talks.

There shall come a time when it will be revealed that the Egyptians worship God with devoted mind and reverence in vain to the Mighty for nothing. All their holy worships will disperse inconclusive; for God will be drawn to the sky from Earth and Egypt shall be abandoned. Country of respect shall fall apart from eminence. When foreigners occupy the country and its territories, they shall not only neglect respect, but a prohibition law of respect, loyalty and divine worship shall be imposed upon. Then this holy country of temples and altars shall be filled with cemetery and corpses. O Egypt, there shall only be stories left from the respectable jobs of Egypt and that shall unbelievable for their children and that Scythians, Indians or other barbaric neighbors shall live in Egypt. Because the Divine Being will have returned to the skies, God and the people shall abandon Egypt? I call on you, O Mighty river and tell you the future; your shores shall be filled with whirls of blood and you shall burst on them; blood shall not only pollute your divine waters, but also it shall shatter them; and the number of the dead shall be much more than of the living. The survivors shall only be recognized as Egyptians for their language; as for their actions they shall be foreigners. O Egypt! There shall only be incredulous stories left for next generations and there shall be nothing more told about you than just words carved into stones...

Why do you cry, Asclepius? Egypt herself shall yield into much more evil and shall sink into conditions much worse. Once upon a time, Egypt being the sole country where Gods settled out of respect for the Divine God, and being the land where blessedness and faith were taught, shall become an example of total infidelity. People shall prefer shadows to light, death to life. No one shall look up to the sky. The respectful shall be crazy, the disrespectful smart, the insane brave, and the imposters shall be respectful. Nevertheless, I, said Hermes, shall furnish the human nature with wisdom, moderation, persuasion and the truth. I shall preserve the mortal life of man forever...'

Hermes, has said the following to his student Asclepius about the First Reason;

"As none of our thoughts can explain the concept of God, nor can any language portray him. Our senses cannot comprehend the intangible, invisible and the formless. The eternal and everlasting cannot be measured with this limited time concept. That is to say, God is not within the boundaries of words and languages. God may favor some of his distinct beings to rise above natural things so that they may be able to perceive a bit, but these chosen people cannot find words to express or explain the non-material form that shiver themselves. These chosen people may only tell other people the secondary cause of creation as an image of their living life that passes in front of their eyes. The first cause is always veiled and we can only begin to understand it once we nourish death and leave it behind."[18]

Neo-platonism, developed in Alexandria of Egypt, in the 3rd century A.D., was the result of the ancient Osiris religion merging with the Greek philosophy. Neoplatonism, nourishing on the esoteric structure that strengthened on Greek soil through the Greeks settling in Egypt, had emerged as the most powerful intellectual focal point of resistance against the Christianity and Islam's orthodox teachings. Coptic language becoming the language of neoplatonism, was an ancient Egyptian dialect expressed in Greek letters. It had emerged during the 3rd century A.D. and Gnostic Christianity was fed from this source.

That the works of Hermes and Gnostic Gospels have been found in coexistence, is an indication of how the first Christians were affected by the Hermetic doctrine. Indeed, it is not possible to find Hermetic expressions found in Gnostic Bibles within the official Bibles.[19]

The knowledge of Jesus addressing Thomas as his 'brother' has reached us. In none of the Bibles, there is no mentioning by Jesus of Thomas as his brother. From this statement, it can be inferred that Thomas was an Essene brother of Jesus and that a group of Essene supporting Jesus may have liaised along with him. Indeed, John the Baptist was also an Essene and had propagandized Jesus. It is highly likely that all the apostles were on the same side. From this expression, which the said Bible was written by Thomas where he is called as 'my brother' by Jesus himself, and that, it is a first-person narrative; seem to appear as to be the truth. Some of the statements of the Thomas Gospel read:

"The Kingdom is both within and outside of us. Once you know your own self, you shall then know that you are the Sons of the Holly Father... The end shall be wherever the beginning is. One who is happy shall be at the beginning; he shall know the end and shall not know death. One who is happy, was present before existence... Once you make two a one, you inner as you outer and your outer as your inner, as you do the one up as the one down, as you make one face as for another one, then you shall go to the Kingdom. Within a being of Light, the whole world is lightened. Love your brother as your soul... If the body is of the soul, this is the truth. But, how such great richness is put within such poverty? The elite, you are happy because you are to find the "Melekut" (Celestial Kingdom). You came from Him, so shall you return to Him...We are of the Light, where the Light is from. The Light has stood up and manifested in his own image. We are the Sons. We are his chosen ones...

His disciples said to him: Is circumcision useful, is not it? If it were useful said he, their fathers would have them born as circumcised from their mother. But the true circumcision of the soul has been found to be very useful... I am from the equal. I was given of what came of my father, said Jesus. I am telling my secrets to ones, worthy of my secrets... The Light over all is me. The whole is me. The whole is out of me. And the whole has reached me. Split the tree, you shall see me. Lift the rock, there you shall find me. Jesus said: Faces are manifesting on men and the Light within is hidden. In the Light of the Father, he shall reveal his veil and his face shall be hidden with his own Light. The living from the live shall see no death or fear. The world is unworthy to one who has found himself... Bodies tied to souls are miserable..."[20]

These statements are the proof of Jesus spreading an esoteric belief of a single God. The Essene, advocating the same belief, had formed an initiation organization of three degrees.[21] According to the rules of this organization, ones born among the Essene or wishing to join the Essene were to be kept under probation for quite some time and if found worthy, would be accepted into the organization with a special ceremony. Ones born into the community but were unworthy, were not allowed in and be only allowed to be the errand boys of the organization. The one accepted to the organization, would spend two of his years as apprentice. The same period was also valid in the second degree. For the apprentice to move up to the second degree, so called 'The Holy Selected of Israel', depended on the ability to be shown by the end of the period. It was quite possible for the period to be extended for this second degree. The same procedure was valid for 'The Son of Light' of the third degree.

The Essene used to make an oath of secrecy of not disclosing the secrets of the sect. The Essene, believing in the immortality of the soul, evolution of men, brotherhood of all men and favoring as to be the most important principle, however, believed of daily swearing to be the greatest sin. Hygiene was essential during all the rituals. Bringing forward the love of man, the hate for lie and the share of wealth were the common features for the Essene. The new member would vow to death not to disclose the secrets to be given to him.[22] There lay the reason behind the Essene rejecting Jesus for not adhering to his oath. The Essene teachings were nothing more than the esoteric doctrines of the Kabbalah of Moses.

Jesus, rising to the higher degrees among the Essene, was not satisfied by means of his character, and wished to learn more. To carry forward his education, he advanced to Alexandria with his cousin John who was older and his teacher among the Essene. Jesus joined the Jewish community in Alexandria with his cousin, later to be known as John the Baptist, who would announce the coming of Jesus as 'Christ' to the Jews. At the time, a large community of Jews was living in Alexandria. The Jews were very influential in the city's trade and culture life. When Alexander the Great conquered Egypt in the 4th century B.C., the Jews had helped him by espionage and as mercenaries and in exchange they had been granted the right to establish and settle in their own territory. It is estimated that half the population in Alexandria is formed of Jews since its establishment. In this city, all kinds of religious tolerance were encouraged, and thus different traditions united and blended in. Thus, the Hellenized Jews of Alexandria, by identifying Jehovah with the Supreme Unity of Plato, had portrayed him as a Universal God.[23]

Egypt had no longer had the old school of Osiris. But esoterical School of Alexandria was very active. Phiolon, heading the School of Alexandria, was one of the leading Jews of Alexandria Community and had close relations also with the Esenne. Philon, who was born in 25 B.C. and died in 50 A.D., was cultivating students with a combined teaching system of both the Kabbalah and Pythagoras (Platon) discipline. Discovering the talent in Jesus, he never hesitated to include him among his students. Philo said, 'God reflects himself as Logos to the world, as Comforter of Jerusalem (Godly word) he is the will of the Godly Man (Son). God has through his son Logos, created the Cosmos out of Chaos. Out of all the creatures on Earth, man is the most competent. Because man has gathered in the Godly will, in other words, in Logos himself. What we perceive is hidden inside our soul of Logos belonging to the inner. The expressionism of the soul is through words. However, intuition is not of words and remains within. God's face is only to be seen by intuition within, in the form light. For this, man should purify himself and glorify his soul with knowledge and light.'[24]

Jewish philosopher Philo, talks of Moses as 'God as his father and Sophia as his mother'. Sophia is the mother of Logos. Logos is the one and only beloved child of God. According to Philo, all the philosophers living on earth, are world citizens and represent an international brotherhood. They secretly keep the spark of wisdom alive. As a part of Logos, all philosophers are on the way to experiment the mystical union with God. Saying that Moses is a Hierophan of a great rite and teacher of Godly things, Philo himself reported to have been initiated just as Moses. Philo, had set up the rule of no disciples of Moses be initiated to Pagan mysteries because they already had mysteries within their religion to pay attention to. He too, just as Moses, had been an initiator, meaning 'teacher of Jewish mysteries'. In other words, Philo was of the pioneer of Kabbalah. He had formed a secret sect in Alexandria. He had made the members of the sect swear never to disclose the secrets to the non-initiated to mysteries. The name of this sect was Therapeutae.[25]

Therapeutae White Brotherhood, was a Gnostic community formed by Egyptians of Jewish origin. Members of Therapeutae dressed in white and used property commonly. It is also known that Jesus was a member and he had risen to the 'masters' degree.[26] It is seen that the group had relations with the Esenne; however, tolerance and love of humanity seemed to be more prominent compared to that of the Essene. Unlike the Essene, all group members were equal, including women. The Therapeutae schools based on Philo's teaching were very effective in Egypt, Palestine and Syria in the early years of Christianity. Among Gnostic philosophers like Valentin and Basilides, his supporters had deeply influenced the Christian communities. The Clement's Christian Gnostic School had emerged from the Therapeutae school.[27]

Jesus, having remained three years in Alexandria, had obtained all the knowledge from his teacher. But both Jesus and Philo were of the fact that this would not be enough for him. Philo with intensive studies on the history of Egypt knew for fact that the documents in Alexandria Library pointed the East, India and Tibet as the source of Light. He instructed his student to reach the source of Light.

Upon this, in order to improve his knowledge, Jesus headed towards yet another source of esoteric teaching, the East. The Saabs and the Saab influenced Nasarians stated that Jesus, in his youth, had been taken to the 'White Mountains' by John, and there he had been taught by 'Anouilh Utra' till he was 22.[28] Traveling to Tibet trespassing India, Jesus remained there for almost ten years and among esoteric teachings, received uppermost knowledge about Eastern sciences.[29] Jesus revealed this knowledge of his on events considered as miracle in the Christian world.

James Churchward provides information in relation to the years of Jesus's Tibetan years. Rishi, who was the priest enlightening Jesus on Naacals, stated that Jesus was up to the highest level among Tibetan monks. According to Churchward, Jesus learned the Naacal language in Tibet and observed the first and only one God religion of Mu at its very source. The English researcher claims that the last words of Jesus proved his knowledge of the Naacal language. Jesus's last words were, 'Eli, eli lama sabachtani' (God, oh God why have you abandoned me). Churchward claims of his words being misunderstood, and that, in truth Jesus had said 'Hele, hele lamat zabac ta ni' (I am being consumed and consumed, darkness covers my face), which he uttered in Naacal language nobody could possibly understand.[30]

And the cross he had chosen for his teachings was also of Mu origin. Jesus had used this sacred symbol of the Naacal, describing the four powers of divine. Rishi had told Churchward that, during his visit to the Himalayan monasteries, Jesus had learned the revealed sacred scriptures, meaning the Naacal Tablets, the language, scripts of the homeland, and the use of the Cosmic Powers.

Russian researcher Nikolaus Notowitsch, in his book 'The Missing Years of Jesus', during his visit to the Mulbek Monastery in Tibet, the head Lama priest of the monastery had said that 'Buddha being a spiritual being, has in fact reincarnated into flesh and bone of Jesus, who has spread our religion all over the world. Jesus is a great messiah. He is the most well known figure of all rebirths of Buddha. Jesus is, Buddha's 22nd reincarnation. He is greater than all Dalai-Lamas; because he is directly from our Lord's spiritual being. His name is written in our holy books too'. Yet another Lama stated that Jesus had been recognized by higher Lamas and that his teachings were spread over India along Palestine, too. According to the Lama's claim, after reaching a certain age, he had come to India, and had learned all the laws of the great Buddha. True knowledge about Buddha was secret and was not known to the public. Only the high ranked priests who has the true knowledge, could learn the life of Jesus in India and Tibet from the ancient manuscripts.[31]

The information given to Notowitsch by the Tibetan monks, date back to the Egyptian adventures of the Jews and of their migration to the holy land. The birth and childhood of Jesus was being told, and that he had left home and gone to Sind from Jerusalem along with merchants, to be close to God. His ambition was to purify his soul, to reach to the Supreme Being and to perfection. Throughout his life, he had wanted to show people how to save their soul from its sheath. In Aryan country, the white priests of Brahma had been his tutors; he had learned to read and understand Vedas, the sacred ancient scriptures of the Nagas and to heal people with his holy powers. During the last years of his six- year learning, he had claimed Vedas being of non-divine origin and had been in contradiction with the Brahma priest. According to him, the eternal power, the creator of the universe and provider of life was the indivisible, universal soul. Following examination of the sacred manuscripts of Sutra, Jesus, a no longer believer of Buddha, had left Nepal and the Himalayas. He also opposed Hinduism which he studied in India. On the way back, he studied the Zoroastrian religion and found missing aspects of this religion too. Jesus, a disciple on his way to the Himalaya, had become a teacher on his return. When he returned to his country, he was 29 years of age. In other words, he had mastered his teachings in 16 years.[32]

Notowitsch, came across a Bible in Tibet's Ladak city in 1887 which included the years Jesus spent in India and Tibet. This Bible which he later named as the Tibetan Gospel, was published in France and Russia. According to this work, Jesus had, with a trade caravan moved to India when he was 14 years old.[33] This was related in the Bible as, "Jesus wishing to be perfect (complete) in divine theology and learn about the teachings of Buddha, he went to India".[34] The white priest of Brahma had taught him how to read and interpret the Vedas. However, by rejecting the idea that Vishnu, Shiva and the other gods were the reflection of the supreme god Brahma, he left India.[35] From there on, he traveled to Tibet and learned the Pali language. Here, he examined the sacred scriptures.[36] Leaving Tibet to return to Palestine, on his way he stopped in Iran and addressed the fire-worshipping people of Persia as 'Wishing to approach the God of Truth, you are creating false gods to yourself'.[37]

Jesus returned to Palestine, and joined the Essene he had previously left. However, after a year, he once again left the Essene and started preaching to spread his teachings to the masses. He had envisaged his teachings reach wider audiences and that the salvation of the Jews was to be this way.

Evaluating the messianic expectations of the people, he announced himself as 'Son of God'. In accordance with the esoteric doctrine, Jesus was a Sage (Kamil One) and had united with God. Indeed, his usage of the 'Son of God' symbol was the expression of this fact.

To understand the life and teachings of Jesus, it is necessary to understand the conditions of his time. In 63 B.C. Palestine had been invaded by Roman armies. Rome, to rule the country in the form of a puppet state, appointed non-Jewish puppet kings. In the year 6 A.D., the country was divided into two: Judaea and Galileo. While Galileo was being ruled by puppet kings, Judea was directly connected to the Roman governor of Cayserium (today City of Kayseri in Turkiye). While Jewish Sadducees, the huge landowners, were collaborating with the Romans, a group called Pharisees was in passive resistance against the rule. However, the Zealots, being in constant close contact with the Essene and gathering revolutionaries from different sects, were continuing their uninterrupted rebellion against Rome. However, much the first uprising of the Zealots led by Judah against Galileo was a short-lived one and thousands of them were crucified. The preparation and struggle for independence of Zealots continued underground. In the year 66 A.D., armed conflicts became inevitable. The ongoing uprising succeeded and the Essene, allied followers of Jesus seized power of Jerusalem for four years. However, in 70 A.D., this initiative was brutally suppressed by the Roman legions. Yet, thousands of Jews were killed once again. The Romans invading the city burned down the Temple of Solomon to its bottoms and the whole city. And the rebellion ended with the fall of the last resistance point of Masada Castle. The Jews were then exiled from Palestine in large numbers. A third uprising in 132 A.D. was also suppressed in the same ruthlessness and the Roman Emperor Hadrian, ordered that all the Jews be expelled from Palestine.[38]

At the time when Jesus was born, the Jewish people were waiting for a messiah to liberate themselves from the hands of oppressors. This awaited messiah, of no holiness, was one traditionally oiled in Mesh oil, and crowned as King of Israel. David, being oiled in Mesh, had taken the title of Messiah, and thus all subsequent kings had retained the same title via the same method. In the eyes of the people, the messiah was the awaited king who was to liberate them not divinely but physically. In the Gospel of Luke, it is said that Jesus was the descendent of David. In the Matthew Gospel, it is also stated that, Jesus had been visited on his birth by kings, and that his family's wealth had always been good. And yet again, in the Matthew Gospel, Jesus was portrayed as a powerful king.

Jesus presented his teaching to the masses in the form of symbols, parables made of sentences, for he knew the people could not have embraced his teachings otherwise. The life and teachings of Jesus reached us in four official Gospels. The biblical history of the writings corresponds to the period of major riots in Judea. The first Gospel, believed to have been written between 66-74 A.D., is the Marcos Gospel. Known to be of Jerusalem, Marcos was a friend of Apostle Paul, however, not directly acquainted to Jesus. St. Paul's aim was to spread Christianity among the Roman world. It has carefully been avoided in this Gospel written in Rome, which addressed the Greek-Roman masses, to show Jesus as opposed to Rome. In regard to this, the Romans were cleared of being accused of the death of Jesus and the responsibility was put on the shoulders of the Jews. Otherwise, it was thought that a contradictory attitude would cause total destruction of Christianity.

The Luke Gospel was also written with similar views in mind in Cayserium (Kayseri) in 80 A.D. This particular policy had been maintained in the Matthew Gospel and in this Gospel of mostly quoted from the Gospel of Mark, the Romans had been appeased and accusations been twirled into another direction. We are under the impression that all three Gospels were of the same source and this source was St. Paul.[39]

The John Gospel being the fourth of all was compiled around 100 A.D. near the Anatolian Greek city of Ephesus. Ephesus was the city where Mary, mother of Jesus, had settled after the crucifixion of Jesus, and where she later died. Today, thousands of pilgrims are visiting the site believed to be the tomb of Virgin Mary. The John Gospel with more mystical properties than the others, was generally of an esoteric character and contained expressions closer to the Apocryphal Gnostic Gospels. The crucifixion in the first three Gospels was described by second parties, whereas in the John Gospel it was described in detail from the first hand. Again in the John Gospel, there are the stories of the Marriage in Kana, Joseph of Arimath and the Rising of Lazarus, that are not found in other Gospels. Scientists today are in agreement with the John Gospel, historically being the most accurate. The esoteric content of Jesus's teachings where love and brotherhood was emphasized more was quite evident in the John Gospel. Sentences such as 'Unless one is reborn, the Devine Layer is not visible' or 'All is born of water and soul' are just two of the sentences with esoteric contents in the John Gospel. (John 3:2-5)

This particular Gospel revealed the esoteric aspects and the inner face of the doctrine. For this reason, the John Gospel, had been the only Gospel accepted by the Knight Orders advocating esoteric teachings. The Gospel adopted by the Protestants and the one Christian Masons swore upon, had always been the John Gospel.[40]

There were no clear indications in the Gospels about the marital status of Jesus. The marriage issue had never been addressed in the first three Gospels, and in the fourth Gospel, it was mentioned that an anonymous marriage took place in Kana. However so, as an Essene, though Jesus may not have been married according to Essene traditions, it should not be forgotten that, he had emerged with Messianic claims. In Jewish tradition, a marriage for a man, especially for a Rabbi is mandatory and the Rabbi title has been used often for Jesus. The sermons and discussions addressed by Jesus are the proof of his very high level of knowledge. It is specifically stated in the Talmud that, a non-married would clearly not be accepted as a teacher, let alone be a Messiah. So, to be accepted as a Messiah, Jesus must be married.

St. Peter, Apostle of Jesus was married. Had Jesus not have been married, the traces of issues of confusion due to him being single, would have clearly been seen in the Gospels. Moreover, in the Matthew Gospel, it read 'Jesus shall leave his father and mother and shall keep to his wife'. (Matthew 19:4-5) From this statement, it can be seen that Jesus had an attitude in favor of marriage. In the John Gospel, a marriage in Kana is spoken of. This marriage where the names of the bride and the groom are kept secret, Jesus and his mother are present and both act as if they are the hosts:

Jesus's mother, said to him: "They have no wines". Jesus's mother, said to servants: "do all I say". (John 2:3-4-5) The host of the banquet called upon the groom and said: "Serve the entire good wine first, and when drunk too much, serve the poor wine". (2:9)' From these statements, it is understood that Jesus and his mother were not guests but hosts and that the words to the groom were directed to Jesus himself. By the presence of a banquet host and numerous servants, it is therefore understood of the banquet to be a sumptuous one among the noble and of many guests due to the lessening wine. Jesus had added water to the wine and had increased the present numbers of bottles to 800, according to John Gospel.

The Benjamin tribe had an important role in the life of Jesus. The tribe was one of twelve Jewish tribes migrating from Egypt to Palestine. Upon reaching the Promised Land, these lands occupied by the Jews were distributed among 12 tribes, and to Benjamin's share, fell the land inclusive of Jerusalem. An insignificant town at the time, Jerusalem gradually developed and became the capital of Israel during the reign of David and Solomon.[41] David had gained Jerusalem after a battle with Saul, a descendent of Benjamin Royalty.

During the exodus from Egypt, a clash between the believers of All Mighty God and polytheistic believers had occurred. When Moses left the tribes to move to the mountain to receive divine revelations, the polytheistic believers, for the sake of the return of the old beliefs, had started a rebellion and made a golden calf as the symbol of the ancient Baal Cult. Among the leaders of the uprising, the Benjamins were the majority. After Moses returned from the mountain, clashes took place between these two groups, resulting in most of the polytheistic believers to be killed, and the rest, providing they swore allegiance to the faith of Moses, the exodus had continued. However, even after the distribution of the Promised Land, the belief of God Baal continued to exist among the Benjamins. The Benjamins, creating a new cult by blending the ancient Sumerian cult and the Jewish teachings, were continuing their calf worshipping rituals. As a result of the killing of Benjamin Rabbis by other Jewish tribes, a war broke out between the Benjamins and the other 11 tribes. This war ended with the defeat of Benjamins resulting in destruction of mostly women and children. Most of the remaining took shelter under their Phoenician allies. The Phoenicians carried most of these refugees to Greece. The story of Danaus, son of King Belus going to Greece with his supporters as in the Greek mythology, verifies this story of migration.[42] In the Sion Monastery documents, as we shall discuss in detail later, it is stated: 'One day the Benjamin tribe left their land. Some remained. After two thousand years, 4th Godfroi (de Bouillon) became King of Jerusalem and founded the Order of Sion".

The Benjamins settling in Peloponnese, Greece, engaged in marriages to Spartans, became descendants of Arkadian Royals. In the period when Christianity emerged, the Benjamins, under the control of Jewish nobles settled in Danube and Rhine regions from Greece, blended in with the Teutonic tribes and the Franks. They were the ancestors of the Movorenj Dynasty, which will be examined later. It is stated in the Apocryphal book Maccabee that the Spartans and the Jews became related. In the Maccabee I, it is stated that both communities were from the Abraham family. There was also some archeological evidence of strong Jewish influence on the Frank culture. The effects of the Franks on Christianity and events occurred shall also be discussed later.

In the Mathew Gospel, Jesus was said to be of noble blood. This bloodline traced all the way back to David. David has seized the kingdom of Jewish state from King Saul of the Benjamin tribe after a wild clash. Despite their expulsion from Palestine, a few members of the Benjamin tribe were left in the Jewish state. St. Paul had stated that he was of the Benjamin family. The David lineage was of the Judah tribe. Judah tribe started their heritage by seizing the Kingdom from the Benjamins. Jesus, engaging in marriage to a noble woman of Benjamin descendent, had revealed a friendship of dynasty and by enabling an old dispute to come to an end had made Jesus a powerful candidate for a priest-king. With this marriage, the Benjamins would have co owned the crown, and thus the throne of Jesus would be strengthened. In Middle Eastern tales, the name Magdalena, frequently mentioned in the Gospels, was said to be a Benjamin descendent and that her bloodline extends to that of King Saul.

In the Gospels, there were the names of two women other than Jesus' mother Mary. The first one of these was Magdalena. She appeared in the first chaplaincy years of Jesus in Galileo. She accompanied him on the way to Yehuda. At the time, it was almost impossible for a woman to travel without any relative accompanying her. Once again, during the crucifixion of Jesus, Magdalena was among the disciples. In the Gospel of Luke, Magdalena was described as 'woman who coped with seven evils'. The cult of Baal, suggests an initiation of seven degrees. Magdalena is an Astarte nun and Astarte nuns were Sacred Temple Prostitutes. The name 'Magdala' of the Magdalena's village is meant the Village of Pigeons, and pigeons are the symbol of Mother Goddess Astarte of the Baal cult. And for being an Astarte nun, Magdalena, in some Christian cycles, had been attributed to as 'prostitute'.

In the Gospels of Mark and Luke, it is stated that an unnamed woman had meshed Jesus by oiling him. Following this oiling ritual, Jesus was widely regarded as a Messiah. The Gnostics believed in the holy marriage between Sophia and Jesus' and celebrated this marriage. In Gnostics myth, Sophia represented the self once fallen and then reborn. Sophia had been portrayed as a lost person seeking the truth in this world. Seeking love in all the wrong places, she had become a prostitute and at the end had begged the Holy Father for help. God had sent his brother Jesus as groom. In this myth, the emphasis of Jesus being the brother of Sophia is reference to both being member of the same fraternity. The sacred marriage is a symbol of the mystical union of the ultimate aim of Gnosticism.[43]

The name of the other woman in the Gospels is Maria of Bethany, sister of Lazarus. In the Gospels, it is stated that there is a grave in the garden of Lazarus' house. At the time, such special graves were only present in the gardens of the aristocrats' houses. It is claimed that Magdalena and Maria of Bethany are the same person. Indeed, during the crucifixion, there is no mention of Maria whatsoever. Absence of ones, known as the disciples of Jesus, during such as important event is unthinkable. Magdalena had always been present during crucifixion and resurrection of Jesus. In the Gospel of John, Maria of Bethany is said to be the person Meshing Jesus with oil. (John 11:12). The person rubbing Jesus of the Messiah oil was his wife Magdalena. It is also said that, Jesus had revived Lazarus from the dead. If Maria or Magdalena were the wife of Jesus, that means Lazarus was his brother-in-law. Lazarus is seen to be closer to Jesus than his other disciples. In the Gospel of John, Lazarus is mentioned as the successor of Jesus. Again in the Gospel of John, in the Raise of Lazarus, Jesus talks about the death of Lazarus to serve certain purposes: 'Lazarus our friend has fallen asleep, I am to wake him up' (11:11) Thomas calls upon his other friends: 'Let's go with him to die, too'. (11:16) From these statements, it is clearly understood that, Lazarus had not physically died but rather was initiated into the school of Jesus by an esoteric ritual executing a re-birth. It is rumored that in Bethany, where Jesus had lived for long years, he had established a school in which esoteric teachings were given to initiates, and that the apostles were also given special teachings at this school.

The writer of the John Gospel, portrays himself as the 'one Jesus loves'. Jesus trusted Lazarus to such an extent that, he entrusted his mother to him before his crucifixion: upon seeing his mother and his disciple beside him he said: 'Woman, here is your son'. Then he said to his disciple: 'Here is your mother'. After that, the disciple took the mother to his home. (John 19:26-27)

After the death sentence of Jesus was heard, Lazarus disappeared. It is understood that, while deploying his other disciples to disperse to various parts of the world and spread the teachings; Jesus had given a special task to his most loved disciple. Before the week Jesus was crucified, he went to Jerusalem as a king, and instructed his beloved Apostle to linger around and wait for his return. It seemed as if Jesus had a plan and this plan was about protecting his family. Because of the fact that, after the death of Jesus', his mother settled in Ephesus and that the Gospel of John was also written there, it appeared that the Gospel of John was narrated by Lazarus and it reflected the story from the horse's mouth.

As claimed by legends of the Middle Ages, after the crucifixion of Jesus, the remaining family; his wife Magdalena, Martha and Joseph of Aramath came to Marseille by boat. Joseph of Aramath, after being baptized by Saint Philip, was sent to England where he established a church in Glastonburg. Magdalena on the other hand, with her daughter Sarah had moved to Axe en Provence in Southern France and had died there. The sister of Lazarus had been the one carrying forward the sacred bloodline, meaning the Holy Grail. The Holy Grail signifies the womb of Magdalena.[44] The bloodline of Jesus had continued through Sarah.

The demand for the Kingdom of Israel by Jesus was not a spiritual kingdom as alleged, but envisaged an earthly one. A man claiming to be descending from the throne of David, and on account of a dynasty he created with his children born of a woman of Saul descent, had created a serious threat to the Roman rule. In his talks with the Roman ruler Pilates, Jesus was addressed as 'King of the Jews'. In the Matthew Gospel, Pilate asks: "Are you the king of Jews?" He answers, "Just as you have said". In the Gospels, although Pilates is portrayed as the authority trying to prevent the crucifixion of Jesus, in fact Jesus was the victim of the Roman rule. Crucifixion was not a method used by the Jews, but was on the contrary, an execution method used by Rome against her enemies and only for crimes against the emperor.

There are doubts about the identity of Barrabas who was pardoned from crucifixion at the last moment when he was about to be crucified along with Jesus. Barrabas was defined as a 'Lestai'. This definition in Greek is defined as 'Bandit'. However, this bandit is not one who commits immoral crimes. According to the Matthew Gospel, he is a 'reputable' bandit. And according to Mark and Luke, Barrabas was a doomed rebellion of political uprising. The Romans use the word 'Lestai' for fanatical Jews. According to Luke, Barrabas had been convicted of being part of a riot in Jerusalem. The two crucified along with Jesus were Lestais, too. Likewise, Simon Petrus, James and John are also known by the same title. It was absolutely natural for the two disciples, who were crucified along with someone like Jesus claiming the Kingdom to share the same opinion.

It is seen that the word Barrabas is derived from the words 'Bar Rabbi-Lord'. This saying was used to describe the children of the Rabbi. Jesus was known as a Rabbi. However, there are indications as "Jesus Barrabas" in the Gospels. In other words, Jesus Barabbas may be expressed as 'Son of Rabbi". The crucifixion age for Jesus was stated as between 33 and 36. According to Jewish traditions, men married between the ages of 13-16. In this case, having been married at the age 13, it was physically quite possible for Jesus to have a young son. The age 13 was enough for a boy to be considered an adolescent, and thus it was also possible for Jesus' son to be in armed struggle and be sentenced. When the Jewish elders were asked to make a choice as to forgive either Jesus or Barrabas, the answer had been Barrabas. The aim for the Kingdom of Israel to continue was to ensure the continuation of the dynasty.

In the method of execution by crucifixion, to speed up the death of people, the feet were not nailed to the cross, rather the ankles were broken. However, in Jesus' case, the ankles were not broken and the feet were nailed to the cross to reduce the pressure to the heart so that the duration of remaining alive would be extended. Even in the case of breaking the ankles, the death of the condemned by crucifixion would take usually 2 to 3 days. However, it is stated that Jesus had died just a few hours after being crucified. Even Pilates was surprised by the report of Jesus' death. The Roman ruler felt the need to ask 'So soon?' and indeed had commissioned a roman officer to verify Jesus' death. The

Roman officer stabbed a spear into Jesus' body and concluded that he was dead, for there had been no response. Meanwhile, Magdalena had gathered the flowing blood of Jesus in a grail and thus, out of this grail emerged the legend of the Holy Grail.

However, bleeding of the place where the spear was stabbed led to the conclusion that Jesus might still have been alive at the time. It is not possible for a corpse to bleed. It is very likely that, by the methods he had learned in Tibet, Jesus had feigned death by undergoing heavy trance. Then, the body of Jesus had been handed over to Joseph of Aramath. This event also shows us another interesting situation. The bodies of the crucified were usually left to the mercy of the vultures and not returned to their families. However, known to have been very rich, it is understood that Joseph had paid a large sum of bribe to the Roman authorities to take back the allegedly dead body of Jesus.

The location of the crucifixion of Jesus is another matter of interest. According to the John Gospel, the place of crucifixion was away from the usual ground of execution and was near a garden where there was an empty grave. This garden and the grave were the private property of Joseph of Aramath. By the same means of bribe, Jesus had been crucified at a place near his disciple's private property and had immediately been moved to this grave. Being a member of the Sandherin Jewish Noble Assembly, Joseph was rather an influential person and had managed to hide his alliance with Jesus from the Roman rule and his Jewish opposition. Joseph was yet another proof of Jesus' being an aristocrat.[45]

The supposedly dead body of Jesus had been buried three hours after the crucifixion and his body had miraculously disappeared. In the Gospel of Mark, it is stated that a young man dressed in white was seen at the tomb of Jesus, and in the Gospel of Luke, it is likewise stated that two angels were seen at the tomb. These people in white were the famous doctors of the Esenne cult who had provided the first medical attention and treated him.

In terms of Gnosticism, the phenomenon of crucifixion is part of initiation. The process of initiation is the representation of the disintegration of the body and bringing it back together. In Pitsis Sophia Jesus says: 'I have torn my body and come to earth. Bring my parts together and carry them to the light.' In a Gnostic hymn, Jesus is begged as: 'Come to us, for we are your parts on the same path. We are your organs. We all are one with you. We and you are the same thing.' In the Gnostic Philip Gospel, it is taught that every Christian is a Christ who has been crucified and later survived.[46]

The secret book of John, it teaches that until the soul reaches Gnosis, it will continue to be reborn, while in Pitsis Sophia, the soul, until it understands all the mysteries shall undergo several lives of experiences, and shall only reach the almighty through Light in a body of virtues. In the Gnostic book called the 'Savior's Book', it is written that, a man of virtue shall in his next life be born without forgetting his previous wisdoms, and as a result of leading intuition and wisdom, the soul shall continue searching the mysteries of the light until found.[47] Gnosis is the mystical experience of truth. The Gnostics believed that through initiation, they would be able to directly experience Gnosis, and that they would know the truth by themselves. Faith was only a tool to reach Gnosis. Knowledge was above faith. In the book of Thomas, there is the expression 'One who knows himself, has reached Gnosis'. Daemon is a Spirit. It is an immortal superego. The spiritual link with God is established though Deamon. The true identity of one is hidden within the Deamon. The aim of the Gnostic initiation is to unite the lower and upper egos. The great Gnostic Master Valentine says; 'When the self being and the Godly being connect, only then may perfection and eternity be accessible.'

Although it seems as if every being has its own Deamon, the enlightened initiate discovers the one Deamon that is shared among all.

The Universal Ego in every being, every soul, is a part of a single Divine Spirit. That is why, to know God, is to know yourself. Clement taught his initiates to try and become God, for the true Gnostic had already become God.[48]

Jesus miraculously was seen in several places after the crucifixion. These appearances had been interpreted as the return of his spiritual body. However, this spiritual body was capable of eating and keeping physical contact with his disciples. Joseph of Aramath and Magdalena were not seen in Palestine ever again after the crucifixion. According to the local legends, Joseph and Magdalena taking with them at least one child of Jesus, Sarah, had first moved to Alexandria and later to Marseilles where Sarah got married to a Gallican prince at the age of 13. It is also claimed that Jesus had been with them all along and lived in France until 45 A.D. His children's lineage is said to have continued here and thus led to the Grail legend to emerge. In these legends, the San Grail, meaning the Holy Grail, is said to carry the blood of Jesus. As a result of San Grail being read as 'Sang Real' (Royal Blood), the claim of the heirs of Jesus being the Kings of Jerusalem and all Christianity was given rise to. Gnostic philosopher Ormus of Egypt claimed that the mummified body of Jesus was hidden in the vicinity of the Castle of Rennes.[49]

It is understood that just as Moses; Jesus too had disseminated his discipline in two ways. The first of these was the hidden truths given in secret through a limited number of disciples. While the apostles accepted to his school in Bethany through initiation from the core team, the illiterate and the uneducated masses accepted this new teaching through the parables. While the protection of Magdalena and the Royal Blood had been the priority for the core team, although being in the same team, Saint Paul taking on the task of teaching the non-Jewish masses himself, had used a different method. For the Saint Paul school, maintaining the blood had no significance. The Orthodox Christianity had been the outcome of applications of this school. The adherents of this school constituting the majority of Christians did not hesitate compromising with the Romans for the sake of spreading this teaching.

Saint Paul or otherwise known as (Pavlus) Paul, in general was considered as the founder of Orthodox Christianity against Gnostic thinking. However, the famous Gnostic Sage (The Kamil One) Valentine, states that Paul had only initiated a few chosen people, and that he had disclosed the secret teachings of God. And even Theudas, teacher of Valentine and the one who initiated him, had been initiated by Paul. Yet another claim was that the famous Gnostic Marcion and his supporters also had a Gnostic Bible said to have been written by Paul. The Nag Hammadi findings also seem to confirm this claim. The most important feature of the Gnostic Bibles was that they revealed the secret teachings of Jesus rising after death. Such expressions are not to be found in any of the four accepted Bibles. Among the Nag Hammadi manuscripts, three text messages containing 'The prayer of Apostle Paul'; The Revelation of Paul' and 'The Ascension of Paul' have been found. In the New Testament, it has been established that at least 7 of the 13 letters said to have been written by Pavlus were not written by him and were fake. It is recognized even by the most conservative theologians that anti-Gnostic 'Pastoral' letters in particular were absolutely fake. Infact Pastoral letters were not mentioned at all until the Ireanus period 190 A.D. It is highly likely that the letters were written by Ireanus in attribution to Pavlus. Even the great Orthodox propagandist Eusebius had avoided including these letters into his Gospel in 325 A.D. In Pastoral letters, Pavlus was pictured as an anti-Gnostic, an enemy of all heretics, and the organizer of the church discipline and system of priests. Within these letters, the supporters of Paul are expected to refrain from unholy superstition in Gnostic texts, to stay away from this endless ungodly nonsense, which in fact, were the direct demands of Ireanus. On the contrary, Pavlus had often used Greek terms from the Pagan mysteries such as 'The Spirit (Pheuma)'; 'Divine Knowledge (Gnosis)'; 'Wisdom (Sophia)' and 'The Initiated (Teleioi)' in his works.

Pavlus was a Jewish who had adopted the common Greek culture of the period. His works were in his native Greek language. Tarsus, the city he grew up was the center of Stoics, one of the most important schools of the Pagan mystery cult. Tarsus was the birth place of the Mitra mystery. It is unthinkable that Pavlus had not noticed the similarities between the Christian mysteries and the Mitra mysteries. On the contrary, all his efforts had been towards placing the Mitra mysteries into Christianity. Pavlus defined himself as the 'Servant of God's Mysteries'. He states 'What we now see is the deceptive reflection of the truth'. There shall come a time when we shall encounter the truth face to face'. Paul argued that the mystery was given to him by revelation and that they were inappropriate words to speak. According to him, to elevate with Jesus was something all initiates had already experienced. In his letter to the Romans, he states, 'Us who have been initiated by him, have also been initiated to his death'. The duty to disclose the God given secrets to the chosen was now his. This secret was about the secret of the spirit of the universe and the mind of God within everyone. Paul writes; 'This is the secret; Christ is within you'. And in his letter to the Ephesians, he teaches; 'Speak the truth, for we are parts of each other'.[50]

In Greek, the word Gnostic means 'Those who know'. For Gnostics, who learn through their own secret and initiatory teachings, the knowledge (Gnosis) is experienced directly from God, the eventual aim is to reach God, to ripen and become 'Christ'.[51]

In Christianity, the Father, Son and the Holy Spirit trilogy, is nothing more than the triple nature of God. However, the replacement of many more concepts such as this holy trinity, had in fact caused the discipline a great deal of loss. The esoteric content of Jesus' teachings is still not known by many Christians of today. However, with concepts like goodness, righteousness, beauty and brotherhood of people, has Christianity managed to provide acceptance of such feelings and thus Christianity has played an important role in the universalization of the esoteric teachings.

Yet another claim is that, after being saved from the crucifixion, Jesus had once again returned to India and that he had settled in Kashmir. The owner of this claim is Iranian Historian Mullah Nadiri. In his work 'Tarik-i Kaschmir', he states that 'Yus Asaf (Uniting Jesus in Hindu), had come to Kashmir from Palestine, and had brought the words of God to the people of Kashmir.[52]

In a temple called the 'Solomon's Throne' in India, it is written that 'Yus Asaf had emerged as messiah in 54 A.D. And he was of Israel descent. This shrine is located on top of a mountain, east of Shirinagar. In the center of Shirinagar, there exists a sacred temple called Ranzabal Khaynar. This word means 'Tomb of the Prophet'.[53]

The temple is a combination of mosque, church and Indian architecture. There are two tombs in the building. One belongs to a senior religious personality, Sayed Nasruddin. The other tomb next to Sayed Nasruddin is regarded by the people of Kashmir as belonging to a prophet, as it is written in a 200 years-old history book called 'Tarik-i-Azim'. In this book, it is told that the name of the prophet is Yus Asaf and that he he had been given the task of preaching by God to the people of Kashmir. Father Weitbrecht, who examined the graves in 1903, had stated that the grave keeper described one of the tombs as belonging to 'Jesus'. On the grave, lies the Arabic statement 'Ziyarat Yus Asaf Khaynar', meaning 'Tomb of Jesus, the Prophet Uniter'. The footprint on the stone located immediately above the grave, which had also been examined by Erich Von Daniken, is believed to have belonged to Jesus.

In a book written in 115 A.D. in Sanskrit, the encounter of Kashmiri King Shalevain with Jesus was mentioned. The King traveling on the way to the Himalayas, encounters a stranger dressed in white. He asks who he is. The stranger answers, 'I am known as born of a virgin, Son of God'. Upon seeing the surprise of the King, the stranger feels the need to further introduce himself. 'I am from a foreign land where evil has no limit. I appeared as the messiah on the land of the Amelia. I have suffered from them.' The man in his 80's gives his name as Jesus Christ.[54]

The somehow withdrawal of Jesus from Palestine history, had not settled the issues in the Jewish land. The Jewish uprising which began in 66 A.D., ended with the fall of Masada Castle in 74 A.D. The 960 people defending the castle, chose to commit suicide rather than surrender to the Romans. Among the defenders of the castle, there were the Esenne, Kabbalas, members of other Jewish sects as well as many Christians and, in particular Barrabas. The speech given by Eleazar, the commanding officer of the castle, just before the mass suicide, had been noted by a woman who somehow had not committed suicide. In this talk, there were a lot of esoteric and anagogic sayings such as: "life is a menace for the people, death liberates the spirit and lets the spirit return home, the spirit is imprisoned within mortal bodies, and that the body is mortal whereas the soul is immortal".[55]

Apart from the Kabalistic and the Essene cults, there were no mention of the spirit and its immortality in Judaism. The superiority of body over the soul and the thought of uniting with God after death, were matters not within the Jewish traditions. This conversation clearly showed that the insurgent at the table and the Christians among them were Gnostics of pro esoteric philosophy and that the early teachings of Christianity were anagogic.

After the first uprising, in Palestine, an ever increasing powerful Judeo-Christian sect named Ebinoit, was accepting Jesus as the prophet. It is known that, in the possession of this Judeo-Christian sect living in Jerusalem around 160 A.D., was an Ebionit Gospel; Gospel of the Hebrews; Gospel of the twelve Apostles and a Nazarene Bible consisting of four Gnostic Gospels. It is proven that the first century Jerusalem Christians were of Gnostics.[56]

The sect's rhetorics were made up of Hermetic, Pythagorean and Mitraik legends. According to them, Jesus was not a God, only his prophet. Similar views had begun to be voiced in Alexandria in 135 A.D. Valentine, a member of the school of Alexandria, was saying that Jesus had been initiated to the secrets doctrine. Moving from Alexandria to Rome, Valentine by rejecting the religious authority of Rome had advocated the esoteric science.[57]

In 140 A.D., yet another philosopher supporting the same opinions was Markinon. Another Alexandrian philosopher Basilides, too claimed that Jesus had not died on the cross, instead Sirenian Siran was crucified in his place. In the Gnostic Bible of Truth, Jesus says; 'I have not been defeated as they planned. I may just seem so. I did not really die on the cross being accused.' The riots and the massacres carried out in Palestine, had led many Christian esoteric thinkers to flee to Alexandria. Thus, Alexandria was made the home of the Christian branch of Esoterizm, too. Indeed, the fact that 'Gnostic Bibles' brought to light at Nag Hammadi surfaced in Egypt confirms this fact.

In the Maria Gospel of the Nag Hammadi collection, the story of Peter complaining about Magdalena is told, and that both share different views: 'Sister, we know that the savior Lord loves you more than other women. Are we now going to listen to this woman? Did the Lord choose this woman over us?'

One of the apprentice's answers Petrus: 'Surely, Jesus Christ knows women well. This is why he has chosen this woman over us.'

In yet another Gnostic Bible, the handwritten Philip Gospel, regarding the matter, it is stated that, 'The Lord did all mysteriously by baptism with holy anointing oil, wine and bread, and with atonement a nuptial ceremony in the bridal chamber. There were three people who always accompanying the Lord. They were, his mother Mary, his sister Mary and Magdalena. Magdalena was known as his comrade.' And all these statements are such as to prove that Magdalena was his wife. Jesus often kissing Magdalena on her lips was mentioned in the Philip Gospel, where marriage or conjugal community was also praised and it was further stated that the creation of the world depended on man, and the existence of man depended on marriage. At the end of this Bible, the statements saying 'Jesus Christ has a son. And that Jesus Christ has a grandson. The son of Jesus is of his descendants (offspring of his loins)'[58] do seem to support the claims made by the Movorenj and the Sion Monastery which we shall discuss later.

In 70 A.D. after Jerusalem had been plundered by the Romans causing the destruction of the temple, a huge influx of Jewish refugees to Europe took place. After the 132 A.D. rebellion, with all the Jews being displaced from Palestine, south of France, under the rule of the Franks, had become a shelter center for the Jews. Among these Jews, there were Cabalists, and this Cabalist opinion by combining with the ancient esoteric teachings through the Benjamins, had strengthened and led the teaching spread.

The Roman rule, for many years, had made every effort to prevent the spread of Christianity. The Christians were being followed and tried to be annihilated. However, the mixture of races accelerated after Alexander the Great, the international intolerance gradually decreased, and the merger trend had spread. As a result, the eastern culture had penetrated into the west, and beginning with Mitraism, the way for Christianity to spread all over the west had been opened. At his point, the Roman Christians encountered Collegium members who were supporting such values as fraternity, brotherhood and goodness just like themselves. During the last eras of the Roman Empire, the ones being educated at the College of Architects were traditionally called 'Comacine Masons'.[59]

In the 1st century A.D., the Roman architect Vitruvius, had stated that the construction workers needed to be organized in Collegiums for their mutual benefits. An architect was known as a kind of magician familiar with all human knowledge with recognition of the basis of the laws of nature. As it could be observed, the members of the Collegium were not merely builders but rather enlightened people with all the knowledge of the period.

The existence of the Collegiums was first found in 715 B.C. during King Numa Pompilius period. In these Collegiums, there were 9 workers' unions including carpenters. It was this period alone that, for the first time, the presence of builders was encountered in the Roman army. While the Collegiums in Rome were active until the barbarian invasions, following the invasion, however, they had flourished in East Rome, and by the end of the 11th century, had confronted by Crusaders. With the Crusades, the artisan unions, within the Guilds once again began to develop in western European countries. The Collegiums were considered as the backbone of the Byzantine state.[60]

First Collegium was located near Lake Como and following this first example, several Collegiums were established in various towns. Following the fall of Rome, members of Collegiums, scattering all over Europe, had passed on their teachings over to generations. From the British Athelstan Palace, to the Byzantine Hagia Sophia church built between 532-537 A.D., most of the architectural structures carried their signatures. In 643 A.D., in a statement issued by King Rotharis, it was observed that the works of the Comani Masons were being praised. The principles of the Comani Masons, had later been named as Mason Mysteries.

Consistent with the discipline of the Collegium, the Divine being could be perceived by the principle of shapes and numbers. Therefore, large structures created by shapes and numbers, were the most important indicators of the presence of God. The synthesis of physics and numbers was geometry. The regular and systematic repetition of geometric models; harmony, order and laws, was in short God itself. Geometry was the master plan available everywhere and anytime. For this reason, it was called the Divine Craft. In these thoughts, the traces of Pythagoras's teachings were obvious. It was therefore understood that the Como College and similar ones had been developed in line with this prediction.

The Collegium members were free people who were given permission to travel anywhere within the Roman Empire to demonstrate their art. Even in regions in Europe outside the Roma Empire, Collegium members were particularly sought for construction works. However, after a while, a feudal system took over in Europe and even these free craftsmen degenerated into the state of serfdom. It was then when the Collegiums joined the monasteries, and to benefit from the rights granted to the clergy, had formed a builder's association of monks called 'Gildea'.[61]

The Gildea Monasteries had been pioneers of the construction of Gothic cathedrals. The Gothic cathedrals were built under the management of a head architect called 'the Master of Craft'. Every single craftsman involved in the construction had used his own geometric knowledge in harmony with the others. As well as all masters having been skilled craftsmen, they were also draftsman. Their artworks represented the degree of high education. For them, the cathedrals symbolized something beyond the house of God. It was clearly stated in the 1410 hand written manuscripts that Pythagoras and Hermes sciences were closely known to these masters of philosophers.[62]

However, because these teachings were in contradiction with Christian dogmas, just as trade secrets, the teachings had been hidden under a veil of secrecy.

In Collegiums where esoteric teachings of Apollo, Dionysus, Orpheus and Pythagoras were well known, not only the ancient Greek doctrines, but the Iranian Mithras cults and the Stoics of Saabi faith had also been effectively applied. After the dissolution of the Pythagorean School in Italy, the school members scattered in various cities of Anatolia and Europe of the Greek-Roman world, and helped spread the teachings, thus preparind the grounds for the emergence of the Mithras cult. The Mithra believers, having learned from the course of the Pythagorean School, had hidden their teachings under a veil of secret and had left no written document behind whatsoever. Mithraism, reaching the peak of existence in the 1st century A.D., had taken its name from the ancient Persian God of Sun.[63]

However, the teaching had nothing more in common in terms of practice, beyond being Persian Mitra and a Sun cult. Because of a secret imposed on not using the real name of the God Almighty, the name had been kept secret, hiding the real name, and the name Persian God of Sun Mitra had been used instead. Most of the knowledge regarding Mithraism was relieved from the glyphs and mosaics of the temples created by this school and a series of higher stages regarding the secrecy and the recruiting of members known to have been in existence. On the glyphs of the temples, the motifs where God Mitra kills a bull with a knife in his hand are often found. Found on or around the arch of the motif called Taurokto, there lies a Zodiac motif depicting the 12 signs of the zodiac. The astrological symbolism in the Mitra belief appeared to be a very important place. On the glyphs, in addition to Zodiac, the symbols of the galaxies, the Earth, water and air elements were present. On all the upper corners of the Tauroktonis, there are busts representing the sun and the moon. Just as the sun being represented as emitting light from the head of God Apollo, the moon is represented in the shape of a crescent. And the planets, as in the Pythagorean Temple of Muses were represented in seven busts and sometimes on the cape of Mitra. The number seven was important in the Mitra system. Mitra was the creator God. The seven planets symbolized the seven degrees' members had to overcome; they were, 1. Crow, 2 Nimphus (Water Nymph); 3. Soldier, 4. Leo, 5. Persian (Perses), 6. Sun (Heliodromo); 7. Father (Pater) degrees.[64]

Tauroktoni of Mitra

In Mitra temples, there are seven doors indicating these seven degrees. There are symbolic links between each degree and nature. The first four degrees, evoke the four basic elements. The crow symbolizes the air, Nimphus the water, soldier the Earth and lion the fire. The next three degrees being Perseus are identified as the moon, and Heliodromos as the sun. And Pater symbolizes the harmony of an initiate relieved of earthly obligations; in other words, the Sage (The Kamil One).

Emperor Neron was an initiate of the Mitra mysteries.[65]

The symbol of the first degree was the crow, for all the Godly knowledge had been brought to mankind by birds. In the second degree, a nymph adorned just like a bride was used as a symbol of adoration to God. In the third degree, the candidate was given a sword and a crown. The candidate would not accept the crown to show as a symbol of his rejection of the financial means. In the fourth degree, the symbol was a Lion dressed in red holding a shovel in his hand filled with coal core, which represented dominance over fire. The fifth degree symbol was a crescent and a star, and war. In this degree where a Persian dressed in silver tunic with a scythe in his hand was the symbol, with which purity and man's identity in relation to the universe was taught. In the sixth degree, the symbols were whips, torches, and a sphere. And in the last, that is the 7th degree, the symbols were an eye, a curvy knife and Phrygian helmets. The mission of the Fathers with the 7th degree was to protect the temples, to convene the ceremonies; make decisions on the acceptance of candidates and to disseminate the Mitra wisdom. The title of the head of the entire Mitra organization was 'The Father of Fathers'.

Candidates wishing to join the Mitra organization had to study on science of astrology in order to grasp the God-Universe-Man oneness identity as a priority. The candidates, following this lengthy training, were then considered into the cult with an initiation ceremony. During the ceremony, the candidate brought to the temple totally naked, would be blindfolded and hands tied, too. In Tauroboli rituals, just as the ones in Luvi and Cybele cults, a bull would be slaughtered on a platform with holes, and the initiate, placed in a pit under this platform, would bathe in the pouring blood.[66] The candidate would be grounded by pushing, and thus would be symbolized as dead. The officers would then proceed with the re-birth of the candidate by lifting him up. The candidate would be covered in mud, exposed to strong wind, passed through a trough filled with water and finally would be pushed forward to jump over burning wood. In other words; he would be tested with earth, air, water and fire. At the end of the ceremony, the candidate would swear on his life to protect all the secrets of the cult. Symbols like compasses, squares, plumbs and scales used in the Mitra cult and also detected on the glyphs of Gallo-Roman tombs, were used in later years by Freemasonry.[67]

*In the picture, on a coin used in Byzantium where the Mitra (Sol Invictus) belief
was widespread, the usage of the square and the compass could have seen to be
used as it is used today by Freemasonry. Justinian I era (527-565 A.D.)*

In the Tauroktonies, Mitra was always pictured over the bull while killing it. Over his head, a helmet recognized as a Phrygian cone was placed which was an indication of him being an Anatolian.

Phrygians were the people who had lived in Anatolia in the post-Luvi era. In sky maps, the constellation standing above the bull and de-effecting it by a fatal blow is seen to be Perseus constellation, one of the Greek mythological heroes. In 4000 B.C. when the spring equinox of the start of zodiac was in the Taurus sign, as a result of equinoxes going back in Zodiac, the vernal equinox had entered the Aries sign. In other words, the leadership, and the effect of the Taurus has disappeared. This is the astronomical event symbolized by Mitra killing of the bull in Taurok.[68]

Perseus, just as Mitra, was wearing a Phrygian conical hat, cap. According to mythology, this cap had been given to him to be invisible and to kill Medusa as his most important mission. According to ancient Persian legends, Perseus had landed the heavenly fire from the skies to earth and had protected this eternal sacred fire in the temple. This was the belief that lay beneath the ancient Persian fire-worship rituals. Perseus had selected talented people as priests, initiated them by fire and as a secret, had thought them how to keep up the fire, and appointed them to protect the fire.

According to historian Pluark, the roots of Mithraism go all the way to the people living at Tarsus in the Cilicia region of Anatolia in the 1st century B.C.[69]

The name Tarsus City comes from the Greek Taurus, meaning the bull. Cilicia located in southern Anatolia, was where the Perseus cult was quite active. However, there, Perseus was considered to be the migrant God. The Perseus cult was united with the local cult.

In the Perseus cult, Perseus was constantly identified with God Apollon. And in Mitra, next to Mitra stood the God of Sun Helios, the Roman derivative of Apollon. As Perseus was identified with Apollon, Mitra was too identified with Helios. Well, were the Apollon belief and other ancient Greek esoteric teachings the only source of the Perseus cult? In the ancient Greek theology, such endeavor with astronomy could not be observed. The answer to this question should be looked for within the ancient belief of Saabism of the Cilicia region. During the invasion of the region by Alexander the Great, the Saabi belief which we shall examine later, affected by the Pythagorean doctrine had influenced the Greek philosophers, too. One of the pioneer movements affected by Saabism was Stoicism.[70]

In the 4th century B.C, shortly after the conquests of Alexander the Great, the effects of stoicism established by Zeno in Athens, was rather strong and wide in Cilicia and Tarsus regions. Tarsus was very close to Harran, the strongest city of the Saabis. An important part of the Stoics had emerged from this region that had been kneaded with the Saabi teachings.

Arato, as one of the founders of Stoicism (315-240 B.C.), was from a Cilicia town of Soli. After Zeno, the Stoic doctrine had been systemized by Krisippus (280-207 B.C.). Yet again, the representatives of the same movement, Atenodorus (74-7 A.D.) was from Tarsus and known to have been in constant contact with one of the best known of all Stoics, Posidonyus (135-50 B.C.). Atenodorus had been in Rome and been an important figure in the emergence of the Mithras cult. After spending thirty years in Rome, as the official representative of Emperor Augustus, he had been sent back to Tarsus and had constructed the city regulations.[71]

Following Tarsusian Zeno, the leadership of the Stoic School had been performed by Seleukos of Tigris and later by Diogenes of Babylon. The university founded in Tarsus, became the most influential representative of the Stoic philosophy. The Stoics had deep interest in astronomy and astrology and like the Saabies, had formed an astral religion.[72]

According to Stoic phenomenon, the faith of human being, that is, the Micro cosmos was directly related to events of the Macro cosmos, meaning the universe. All planets and stars including the Sun and the Moon had an impact on people. The Stoic soothsayers were famous for their prophesy and star fortune telling. The fact that faith could not be stood against was a primary thought. All beings in the universe were alive. The planets and the stars were alive and sacred too. It was believed that the Sun, the Earth, and all the planets and the stars had spirits. The cosmos is a God. The stars are God. However, the biggest of all the Gods, was the Mind in Heaven. In his 'About God' work, Stoic philosopher Krisippus had argued that the cosmos is a living creature with its own soul and intelligence. The famous Greek philosopher Cicero described the thoughts of the Stoics as such:

'Since the universe is sacred, the stars made out of the purest and liveliest materials are also sacred. That they are constantly hot is the proof of their intelligence and their conscious'.

Stoic Posidonyus, was one of the most ardent advocates of the idea that the stars determined the fate of everything. He had theorized this thought in his work the 'Cosmic Sympathy' and had tried to prove his theory by making a crescent presenting all the movements of the Moon and of the Planets. He also had not fallen back from defending the beliefs of the ancient Babylon that the faith of a war was to be read from the lungs of sacrificed animals. The Stoics believed in cosmic cycling and as a result of this cycling, everything disappeared and then re-created. The entire universe periodically ending in a doomsday event was beginning to recuperate, which would last until another doomsday. According to Cicero, who had been accounted for transferring the ideas of the Stoics, the universe being destroyed by a sacred fire, was returning to its starting point, then without any change, the same cycle of life was repeating. Kleantes and Krisippus argued that it was inevitable that the universe was a seed and that it turned into a sacred fire from within.[73]

The Stoics used the Babylonian concept of the 'Great Year'. There was, however, much controversy over the length of the "Great Year", which covered the entire duration of the universe, the Earth, and other five planets, all of which completed their entire cycle and returned to their starting point at the beginning; however, all Stoics agreed that there was a specific time for it. The Stoics had created many gods and mythological figures by allegorizing cosmic and natural forces. Cicero, stated that 'The gods were derived from theories of nature. In the Mitra belief, Saturn was the God of the seasons and the repeated time periods; Jupiter was of the sky; and Juan was of the air. Helios, the God of the Sun, traveled in the sky riding on fire.

Astronomer Hipparkus argued that our souls were part of the sacred fire that created the whole universe. Like all material beings, our souls would return to their main source. Hipparkus had discovered that the entire universe was in motion, and had said that it had a sacred meaning. According to Hipparkus, as a result of this movement, the cycle of the Great Year of the universe was completed in 36 thousand years.

Hipparkus and his contemporary friend Posidonyus living in Rhodes, had been the important figures in the development of the Stoic philosophy and teachings in the Roman Empire.

These interactions continued to exist as the most effective form of religious belief until the 4th century, when Stoic philosophy, which received the name of Mitra culture, spread all over Europe, especially to the Collegia school and became the most widely practiced religious belief until the 4th century when it dissolved the Mitra beliefs within its own framework.

Christians regarded the gods of Mitraist Collegia members as saints and thus the Collegia were able to sustain their existence by finding shelter in the Colleges. In Byzantium, Christians continued to exist under the auspices of the Collegias, and over time they succeeded in forming a powerful organization and their religion was recognized as an official state religion. Sol Invictus (The Invincible Sun), was the most important god of pre-Christian Byzantine times. Sol Invctus was the Byzantine version of Mitra. The Byzantine Emperor Constantine, who was an initiating member of Sol Invictus, was also the head priest of this religion.[74]

During the reign of the Mitraist Constantine, the other name of Byzantine was the 'Sun Empire'. The invincible Sun figure was placed on all the empire flags and the currency. In this cult, Sol Invictus was regarded as the Almighty God, possessing all of the qualities of all the gods. In other words, Sol Invictus was in a way overlapping with the monotheistic Abrahamic religion and was the transition from polytheistic to monotheistic belief. Christianity, which begun to appear in such environment, grew up and prospered under a large umbrella of tolerance, through the Collegia, who operated extensively in the country.

Constantine, in 321 A.D., declared Sunday the blessing day of the sun as a day of resting. Until that day, Christians who had adopted the Jewish tradition of resting on Saturdays, accepted this practice and thus Sunday was accepted as the sacred day of resting. 25th of December as the day of the Rising Sun was the most sacred day in the Sol Invictus cult. This practice was also adopted by the Christians and began to be celebrated as Jesus' birthday. Subsequently, Christianity had adorned itself with the present religion and gradually began to take its place. The beliefs of re-birth and resurrection of Mithraism were adapted for Jesus. Constantine tried to remove the differences between Christianity and Mithraism throughout his lifetime and did succeed in doing so. Thus, Constantine adopted Jesus as the earthly manifestation of the Sol Invictus and had it adopted by his people. For Constantine, belief was a political instrument and any belief that helped the integrity of the state had to be freely practiced.[75]

Constantine, in 325 A.D., gathered the Iznik council. The rules of Christianity were adopted within the framework drawn by the priests. The council of Iznik, decided on Jesus to be not a mortal prophet but rather a God and thus Sol Invictus as God and the Lord, was transformed into Jesus. As a result of the Council's meeting, the 'Iznik Faith Confession' was published, and the discrepancies between various Christian groups were eliminated.[76]

A year after the Council of Iznik, Constantine decided to destroy all practices against Orthodox teachings. He allocated a steady income to the Byzantine Church and also decided to establish the Roman Church. Later, the bishop of Rome declared his first 'Pontificate' in the year 384. Constantine, after identifying Christianity with the Sol Invictus, agreed to be baptized in the deathbed and became a Christian.[77]

Julianus, who rose to the throne after Constantine, initiated a desperate attempt to return to the Mitraic religion. Julianus, who initiated to the Mitra religion in 361, founded the Mitraemum, the Mitraic temple in Istanbul. Seeing himself as the reincarnation of Mitra, Julianus blamed his uncle Constantine for leaving the religion of his ancestors in the hands of ignorant Christians.[78] But his efforts did not suffice. After his death, Christianity continued to develop in an even more powerful pace.

Half a century later, Theodosius declared that Christianity was the only accepted official religion, while Christianity was equal to pagan religions during the Constantine era. Following the declaration of Christianity as the official Roman religion, the church began to implement intimidation policies for all pagans and Gnostics. Pagan seers were caught, and tortured to death. The Pagan priests were chained to their temples and left starving to death. While some temples were being demolished, others were being converted into churches. Theodosius, in 391 A.D., issued an order to shut-down the whole of pagan temples.

The temple of Eluisis, where thousands of people had been initiated for more than 11 centuries, was destroyed by fanatic Christian monk communities in 396 A.D. All temples, including the Serapis Temple of Alexandria was also destroyed. All books in the Alexandria library were burnt upon the orders of the Alexandrian Archbishop Cyril. The Emperor had said, 'Burn all books hostile to Christianity'. Head nun Hypatia was torn to pieces and killed. Cyril was declared saint. Theodosius initiated action against Gnostics too. He issued 100 legislations to prevent them from spreading their beliefs, holding meetings and converting others into their own religion. He also forbade them to own property. At the end, in 381 A.D., he declared all heretic activity as a crime against the state. This official order stated; 'Novatians, Valentinans, Marcians, Pauls, understand by this law that, your teachings are filled with a lot of lies, destructive and poisonous thoughts. We are warning you that none of you should build up communities from now on, and to prevent you from doing so, we order you to immediately transfer all the property you own to the Catholic Church'. In conclusion, the Gnostics were not only forbidden, but were declared as heretics to be completely destroyed and burned on fire. Despite this policy, Gnosticism continued to exist as a great force in the Christian world. In the fourth century, heretic Christians were so widespread that Cyril of Jerusalem had to warn believers not to go to a Gnostic church by mistake.[79]

As a result of the work of the Orthodox Church, the book known today as the New Testament appeared. It was not possible to talk about the New Testament before the 4th century. Various books which were bound to the Old Testament, but not included in the Bible, because they were not Hebrew manuscripts, were declared 'apocryphal', in other words, not regarded as true or certain. Although these were books tried to divine Jesus, such as the Paul's Gospel and the Childhood Bible of Jesus, the Orthodox Church did not consider them reliable enough. In addition, numerous sacred manuscripts were proclaimed as Gnostic and were removed from Christianity belief.[80]

The Western Christian Church had struggled for 400 years to distinguish between the sacred texts of Christianity as Canonic i.e., those accepted and Apocryphal ones; i.e., those that are not acceptable. The Canonical texts were claimed to be taken from a total of 27 sources. The fact that the Eastern Church recognized some apocryphal texts as sacred brings about the most important difference between the two churches.[81]

Since the Roman rulers were defined as divine, so had Jesus to be a newly emerged God. He was supposed to emerge as God and not as priest-king, nor a Christ. It was imperative that Jesus be re-born to appear as God. Therefore, Jesus was made equal to the reincarnated gods, such as Osiris, Attis, and July. In harmony with the same thinking path, the doctrine of having been given birth by a virgin mother was put forward. In the 9th century A.D., the title of 'Theotokos' meaning the 'The mother of God' was found suitable for Mary by the Orthodox clerics. Thus, Mary was being regarded as the 'wife' of the Father God. On the other hand, the Catholic Church identified Mary with Sophia (wisdom). Thus, Mary was the second identity in the triple god (the Trinity), and the symbol of Mary was also accepted as 'rose'. Coicidentally, Rose was accepted as a symbol of 'secret' and 'hiding of secrets' in Greek mythology. The five-pointed red rose had become the symbol of the Masonic 'Subrose' tradition in the sense of hiding secrets. The symbol known as the Philosopher's Stone in alchemy was named as 'Rosaettastone' (Rose Stone) in free masonry. Again, in the tomb of every Mason who has died, three white roses symbolizing the light, the love, and the life are planted.[82]

The origin of the concept of God's trinity in Christianity was Egypt. In an ancient Egyptian text, it was stated that, 'As one, I came to be three' while in another, "Amon, Ra and Ptah, all three are one God. What is hidden in Ra is Amon, whose body is Ptah. He appears in Amon, Ra and Ptah. All three are united'. According to Hermes, a logo was the Son of God and thus had created the universe. Father and Son were in fact one just as the case with intelligence and thought. Logos was God in his own consciousness. He was the sole spirit of the universe. Logos was the common identity of all mankind.[83]

In Christianity's new triad of the 'Holy Father, Son and the Spirit' system, the corporeal family of God was unnecessary, and even more than that, it had un favorable drawbacks. Keeping with such a material family would contradict with the claim of being universal.

As a result of such activities taking place at the end of the 4th century, Mithraism, which had created the appropriate environment for the development of Christianity, was defeated by the very Christianity it had flourished with its own hands and was dissolved within this new religion. Nevertheless, the teachings of Mitra could not be totally destroyed among the people, and continued to exist in schools such as Cathars and Arianism and in organizations of Knights which were to emerge in the future.

However, at this point it is necessary to go back in history and examine the role of Islam, a new religion in the Middle East, on the History of the Esoteric-Anagogic Doctrines.

References

1   Schure Edouard, - *Great Initiatives (Büyük İnisiyeler)*, RM Pub, Istanbul 1989, p. 60

2   Santesson Hans Stephan, - *Sunken Country Mu Civilization (Batık Ülke Mu Uygarlığı)*, RM Pub., Istanbul 1989, p. 137

3   Signier, Jean Francois/ Thomazo, Renaud - *Secret Organizations (Gizli Örgütler)* Larousse Oğlak Güzel Kitaplar, Istanbul 2006, p. 33

4   Kutluay Doç. Dr. Yaşar, - *Islamic and Jewish Sects (İslam ve Yahudi Mezhepleri)*, Anka Pub., Istanbul 2001, p. 238

5   Knight, Christopher; Lomas, Robert - *The Hiram Book (Hiramın Kitabı)*, Bilge Karınca Pub., Istanbul 2008, p. 261

6   Knight, Christopher; Lomas, Robert- r.w., p. 304

7   Erentay İbrahim, - Hiram Abif, Irmak Pub., Istanbul 2000, p. 88

8   Erentay İ., r.w., p. 80.

9   Baigent Michael/Leigh Richard, - *Holy Grail, Holy Blood (Kutsal Kâse, Kutsal Kan)*, Emre Pub., Istanbul 1996, p. 313

10   Freke, Timothy & Gandy, Peter - *The Secrets of Jesus (İsa'nın Gizemleri)* Ayna Pub., Istanbul 2005, p. 381

11   De Suarez Philippe, - *The Bible of Thomas (Thomas'ın İncil'i)*, RM Pub., Istanbul 1988

12   Freke, Timothy & Gandy, Peter, r.w., p. 149

13   Erentay İ., r.w., p. 63

14   Özbudun Sibel, - *Transformation Dynamics of a Religious Tradition from Hermes to Idris (Hermes'ten İdris'e Bir Dinsel Geleneğin Dönüşüm Dinamikleri)*, Ütopya Pub., Ankara p. 148

15   Özbudun P., r.w., p. 156

16   Özbudun P., r.w., p. 155

17   Özbudun P., r.w., p. 163

18   Özbudun P., r.w., p. 164

19   De Suarez P., r.w., p. 27

20   Kutluay Y., r.w., p. 239

21   Kutluay Y., r.w., p. 242

22   Bobaroğlu Metin, - *Anagogic Tradition (Batıni Gelenek)*, Ayna Pub., Istanbul 2002, p. 64

23   Freke, Timothy & Gandy, Peter r.w., p. 237

24   Churchward James, - Sacred Symbols of Mu, England, p. 52

25   Freke, Timothy & Gandy, Peter, r.w., p. 243

26   Benson, Michael - *Glossary of Secret Communities (Gizli Topluluklar Sözlüğü)* Neden Pub., Istanbul 2005, p. 38

27   Freke, Timothy & Gandy, Peter r.w., p. 380

28   Ada, Ural - *Cultural Origin of Turks (Türklerin Kültür Kökeni)* HKEMBL Pub. Istanbul 2006, p. 258

29   Churchward J., r.w., p. 55

30   Obermeier Siegfried, - *Did Jesus die in Kashmir? (İsa Keşmir'de mi Öldü?)*, RM Pub., Istanbul 1996, p. 30

31   Obermeier P., r.w., p. 52

32   Baigent M./Leigh R., r.w.,p. 319

33   *Tibetan Bible (Tibet İncili)*- Itil Pub., Istanbul 2004, Back Cover Text

34   *Tibetan Bible (Tibet İncili)*- Itil Pub., Istanbul 2004, p. 20

35   *Tibetan Bible (Tibet İncili)*- Itil Pub., Istanbul 2004, p. 23

36   *Tibetan Bible (Tibet İncili)*- Itil Pub., Istanbul 2004, p. 26

37   *Tibetan Bible (Tibet İncili)*- Itil Pub., Istanbul 2004, p. 36

38   Baigent M./Leigh R., r.w., p. 324

39   Nauodon Paul, - *Freemasonry in History and Present (Tarihte ve Günümüze Masonluk)*, Varlık Pub., Istanbul 1968, p. 122

40   Baigent M./Leigh R., r.w., p. 271

41   Baigent M/Leigh R., r.w., p. 273

42   Baigent M/Leigh R., r.w., p. 343

43   Freke, Timothy & Gandy, Peter r.w., p. 165

44   Baigent M/Leigh R., r.w., p. 310

45   Baigent M/Leigh R., r.w., p. 350

46   Freke, Timothy & Gandy, Peter - r.w., p. 167

47   Freke, Timothy & Gandy, Peter - r.w., p. 140

48   Freke, Timothy & Gandy, Peter - r.w., p. 139

49   Baigent M./Leigh R., r.w., p. 303

50   Freke, Timothy & Gandy, Peter r.w., p. 222

51   Freke, Timothy & Gandy, Peter r.w., p. 18

52   Obermeier P., r.w., p. 137

53   Obermeier P., r.w., p. 165

54   Obermeier P., r.w., p. 156

55   Baigent M./Leigh R., r.w., p. 378

56   Freke, Timothy & Gandy, Peter r.w., p. 229

57   Baigent M./Leigh R., r.w., p. 381

58   Baigent M./Leigh R., r.w., p. 383

59   Baigent Michael/Leigh Richard, - *Temple and Lodge (Mabet ve Loca)*, Emre Pub., Istanbul 2000, p. 147

60   Naudon, Paul - *The Roots of Freemasonry (Masonluğun Kökenleri)* Homer Pub., Istanbul 2007, p. 45

61   Naudon Paul, *Freemasonry in History and Present (Tarihte ve Günümüze Masonluk)*, p. 28

62   Akin Asım, - *Freemasonry Throughout History (Tarih Boyunca Masonluk)*, Hacettepe Pub., Ankara, p. 136.

63   Ulansey David, - *Origin of Mitras Mysteries (Mitras Gizlerinin Kökeni)*, Arkeoloji ve Sanat Pub., Istanbul 1998, p. 15

64   Ulansey D., r.w., p. 48

65   Signier, J. F. / Thomazo, R., r.w., p. 27

66   Freke, Timothy & Gandy, Peter r.w., p. 75

67   Akin A., r.w., p. 74

68   Ulansey D., r.w., p. 60

69   Ulansey D., r.w., p. 50

70   Ulansey D., r.w., p. 82

71   Ulansey D., r.w., p. 83

72   Ulansey D., r.w., p. 85

73   Ulansey D., r.w., p. 96

74   Baigent M./Leigh R., r.w., p. 369

75   Baigent M./Leigh R., r.w., p. 370

76   Baigent M./Leigh R., r.w., p. 371

77   Erentay İ., r.w., p. 73

78   Altındal, Aytunç - *Which Jesus? (Hangi Isa?)* Destek Pub., Ankara 2006, p. 99

79   Freke, Timothy & Gandy, Peter - r.w., p. 328

80   Erentay İ., r.w., p. 75.

81   Obermeier P., r.w., p. 14.

82   Altındal, Aytunç - *Brotherhood of Rose and Cross (Gül ve Haç Kardeşliği)* Alfa Pub., Istanbul, 2004, p. 33

83   Freke, Timothy & Gandy, Peter - r.w., p. 114

CHAPTER VIII

ISLAM AND ANAGOGICS

In examining Moses and the Jewish Esotericism, we saw that some of the Saabian religious people living in Mesopotamia and especially in the Harran Plain had been expelled from the society due to the call of their leader Abraham to return to Monotheistic belief, and had emigrated to Egypt. Ismael, the son of Abraham born of a concubine and a small group have been distanced from the group due to the great reaction of Sarah, wife of Abraham. Sarah, as the heir of leadership of the people, has send Ismael and his friends to exile to the deserts of Arabia to prevent him from claiming inheritance in the future, and only allowed her rightful son Ishak to remain behind.

Hajjar and her son Ismael were obliged to abandon the house of Abraham to live near the source of the Shur. According to the Qurayshlars, this area is where Mecca and Zemzem water is located.[1] Ismael, a Saabism believer, settled in the southern shore of the Arabian Peninsula and established the first pillar of the Yemeni Nation State. Dams and waterways were built as a result of intensive works of this people who controlled a significant part of the Arabian Peninsula in a short period of time. The Saban rule built the Maghreb Wall and made the land cultivable. The desert was transformed into green, and several temples were built, which were the basis of Saabi belief in the nature of a sun cult. And Kaaba, being one of those temples, possibly the most important one for being built for the sun.[2]

The Babylonian inscriptions from two thousand B.C., indicate that the Meagan people had lived in Mesopotamia. After the collapse of the first Bablionian State in 18th century B.C., the Meagans by moving south of Arabia, have established Main State. The Main inscriptions found in Yemen have indicated that, the Saba state established in 700s B.C. and continued in existence until the year 115, was a trading state just as the Phoenicians, that the expansion of the state was of trade and not of wars, and that monarchs of the Sabas called 'Mekrup' or 'Mukarrip' were in fact Priest-King. The same inscriptions show that Saba religious beliefs are worships to celestial bodies. The worshipped gods are, Shems the Sun God, Sin the Moon God, Ashtar the Venus God, Nekruh the Mars God and so on. However, according to Abraham, the idols representing these gods themselves are not gods but merely symbols of the Almighty Creator God.[3] Hadj visits are made certain periods of the year to almost 100 mosques established for these Gods; and each one is tauted and scarification takes place. Kaaba is one of those places and is dedicated to the God of Sun. The God of Sun is the Supreme God as the first cause and creator of all things. Everything is at his command and is subject to him. In other words, the Sabbath's religion is a monotheistic religion. Other gods are secondary beings that he has created and are under his command.

The Yemen Sabas are the branch of the believers of the supreme god Allah symbolized by the sun.[4] Hacer and Ishmael were he first ones leaving in Egypt from the group which was separated from the Saabs with Abraham and moved to Yemen, and later Esen having been deprived of the heritage by Yakoup, joined Ishmael with all his followers. Esev marries Ishmael's daughter Mikale and the faith of Abraham begins to spread steadily.[5] The Saab Meagan people of the region worship a great number of idols, however with the influence of Ismael, they embrace the idea that God is an absolute force over all these idols. Yet they continue to place second degree gods they believe that they will intercede with Allah, because they conceive of Allah as a passive force.[6] God is the Supreme Being. However, since Allah is far from them, they pray to lower-ranking gods such as Lat, Menat, Uzza, Hubel, and they pray directly to Allah when they do not receive help from them.[7] The Greek historian Herodotus says that one of these idols is in the Kaaba and is called "'El-ilat'. In ancient Mesopotamia, 'Al', 'El', 'Il' indicate divinity. Al-ilahat is the Sun god. The name Harranans give to this God is 'Alla'. When Abraham said that only Alla should be worshiped, he pointed to the Sun god. His son Ismael and his successors followed the same path and argued that only 'Allah' should be worshiped. This is the truth behind the construction of the Kaaba as a sun temple. 'Al' is height in Sumer language, 'Elu' is the most supreme in Akhat, and 'Ali' means supreme in Arabic. The names of the 4 angels in the heavenly religions are Azrael, Gabriel, Israfel and Michael, and the el ending of the names is the expression of their divinity.[8]

After the destruction of the dams that the locals called the Arabul Baide (Arabs from the North) and as a result of the great drought, migration towards the oasis took place and commercial princedoms such as Mecca, Taif and Medina around the temples emerged.[9] The family of the Prophet Muhammad were the priests controlling the rule of the Sun Temple and the Kaaba for generations. The family of Muhammed and the religious faith they advocated were called 'Hanif Religion' meaning 'Monotheistic Believers'.[10]

The Qurayshlars tell us that they are descendants of the Ishmaels. After Ishmael settled in Hijaz, he married a Sami woman from the Churham tribe and built the Kaaba with his father Abraham. The Arab legends say that the first Kaaba was built by Adam, and that this first Kaaba was destroyed by the Great Flood and the second was built by Abraham and Ishmael at the same place.[11] In the first construction of the Kaaba, there are no ceilings, thresholds, windows, gates as in the ancient Mu temples. Kuyas bin Klab, from the Ismael family, built a new building from palm trees, covered with tannery lumber, destroying the old building during the guard duty of the Kaaba. For the first time, the veil of Kaaba is covered during the during the period of one Saba-Himyer King Esad Thuba, of Ismael descendant. Throughout history the care of the Kaaba has been in the hands of the Abrahams.[12]

Turning seven times around the Kaaba (Tavaf) is an ancient worshiping method. The tavaf of Kaaba has been is existence since Ismael. The name of this worship is called 'Hajj'. It is imperative for the Hajj to wear a two-piece dress made of seamless white fabric.[13] for the purpose of protecting the Kaaba, Abraham and his sons have established an anagogic organization under the name of 'The Order of the Kaaba'.[14] The roots of the Yemen Saba rulers and the ancestors of Muhammed are based on this organization.

As a matter of fact, Muhammed, whose family protected the Kaaba for centuries, is said to have been an initiate of Knight like sect in charge of securing the Kaaba. The aim of the Kaaba cult founded by Abraham is to protect the faith of a monotheistic religion. The believers of this religion in Hicaz are called Hanif Religous Priests.[15] Muhammad was a student of a Hanif religious priest named Bin Kashi in Mecca when he was thirty years old and learned from him for many years. Muhammad is also said to have been a teacher of some Hanif religious students before he started to spread the Islam religion. Ebru Bekir and Ali are among these students.[16] Ez Zubayr, one of the uncles of Muhammed, in order to prevent conflicts between the tribes during the Hajj period, to develop the trade and to protect the peace, has founded the organization of 'Hilful Fudul' (Allah's

Peace Months). Hilful Fudul, an organization similar to the Christian Knight Sects and based on the Sabbath of Abraham's roots, was made up of those who vowed to defend the oppressed against the cruel. The Hilful Fudul oath text reads: 'From now on, we shall not leave anyone who is under persecution, regardless of being local or not, in Mecca. We shall never allow persecution. We shall be with the oppressed until the right of the oppressors is received. Until there is no water left in the seas to even soak a piece of hair, and until the Sebir Mountain in wiped from the face of earth, we shall stand by our decision.' All the initiates members are believers of the Hanif religion. In addition to the art of war, the members are also given the teachings of Hanif religion. The family of Muhammad, Beni Hashim, the family of Muhammad's mother, Beni Zühre, the family of Abu Bakr, Beni Teym, the relative family of Beni Muttalip, constitute the backbone of this organization. Muhammed nicknamed 'El Emin' among the people of Mecca, is known to be frequently stating of him being proud to be a member of this organization. When Muhammad was asked about his opinion about Hilfül Füdul after the prophethood, he said, 'If I am invited to such a contract today, no doubt I shall oblige.'[17]

The Hashemites, the family of Muhammad, have been carrying on the duty of guarding the Kaaba for centuries. Grandfather Abdülmüttalip, who took care of Muhammad after his father Abdullah's death, was taking care in the administration of the Kaaba. Upon his death, the sacred duties of the Kaaba and the care of Muhammad remained in his uncle Abu Talib.[18] Abdulmuttalip was one of the ten of the Makkah oligarchs and the head of the Kaaba. However, Muhammad's father, Abdullah, was not the first son of Abdulmuttalip. For this reason, he had no say in the administration.[19] In Arabic, the word Abd means 'servant'. Abdullah means 'the servant of God', 'the worshiper of God'. Muhammad's father's name is another indication that his family is of Hanif religion.[20]

Varaka bin Nevfel, the son of uncle of Hatice, wife of Muhammed, and Ubeydullah bin Jahsh, son of Hatice's uncle, and Zeyd bin Amr, son of Omar's uncle are all believers of Hanif Religion and members of Hilful Fudul organization. During the first years of Islam, Muhammad had tremendous help from this organization, which was a considerable force. In the process of spreading the teachings, the attempts of Muhammad opponents to assassinate him, have been left inert due to the help of the members of this organization. Hilful Fudul member Varaka bin Nevfel, went to Damascus, conducted research on the Christian religion, and translated the Torah and the Bible into Arabic. In the month of Ramadan, Abdulmuttalip used to retreat in Hira cave. Muhammad also continued this tradition and every year he spent the month of Ramadan contemplating in the cave. After this incitement, he was tauting the Kaaba seven times and returning home afterwords. The result of these contemplations were the Quran and the Islam religion.[21] The Qurayshalls call the first Muslims along with Muhammed as 'Sabi'. This word means 'the turncoat, renegade' in Arabic, and in Aramaic language, it means 'washed with water, baptized'. The Sabi of El Shahristan describes as the munificence of Hunefa bound to Prophet Abraham.[22] In the Al'i Imran sura of the Quran is said, 'Abraham was neither a Jew nor a Christian. He was a Hanif and a Muslim'. The terms Hanif and Sabi are used as synonymously in the Quran. Hanif is derived from the word 'Hanpe' (Pagan) in Arabic. The El Yakubi, 'Star worshiper Palestinians' are named as 'Hunafa'. It is said that the Greek Kings, before becoming Christians, were Hunafa and Saabi.

The most important law maker outside the holy book of Islam, are the principles of the Hanif religion. The practice of the circumcision of a child, the burying of those who believe that they will be resurrected after death, three obligatory prayers and seven prayers, pre-prayer length ablution applications are all practices of the Hanif Religion. These practices have been passed on to Islam by preserving some and giving new formats to some also. It is known that Muhammad prayed three times a day, morning, noon and night before Islam made praying 5 times a day obligatory. It is known that Hanifs usually pray three times a day, and in some cases seven times a day.[23]

The Saab words such as Allah, Rahman, Quran, Furkan, angel, human, book, Adam, Eve, Nebi, Savm (fasting), Salat (prayer) passed on to Arabic show the influence of Saabs over Islam.[24] For this reason, although it has become very different over time, due to the first source being esoteric, the traces of this teaching are frequently found in Islam. The reason behind the emergence of a large number of Anagogic sects in Islam is that, there is a teaching of the Anagogic at the root of the system of thoughts on which religion is based. All the Anagogic sects in Islam, have found themselves in the holy book, the Qur'an, and the Hanife faith before that. However, the Orthodox believers of the religion, have always tried to annihilate such ideas by declaring them as heresy, as it happened to Islam and other Esoteric origin beliefs.

The next encounter of Islam with the esoteric doctrine came to fruition was during the Egypt's conquest by the Muslim forces. While Islam began to spread out of the Arabian Peninsula and throughout the Middle East, part of the people in Egypt were Christians, partly Jewish, but the vast majority were of the ancient polytheistic religionists. Though Osiris Temple was destroyed and most of the priests had moved to Jerusalem; however, Esoteric doctrine continued to exist from generation to generation. The main source of the doctrine was the New Platonist Alexandria School in Alexandria, which continued to exist despite everything. Far from being a powerful state for a long time, Egypt surrendered to the powerful Islamic armies without much resistance. The public was offered two options; 'Either be Muslim, or consent to being killed by the sword' ... They did not have the luxury of protecting their religion like the Christians or the Jews. Because in the eyes of the Muslims, they were pagan infidels that had to be converted on the path to God. They had no other choice, they became Muslims.[25]

In Egypt, concurred during the Khalifa Omar period, the first thing the Muslims did was to demolish the Alexandria School and to burn down the Alexandria Library which has been collected for centuries and contained the art works from the previous fires. There was only one thing to do for the philosopher of the school: to look like a Muslim, to provide an Islamic cover for their teachings. There was the only thing they could do: For this, philosophers benefited from the opposition of Ali Sect within Islam and thus succeeded in getting a little bit out of the strict rules of Islam. Because of the caliphate claims, they stood by the prophet's son-in-law, Ali, who was in confrontation with Omar. In addition, Ali was the representative of the ancient Hanif religion and Anagogic school within Islam. For this reason, he was closer to them. These philosophers brought an entirely different dimension to Islam under the appearance of Ali's followers.[26]

The orthodox Sunni viewpoint imposed by the Islamic religion changed within the Ismaeli, Shiite and Alevism texture. The creation of worship left its place in the union of God-universe-human triune. This situation was immediately referred to as heresy by the Sunni Muslims. But there was nothing they could do. They were the followers of the Prophet's mother-in-law, and they were all Muslim in appearance. This form of belief has spread among the forcibly made Muslims by Arabs so much that Zoroastrian Iranians, Egyptian Fatimans and Shamanist Turks, whose ideas are not similar to each other at all, are gathered under the same patronage of Ali. Although all seem to be pro

Ali, this is the truth where Shi'ism resembles with Alevism, Anagogism and Druzhism. Zarathustra followers have become members of the Fatimid, Ismaeli, Druze, or some other Western sects of Shia.

Let's go back to Anagogism to examine later the role of Shamanist Turks in Islam.

The members of the Alexandria School, who seem to accept Islam, immediately began to spread the works of Greek philosophers, especially Pythagorean and Plato, in the Islamic world. The philosophers who are well informed of the benefits of the Quran, say that 'One of God's attributes is Knowledge. Therefore, we the closest people to God are the scholars.' they found a shield for them and found the opportunity to spread their teachings more comfortably within these contexts. From these philosophers, Veysel Karani was raised to such a degree that there was even a rumor that was the teacher of the prophet.[27]

Du'l Nun, a 9th century representative of the School of Alexandria, is known as a philosopher who brought Greek philosophy into Islam. Tustari, another Egyptian philosopher, also went from Egypt to Basra and was the founder of the Sufi doctrine.[28] The philosopher, Tustari, was the first to say that Muhammad, was created as a light of light before all beings by God, and that those who perform sacred works in this world shall be united with Allah. He is the first to use the important concepts in mysticism such as Nur-el Yakin, Ilm-el Yakin, Ayn-el Yakin and Hakk-el Yakin. Like Tustari, many philosophers from the Alexandria School have spread to the Islamic world, particularly Harran, Basra and Baghdad, and have begun to spread their views of the West.

The effects of the new Platonist philosophers continued, spreading throughout generations. Many people and sects were affected by their views. The philosophers gave this flow the name of Sufism and Sufi to themselves. Some sources suggest that the word Sufi originated from the clothing that these philosophers wore. This, however, has been adapted by Sunni Muslims to humiliate philosophers, the most powerful scholars of the time, and to despise Esoteric teachings. The claim that the name of the Sufis comes from the so-called Suf clothing is totally invalid. What philosophical school until today has received the name of the dress the disciples wore? On the contrary, the Sufi word is the source of this thought movement of the Greek philosophy, and that the evidence of its roots is in Pythagoras and Plato. In Greek, the word Sofos means devine-wisdom or the Wise One (Kamil Man). The word Sufi coming from the same roots is chosen because of the significance by the supporters of School of Alexandria.[29] Again the words philosophy and philosopher are derived from the same root. These words originated from the combination of 'Pilos' and 'Sofos', which mean love and beauty in Greek. In other words, philosophy is beauty and love led by reason and wisdom. Meanwhile, a group in Greece, just to show how clever and knowledgeable they are, calling themselves 'Sophists' were in fact very conservative and even bigoted which caused the birth of a new word, asceticism (Sofu). Sofu has been the word to describe the extreme fanatics in all religions.

While these developments occurred in Egypt and Sufism spread throughout the whole Islamic world, another source of reaction against Islam emerged in Iran. At that time in Iran, a group called the 'St. Jan Babtis' Christians, who believed in the Yuanna Bible as well as the Zoroastrian beliefs, were living.[30] The Muslim invaders called all of the groups of Iranian people who opposed them as 'the outsiders'. The outsiders and the St. Jan Babtis' Christians, although seemed to accept Islam within time, were a leading source of Ismailism spreading in Iran and of the Mausoleum movement that emerged in the 10th century. The outsiders argued that Muhammad was a sacred word, in other words, a reincarnation of Jesus. The outsiders, who saw the Arctic star as a symbol of tolerance and worshiped a God trinity called 'Nubuka', were ruled by a parliament of three hundred priests, called

'Ahyar', resembling the Three Pillar House of Pythagoras. And the seven-man government chosen within Ahyar was also called 'Abrar'.

The Sufis were very influential in Egypt, as well as in Mesopotamia. Resembling the ancient Babylon School, a powerful 'Ihvan-i Sefa' Sufi center had established.[31] Ihvan-i Sefa meaning the 'brethren of purity and cleanliness', united the Hanif, Ancient Greek, Persian and Indian Anagogic doctrines and created and encyclopedia style texts. According to Ihvan-i Sefa members, Muhammed came to tell the people the Anagogic message written in the Quran. Ihvan-i Sefa, which means 'Purity Brothers' is divided into four groups; Princes, merchants, scholars and artists. The initiation first begins with 'artisan'; after forming rationalism 'administrator'; after being acquainted with the secrets of creation 'truthful' and lastly passes through the 'abdal' stage accepted as being close to the Imam.[32]

Ihvan-i Sefa, who adapted the Pythagorean numbers system to Islam, secretly formed a quadrature degree system.[33] The disciples having been accepted to the association at the age of 15, in the first degree, are taught cleaning of physical matter; in the second degree, to show compassion to people; and in the third degree, they are given lectures on methods of evolution. However, it was believed that the disciples reached Hak (God) on the scale of Wisdom (Kemal), which is the highest grade that can be reached after 50 years of age. According to Ihvan; Prophets such as Abraham, Joseph, Jesus, and Muhammad, as well as philosophers such as Pythagoras, Socrates and Plato, were people who reached the level of the Kamil One.

There are many reasons why people should be 'clean brethren'. They need to freed of the obstacles preventing them from becoming the Kamil (Wise) One, achieve perfection, and they can only be freed of their ignorance with the knowledge of their brothers. According to Ihvan, man's constant acquisition of knowledge is the only means of self evolution. People are born with innate knowledge; however, this knowledge is an abstract knowledge hidden in their soul. This information comes out only through a guide, a teacher. As learning progresses, the souls are purified. Soul is fed by knowledge. There are three kinds of source of knowledge. The first is the senses and the second is the mind. But the mind itself is not enough to obtain the knowledge of God, and here the third source, the intuition, enters the circle. The only way to improve intuition is to acquire knowledge from a competent teacher. The teacher's knowledge is obtained within from the Imam, the Imam's from the Prophets, and their source of knowledge is Allah.[34]

According to Ihvan, philosophical sciences are divided in four; 1. Mathematics; 2. Logic; 3. Nature; and 4. Theology.

Ihvan, who states 'Philosophy starts with knowledge of mathematics, mathematics begins with knowledge of the characteristics of numbers', has given the teachings of geometry followed by mathematics, and then logic, physics and metaphysical to his followers. Pythagoras, who is regarded as the creator of the Science of Numbers by Ihvan, is the 'Muallim-i Ekber' meaning the most supreme teacher. According to Ihvan, the origin of beings depends on the nature of the numbers. The science of numbers is the foundation of all sciences, and the essence of wisdom. For this reason, Ihvan who has received the Pythagorean teachings through the Saabs, is called the 'New Pythagorian'.[35]

According to Ihvan, whose system is based on quaternions, the first four numbers are the basic and base numbers that are based on the entire universe. All other numbers are derived from one, two, three and four numbers. One is Almighty God. Two is the First Mind that emerged from it, and three is the Universal Spirit, which is the sort of combination of one and the other. The number four represent the first material created, hence the Divine Justice, the Universe. Within the natural order, there is a quadruple rating;

1. Creator; 2. Universal Mind, 3. Universal Spirit, and 4. First Matter.

Thanks to the numbers, it is possible to understand the harmony that exists within the world and to connect multitude unity, that is to say. The relation of God to the universe is the relation of the number one with the other numbers. For this reason, numbers are a path that leads people to understanding of unity. Ihvan has explained the geometrical shapes as concentric numbers and accepted the geometric forms as a sign of unity. According to Ihvan, triangular harmony is the symbol of square persistence.

Ivan-i Safa explains the first nine numbers as follows:

1. God: He is eternal and everlasting.
2. Mind: Has two types; one of creation and one of subsequently acquired.
3. Spirit: Has three types; Vegetal, animal and human.
4. Matter: Has four types; First substance, ash, physical substance and hand product substance.
5. Nature: Has five types; Semantic Nature and natures that are connected to the four elements.
6. Object: Has six directions; Up, down, front, rear, right, and left.
7. Sky: Has seven planets.
8. Elements: Have eight qualities. It is made of the combination of four qualities by two; Soil: Cold and dry; Water: Cold and humid; Air: Hot and humid; Fire: Hot and dry.
9. World Existance: Minerals, plants and animals, each consisting of three parts.[36]

Ihvan-i-Safa has adopted the Theory of Emanation (Sudur). According to Ihvan, the universe has emanated from God, however not directly. There is a spiritual hierarchy among mediators. The first thing God created is the First Mind. From this mind ore, the Külli Nafs (universal soul) was born, and the first matter came to the existence from this universal spirit. The first matter has given birth to the second, and thus the universe has come to existence. For this reason, the whole universe is in love with its creator and constantly looking for it.

Ihvan has a liberal understanding of religion. He advises his followers not to be prejudiced in any religion. However, the members must definitely choose a religion. The worst religion is better than no religion. Atheism is never acceptable. For their own sake, for being the last religion, Islam is the best religion. Let's follow Ihvan's views on this and other issues from his own documentations:

'It is necessary for our brothers and sisters not to front just to one science and to just one book, and not to have interest in just one sect; for our vision and sect covers all religions and sciences. O brother; Know that we are not hiding our secrets because we are afraid of the sultans of the earth or that we are disturbed by the people. We hide our secrets to protect the guidelines that God has given us. Indeed, God has given such an advice to Holy Messiah: 'do not talk of wisdom next to someone unworthy, you would be punishing wisdom itself.' Do not hesitate to give wisdom to the competent, for this time, you shall be punishing the competent. 'We are not asking for the reigns of the world, but for the reigns of the heavens. In this world, we are the servants under the captivity of nature. The cooperation between the people of the world is of the physical forces. The cooperation between our brothers on the other hand, are the work of religion and the demands of the hereafter, which can only be achieved through knowledge and ingenuity. It is also suitable for those seeking religion and worship. Our enrollment includes everything that will enable us to reclaim humanity in this world, and to ensure that in the Hereafter it will provide for its happiness and salvation.

Man should try to resemble Allah as much as he can. Philosophy is a tool that brings the elite people on earth closer to the Supreme Creator. With philosophy, man realizes his virtues. The start of philosophy is love for sciences; the middle, knowing the truths of the beings in terms of human power; and the end is to have the act and the thought that is required by the sciences. The prophets are the messenger between Allah and those created; the scholars are the heirs of the prophets; and the philosophers are the most virtuous of scholars.

A philosopher must have seven attributes in himself: 1. Things he does must be wise.2. His arts should be enough and competent.3. His words must be true, 4. His moral beautiful, 5. His opinions correct, 6. His amber clean, and 7. His knowledge should be true.

'O brother; know that serial science with a prophet and philosophical sciences are both divine. Their purpose is one and their disputes are in the details. The ultimate goal in philosophy is to resemble God as much as possible. To achieve this, one must have the following four qualities: 1. Know the truths of the beings, 2. Believe in the right views, 3. Have good morals, 4. Have clean and beautiful actions. After all, the purpose of all this is to purify the soul and to reach a state of being the wise one.[37]

During the Abbass period, Baghdad becoming the capital of the Islamic world led to the spread of Sufis in the whole Muslim world. The Karami sect, in which the Sufi leaders are members of, set up Tekkes in Jerusalem, as well as in Alexandria, Cairo, Baghdad, Basra, in many cities of Turkistan and in almost every corner of the Gaza Strip.[38] The Shiites, who were openly opposed to the Sunnis, did not escape being defeated after a while, while the Sufis were fighting against the strict supporters of Orthodox Sunni Muslims in a very rational and secret warfare. In contrast, the persecution and oppression they imposed during the reign of the caused the forced Muslims to engage in hatred against Sunnis. This hatred has reached its peak with the Ismaili and Fatimid revolts.

The Ismael movement is a derivative of the Ali opposition movement, which is an Islamic opposition movement. Following Muhammad's death, Hanifs, the pro-Batinism group of the new religion, wanted the election of the son-in-law, Ali, but the adoption of the Sunni majority led to the election of AbuBakr caliph. The followers of Ali did not accept the caliphate of Omar and Osman too, and after Ali's short and interrupted caliphate, the slaughter of his sons, drove Islam into a day-to-day division and conflict. The Ismael movement also became the organization of the Anagogic's who accepted Ismael as Imam, the son of Cafer Sadik, who came from the descendant of Zeynelabidin, the grandson of Ali who was saved from the massacre. The Ismael movement and other Anagogic schools, have accepted the Islam religion through being Ali supporters. However, the general attitude of these schools is nothing more than the expression of different beliefs and ideologies, which do not accept the Orthodox Sunni system of Muslims in their efforts to maintain their own beliefs within the Muslim world. Indeed, the philosophical and organizational dimension of the Ismael movement's teaching clearly demonstrates that Saabi beliefs, Neo Platonism and Hermeticism, are briefly based on the teachings of Babylon and Pythagorean teachings and are a continuation of the Anagogic schools that existed until that day.

Sunni rulers accepted that after the murder of two of Ali's sons and many of his followers in Karbala, the only surviving grandson, Zeynelabidin and his followers, are Imams in Shiite sect beliefs. But they were doing it to keep the Shiites under control, and all Imams were puppets in the hands of the administration. The Ismael movement known as the 'Ismailis' was the name given to Karamils, who accepted Ismael as the imam, the son of Imam Cafer Sadiq. The Ismailis on their hand, the Egyptian supporters of Ali were called "Fatimis" because they carried their roots to the daughter of the Prophet's Sunnis, to Ali's wife Fatma.[39]

The goal of the Ismailis was to establish a republic based on the real philosophy, brotherhood and equality of the philosopher Farabi. As the death of Imam Ismael is M.S. 760 A.D., it is believed that the İsmaili sect was also founded in those days. However, it is known that the Ismaili organization based on a 7-degree initiative, Ishmael Sheikh al-Jabel, has began in the period of Abdullah, the son of Meymun.[40]

The first Ismaili State, was founded by Hamat in Lasha, south of the Persian Gulf in 874 A.D.[41] This state, which lasted for about 150 years, was completely secular. In Lasha, there was no fasting, no prayer, and there was not a single mosque. The armies of this state, called the Karmats, led by a parliament, invaded Mecca and took the sacred black stone at Kaaba called 'Hajeri Esved' to Lasha in 929 A.D. Meanwhile, the other branches of the sect spread to the Middle East were not settled; They were being organized in secret as İhvan-ı Safa associations in all major Islamic cities, especially in Baghdad. After a while, the Karmats came to control of Baghdad and all Mesopotamia. The caliph in Baghdad had literally turned into a puppet, and the control was in Lasha. The emergence of the Mutezile movement in Baghdad was in such an environment.[42] The Sufis, benefiting from the absence of the Sunni Islamic authority, have come to discuss all kinds of religious and political ideas. Such that, even the presence of God in the Muslim lands, could be discussed for the first time. In the 10th century, the Baghdad caliphate had to secularize the administration. In addition to many theocratic privileges, the caliphs, even in the name of Friday prayers for instance, gave up a sermon to be read to their name. Requirements such as praying, fasting, and pilgrimage were lifted. The sale of alcoholic beverages was permitted and even allowed to sell pork that was prohibited to be eaten within the framework of Islamic rules. In the mean time, it was declared that women and men were equal.

The Karmats have agreed to replace Hajeri Esved for the former position of the Kaaba upon the succession of the Khanate of Baghdad. In Baghdad, the administration was in the hands of the Sufis, who were based on the Ivana-Safa associations, called 'Umera'.[43] The atmosphere in the capital of Islam found its echoes in many places, from Iran to Turkestan and Andalusia.

In 909 A.D. The Fatimies State of another Ismaili faith was founded in Egypt. Just as Karmets, the Fatimies were were being ruled by a council made up of brethren of the sixth degree of the Ismaili sect. These councils were headed by sheikhs of the seventh degree as head of state.

The Fatimans revived the old Egyptian craftsmen who built the pyramids and temples, and they developed these guilds with a new organization. A tremendous military force, formed by young Ismaili artisans, was created under the name of 'Futuveve', which means 'scouts'.[44] Just as in all other Anagogic organizations, Futuveve also had a degree-based system. The first degree of the 9 degree Futuveve organization was Nazil, the second was Tim Tarik, the third was Meyan Beste grade. The 4th was Deputy Nakip, the 5th Nakip and the 6th degree was Head Nakip, which the most important tasks of these grades, was organizing the military organization and conducting all kinds of ceremonies. The 7th degree was called 'Ahi' meaning brethren.

Futuveve's subsidiary Ahisizm, which became widespread among the Turks, received its name from this source. The organization that took the name of 'Ahis' developed quickly among the Turks in a short time. The tasks of the Ahis in Futuveve were in the position of sheikh assistance. The

8th degree was the level of the sheikhs, each at the head of their own organization. The 9th degree was given just to one person, to the sheikh of all sheikhs, just as it was in the Ismaili organization. The title of the leader of the entire Futuveve organization who was only responsible to the head of state Sheikh al-Jabel, was called 'Sheikhssi'. It was aimed that Futuveve would be a force that could oppose the increasingly strong Sunni religious Seljuks.[45] This organization was later adopted by Sunni Muslims during the Selahattin Ayyubi period and the Sunnis implemented the organization with the same name.

As in other anagogic belief organizations, discretion was essential and the oath would not be broken under torture. In Ismaili cult, it was believed that the Imam was the manifestation of God on earth. Sheikh al-Jabel (Sheikh of Nature), leader of the sect, came from the line of Imams. The name of the sacred book of İsmailis was Umm el Kitab (Main Book) and this book was the main source of the ihvan-i Safa teachings:

According to İsmailism, heaven and earth are made up of seven layers.[46] For this reason, perfection in the sect is reached with the 7th and the last degree. It is based on the belief that it is only given to Sheikh al-Jabel, for he is the perfection and God. Other Ismailians could reach up to the 6th degree. Meaning, they could only approach perfection, but they would fail to get it when they're alive.

The Ismailians believed that God was a Supreme Being, a mere light, that all the souls that had emerged from him would return to him. According to them, while the spirits of those who could have received the sixth degree, had access to the happiness of returning to God after death, the souls of lower-ranking siblings and ordinary people would continue to suffer in the world, passing through body to body. However, it was believed that a brother who not yet completed his mission, would return to earth in the next life of his soul, as being evolved. For the Ismailians, the earth was the very hell itself. For this reason, they did not hesitate to sacrifice themselves on the orders of their sheikhs; because they believed that a better life would be born or if they possessed enough degrees, they would reach God.

This idea lies beneath the assassinations of the Ismaili federal forces against Hasan Sabbah and the Sunni rulers at the expense of their own deaths. Sunni rulers who do not understand the idea of sacrificing their own lives for a better life have assumed that such actions can only be the result of those without conscious. For this reason, people spread rumors that the bodyguards are drugged before their actions and are fooled by a false paradise. Ismaili doctrine argue that the soul is responsible for what they do during the time they are in the body. If you have lived as a good person, the next coming to life will be a higher person and thus all stages will be possible to complete. Heaven and hell are in this world. He who has spent his life happy is in heaven, and the unhappy person is in hell. As claimed in the Qur'an, God has no judicial power. Worshiping such as prayer, fasting, pilgrimage and alms is unnecessary. The first practitioners of the 'ploy' of the Muslim-looking tradition became the Ismailis living in the Sunni communities.[47] The Ismailis also improved the organization of Futuveh and ensured its widespread use with the guild system in all territories conquered by Islamic forces. The Ismaili cult is a kind of continuation of Pythagoreanism. The Ismailis have received the holiness of the number 7, among their views, as well as their white clothing of Pythagoreanism from Saabism which has been influenced by Macedonian Alexander the Great during his occupation of Mesopotamia.

The clothes of the Ismailis are made of a red waistband over a white tunic. This outfit has passed on to the Templar Knights affected by the Ismailis, transformed into a red cross added white tunic.

The Ismaili doctrine contains a 7-level evolution chain. A candidate wishing to become a member of the organization would be taken under examination for a year and accepted by a special ceremony if deemed appropriate. The accepted member called 'believer' would wear a white outfit, and sworn in to obedience and complete discretion. Second-degree owners were called 'The Responsible'. In addition to Islamic religion, other religions were taught to 'The Responsible' and it was demonstrated that the only valid religion is not Islam, but that all religions are directed to the same goal. 'The Responsible' were expected to be in contact with the people who could be candidates in the outside world and to attract them. The duration for a higher rank in this degree was two years. In latter years, the disciples would rise up to the sixth grade as early as a year.

The third degree was called 'Dai's. This degree where discretion and secrecy were taught, the disciples were gradually driven the doctrine of the prophet Mohammed's life and ideas as well as the sect secrets of the seven prophets before him.

The Dais of the 'Talent Gate' degree would investigate those who wish to enter the sect and make decisions. Yet another task of the Dais was to propagating about the sect. The word 'Dai' means 'The Caller' in Arabic. The Dais were responsible for the previous two-grade disciples and would decide among whom should rise to a higher degree. The Dais would work in complete secrecy, and make decisions about the sect during their meetings called 'Mecalis el Hikme'. The newly entered disciples, following their oath, would dress up in their Ismaili outfits. It is essential to keep secrets in hierarchical organization.

The Ismaili teaching targeted individuals, and not masses. For this reason, candidates were carefully selected by Dais. However, only individuals with high educational levels and high moral standards were accepted to the sect. A Dai's intellectual level was to be adequate, and the knowledge on the subject of religions and sects were to be complete. He should have mastered the languages and the traditions in the regions he was assigned to, so that he can adequately represent the Ismaili sect. For this reason, all of Dais became superior philosophers of the period and created valuable philosophical works.[48] In Ismailians, a gradual education system was applied and a gradual sequence of the Anagogic sciences was followed. The most important educational institution teaching anagogic sciences of the era has been the El Ezher University in Cairo.

The forth degree was the 'Dai Ekber' meaning the Great Dai degree. Disciples of the 'Dai Ekber' degree were called 'Father'. They were entitled to enter the Cult through the 'Gate of Truth'. In later years the 'Father' title given in Yesevism and Bektashism is based on this tradition of the Ismaili cult. The Dai Ekbers were the head of all Dais. They ruled the Mecalis el Hikmels.

The degree in which the true secrets of the order began to be given was the fifth grade, called the 'Order of the Cross'. At this stage, the insufficiency of religions including Islam would be taught and the disciples be called 'Zu Massa' meaning 'Sippers'[49]

The sixth degree, called the 'The gate of Truth', was the ultimate truth that an Ismaili could attain. At this stage, the most important secrets of the Doctrine were given, such as the duality existing in the world, the triple qualities of God and the four great powers bringing to the universe, and that all prophets just like in all other religion founders, are just a 'Kamil Ones'. At this point, where the Divine Glory is taught as 'Light', and to reach it, they are obliged to purify their souls and and ascend to the rank of the 'Kamil One'. The Ismailis believed that only the sixth degree members after having lived a perfect life, could reach it when dead.

The seventh degree was the most perfect and had a divine character. Only Sheihk Al Cebel (The Sheihk of Nature) who possesses this degree, is believed to be the manifestation of God on earth. Other titles of the Sheikh, the ruler of all the Ishmais, were Belag-i Azam (Sacred Wise Master) and Namus-ül Ekber (Grand Secret Master).

In Ismailis, religions have always remained as secondary whereas the teachings of Anagogic doctrines have been considered as primary. The teachings have been divided into 12 regions of the world to spread to the known world of those days. These regions were called Jezire (Island); El Arab (Arabia), El Berber (The Berbers), El Rum (Byzantium), El Turk (Turkistan), El Deylem (Iran), El Hazar (Africa), El Habesh (Ethiopia), El Sind (China) and El Sekalibe (Christian Europe). Each region was left to the administration of Hücce (Cells), who were the Chief Dai and who were directly responsible to Dai El Duat.[50] It is highly probable that the Ismailis, had accepted the Grand Master of Tamplier, as a Hücce of El Sekalibe.

Although the Ismailis have continued their influence over the Muslim world for a long time, they have fallen back in the face of the Sunni Seljuks taking control.

After the collapse of the Karmeti State, the Fatimans were first shattered by the attacks of the Crusaders, then by internal rebellions, and finally destroyed by the Sunni forces under the command of Selahattin Ayyubi. The most famous of these was the Alamut Castle under the command of Hasan Sabbah.[51]

Sabbah and his guards were constantly struggled against the Seljuk rule and became a fearful dream of both Arab and Turkish Sunni elders. From 874 A.D. to 1256 A.D., the Ismailis were very active in the Middle East. Their power increased to such an extent in 1164 A.D., the Ismaili Imam, 2nd Hasan, announced that he had removed the shari'ah in the middle of the month of Ramadan. In addition to fasting, prayer and other worshiping obligations have also been announced void. His son, Imam 2. Muhammad continued his system.[52] The obligatory worship required by the Sunni Islamic concept was passed only by the Seljuk Rule's lifting of the Ismaili pressure on the Baghdad caliphate.

After the Seljuk occupation, Hasan Sabbah became the one who was able to maintain the presence as an important force in Iran. Sabbah, alleged to have come from the descendants of the Himeyri kings, who ruled Yemen before Islam, was educated at El Ezher University in Cairo under the auspices of the Fatimid State. Hasan Sabah participated in the Great Cairo Lodge in Egypt, a Kabbalist organization with cadets and secret knowledge that had been passed on since the earliest times of the Old Testament, and after learning the working system of this secret society, he took it as an example for the formation of his Assassin organization.[53]

In 1090, he returned from Egypt to Iran, and with the help of his Ismaili followers, he conquered the Alamut Fortress in Teberistan.[54] Having conquered Alamut, applying a new system that transformed Ismaili disciples into assassins, Sabbah began his attempts to overthrow the Seljuk government with the Abbasi caliphate, and named his disciples 'Assassins'. This word which means 'Protector' or else known as 'Protector of Secrets' in the Arabic language, was misinterpreted by the Sunni Muslims as 'users of hashhiss' (opium) and was garbled as 'Hashhisies' as explained above.

Because of the assassinations they attempted against the Sunni rulers, the same word entered the western languages, as 'Assassins'.[55] The Protector of Secrets of Sabbah, were assassins raised with unlimited obedience through reincarnation. For this reason, the other name of the organization was named 'Fedayiin' (Sacrifiers). Several assassins chosen to frighten the envoy of Seljuk Sultan Melikshah, who had to throw themselves down the castle bastions as well as the assassinations against the rulers at the expense of their lives, caused great repercussions in those days. The Seljuk administration declared Hasan Sabbah and his organization illegal and eliminated thousands of Sabbad's supporters in the cities.

Although the strong Seljuk army under the command of the Vizar (minister) Nizamülmülk, the most prominent enemy of Sabbah, started an attack on İsmailis, the killing of Nizamülmülk by an assassin and the death of Sultan Melikshah, caused the siege to be abolished. Considering this disturbance well, Sabbah, did spread Ismailism in all of Iran, Syria, and especially in all the Turkish states, including Khorasan. Ismailism continued its power at its peek until the death of Hassan Sabbah in 1124.

Taking advantage of the death of Sabbah, minister Kashani ordered the killing of all anagogic believers wherever seen. Again, thousands of Ismailis were sworded. The aim was to eliminate this belief, which was accepted as heretic, from the face of the world. However, the revenge of the Ismailis was also great, and hundreds of Sunni leaders, especially minister Kashani, were killed by the assassins. The issue for the Ismailians was the problem of existence or vanish. Just as the assassins were believed to be non-existent, the assassinations they carried out, forced the Seljuk Sultan to negotiate peace with the Ismailis. Thus, anagogism was officially recognized as a sect and maintained its effective power until the Mongolian conquered Alamut.[56]

Sabbah's assassins, who organized assassinations of the Sunni leaders at the expense of their lives, caused the Crusaders, especially the Templiers, who were allied with the Ismailians to be greatly influenced by them. The history of the Druzes, considered to be the continuation of the Ismailis, states their alliance with Christians and specially with the Templier knights.[57] The Druzes, moving away from the doctrine of the anagogics, towards to the dogma of their founder al-Hakim as God, would wear white just as the Ismailis. According to Druzes, who divided people as clever and ignorant, they are the wise and the rest ignorant. The 'accepted' are called 'Akel'. It is explicitly stated in the rituals of the Druze, called 'Darasin' that they especially hide their true identities and pretend to be Muslims.

Any Druze can be initiated if he wants. The trials are tough. The candidate should be able to learn secret books to be accepted into the 'Wise' category, and to demonstrate their will to achieve perfection. The initiates swear not to reveal any secrets. Additionally, they are to comply with the seven testament of Islamic law. They are; To be honest with each other; To protect and promise of help each other; To give up all previous religious beliefs; To acknowledge only El Hakim and to accept his decisions; To Obey the orders of those he sends; To abide by these orders without exception. To be reincarnated is a belief of the Druze. Souls not reaching perfection should come back to the world over and over again.[58]

Let's take a look at the influence of the Ismailis on the shamanist believer Turks, putting aside to reconsider later the relation between the Ismailis with Templars and its consequences.[59]

References

1. Bulut Faik, - *Democracy in the State of Allah (Allah Devleti'nde Demokrasi)*, Tüm Zamanlar Pub., Istanbul 1993, p. 71

2. Hamidullah Prf. Dr. Muhammad, - *Life of the Prophet of Islam (İslam Peygamberinin Hayatı)*, İrfan Pub., Istanbul 1966, p. 33

3. *Prophet Muhammad and His Life (Hazreti Muhammed ve Hayatı)*, Diyanet İşleri Başkanlığı Pub., Ankara 1966, # 67, p. 15

4. Tabbara Afif Abdülfettah, - *Islam in the Light of Science (İlmin Işığında İslamiyet)*, Istanbul 1977, p. 107

5. Bodley R.C.V, - *The Prophet of God, Mohammed (Tanrı Elçisi Hz. Muhammed)*, Nebioğlu Pub., Istanbul 1943, p. 23

6. Yurdakök Murat, - *Traces of Old Beliefs (Eski İnançlardaki İzler)*, Ankara 1994, p. 3

7. Yurdakök Murat, r.w., p. 27

8. Yurdakök Murat, r.w., p. 22

9. Bulut F., r.w., p. 61

10. Bulut F., r.w., p. 56

11. Bodley R.C.V., r.w., p. 26

12. *Prophet Muhammad and His Life (Hazreti Muhammed ve Hayatı)*, p. 20

13. Bodley R.C.V., r.w., p. 346

14. Şeşen Ramazan, - *History of Harran (Harran Tarihi)*, Diyanet Vakfı Pub., Ankara 1996, p. 41

15. Hamidullah Muhammed, r.w., p. 49

16. Hamidullah M., r.w., p. 36

17. Von Sebottendorf Baron Rudolf, - *Practices of Old Turkish Masons (Eski Türk Masonlarının Uygulamaları)*, Hermes Pub., Istanbul 2006, p. 128

18. Bodley R.C.V., r.w., p. 39

19. Hamidullah Prf. Dr. Muhammad, r.w., p. 32

20.

21. Hamidullah Prf. Dr. Muhammad, r.w., p. 64

22. Yıldırım Remzi, - *Life with Principlesi (İlkeli Hayat)*, Moralite Pub., 2004, p. 113

23. Yurdakök Murat, r.w., p. 81

24. Özbudun Sibel, - *Transformation Dynamics of a Religious Tradition from Hermes to Idris (Hermes'ten İdris'e Bir Dinsel Geleneğin Dönüşüm Dinamikleri)*, Ütopya Pub., Ankara, Ütopya Pub., Ankara 2004, p. 198

25. Bulut F., r.w., p. 101

26. Dursun Turan, - *This is Religion (Din Bu)*, Kaynak Pub., Istanbul, 1991, Vol. 2, p. 52

27. Eyüboğlu İsmet Zeki, - *History of Sufism, Sects and Cults (Tasavvuf, Tarikatlar, Mezhepler Tarihi)*, Der Pub., Istanbul 1990, p. 94

28. Eyüboğlu İ.Z., r.w., p. 5

29. Baldick Julian, - *Mystical Islam (Mistik İslâm)*, Birey Pub., Istanbul., 2002, p. 56

30. Sever Erol, - *Yezidism and the Origin of Yezidism (Yezidilik ve Yezidiliğin Kökeni)*, Berfin Pub., Istanbul 1991, p. 48.

31. Mezaheri Ali, - *The Lives of Muslims in the Middle Ages (Ortaçağda Müslümanların Yaşayışları)*, Varlık Pub., Istanbul 1972, p. 6

32. Mazaheri A., r.w., p. 7.

33. Signier, Jean Francois/Thomazo, Renaud - *Secret Organizations (Gizli Örgütler)* Larousse Oğlak Güzel Kitaplar, Istanbul 2006, p. 41

34. Sarıkavak Doç. Dr. Kazım, - *Urfa and Harran in the History of Thought (Düşünce Tarihinde Urfa ve Harran)*, Diyanet Vakfı Pub., Ankara 1997, p. 112

35. Sarıkavak K, r.w., p. 127

36. Sarıkavak K, r.w., p. 120

37. Sarıkavak K, r.w., p. 124

38   Sarıkavak K, r.w., p. 115

39   Eyüboğlu İ.Z., r.w., p. 385

40   Mazaheri A., r.w., p. 11

41   Eyüboğlu İ.Z., r.w., p. 379

42   Mazaheri A., r.w., p. 119

43   Eyüboğlu İ.Z., r.w., p. 409

44   Mazaheri A., r.w., p. 122

45   Mazaheri A., r.w., p. 133

46   Köprülü Fuad, - *First Sufis in Turkish Literature (Türk Edebiyatında İlk Mutasavvıflar)*, Diyanet İşleri Başkanlığı Pub., Ankara 1984, p. 213

47   Doğrul Ömer Rıza, - *Hasan Sabbah's Heavenly Bodyguards (Hasan Sabbah'in Cennet Fedaileri)*, Can Pub., Konya 1982, p. 18

48   Daftary Farhad, - *The Ismailies, History and Theory (İsmaililer, Tarih ve Kuram)*, Rastlantı Pub., Ankara 2001, p. 368

49   Daftary F., r.w., p. 265.

50   Doğrul Ö.R., r.w., p. 20

51   Daftary F., r.w., p. 262

52   Bulut Faik, - *The Truth of Hasan Sabbah (Hasan Sabbah Gerçeği)*, Berfin Pub., Istanbul 2000, p. 150

53   Dierl Anton Josef, - *Anatolian Alevism (Anadolu Aleviliği)*, Ant Pub., Istanbul 1991, p. 33

54   Benson, Michael, - *Secret Communities Glossary (Gizli Topluluklar Sözlü*ğü) Neden Pub., Istanbul 2005, p. 38

55   Zelyut Rıza, - *Alevism by Essence* (Öz Kaynaklarına Göre Alevilik), Yön Pub., Istanbul 1992, p. 42

56   Eyüboğlu İ.Z., r.w., p. 343

57   Bulut F., r.w., p. 184

58   Daftary F., r.w., p. 235

59   Signier Jean Francois / Thomazo Renaud, r.w., p. 47, 274

CHAPTER IX

SUFIS, ALEVIS, BEKTASHIS

We should examine the belief systems in the Middle East, Anatolia and Central Asia before the Sufis, their representatives among the Turks, the Alevis and the Bektashis who are the followers of the Anagogic doctrine.

How the Sumerian civilization, which is considered to be the oldest known civilizations of Mesopotamia and Anatolia, emerged just like a Maya and Egypt civilizations is a mystery. As mentioned earlier, it is seen that in the Sumerian Royal List, which is the most important document written in cuneiform script, that at least ten kingdoms existed during the pre-flood period and that each of kingdoms continued its existence for 10 to 60 thousand years.[1] It is seen in the Sumerian and its successor, the Babylonian civilization that, Esoteric initiations and secret teachings are constantly being protected by the priests and by the rulers.

Wisdoms such as music, writing, carpentry, iron workmanship and masonry were presented to humanity by the gods, and the organization of the priests called the 'Servants of the Skies' were responsible for the protection of these wisdoms. This organization has transformed into being the Babylonian and Kalda schools in later years. In an inscription found about these schools, where the famous Ziggurats were the pioneers in the construction of, the phrase 'whether a prince or a slave, the door would open to all and all would enter the temple directly. All were equal under the eyes of the Heavenly Father of all. They were truly brothers here'.[2]

King Hammurabi of Babylon, in 1750 B.C. took his famous codes from Shamas the Sun God and announced them to the people, just as Moses' Ten Commandments. In Hammurabi codes, there is mention of privileges granted to architects, sculptors, stone sculptors, and masters of masonry.[3] A tablet found in the Assyrian capital of Ninova, attributed to the Assyrian King, has the following expressions:

"The God of the Clerks has given me the knowledge of the art and gave it as a gift, I have been initiated into the secrets of the writing, and I can even read the tablets written in Assyrian, I understand the enigmatically written words of the days before the flood." The word 'Babylonian' given to the Babylonian School means 'Gate of the Gods' and the word 'Kaldi' given the School of the Kalda also means 'The Watchers of the Stars.'[4]

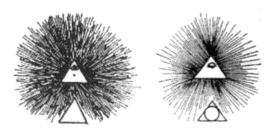

Babilonian and Kalda Cosmic Diagrams

On the cosmic diagrams which are the introductory symbols of the Babylonian and Kalda schools, it is seen that both Babel and Kalda teachings have chosen the 'eye within a triangle' symbol. The Babylonian and Kalda Cosmic Diagrams that had great importance in Sumer, were it was believed that, where astrology was of great importance, the cosmos surrounding the earth and its surroundings was Devine, with the sun being the big light in the center, and of 7 planets, the sky being divided to seven astrological signs, and that the universe around the earth being universal. The Gods of the Earth, the Sky, the Air, and the Water were creative, others were rulers and guardians. Concepts such as circles and dozens were first used in Sumer after the flood. Again, the double headed eagle and the triple use of the moon, sun and the star symbols and the cross symbol known as the Templar Cross are found in the Sumerian tablets. As seen in all the Sun Cultures around the world, the Sumerian beliefs have also changed over time and have been transformed from worshiping the Sun into a polytheistic religion. However, in Harran, known to be a part of the Sumerian civilization, the Saabi belief which is much closer to the first belief, has maintained its existence and after a long period of time, has played an active role in the world of transformation to a monotheist order. In the years of the spread of Islam, in Anatolia and in Mesopotamia, the Saabi beliefs stemming from the Anagogic doctrine were in rule.[5]

Although Christianity was on the forefront on the lands of the Byzantine rule of Anatolia, especially in Eastern Anatolia and around Euphrates, the Saabs were the majority. During the Christian Era, the Harranities were called Heliopolis by the rulers of the Harran Church because of their lack of Christianity and resistance to polytheistic religion. Sabian scientist Sabit Bin Kura has once said, "This city has never been contaminated by Christianity." Urfa on the other hand, became an important center of power with King Abgar's acceptance of Christianity in the 1st century A.D. and began to fight against Harran paganism. In this process, Harran's religious importance had quickly disappeared and thus Urfa was at the forefront. The Harranans were determined to maintain their pagan characteristics during the Islamic period too. The Saabians pay vital importance to baptism in the stream. The Euphrates and Dicle rivers are holy baptisms locations for them that connect the Realm of Gods with the World.[6]

Saabism was a public version of Babylonian School teaching, that dates back to the Uighur Empire. Saabism, which has been the source of all the monotheistic heavenly religions in one way or another, has encountered Pythagoreanism during the conquest of Alexander the Great, and the Saabi doctrine has gained a new pace. In the 4th century B.C. with the invasion of Alexander the Great, the region of Harran and surroundings went under the influence of the Greek culture. With the influence of Hellenism, many historical or mythological personalities of the ancient Greek tradition were also interpreted in the context of Harran's belief. Philosophers and Gods such as Hermes, Solon, Plato and Pythagorean transformed into being one of Harran's Prophets. Ideas of these people were reinterpreted with Saabi faith and by this way adapted into the eastern culture. Especially from the 10th century A.D. onwards, these translations, interpretations and syntheses also laid the groundwork for a new philosophical tradition.[7]

The Pythagorean doctrine has played a role in the reformation of beliefs that already existed between the Saabs and in the formation of the so-called İsmailism, after the merging of both streams. During the invasion of the region by Alexander the Great, many Greeks settled in the region. Along with the Greek occupation, The Greek doctrines have also reached the region and many philosophical trends, especially Stoicism and Pythagorean doctrine, have begun to be influential on the Saabi religion.

Saabism like Shamanism which we shall examine later, is a Sun Cult that replaced the Sun God accepted as the Supreme God's symbol of the first monotheistic religion of Mu, with itself. The Saabs worshiped the Seven Stars, especially the Sun. These included 'Shamas' the supreme god being the Sun God, his wife the Moon Goddess Sin, Nabu the Mars God, Marduk the Jupiter God and Ninutra the Saturn God. All of which are Babylon Gods. The Saabs, along with all these gods and goddesses, regarded Hermes, Pythagor, Orfeus as half gods.[8]

In Saabic, Sin (Moon), Shamas (Sun), Isthar (Venus) and other stars were worshipped not their matter but their souls. The traces of this belief are still seen today in the Yezidies who are the successors of the Saabs.

The most important god in the Saabi faith is Moon God Sin. The gender of Sin was changed from feminen to masculen in an unknown historical period after the great flood. It is often called the Lord, Master of Harran. Titles such as Sin, the Lord of the Gods, or the King of the Gods have been given to him. In the Harran language it is in the form of 'Mar Alahe' which later is transformed to the form of 'Allah'. The other names of Sin are 'Ilahul Alileh' and 'Rabbul Aliheh'. Sin is symbolized with a crescent. Along with Sin, Sin's son, the Sun god Shamas and his daughter the Venus Goddess Ishtar, form a divine trio. Shamas is symbolized by a circle that emits rays, and Ishar is symbolized by a star figure in a circle. All three symbols are still used in Freemasonry. Sin's wife Nigal, the god of fire Nusku, god of literature and wisdom Nabu and many other gods are important gods at secondary level. It appears that the upward facing crescent and one or two star symbols in front of it frequently appear on the coins of Harran. It is observed that because of the belief of the Yemen Sabas, the Crescent entered Islam as a symbol of the religion and that many celestial objects, especially the use of crescent and star together were used as national symbols from the ancient Turk and Asian tribes.[9]

Shamas, the son of the Moon God, is called Rabbul Azim (Almighty Lord). Another name given to the Ishtar is Uzuz and this name has passed as Uzza to the Yemen Sabas. It is mandatory to worship the sun three times a day, at dawn, noon and at sunset. A water purification ceremony is performed before the prayer and south is faced during prayer. There are also three voluntary prayer ceremonies held at certain three periods at night.[10]

According to the narrations circulating among the local people, Harran city is the first settlement center established on earth after the flood. It was built by Kayan the grandson of prophet Noah.[11]

Harran is mentioned in historical sources for the first time in Kultepe and in Hittite tablets in Mari. In these tablets, it is stated that an agreement has been signed at the Moon God Sin's Temple in Harran around 6000 B.C. Sin is the protector God of Harran. It is also understood that in the Hittite tablets, an agreement between the Hittites and the Mittanies is signed around the mid 2000 B.C. It is seen that one of the first sources of the Saabi beliefs is the Luvies. During the Hittite rule, the Luvi beliefs have blended in to ancient Babylon doctrines thus creating the Saabi culture. As a matter of fact, the word 'Saba', which is the name of the Saabian doctrine, means 'baptized in Mandence (to perform ablution)' which is truly of Luvi origin.[12]

There are temples of Saab, which are built after the names of the forms of the stars of the sky. The greatest of these is the 'First Reason Temple'. It is also called the Sun Temple. After that, there are the Mind Temple, Politics Temple, Face Temple and the Naves Temple respectively. They are all in the shape of a circle. The Saturn Temple is in the shape of a square; The Mind Temple square; Star of the Shepherd (Venus) Temple a triangle in the middle of a square; the Mercure Temple is a triangle in the middle of a rectangle; and the Moon Temple is in the shape of an is octagonal. On Sunday, the sun is worshiped, the Moon on Mondays, Mars on Tuesdays, Mercury on Wednesdays, Jupiter on Thursdays, Venus on Fridays, and Saturn on Saturdays. The temples foraged to these planets are built in geometric shapes such as a square, circle, rectangle and a triangle. The temples according to the narratives of the medieval authors such as Mesudi, Sehristani and Dimiskhi are as: 'The Temple of the Sun was square, and the colour of the building was yellow, in the middle of the temple there was a statue decorated with crown and jewels on a six-stepped throne.'; 'The Moon Temple was a pentagon-shaped structure, it was white in colour, with various inscriptions and there was a silver statue sitting on a stepped throne.'; 'The Mars Temple was a rectangular structure. In the middle of this temple there stood a sculpture made of iron, holding a bloody sword in one hand and a be headed 'hanging from the other, sitting on a throne with a stepped stairway.'; 'The Mercury Temple was a triangular structure built on a square floor. There was a sculpture made of clay on a four-step throne.'; 'The Venus Temple was a triangular structure built on a rectangular floor. The building was red colour and there was a sculpture made of copper. During the worship of Venus, various instruments and music were played.'; 'The Jupiter Temple was a green-coloured structure built like a triangle. There was a sculpture in the Temple inside the temple.' The Saturn temple was a hexagon and was built of black stones. There were four sculptures in the temple. These sculptures were a man sitting on an elephant with cattle around him, a man holding an axe in his hand, a man sitting on a nine-stepped throne, and a man made of black stone. Saturn was worshiped in black dresses, while worship of all planets was performed with white clothes.[13]

Between 1950 and 1959, Brice excavations were carried out by archaeologist W.C. Brice in the Moon Temple, which was transformed into a mosque.[14] The Temple has three entrances. On all three entrances, there are stone reliefs dating from the 5th century B.C., believed to have been made during the Babylonian period. These symbols are the Moon God Sin; The Sun God Shamas and an Eye in a Triangle. It seems that the first use of the minarets in the temples also belonged to Saabs. In Saabian literature, the word 'Haran' refers to the supreme and divine country where the souls have reached perfection. Saabians claim that the ancient Egyptians are from the Saab religion. This is the belief that lies beneath of accepting Hermes as a prophet. The Harranians are also called Hermetics. In the Sumerian-Assyrian-Babylonian tradition, the Moon meaning Sin, is the tablet on which the master of knowledge Nebo, wrote the divine commandments on. Nebo is also the inventor of writing and the guardian god of all arts. Nebo is the Sumerian opposite of the Toth figure. The Hermes identify that reached Mesopotamia after the conquest by Alexander the Great, is immediately adopted and honoured by the Harrans.[15]

In Saabism, for each planet, each day of the week, as well as the daily prayer, were reserved for the arrangement of special planetary rites. Sundays are reserved for Sun rituals, Mondays for Moon rituals, Tuesdays for Mars, Wednesdays for Mercury, Thursdays for Jupiter, Fridays for Venus and Saturdays were reserved for Saturn rituals. The names of the days in Latin originated western tongues are nothing more than the reflection of this Sun cult. Forinstance 'Sunday' is the day of the Sun, 'Monday' is the day of the moon and 'Saturday' is the day of Saturn. This type of worship has changed slightly in the face of the Pythagorean doctrine during the Occupation of Alexander the Great, and Saabism begun to believe to a Supreme Being and the six assistants under his rule. In the same period, the anagogic belief forms also settled in Saabism, such as believing that there are four basic elements as air, water, earth and fire, and that plants, animals and lifeless beings have souls, and that the Supreme Being can only not be reached through love. Hereafter for the Saabs, Azmoun, Hermes, Orfeus and Pythagoras are Supreme Spirits and half gods. In Saabism, it is imperative to keep secrets as it is in other anagogic doctrines. The Saabs never give their secrets to those who are not from them. Yezidism today, which is the corrupt continuation of Saabism preserve the same principle of keeping secrets and never accept the foreigners into their community. Saab's secret rituals were conducted in the lounges under the temples dedicated to the planets. These halls were filled with sculptures of planets that had first become worshiped and transformed into symbols after the Pythagorean interaction. A part of Saabism was in the Arabian Peninsula. And part of Saabs who migrated to Egypt, had moved to Yemen. Belkis the Saabian Melike, with whom the Jewish King Solomon was in love with, was one of the queens of the Yemeni Saabs.[16]

The Quran also refers to this Yemeni belief and they are referred to as the monotheistic 'Hanif Religion' believers. It is this branch of Saabism that is effective on Islam with its doctrines. It is expressed in the Islamic, Vajayat al-Ayan and Kutr al-Muhit books that the word Saabi has the same meaning with the word 'Hanif'.[17]

It is stated in the books by the Quraysh tribe that, Muhammed is a Saabian as well as Abraham. During the leave of Abraham from Harran, some of his relatives remained in Harran. As a matter of fackt Ishak, son of Abraham, is sent to Harran for his marriage. Again, Isaac's son Yakub came to Harran and served his uncle and married his daughters. El Dimishk who died in 1327 A.D. writes that the true Saabs are the ones who live in Southern Arabia and who have nothing to do with the Harrans. According to him, the Saabs living in Arabia are believers of monotheistic Hanif, while the Harrans are pagans.[18]

The Harran Saabs do not provide positive for Abraham in their belief systems. To them, Abraham is pervert and a heretic. According to Harrans, Abraham a Saabi by origin, to get rid of an infection on his sexual organ, he had been circumcised and thus has been considered dirty by religion because of a deficiency of an organ.

Abraham, who was removed from society, was also expelled from the temples due to this spiritual non-purity. Abraham, then, destroyed the sculptures of gods in a temple and left the Saabs. It is believed that Abraham later regretted what he did and attempted to sacrifice his son to Saturn in order to be able to return. This request was rejected by the Saabian clergy.[19] In the Qur'an, Saabism is regarded among monotheistic religions.[20]

Behind this lies the reason that many of Islamic rhetoric and worshiping styles come from Saabs. Prayer, fasting, sacrifice and visiting sacred places.

The reason for this is that many of the customs in Islam such as prayer, fasting, pilgrimage, ablution and scarification before prayers are all customs originated from Saabs. While seven praying for seven planets are done in Saabism, this number is reduced to five in Islam. Fasting with the beginning of the month and ending at the beginning of the following month is a tradition of the Saabs long before Islam. In the period of Caliph Memun, Muslim invaders were confronted with Saabs in Harran; however, they were given the right to remain in their own belief systems in the face of giving a certain amount of money to Saab, Christians, and Jews, while characterizing other Sun cult believers as idolatrous and force them to accept Islam. Harran has been conquered by the Muslims in 640 A.D. and the Sin Temple converted to a Mosque. The Saab and Hanif expressions are used to describe the community living in Harran who are reacted to the Magan people.[21]

Because of the pressure by the Christians, the Harrans surrendered to the Islamic armies under the command of Iyad Ibn-i Ganam, who occupied the area, without any difficulty. In the sources of Islamic history, the Byzantine Emperor Julian, who left Christianity and returned to the Mithra religion, is secretly given a Saabi and Hanifi characterization. Saabs considered to be monotheistic, have been shown another place for rebuilding their temples, and the newly built temple has survived until the end of the 11th century. In 1081, this last temple has been destroyed by the Numeyries, and the Saabs expelled from the city.[22]

Ibn Nedimi has said that the Saabs had two important books of religions. 'Malakatu Hermes' (The sayings of Hermes) and 'Safvet el Ukala'.[23]

El Kindi said that he has seen the sacred book of Malakatu Hermes of Saabs and that it is the only book totally in line and appropriate with monotheistic God belief and that no philosopher can find anything missing in this book.

The information given by Tayyib al-Serahsi, student of El Kindi, about Saabs is as follows: 'In order to reach the divine wisdom of the light sphere, it is essential for the individual to work to purify the soul, from the beginning towards the wise. The Divine Being is the master of everything. All being living or lifeless have souls. The souls of the Sun, Moon, and the other five planets are intercessions in the presence of God, and people must purify their souls with these intercessory souls, in the temples appointed to them, through worship for the evolution of their own souls. The divine light must be reached from the living to lifeless to the wise through these intercessory souls.

Fire, water, air and earth are considered sacred. intercessory souls of the sky are called 'Fathers of the above', and the four basic elements are called 'Mothers of the below'. Fathers of the above Influencing the Mothers of the below bring about the Lifeless, the Plants and the Animals called the Three Borns. The Fathers of the above are the ones who affect people's behavior and create the storms, earthquake and all kinds of earthly events. For this reason, people should worship the 7 heavenly powers, the planets and other heavenly elements. That's why astrology has an important place in the Saab culture. Study on astrology and laws of physics has been done and Aristotle's laws of physics are adopted. Thera are three prayer sessions, one when the sun is rising, second when its noon and thirdly at sunset. Women cannot under any circumstances participate in these secret ceremonies. The Pole Star is the Keble. The language used for worship is Syriac. An ablution is taken before any prayer. Circumcision is forbidden. The Saabs oppose circumcision for it does alter the natural structure of the body. They see women's menstruation and sexual relations as reasons for impurity and therefore hold it mandatory to take ablution with water in order to be purified. They definitely clean themselves with water after sexual contact or touching a dead body. It is forbidden to have sexual intercourse with a women during menstruation. Men and women are equal. Monogamy is mandatory. Interrelated marriages are forbidden. Divorce is allowed only with the decision of a priest. One cannot remarry his once divorced wife again. Men and women receive equal inheritance. Every year, fasting is held for 30 days. Sacrifices are held for the Great Fathers. The sacrifice should be carried out by means of cutting the carotid artery. Cattle, sheep and goats can be sacrificed. The meat of an uncut animal is not to be eaten. Pigs, dogs, ravenous birds and pigeon meat are inedible.[24]

The El Bruni, has said for the Saabs that 'They are also called Harranies'. They believe in the unity of God, and that he is not short of any capacity. God has sent prophets to guide those whom he has given the ability to distinguish between good and evil in order to accept himself. Through these prophets, people are ordered to do good and to stay away from evil. The Saabian prophets have said that blessings will be given to those who obey Allah, and those who rebel will be punished. These beliefs are the bases to those who are on the path of Allah and Hanif. Their prophets are Arani, Agathedemon, and Hercules.[25]

Nedimi states that some Saabians see Solon who is said to be the grandfather of platoon on his Matthew reside, as a prophet too. Sehristani says that rebirth is believed in Saabism. In his book of 'El M'lel Vel Nihal' Sehristani states the following for the Saabs: The Saabs are divide into three; The Spiritors, Templers and the Harrans. Some disagreements between the Saabs have occurred. Various branches of Saabism have been established from these divergences. The creator God is one and many. His being, him being eternal and immortal is one. On the other hand, he is many; because people do multiply. Humans are the worthiest, intelligent and virtuous among all living things. God appears in them. He, in their presence becomes a person. In this way, his unity of existence does not disappear. In Harran theology, it is seen that the idea of a Superior Power is emphasized above all divine beings. According to them, this Superior Being is the first cause of all things. This cannot be totally understood or comprehended by people. He is the one that creates and regulates everything. After completing his work, he has chosen to pull himself back and to stay away from people. After his withdrawal to his quarters, his other work, are being carried away by secondary godly beings. These divine beings have emerged within the Supreme Power. The first five beings emerging from them are the mind, soul, order, form and necessity. As can be seen, this definition is an early expression of the philosophy which will after centuries be defined as Deism. In deism, God has created everything, and after completing his work he was drawn to his corner.[26]

Allah is far from creating evil and ugliness. All of this is the result of the sinister relationships of the stars and the blurred unity. The purpose of creation is good and purity. God has created the skies, the objects and the stars therein, and made them the rulers of the world. The heavenly being are called fathers. The Earthly elements are called Mothers and are fire, water, air and soil. The lifeless, plants and the animals born from the unity of the Fathers and Mothers are called The Born. From these Born, if a pure and solid person is formed, as a result, a highly talented personality arises. And in the form of this Wise One, God appears in this world. Every cycle of the world is 36 thousand 425 years. At the end of each revolution, the apocalypse breaks and a new era begins. (It has already been stated that this belief has also been adopted by the Stoics.) Saabs would accept the young people entitled to enter the religion by an initiation held at various Temples. The 'The Book of Five Secrets' of this initiation ceremony, has not reach as far as today. However, it seems that in the work of the Arab philosopher Innu Nedim, there are some references to the acceptance ceremonies of the Secret Rituals. According to this source, the initiation ceremony takes place in the underground rooms of the Secrets Temple. The ceremony is held only for boys and takes seven days. The children definitely do not come out of the Temple for such a period of time. It is also forbidden for the women to see them. The candidate drink a liquid called 'Yusur' from seven cups and wash their eyes with it. The contents of Yusur is not known. They eat from the same cups they eat chicken, bread and salt prepared by the priests. On the last day a sacred wine ceremony takes place. In this seven-day period, candidates are taught in five stages of Secrets.[27]

For the Saabs the soul is not an object but a substance. The body dies. The resurrection or revival of the dead body is unthinkable. The ore, however, passes from one body to another and is born again. The Spirit is born and dies several times in new bodies to reach the Divine Light. Hulul is the form of existence of ore in other bodies. Punishment and reward are in this world, not in another world. Our lives are the events of the ones who have lived before us. The comfort, joy and abundance we experience in this life are the good things of our past life. Troubles, worries and hardship are the punishments of the evils we have experienced in previous lives. That was the case in the past, and it will be the case in the future.[28]

Saab philosophers and scholars such as, Sabit bin Kura, Cabir bin Hayyan, Rabbi Vahshiyye and Abu Cafer el Hazin have played an important role in the translation and development of mathematics, astronomy, medicine, philosophy and natural sciences from Greek to Arabic. In Islamic sources, this philosophy school and its followers are called Deysaniye.

This school which is the continuation of ancient Harran School, at the beginning of the 4th century A.D. became a Christian School under the name of Urfa School, and in 640 A.D. after the Islam religion came to the region, it transformed into a school where archaic interpretation of thoughts of Christians, Saabs, Mani supporters and Muslims' gathered together. In 6 A.D. After the order of closure of the Athens School which he regarded as a Pagan belief center against the Christian religion which was the official state religion, many philosophers and philosophers of the Neo-Platonist movement were settled in Harran and took part in the academy. The Neo-Platonist doctrine had a strong influence over Harran that affected all eastern countries.[29]

Later on, during the invasion of Egypt by the Islamic forces, upon the collapse of the Alexandrian School, some philosophers went on to Harran and continued to teach at the Harran School. Thanks to the participation of the Alexander philosophers, the school has empowered and thanks to the philosophers who passed from Harran to Baghdad and Basra, the Saabian doctrine had an active place in Islam.[30]

Harranian thinkers have emerged from the existence of new schools in the Islamic centers such as Basra, Baghdad, Küfe, Samarkand, Khorasan, Cairo and Kurtuba, for Sufi thinkers to appear in these cities under the name Ihvan-i Safa. In other words, in Harran Sabi belief, 'Hanif' is the name of the wife of Sin, one of the greatest gods, the god of the moon. And the Christians also define the as pagan Harranians as Hanif. The most famous Harran scholar and translator of Greek works to Arabic, Sabit bin Kurra, states his opinion regarding his religion as: 'We are the children and inheritors of the victoriously spread Hanif religion of the world. How happy is who carries his burden for the sake of Saabism. Are not the Saabi chiefs and kings who civilized the world and built cities? Who built the harbors? Who drew the channels? All is built by victorious Saabs. They are the ones who found the art of cleansing the souls, who promoted the art of body-healing, and who equiped the world with civilized institutions and wisdom and with the greatest of the good. If it were not for Khanif religion, the world would be empty and in poverty.' It is known that Abu Sait Sinan, the son of Sabit bin Kurra, went to Horasan in 932 and taught in the Ismaili Khorasan tekke.[31]

Muslim historians who have identified some differences between Harran faith and Yemen belief in the process have used the Saabi word for the Harran worshipers of the stars and Hanif word for the Yemeni Sabbaths of the Abraham descendant who believed in One God.[32]

Hermes/Idris beliefs have great importance in both schools. Hermes was thought of being a prophet as both a divine being and a wisdom teacher by the Saabs. Harrans believed that their religion was taught to them by Hermes.

It is said in the Qur'an that thirty books have been send to prophet Idris (Hermes) after Sit, son of Adam, and that the secrets of the heavens have unveiled to him, and while alive, he has been taken to the skies by Allah. In Hanok's book written in Ethiopian which survived till today, it states that Hanok (Hermes) has seen the heaven and the hell while still alive, and that God allowed him to remain in heaven without surrendering his soul. In the same source, Hanoi is seen as the founder of astrology. According to some Arab sources, Idris is the son of Kabul, not Sit.

The French writer Gerar De Nerval, in his 'Travel to East' book written during his visit to the Ottoman Empire, has written about the Hiram story as known to the Saabs. According to this narrative, Hiram is given the secrets of Freemasonry by his predecessor Enoch (Hanok)/Hermes. These secrets are said to be learned which are passed on from Adam's son Kabul to his son the first blacksmith, Tubal Kain. The etymology of the word Idris show that this name has emerged due to the origin of Arabic DSR which refers to the transfer of information and techniques. For example, the word 'Ders' (study) in Arabic means examination and comprehension. It has also settled to Turkish language as a doctrine. The word 'Idris' can also be described as deepening and the examination of the religious laws.[33]

One of the first sources of the Hermes tradition to reach Islam is the Christian Gnostic 'Copts', which are based on the Hermetic tradition, that conducts Guild activities in Egypt. The Guild system that is passed to Islam through the Copts, who are the precursors of today's Coptic belief, continued its existence for many years, taking the name Futuvve.[34]

The transfer of the teachings of Hermes/Idris in the Islamic world has been made through professional associations such as Futuvve (guilds) and Sufi orders, just like its predecessors. It is seen that the sufi order in the east occasionally occupy the professional associations or the professional organizations in which the local artisans and tradesman come together are themselves of sufi sects. According to Tabari, the patriarch role of craftsmen attributed to Idris is to his craftsmanship. Sohraverdi, who states that Idris is one of the seven pitfalls accepted by the guilds: 'From the time of the Egyptian Hermes, also known as the Idris prophet, to the time of Plato, all the wisdom has had mysterious experiences. Among them the main living sources of are Empedocles, Pythagoras, his student Socrates, and finally his student and the ultimate seal of wisdom Plato. Idris is called Father because he is the first to organize the Wisdom Corpus and many extraordinary pieces of knowledge, has passed the wisdom to his students and has reached to the master degree of the above. All foundations rest on the pillars he has built. His teachings are the bases of the entire Wisdom Structure. That is why these foundations are called the 'Wisdom Columns'.[35]

Muslim historian El Nedim in his famous work, 'Index' states that, Hermes is originally form Babylon, and for several reasons he settled in Egypt, and that he was king of the city, and was buried in a building known as Abu Hermes when he died.[36] This location is later known as the El Harameyn (Double Pyramids - Keops and Kefren). Hermes is buried in one those pyramids and his wife and son in the other. According to Yemen Saabs, the name of the pharaoh who is the son of Hermes, is Sab (Sab ibni-Hermes) and they come the same blood line. During the Egyptian Queen Hachepsut era, was noted that the Yemeni Sabas visited the pyramids for crucifix and Tavaf around both pyramids. It is possible that the Saabian word came from the Pharaoh Sab. The tradition of visiting the sacred place called the Kaaba by Islam still continues today. El Kindi wrote that Saabs went from Harran to the pyramids for crucifix, while El Kajrazi wrote that Saabs believe that in one of the pyramids Hermes is buried and his son Agathodaimon in the other. Markizi also stated that Saabs named the Great Sphinx as 'Ebul Hul' and sacrificed vows. It was believed that Agathodaimon, Hermes and another god-prophet, were teachers of the truth and wisdom. Agathodaimon is a godly being believed to be the teacher of Hermes. The Harrans, like Hermes, accepted him as Egyptian.[37]

The famous Islamic geographer Idris (1100 A.D.) talks about Hermes as: 'Before the flood, there was a building called El-Berba, built by the glorious Hermes, who foresaw that the world would be destroyed by a disaster, but he did not know it would be with water or fire. For this reason, he built a temple surrounded by unburnt soil and filled it with scientific pictures and symbols, even though the earth was burned with fire, tnhewy would survive. He then built a building that was completely waterproofed with stones and stored all the information useful for the people. If the earth would collapse, the soil build would collapse but the stone building will remain intact, protecting the sciences from destruction. Everything happened as Hermes predicted. The title used by the Kaldelians for Hermes is 'Grand Master'. The Arabs too call him as 'Hermes ul Ekber' (Hermes the Great) and El Muselles which also means (Three times great).[38]

Ibn-ul Arabi describes Hermes as the 'Prophet of the Philosophers'. He is also the protective sheikh of the craftsman guilds and of the futuvve. The sayings in the Emerald Plate, whose original form of Hermes Trimegistus is said to have been in a cave and is written in the Phoenician language, are translated first to Syriac and then to Greek. The Emerald Plate which has been translated from Greek to Arabic and has survived present day in the Cabir Collection, includes the following:

'It is the truth. It is without any wrong. It is definite and just. They are like the one above up and down below and they realize something miraculous. And as everything is derived from One thing, everything is derived by one implementation from this One thing. His father is the Sun and mother is the Moon.the wind has carried him in its womb, and the soil has breastfed him. He is the father of all wonders of the Earth. His authority is mighty. If he is to be thrown to Earth, he would separate the earth from fire and the delicate from the rough. With great wisdom, he glides into the sky. He descends again back to earth and unites in himself the strength of the high things and the low things. Thus you have the brightness of the whole world and all darkness shall run away from you.

Just as it is the one of the One, and his father is the sun, the wind blows him in his womb, he sucks the earth, he is the father of all the wonders of the earth, the mighty authority, and he will divide the earth from the fire, and the wicked from the fire, with great wisdom. So that you have the brightness of the whole world and all the darkness will escape you.[39]

Sabit bin Kurra introduced the Pythagorean numerology and arithmetic understanding into the Islam mathematics and ensured the settling of the number mysticism. Number mysticism was later developed by Ihvan-i Safa. Sinan bin Sabit, the son of Sabit bin Kurra, translated Kitabul Hermes, the basic book of Saabism, into Arabic.[40]

The Harranian scientist Teymiye El Harrani (1261-1327 A.D.) is written that, there are Temples and statues in Harran, the home of the Saabs, attributed to the 'First Reason', 'First Mind', 'Self Control', Zuhal, Zühre, Mars, The Sun and the Moon and that the Saabs are divided into two as Hanif Saabs and Polytheistic Saabs, and that prophet Abraham is the Imam of the Hanif Saabs. The beliefs of the Polytheistic Saabs are very similar to the beliefs of Indian polytheists. Teymiye also reports that the Turkish philosopher Abu-nasir al-Farabi (870-950) took lessons from Yuanona bin Haylan, a Saab of Harran. Farabi is among those who lead the Harran school to settle in Baghdad. An important part of the scholars, philosophers and interpreters who brought about the Baghdad School came to Harran from Baghdad. Farabi, a philosopher who influenced the Christian world as much the Islamic world with his thoughts, tried to make a synthesis of Sunni Islamic thoughts with the New Platonic Anagogic philosophy.[41]

According to Farabi, blending his theory of Anagogic being water and his idea of Divine Revelation, God is one and is all. He is a being beyond and above the cosmos. He is before of every being other than himself emerging from himself, and he is the end in terms of being the true purpose of every being. Every being carries a part of him. Matter has appeared from him. He is connected to the cosmos with his enemation The substance that looks as if to end, can also be regarded as eternal because of the ongoing enemation God is the foundation of all existence. From this single and absolute being; first the mind, then the holly spirits, then the human soul, and finally the universe meaning the material realm has emerged. This universe which in essence is a unity and is One, shall surely return to being One again. All have emerged from Allah. According to Farabi, the order of existance is: 1. Allah; 2. The First mind; 3. Active mind; 4. Domination; 5. Apperance; 6. Matter.

Matter is the common essence of four basic elements. The very first thing that emerge from it, is the First Mind. The Active Mind which is the result of the First Mind, is the reason for the existence of the four basic elements meaning the universe. The soul is the existence of the body, and the mind provides the existence of the being of the soul. The soul is from the abstract world and is different from appearance. The soul continues after the body. Active Mind is the result of First Being. To a Kamil Man, where there is nothing left between him and his Active Mind, revelation comes.

Therefore, it can be said that, through the Active Mind, it is the First Reason meaning God that courses revelation to a Kamil man. A Kamil man is an excellent philosopher who uses the Godly mind. Prophets on the other hand, are Kamil (Wise) Ones that inform, provide and warn. Both the prophets and the philosophers have the purpose of showing the truth to the people. According to Farabi, without the creation of the body, the soul alone is not the subject of existence.

After the body is created, the soul is blown into the body through the Active Mind. And after the body is dead, it transforms itself to the afterworld. Rebirth is not the case. On one hand, the Sufis originating from the Egyptian School of Alexandria, and on the other, İsmailism based on Saâfili, have led to the spread of the anagogic belief in the whole of Islamic world. Ismailism has spread among the Shamanist Turks much more rapidly; because there is already an anagogic side to Shamanism. Before moving to Turkistan and the Turkish mystics, it is necessary to examine some other Sufis who have had great influence in the Islamic world. Leading these Sufis, is Hallac-i Mansur, who for stating ‹Enel Hak› (I am God) has been stripped of his skin by the Sunni rulers.[42] Born in the 850s A.D., Mansur is killed by the order of Caliph Mukhtedir in Baghdad. Mansur defended the unity of being that included the God-Cosmos-Men trio. Spending his youth in Cairo, met the descendants of the Alexandria School and adopted their views. Later, he wandered through Turkestan and spread his views to Sufi tekkes.

According to Mansur, the truth is ‘One’. The multitude is the reflection of this ‘One’ in different forms and qualities. The universe and men are not on the out but rather in the ‘One’. For this reason, it is true to say that a person is ‘Enel Hak’. Men is God, a part of God. However, God is not merely men but he is the entire universe.

According to Mansur, the universe is not created, it is a splash of God, a combination of light and love. The word ‘Işk’ he uses, covers both the divine light (ışık) and divine love (aşk).

The creation that all the semantic religions claim is a misinterpretation of existence. Those who lack the power to comprehend the truth, suggest that all beings are separate beings from God. It is only by intuition that it is possible to perceive that this is a mistake that every individual can turn into himself and reveal this intuition. As a result of this self closure, the Divine love awakens, later the Divine Light appears within ones' heart. The real secret is to see God in ones' heart. Mansur who states 'One who knows himself knows God. One who loves himself loves God.' has been described by the Sunnis as a heretic and was first whipped to give up his ideas, later skinned and finally stoned to death by the Sunnis:

'Mansur, 65, was crucified in Baghdad at the Tak Gate Square. Stoning him was allowed. After a session of stoning, whips came into action. Blood began to come out, but it was inadequate, his hands were cut and then his tongue and his eyes were cut off. They brought him down from the crucification and with a blow they beheaded him, but he was parted into two. They cut off his arms and legs, now there were six pieces but he still was dangerous. They burned parts of his body in a big fire, and slammed his ashes into the river Dicle.' The rumour is that, the reason for his vicious murder was the answer he gave to Mansur when asked about the 'secret': 'the word is to be given the competent. So that the secret of the God doesn't become unworthy. To pass on the secret to someone not competent, is to give him a load he can not carry.'[43] Mansur's choice of death for the sake of his own faith, left deep traces among the Sufis, and with his death, and instead of falling back, Sufism greatened.

For centuries, the influence of the Mansur, who combined all thoughts on Human-Universe-God trio, spread throughout all Islamic countries and fled all branches of Islamic mysticism. Especially in Iran, all intellectuals who embraced mysticism in the Turkish poetry were inspired and illuminated by Mansur. Turkish poets such as Yunus Emre, Imaddeddin Nesimi and Iranian poets such as Senai, Attar, Sadi and Camii have followed in his footsteps and brought his opinion to be the center-point of their poetry. The ceremony called 'Dar-ı Mansur' in Bektashism, the instrument that is called 'Nay-ı Mansur' by the Mevlevis continue the memory of Hallac-ı Mansur today.[44]

Another Islamic philosopher that is particularly important in terms of the influence over the Anatolian Sufis is Feradettin Attar.[45] The importance of Attar who is born in 1119 A.D. in Nishapur and has died in 1193 A.D. at the same place, is the work called 'Mahzar-ul Acaib' that contains anagogic views. Because of this work, he has been accused of paganism by the authorities of the period, and under the threat of being killed, he left his country for a period. Taking advantage of the change in the administration, Attar returned to Nishapur and continued to spread his teachings.

According to Attar, who played a very influential role in the spreading of the concept of 'Vahdat-i Vucud' (unity of being) among the Sufis, to exist is to rise from the supreme light of God, to the field of view. Being, is to come out and to return to God. The divine light comes into focus step by step all the way from the most divine to the lowest level. These step make up the various forms of qualified beings. Existence does not mean creation from nothing. It represents the appearance from the non appearance stage. Men is God-identical, a divine being. Among all kinds of beings, the human being is the closest to God, and by these these qualities is the center of the unity of being, 'Vahdat-i Vucud'. The individual will be the reflection of the total will. The soul is immortal. It is from God and shall return to God. The body itself is reflection of soul on earth. The soul shall out wear as many bodies as necessary to in order to evolve and reach God.

In his famous work 'Mahzar-ul Acaib', Attar states that 'God while invisible, wanted to be visible to him because of his love for him. Thus divine appearance began and all kinds of beings were formed. Love is the source of this formation, it is the first reason.' Attar, like all pro anagogic doctrine people, argues that the spirit has matured through various stages and eventually has become God as the Kamil (Wise) One. These views of Attar deeply affected the Anatolian sufis, Yunus Emre and Mevlana.

Ishak al-Kindi, a 9th century philosopher who is also an Anagogic believer, was born in Basra and educated in Baghdad.[46] Kindi too believed that the spirit should be purified for evolution, and like Farabi, has strived to reconcile Anagogic thoughts with Sunni philosophy. But Kindi, arguing that Revelation is beyond reason, rejected the theory of Appearance, and argued that God is the creator out of nothing. Although he accepted the Alim (All Mighty) and Kadir (Creator) attributes of Allah, he has been accused of denying the qualities of Allah by the Sunnis.

Kindi, close to the homiletical movement, argued that objects have an ending, and are not eternal, and that object needed to be created. 'If there is one created, then there must be a Creator. Creator is one, but created ones are many. He is permanent but the rest are variable. As of self, he is perfect, and true One, he is eternal and everlasting. Allah is the first reason. The spirit is the appearance of God as a divine essence and is not related to matter. Even with its temporary unity with the body, it is independent. Once separated from the body, the spirit returns to the world of reason and unites with Allah.'

Another important name for Islamic philosophy is Ibni Sina, who was born in Buhara in 980. Known for his contemptuous view of traditional religiosity and aboriginalism, İbni Sina, with his short symbolic narratives, emerges as one of the most prominent advocates of New Platonicism in the Islamic world.[47] His philosophy which he defines as 'Orientalist Enlightenment' is a structure of thought that is understandable only by high-level elites. Due to his views, he has been accused by many Sufis as well as the Sunnis, as the representative of the Greek philosophy. In addition to his medical studies, Ibni Sina, who studied Zoology and Botany, advocates the immortality of the soul. The body dies, the spirit matures. For a man to distant himself from bodily passions, causes his spiritual perfection to strengthen. When the body dies, the spirit of the Wise One, lives forever next to Almighty Allah.

Known as the most important systematic of the Sufi tradition, Ibni Arabi was born in Seville, Spain, in 1165, moved east in 1202 and died in Damascus in 1240.[48]

Ibn Arabi, who invented a synthesis by combining Platonism with Islamic theology, argues of a single ultimate truth in the whole of a being. The unity of being (Vahdet-i Vucut), sometimes represent El-Hakk (Allah as the essence of all), and sometimes Mahlukat (the created ones). All in the universe is Allah's. However, he cannot in any way degraded even as affinity to the created ones. Allah can also not be held one with the universe which is the total of all parts that create him. There is only one essence in the universe, and that is Allah's himself. Only the Kamil (Wise) One can reach to the truth. The Kamil One, perfecting all the qualities of Allah, is the link between God and the world. Thus, the Kamil One is the true cause of the existence of the universe alone. However, the highest level that can be reached by the Kamil One is not the level of the Unity (Uniqueness) which belong to the Self, but the level of Kemal (Unity with God).

Another Sufi that leads to the recognition of anagogic view's popularization and popularity among the masses is Omer Hayyam, whose thoughts are poetry are still being spoken of by generations.[49]

Hayyam was born in Nishapur in 1050 A.D., the light source of Iran at the time.

Hayyam of artistic soul, chose a different life than the other Sufis. Hayyam, known for his fondness for wine and visiting winery instead of Sufi Tekkes, visited Turkish cities, Semerkant and Isfahan. Although Hayyam worked in algebra, he conveyed his views with his poetry meaning his rubais.

If we are to line up some of the rubais of Hayyam who died in 1122 A.D., there shall be no need for any further word:

'If you knew the secrets of your life,
You would unveil the secrets of death.
Today you a mind, but you know nothing,
What would you know tomorrow without your mind?
There is no other world apart from this world, do not search.
There is no one else but you and I that question, do not search.
Give up the beyonds, do not tire yourself.
What you think exist, does not, do not search.
Some found wisdom in faith and some in religion,
Some found it in science and reason.
Then a voice came from the darkness;
The unwary, the right way is neither this nor that...
I still search since I my birth
The fate, heaven, hell.
My tutor cut it short with his solid knowledge:
Fate, heaven and hell, is all in you.
We worship love, and are not Muslims,
We are tiny ants, and are not Solomon.
We are pale faces wearing oldies,
And not merchants selling seams at the market.
I myself am not existent with my self existence,
Surely am not on this dark path by myself.
My self being is of a different being.
Who am I, where and how am I to be?
I can not cleave the Sun with clay.
I am not to tell the secrets I have come to.
My mind is deep in the sea of thoughts,
I am not to hole a pearl of the sea.
Seventytwo nationalities and similarly same amount of religions.
The only concern of my nation is to love you.
What is infidelity, Islam, mitzvah and sin?
You are the purpose, let no one in between.
I did miss you yesterday, I was over excited,
Climbed up to the place said to be yours.
A voice rose from above the skies:
'Unwary' he said, 'The God you think we are, is you'.

YESEVISM

Another Sufi who is important in terms of the history of the anagogic doctrines, is the Turkish Sufi Ahmet Yesevi who put forth the direction for the ones after him. Before moving on to Yesevi's life and views, it is necessary to take a look at the situation and beliefs of the Central Asian Turks during the years of Islam's expansion. The Central Asian Turks, who are the heirs of the ancient Uighur Empire, were attached to the Shaman religion, a sun cult.[50] According to Shaman religion, which is a distorted expression of Naacal's teachings within thousands of years, the Turks were born of both masculine and feminine expressions of the sun and the moon. The priests of Shamanism, the Shamans, wore red cones during the worship ceremonies of the sun and the moon, play kopuz and drums, and danced. A similar application is seen in the Anatolian Alevis, which is the continuation of Shamanist Turks, and also in the Mevlevis today.

Being a Shaman required a long, incisive path. Shaman candidates were admitted to the priesthood with special ceremonies and, after many years of acquiring their visual secrets, could earn the title of a Shaman. According to Shamanism, everything in the world had a soul and a life. Mountains, lakes, rivers, forests, are always considered alive and trees were considered holy. The Sun and the Moon were the symbols of the great God, the Son of the Black Han, the Sky God 'Ulgen', who was the cause of their existence.[51] The Shamans would close in to themselves in torero to reach to Ulgen the Sky God and to reach a state of ecstatics. The term Shaman came from states of the priests and meant 'one who is ecstatic'.

It was impossible to comprehend the Sky God by reason. Therefore, the Sun and the Moon, as representatives of the Sky God, required to be respected and worshiped. The relationship between humans and nature needed to be treated as careful as the relationship between humans themselves; because the spirit of a stone, tree, or river was not any lower than the spirit of a man. Previously, the symbol of the double-headed eagle we discussed in the Uighur Empire before the flood, is seen to emerge as a result of the recreation of power and force not found in nature, with human mind power and intuition. This symbol deriving by adding one more head to a normal eagle, has increased the ability to see and sense, and the exaggerated ears have increased its hearing. It's one head is related to this world, and the other head to the other world. The relation of the double headed eagle to the both worlds is observed most intensively in the Shamanistic practices. According to the Shamanic tradition, no one who is not eaten by the powerful beings, and is not separated from his flesh, and who does not come back to the world at least twice by the bones being fleshed, can not be a good shaman.

In the legend of 'Er Toshuk' of the Turkish Ilmen tribe, the powerful being that brings Shaman back to the world by eating it, is a double headed eagle. This eagle is so big that the left wing covers the moon and the right wing covers the sun. Since the sun is the symbol of the east and the moon of the west, the two heads of the eagle look at these directions. It hunts in the skies and in the underground (the world beyond) for seven days each. The Shaman candidate hunts 'Er Toshuk' and swallows it. Later by giving it life, brings it back to the world. The aim is to make him a good shaman, to be a communicator between the world of the spirits and the beings of the world. However, the process is not completed. He once again swallows 'Er Toshuk' so that its bones are as strong as steel and that it can no longer be harmed. Er Toshuk, being underground for quite some time, and months after, returns to earth on the back of the eagle and become as a very powerful Shaman. The eagle presents him a feather as a gesture of friendship. From that day Onno all Shamans start using feathers to dispose all troubles, and to protect themselves from the damages of lightnings.

The same tradition is also seen among North American natives. The Yakuts living in Siberia and the double-headed eagle symbols used by North American Indians are identical. Hida Indians accepts the double headed eagle as sacred bird. This symbol found on top of the totems is called Helinga and as in Sumerians, it means the Storm Bird. The name of the double-headed storm bird in the Zuni tribe using the same symbol is called 'Sikyati'. Since the eagle is seen as in relation with the source of light, it is regarded as a symbol of the light of physical and spiritual enlightenment for the North American Indians. At the same time, he is the serpent of the heavenly kingdom. In America there are many double-headed eagle figures found in many tribes, especially the ancient Inca, Aztec, Mayan civilizations. Aztecs and Northern Indian Shamans use whistles and eagle feathers made of eagle bones, just like the Japanese, Mongolian, and Turkish shamans in their Sun Worship rituals. Wings made of eagle feathers are worn, dances are made to remake flying in the sky. Eagle as a sacred bird, is believed to have therapeutic features. One of the two strongest cults in Aztecs is the Panther, the other is the Order of the Eagle Brotherhood. The Brotherhood of the Panther is the lord of the earthly forces and the Eagle Brotherhood is the lord of the spiritual forces. The Aztec emperors sit on thrones covered with eagle feathers because of their spiritual powers.

The birth of the first Shaman is described in the legend of the Bouryat tribe of the Mongols as:

'God sent the eagle to earth to help people, and guard them against diseases, but people did not understand the language that the eagle spoke, so the eagle got a woman as his wife, the woman got pregnant and gave birth to a boy who learned the eagle language from the eagle father and in time learned all the Shamanic knowledge. The child who grew with time became the first great Shaman in the world and also became the father of all the Shamans.'

In Shaman rituals, the eagle symbolizes the Shaman fly to the spiritual world. Symbolically the Shaman falls while dancing and dies. His spirit is carried away towards the skies in a cart pulled by eagles. That the Shaman's dress is winged and decorated with eagle feathers and bones, provides the imaginary flight. A Shaman, wearing as eagle-winged dress, may go to any level of the skies. In Asian mythologies, the eagle is depicted as the symbol of sun. The Shaman, therefore, reaches the sun, the competent symbol of the greatest God. In Central Asian Shamanism, there is a double-headed eagle on top of a pole called the world column. This column is erected in the middle of all settlements. This column, which contains the double-headed eagle called Hamca, meaning 'Master Bird', is accepted as to never decay or be destroyed. This column carries the meaning 'Shall always stand with God's might and power'. It has also been observed that some of the derivatives of this column, called the world stump, the sky pillar or the sky pole, have seven or nine arms. These arms represent the layers of the skies. The sky pols are the cosmic tree. The sky pols are the same as the cosmic life tree. The double-headed eagle figure on the symbol of the tree of life, found in almost every cult of the world, is also called the 'Sky Bird'. The same application is observed in Indian Totems too. The pole of the sky accepted as the foundation of the world, expresses the might and power of God. The double-headed eagle on the top with its large wings, keeps the door between the earth and the sky close for men. When a child is to be born, the double-headed eagle would get a spirit from the other world with his beak, and then place it in the body of the child with his other beak. For this reason, the double-headed eagle is regarded as the guardian of the children.

The Indian's double-headed eagle named 'Daruga Khan' lives on the tree of life, on the fifth floor of the chorus, and is the most powerful guardian of God and protector of the heavens. One of its heads is north, white, cold, dry and male and the other is south, red, hot and female. In Indian mythology, the creature that carries the fire first and brings humanity is also an eagle. The name of this creature whose symbol is the sun is 'Garuda'. It represents the honor of Vishnu, the God of Sun and is depicted as roosted on his arm. Garuda's head, beak, wings and claws are in the shape of an eagle and its body, arms and legs are depicted as human.

The eagle has a very important place in Persian culture too. The winged sun symbol is the symbol of Ahura Mazda, the first God of the Zoroastrian religion. For this reason, it was used by the Persian king Dara in the reign of the Kingdom. In Mazdek religion the eagle is the symbol of victory and glory. The Iranian Sasani is another state that uses the double headed Eagle in the reign of their Kingdom. In Sasanids, the Double Headed Eagle is regarded as looking to the bright east on one side and to the dark west on the other. The Sasani King is also the head priest of the religion cult. It is accepted that the Sassan double-headed eagle's one head symbolizes the authority of the material world, and the other the spiritual world. Gaznelles have used the same symbol too.

The Greater Seljuks and later the Anatolian Seljuks, the lhans and some Anatolian principalities have used the double headed eagle for their empire or principality arms. The bow of the Seljuk flag and the arrow symbolizes the envoy of God.[52] This arm is known to have been used by Sultan Alaaddin Keykubat after receiving the title of Sultan'ul Azam. It has never seen to be used as intensively anywhere in the world as in flags, on walls, arcs and other ornaments as it has by the Anatolian Seljuks. The Anatolian Selcuks have usually used the double headed eagle as the other Turkish principalities.

Anatolian Seljuks have usually depicted the double-headed eagles in the form of birds with big ears, and sometimes eagles with a head of owls. The double headed eagle is found in Diyarbakir, Urfa, Konya, Beysehir, Denizli, Sivas, Kayseri, Erzurum, Niğde, Amasya and many other settlements, shortly almost in all Anatolia. In some of these motifs, the wings of the eagle are drawn as the heads of a dragon. Another symbol, usually depicted with a double-headed eagle and a dragon, is the tree of life. The double headed eagle motifs created after the adoption of Islam, although being in overly stylised, carry in the very source, extremely prominent effects and beliefs of Shamanism.[53] In the legend of 'Oguz Kaan', an ancient Turkish legend, the legend of the birth of the Turks is described as follows:[54]

'When Oguz Kaan was invoking to God Ulgen, there appeared a light from the sky. And there was a girl in the middle of this celestial light. This girl gave birth to three children for Oguz. They beamed them as Sun, Moon and Star.' These are symbolized by a downward triangle to remind the soul descending from heaven. 'Later on, while Oguz Kaan roamed in the forest, another girl came out of a tree bark, and he had three sons from this girl too. They were named as Sky, Mountain and Sea. From these six children came about the Turkish generation.' In the second part of the legend, the girl from the tree peg is therefore the symbol of the universe. And the children born of her, Sky is the symbol of air, Mountain the symbol of soil and Sea is the symbol of water and the symbol of these three children is an upward triangle representing their return to the soul to the heavens measuring to God. The combination of the two triangles gives the six-pointed star, a former Mu symbol, the star of divine justice. All these clues indicate that the Central Asian Turks believed in the religion of the 'Sky God', which can be regarded as a monotheistic belief. The gods under Ulgen are secondary grade gods.

155

However, this monotheistic belief did not satisfy the Muslims. Already the Prophet Muhammad had declared them as enemies, even though he did not recognize the Turks. In one of his Hadis called 'Kitat Ul Türk', Muhammed has stated that there is a special meaning in fighting the Turks and that doomsday shall only happen after Muslims killing the Turks.[55] In Buhari's book called 'Es Sahih Kitabul Jihad' which compiles the Hadis' (Sayings) of the prophet, states that 'Doomsday shall not come until the broad faced, small eyed, flat nosed Turks with shield like faces are not killed'. According to this Hadis, the Arab armies entered the Turkish territory and 'killed the infidel Turks.' However, doomsday had not come; as a result, majority of the Turks had accepted Islam.

Arab armies that entered Turkistan during the rule of the Emevis, acted extremely racist and their attitude led to the great reaction of the Turkish people.[56] Very long bloody battles have taken place between the two nations. While Turks living in towns accepted Islam quicker due to some tax exemptions and under intense pressure from Arabs; it has taken a longer time for the nomads to leave Shamanism and accept Islam. At the end, the Islam tray have accepted remained as mere appearance.

The occupancy of Central Asian Cities by the Arabs begun during the 630s A.D. Especially during the Caliph II Yazid period, the defeat of the Turkish Hakan Su-Lu to the Arab armies led Islam to settle on Turkish territories never to leave again.[57] The Arabs took some of the Central Asian Turks to their countries to use as slave-soldiers. This attitude of the Arabs led to an unexpected result. A great Turkish immigration started and over time, all of the lands under the Arab sovereignty went to the rule of the Turks. For the Arabs, the Turkish sovereignty, which did not end until the end of the last century, had began. The resistance of the Turks to the colonial Islam, which the Umayyads brought, led to bloody battles and hostility between the two nations. Under this strong resistance, besides the desire to preserve their old beliefs, the Umayyads, extreme Arab nationalism, were also lurking. The Turks, the race to be destroyed, the Umayyads, who saw themselves as superior races, exhibited their racist policies in all the non-Arab cities they occupied. In an Iranian or Turkestan city, indigenous people even forbade Arab walkers to walk on the same pavement.[58] The native, who saw an Arab come, had to change the pavement he walked on. For the Umayyads, they were the masters, the other nations were slaves. Non-Arabs could not marry Arab women. Those who act against it were beheaded. The Abbasids who emerged after the fall of the Umayyad State, could not trust the Arab elements that supported the Umayyads. For this reason, they had to entrust their security to the Turkish mercenaries. This obligation brought all the nations to the equality of the Arabs, provided that the Abbasids accepted Islam.

In the meantime, a phenomenon that has come to the fore has helped the Turkish-Arab rapprochement and more Turks accepted the Islam religion. In Central Asia, the Chinese-Turkish competition has been going on for centuries and in the 700's A.D., China seized an important part of Western Turkistan. About 50 years later, after the Chinese had begun a new attack, the Turks asked the Abbasids for help. With the help of the Arab army in the region, the Turkish forces used the Chinese at the Battle of Talas Square, and Western Turkistan was rescued from China.

The success of the army that the Abbasid caliphs brought together from the Turkish mercenaries, increased the demand for the Turks, and this demand was the beginning of an immense immigration that could not be prevented. By the 9th century Turks had already reached the majority in the vicinity of Khorasan. However, the Turks who settled in the region to establish dominion in Khorasan, were forced to convert to Islam. Because the inhabitants of the region, who had previously accepted Islam, were not accepting ones from other religions among themselves. The Turks, converted to Islam in masses. However, the majority chose the Ismaili sect, which was much closer to the Shaman religion of Muslims. The Ismailis were also very organized and powerful in the region. Ahmet Yesevi was born into such a world in the 12th century.[59] In addition to the Ismaili Dais, the Futuvve organisation of the same sect was also very much spread in Khorasan and its vicinity.

Yesevi, who also was an initiated Ismaili Dais himself, rose to the position of the Sheikh of the Khorasan Ismaili monks. Yesevi disciples were recognized among the people as Horasan Erens or 'The Father Eren'.[60] As in other Ismaili dervish lodges, it was expected that the followers of the Khurasan should strictly adhere to the orders of the sheikhs, to listen to the teachers in order to understand the symbols and the secrets, to listen and to be absolutely worthy in their words and actions.

Ahmet Yesevi, although he was an Ismaili Dai, made some changes in his own sect in line with the Shamanist traditions. For example, the six-stage teaching became as nine stages, as in the Futuvve organization. In order for a Yesevi mentor to get the title of Sheikh, he must have pass these nine stages and achieve salvation. These nine stages were as follows:

1. Those who repent,
2. Scholars,
3. Zahid's,
4. Those who have patience,
5. Salihs (Survivors),
6. Razis (Acceptors)
7. Shakirds (Students),
8. Muhibs (Willings),
9. Arifs (Kamil Ones)[61]

The names given to each owner of these stages, which are each a grade, indicative Yesevi of being an Ismaeli.

The goal of Arifs being the last step of Yesevi is to reach to Divine truth and to be with God by providing the spiritual evolution. According to Yesevi, the only way to do this is to close within. There is no way to understand the Almighty God with the mind. For this, Arif must turn into himself and through intuition seek the God that exists within him. To introvert requires to discard your own self, think nothing but God and to content oneself with as little as possible so not to disrupt the flow of this thought.

The closing in of self requires that you discard your own self, not to think of any other being than God, and make as little as possible of the flow of this thought. Deep intuition provided by self closure; allows the waking of the soul to reach God. Arif (Kamil Man) passes through three stages: Knowing Self; Understanding the Truth; Reaching God. At this point, the Kamil Man is already with God.

Yesevism adopted the closing-in method from the Shamanist clergy and applied it to the Batiani. For this reason, the sect was not at all alien to the masses of Shamanism, and the Turks who sought a solution to escape the rigid rules of Islam found salvation in Yesevism. However, while the nomadic people choose Alevism through İsmailisism, Yesevism and Futuevve, the settled Turks in the cities and their rulers preferred the Sunni view for these methods provided much greater opportunities in terms of governing and directing the masses. From these rulers, Gaza and Seljuks were at the forefront of those who helped the Sunnism to become institutionalized among urban the Turks.

As we have seen, the Baghdad Caliphate was under the pressure of the Mutezile and Ismaili movements. When the Seljuks strengthened and defeated the Gazze and Byzantine forces, the Abbasi Caliphate Kaim sent a call to the Seljuk Sultan Tuğrul to be freed of the Ismaili pressure. The Seljuk forces under Tuğrul command, in 1055 A.D. entered Baghdad. The Baghdad Brotherhood Ihvan-i Sefa which included famous Sufis such as Ebu Hamid Al-Ghazali and had been stroked a major blow. The Ismaili Dais and the Sufis were forced to leave the city. Caliph Müstencid, who supported the war against the Mutezile, ordered in 1150 that all the books of Ibni Sina and the Ihvan-i Sefa leaflets were to be incinerated and burned.

However, the leaflets and works of Ibni Sinai were abducted to Spain along with the translations of Greek through the El Mecriti and El Kirmani, thus reaching the present day.[62]

Just 45 years after the Turks settled heavily on the Anatolian soil, the whole country went under Turkish control.[63] During the Turkish invasion from the east of Anatolia to the west, not even the smallest reaction from the ancient Anatolian people occurred.[64] On the contrary, the olds showed the path to the newcomers. How was this possible?

The olds were knotted with Anatolian polytheism and Apollonian religion, Pythagorean and Saabic teachings. Their greatest fear was the Sunni Muslim occupation. Even if the newcomers declared saying that they were Muslims, they had little to do with Islam.

The olds and the newcomers were very close to each other in terms of faith. The local people saw that they could get along well with the Turkmens. In addition, some historians point out that among the people living in Anatolia, there were also Turks who came to these lands for the very first time. Scythians, a branch of the Turks, are known to have settled on Anatolian soil in 4.000s B.C., additionally it is believed that Sumerians, a branch of the ancient Uighur Empire, are in fact of Turkish origin.[65] The presence of these old Turk tribes has been a factor in the easy acceptance of new Turks. As a matter of fact, before a 100 years passed, following the entrance of the Mongols into Anatolia with their strong army, they had never been accepted by the Anatolian people, and while a large number of them had to return back home, very few were able to settle in these lands by assimilation among the Turkmen.

As a result of these developments, together with the Crusades, the name of Anatolia began to be pronounced as "Turchia" (Turkish Soil).

Turkmen immigrants were extremely fond of their freedom. There was no separation between them. Even a simple shepherd was equal and brother with the tribal leader. Their women were with their men everywhere, and they never wore veil that Islam required. This attitude was expressed by the Bektashi Father Kunci, a Turkmen apostle; "Arifs, chastity does not give honor, nor does veiling oneself" …

However, the Seljuks had no intention of defining a broad freedom for the Turkmen. The Sunni rulers applied all kinds of oppression in order to allow the Turkmen to come to the same view, and they considered Alevism as heresy. In contrast to the Turkmens who have been uprooted by these oppression, instead of the Great Seljuks who were eventually destroyed by the Mongolian invasions, the weaker Anatolian Seljuks had remained in Anatolia. The constant Mongolian invasions had devastated the trade and by spreading to Turkestan, days of distress had begun for Futuve groups called Ahism. In this setting, during the reign of Keykubat II, Gıyasettin, Yesevi Sheikh Father Elias of Horasan called the people up for rebellion against the Sultan.[66] This call of Father Elias, who had migrated from Khorasan to Amasya, found attention among the nomad Turkmens. According to

Elias, who has reached the highest rank of the Yesevi order called 'Father', this was the real world. After life, there was no reward or punishment in other worlds. Elias who said, "There is no need to obey the absurd provisions of Shari'a." Stated that in society men and women are equal in society, and that the sultans destroyed this equality based on power. Elias who believed in all the institutions of anagogic institutions, the immortality of the soul and evolution, reincarnation and unity with God being the final destination, said that 'All is equal. However, the ones developing their souls and closer to God.'

The settlers running to the call to rebel, at the forefront of the immigrants who ran to the call to rebel was yet another Father of Elias, Father Isaac. Thousands of Alevis Turcomans, Ismailis, Saabi believers and Ahis were soon gathered around Father Isaac. This force under Isaac command won several victories over the Seljuk armies. At the time Father Elias was in captivity in the City of Amasya by the Seljuks. When the Isaac forces headed for Amasya to rescue him, the Seljuks established a new army and slaughtered almost all the Isaac forces. Thus, the popular uprising, which in history is referred to as the 'Babylon Rebellion', was suppressed.[67]

Although the Babylon Rebellion ended with defeat, it also revealed how widespread and settled Alevism was as an institution in Anatolia. In the following centuries, the Ottomans as the continuation of the Seljuks, rose to the position as the leader of the Sunni Islamic world when Yavuz Sultan Selim captured the caliphate. In the Ottoman Empire, however, the Alevis rebellions never stopped. In 1519, Celali Rebellions, which began with the rebellion of the Babai monotheistic Father Celal in Yozgat, lasted for centuries. The famous Sheik Bedrettin uprising was another Anagogic uprising that shook the Ottomans. Most of the Ismaili and Yesevi dervishes who survived the Babylon Uprising came together under the leadership of Hacı Bektash Veli and founded the Bektashism sect. Bektashism thus emerged as the organized superstructure of the Alevi faith.[68]

The Alevi teachings can be grouped under four main headings. The first of those beliefs is that all beings are realisation from God; Second, the Kamil Human theory; third, the love of Ali, and the last is rejection of sharia.[69]

They say, 'once you know that everything is part of God, you do not have to give up what is forbidden by the shari'a, for example, to abstain from drinking.' According to Alevis, the Qur'an used today is not the true Qur'an. The Quran of Prophet Muhammad was changed in the Caliph Osman era, in the interests of Osman and his followers.

The Anatolian Alevis and the Iranian Shiites are two separate communities with very different belief systems. That both sects have supporters of Ali, have led them to be treated as claiming that they are always in the same camp. However, while the Shiites, under the influence of Zarathustra's religion and making parts of this religion into the system of belief in Islam, have accepted a large part of Shari'a over time, however on the other hand, the Alevis in favor of anagogic doctrine, have never accepted Shari'a.

The Alevis and the Bektashis accepted the Turkish language as a language of worship, and due to this, they have provided the use of the Turkish language in Anatolia until today. Thanks to the adherence of the Alevis to the Turkish language, the Arabization of the Anatolian Turkish people or the Iranianization was also prevented.

Becoming a member of Bektashism depends on self request. Anyone who wishes can enter the cult if deemed appropriate. However, outsourcing to Alevism is generally not accepted. A large part of Alevis are defending that one can only be born as an Alevi and not become one.

Young people born to an Alevi family have to enter the community through a ceremony called the 'Pledge Ceremony' when they come to know themselves at a certain age. In this ceremony, which can be considered as a transition from childhood to youth, in other words maturation, the young participating in the congregation is accepted to the society and has obtained all kinds of rights against the congregation, and is assumed to have accepted all social obligations.[70]

Before the 'Pledge Ceremony', the Alevi community confirms the young people who are to enter the road during a Cem ceremony where they come together. On the day of the ceremony to be held, the young who have received confirmation, are brought to the Cem (Gathering) Ceremony by a guide, with a rope tied to their neck. Here every candidate leans and kisses the threshold. The threshold is the symbol of Ali and the entering the road. Threshold kissing is a sign of candidates submitting themselves to modestly. The guide stood at the door and said, 'I am bringing sacrifices to the truth, from the cults of the order, to the shariat, to the sacrifice, to the truth, and will accept the inclusion of our orders. Do you accept?' he asks.

Dede, who manages the meeting, asks to the participants of the meeting, 'Cem brothers, they are eager to enter our way, and are assuring to bear their obligations. Do you accept?' If there is no appeal, he approves the newcomers by saying 'We accept them as brothers'. Upon receipt of the confirmation, the guide shouts three times, "Hey the wise, I extend the string'. Candidates enter the ceremony hall collectively and wish. The guide hand overs the candidates to Murshid and moves away. After that, the rights and responsibilities are explained to the new participants by Dede Murshid (Grand Master):

'The door you have come to is the door of God. This the where the people are. Fill if you have poured. Make one smile if you made cry. Pick if you have destroyed. Do not come, don't come! Do not turn back, don't turn back! Cover what you have seen, do not talk of what you haven't seen. Know how to keep secrets. You, posses yourself. We took you away from and, and returned back.

Be known that, in the Gathering (Cem) of God, there is no you and me. You are always the mother, the father, the brother. This path of God, sharpened by a thin sword that is thinner than a hair. Servants are never without sins. May God forgive the sins. However, ones on this path shall not be in illicit activities nor lie or commit adultery. Be in control of your hand, mouth and urges. Do not commit crime. Honor your word. One who commit adultery can never be cleaned of that sin. Do not commit adultery. Take care of your wife and food. Treat all as one and as brother. This road is a long road; you can not go. You can not eat. It is a shirt made of fire, you can not wear it. You came and saw. Do not come, don't come, if you do come, do not go back. If you go back on your cognovit, let this be a lesson to you. Let the month and day be witness you not to go back on your cognovit. Shall the Cem wises be witness? Do you trust in God?

The question is asked three times. After taking the words of the participants, Dede replies, 'Let your head be high and up. Good fortune, good state. Let luck be with you. Have good foreordination.' and turns to the crowd by saying 'Hu to the truth. New blood has arrived to the Wise Cem. He removes the rope around the candidates while saying 'they are now your brothers. Protect them.' Then makes three knots and ties it around their waist as a girdle. This three knotted girdle symbolizes the trinity of God, Muhammed and Ali. The new participants have now become members of the community who are fully authoritative and responsible.[71]

Alevism believes in Allah-Muhammad-Ali trilogy. This belief is a continuation of a kind of triangle consisting 'God-Nature-Man's unity'. In Alevism, the woman, unlike the Sunnis, is certainly not isolated from the society. She is an equal parter of the society. Does not cover her head in ceremonies. These women and men pray together and even can drink wine together respecting the rules of the community.

The Alevis do not believe in divine revelation. According to them, God's greatest revelation is nature and thinking men. Everything written until now is the work of men. Especially, the writers of sacred texts are Kamil Men. For this reason, they are absolutely opposed to the dogmatization of these texts, and that some parts of which are taken and a mandatory lifestyle is determined.

The Alevis believe that in every period of history, there are around 300 Kamil Men living in the world, and that today there are more or less the same number of people are living on earth. The most important analoggic belief in Alevism is the theory of suddenism and the beliefs of the Wise. Although these topics have been addressed several times throughout the book, it will be useful to examine their interpretation of these theories in order to better understand the structure of thought of the Alevis.

According to Alevis, Godly enemation has happened as follows: God was not in his own consciousness during the first phase. God, who loves himself and is in need of self-knowing, stranged himself to reach a higher level of consciousness. Without losing anything from his essence, the whole universe sprang from God, aa a wave of light and love.

In the second phase, three different aspects of God's personality appeared. The Hermes priests were described these aspects as Osiris, Isis, and Horus whereas Christians accepted this trinity it as Father-Son, and Holy Spirit. The Alevis, as we have seen before, named this trinity as Allah-Muhammed-Ali.

In the third phase, 'the smart mind' appeared. The smart mind was the sacred force that formed the entire universe and saved the world from chaos and for this he was called 'the master of the creator of the universe'.

Adam was the divine Godly reflection on earth. Meaning he was the Microcosmos. In order for God to know Himself, he needed men, especially Kamil Men. Because when combined with the Divine Light, the only being that would increase the divine consciousness through his experiences, thoughts were the Kamil Men. The Alevis believe that souls gushing out of God have to thrive in order to reach their goal of being the Kamil One. As the first result of Enemation, minerals were formed. The process had to continue forward. Plants emerged from minerals, then the animals and as a result, men at the top of the animal stage, emerged. It is believed that the Kamil have to be good and honest because the spirit changes their body continuously until they reach their goal, that the lives of people on earth are the only way to reach the goal of becoming the Kamil Man.

According to Alevi belief, every soul must pass these 14 stages before reaching the Divine Light:

1. The spirit of inanimate objects,
2. The spirit of the plants,
3. The spirit of animals,
4. The spirit of the demons,
5. The spirit of the genie,
6. The spirit of the unbelievers,
7. The spirit of believers,
8. The spirit of the pious,
9. The spirit of the people,
10. The spirit of the married,
11. The spirit of the Prophets,

12. The spirit of angels,
13. The universal soul,
14. Universal Wisdom[72]

Ali and 12 Imam beliefs of the Alevi are out of our context. But let's just content ourselves that Alevis believe that Ali is not an individual but a Divine Law, and let's examine this institution, its organized form of Bektashism and the founder Hadji Bektashi Veli.

BEKTASHISM

There are two different claims regarding the history of Haci Bektashi Veli's birth about. According to one claim, Veli was born in Horasan in 1210.[73]

Veli, who joined the Yesevi order and rose up to the 'Father' position came to Anatolia together with other Yesevi Dervishes and Ismaili Dais in 1240. He settled along with Father Elias, who had previously come to Anatolia and settled in Amasya. Leaving Amasya before the Babylon Rebellion, Veli survived the conflict by distancing himself from a huge massacre. Having traveled to many parts of Anatolia, Veli eventually settled in Kırşehir's Sulucakaracahoyuk township and began to spread his teaching as the continuing character of Yesevism. The Yesevis and the Ismailis, who survived the Rebellion of Babylon, gathered around Hacı Bektas in a short period of time. When he died in 1271, he already had thousands of followers around him.

According to yet another claim, Hacı Bektashi Veli was born in 1240. His father was Sayyid Muhammad Ibrahim El Sani, the Sultan of Bel City, and his mother was Fatima Hatem. The linage rests all the way back to Muhammad's son-in-law, Ali, and is the 10th grandson of Ali. According to Bektashi Caliph's Father Teoman Inspired Gure, the ancestry of Veli is as follows:

1. Ali
2. Hussein (3rd Imam)
3. Zeynel Abidin (4th Imam)
4. Muhammad al-Bakr (5th Imam)
5. Cafer el Sadık (6th Imam)
6. Musa Kazim (7th Imam)
7. Ibrahim Mükerrem el Mucab
8. Musa-i Sani
9. Muhammad Ibrahim el Sani
10. Haci Bektashi Veli

Caliph Baba Gure intentionally says that the date of death was changed to 1271 in order to show that the birth and death dates of Veli were particularly diverted and that Haci Bektashi Veli had died before the founding year of the Ottoman Empire 1299. According to Gure, it is not feasible that Veli could have been involved in the events because he was 4 years old during the Babylon Rebellion, and that he had not personally meet with Father Elias. Vali came to Anatolia years after the massacre and in 1299 and personally made important contributions in the foundation of the Ottoman Empire. He was alive during the conquer of Bursa by Sultan Murat and died at the age of 80 in 1320.

Haci Bektashi Veli, stating that 'religions are the cause of disagreements among people, in fact, all religions are for the purpose of providing peace and brotherhood in the world' has put these views in his Velayetnâme' work.

Haci Bektashi gathers the people of God in four groups. These are the people who practice different methods of reaching God. In the first group, there are people who are looking for the truth in God's worship, and this is a very important majority of the people on earth. In the second group, those who apply the path of the order but can not escape from the follis; in the third group are the dervishes who have the privilege of knowing the secrets about God, and finally those who are united with God in the last group. This four-fold form of belief in Bektashis is called 'Four Door-Forty Teachings of the Authority'. A Bektashi can not be a Kamil Man without passing through these forty positions and four doors.

The institutionalization of Bektashism in its final form has been possible in the 1500s A.D. with some amendments done by the Bektashi leader of the period known as the Father of Dede (Grand Master) The Balım Sultan.

The primary goal of Bektashism is to recognize the 'God-Universe-Human' unity, which is based on love. Man is a being of love. Man is equipped with divine qualities. The first step of success is to know and love yourself. 'He who loves himself, loves God ...'[74]

One of the most beautiful expressions of the love of God in Bektashism is put forth in the following famous quatra: "Shakirdis (Followers) carve stones, and present it to their Master, and cite the name Calab (God), in every part of that stone' ...

Bektashism accepts that the universe is the reflection of God's, and that man is the inner part of God. Since God is in men, Godly abilities to think, will, freedom of action is also present in men.

True worship; is people concentrating their thoughts on themselves. It is unnecessary for a person to worship a fact outside his own. The thinking of one's own being will enable him to develop spiritually and the individual and by so men will be able to reach the position of Kamil men. God Almighty reaches the highest point of his own consciousness in this world through Kamil men. Only the Kamil can return to God and be internalized by God.

In other words, Bektashism is the name of Kamil Men's faith school at the point of intersection (point of intersection between two realms), because of looking at society in terms of the ones that are visible and looking at God with wisdom. This Kamil Man manifests the wisdom of mankind with the symbol, the manifestation of mankind with the model, the symbol of the libation (divine world), and the manifestation (visible world) of the world model. For this reason, Bektashi speaks with every language and colors with every color in the way of telling the truth.

The expression of the God-man union is also apparent in the following quadrants:

'Allah is Allah (God is God),
Adam is Allah (Adam is God)
I believed too,
Amentü Billah (In the name of God) ...'

Just as in the other anagogic teachings, in Bektashism, the soul is immortal. The soul has subsequently entered the body and will return to the Divine source from which it came. The spirit does not only provide the body with freshness; but also is the source of understanding, remembering, knowing, recognizing, thinking and wisdom.

For Bektashism has manifested all of God's attributes in men, valuing man and calling men 'the Qur'an-Natık' (Talking Qur'an). Men is an independent entity from the living environment. His duty is to act modestly; to purify his soul from the after-grown filth, to maturate, stay away from pretension, and to fill his heart with the love of nature, man and God. The humanly bodies are only one medium for a purpose. For this reason, it is the greatest mistake to divide people into men or women, or to look at their social position or race. All people, men and women are equal. All religions are meant to mature, and to spread peace and brotherhood. However, over time, these meanings of religions have been changed and the lives of people have been restricted and self-development has been set in front of them by introducing strict and unbearable rules. Actual prohibitions are not contradictory to Shari'ah, but contrary to the basic principles of the order. The five conditions of Islam are not religion's essence, but fera (important in secondary order).

Secretiveness is essential in Bektashism. They have special rituals that are not open to the public and their 'Bektashi Secret' is protected with great care. In terms of rituals, the 'Bektashi Erkanna' has a special significance.

A Bektashi can only understand the teaching with the help of another Murshid (guide/teacher). The presence of a murshid and the presence of a guide is absolutely necessary. For this reason, it is perfectly natural that the new disciples, will comply the murshid in complete and absolute obedience. Understanding of the symbols and practices of the sect is only possible with the murshid and guide. Because the Bektashi doctrine was often counterproductive with the learning of the society in which the migrant lived, and especially because it was incompatible with Shari'a teachings, great importance was given to the guidance system in order to protect the new disciple from a possible shock. Murshid can be described by three adjectives; Dede's representative, master tutor and person to be taken as an example in the art of spiritual life. Bektashism with the presence of murshids becomes a living fact. The only thing expected from the disciples is to keep their minds open and keep them as their greatest secret.

Bedri Noyan Dede Baba, the 36th spiritual leader of the Bektashi World, relates to the entrance ceremony of the cult; 'The first stage in the acceptance ceremony is the repentance of the candidate, this never failing repentance is called the 'Nasuh Repentance'. The repetend is as innocent as a new born child. The candidate is asked three times during the ceremony as; 'Have you received the advice given to you, have you accepted it?' Should the candidate answer three times as 'Yes, I did', the guide (murshid) appointed to him prostrates before him. It is in fact the humanity that is being prostrated before him. Thus, we take him from himself and return back to him. It is said that 'He is now a Bektashi disciple.'[75] In Bektashism, it appears that, as in the other anagogic schools, there is a symbolic death and rebirth ceremony.

The first gate after the rebirth, is the Shari'ah Gate, where religious laws are taught. This is followed by the Cult Gate, where the secret practices and symbols of the order are given, and the Ingenuity Gate, where the mystical science of God is taught. The Truth for Bektashi is revealed only with the forth gate, the Truth Gate. However, only the one who completes all the levels of the fourth gate is considered to have reached the level of Truth through his skill, and the truth he has found enables him to present skill.

Each of the four doors are made up of ten stairs, and one intending to become wise (Kamil), has to climb these stairs.

At the Shari'ah Gate, the basic principles of Islamic religion, the general conditions of Alevism and the mystery of the God-Muhammad-Ali trinity is taught. The disciples of this door (level) are called 'Beloglu' or 'Asik'. The 'Asik' is the one who has not yet received foreordination. The 10 levels of the Shari'ah Gate are as follows:

1. To have faith,
2. To learn science,
3. Prayer, fasting, pilgrimage, alming
4. To make halal money,
5. To avoid haram (forbidden by religion),
6. Not to approach women with Hayz and Nifas (period of regl)
7. To enter the house of Shari'ah, not to despise the adept of Shari'a,
8. To be compassionate,
9. To eat and dress clean,
10. To act with obedience (Emr-i Ma'ruf).

The title given to the disciple who successfully implements the conditions of Shari'ah and is approved by the Murshid and passes to the second degree being the Gate of the Sect, is 'Son of the Path' or 'Muhip' meaning a loving friend. A muhip will be forced to repent for all his previous sins and show his devotion to Pir (Saint). After that, the Muhip is educated about the rules of the order by the Murshid, and to show that he understands and accepts them, he simplifies his clothing and cuts his hair. The fourth step of this stage consist of a very strict work and discipline training, where the fifth step is to service all the brothers and sisters. In the sixth step, the Muhip, is to behave humbly and to foster his fear of God. In the seventh stage where the Muhip is liberated from the fear of God through harboring God, is to learn to act cautiously and meticulously. In the ninth step, the Muhip, by intensifying his knowledge of spirituality and love, will recognize the divine direction of love and qualify for a higher degree.

As seen, the obligation to comply with the Islamic Shari'a ends in the second degree. The ceremonies held at this degree, where men and women attended together, are called 'Affirmation Ritual' or "The Ritual of Cem".

The Ten rules of the second degree, Gate of Sect are as follows:

1. To take the hand of Murshid and repent,
2. To be talib (willing) and discipleship,
3. To keep the hair, beard and garment clean,
4. To fight against the self (Jihad-i Ekber),
5. To respect,
6. To havf (to learn to fear from Allah),
7. Not to give up hope from God.
8. To be of prophecy and guidance
9. To be social, of advice and of conversation.
10. Not to complain about love, enthusiasm, pride and poverty.

The third degree is the Gate of Skill. The members of the degree are called 'Dervish'. The name of the ceremony of the Gate go Skill is 'Vakfı Vucut' meaning 'bodily present'. In this ceremony, the Dervishes, sometimes waiting for ten years to get this degree, are crowned with the official crown of the order. At the gate of Skill; people, God, the secrets of the universe, values and meanings are emphasized. The leading teaching of the doctrine of the 'Union Law' mystery is realized.

The ten steps that should be taken up this door by the Dervish are as follows:

1. Decency,
2. Fear
3. Patience
4. Opinion,
5. Shame,
6. Generosity
7. To learn science,
8. To examine anagogic science
9. To include anagogic science in the application (Skill),
10. To know your own self. (One who knows himself knows God)

The person who knows himself and therefore knows God, is the one who is entitled to pass on to the last stage of the Bektashi teaching. The final stage of your Bektashism, as in Yesevi, is the 'Truth Gate' where the title of 'Father' is obtained, which likewise is called the Kamil Man. The Father, who is given a special ceremony at the Gate of Truth, also gets the right to be a martyr. The directors of the Bektashi monks are appointed among the Fathers. The Bektashi Fathers also have ten duties:

1. Being a Turab (learning the Union of Being),
2. To be tolerant of other forms of belief, not to interfere. To recognize all people as one and not to be against anyone,
3. Avoid actions that would disrupt the nature and the natural balance, to know all living beings as God's will, and to be abstinent,
4. To recognize the universe and to recognize the unity of the world and the entity,
5. To bow before God's glory, to ask for help and success from him, to trust and revere Allah in all his work,
6. To discuss the secrets of the degree only with other Fathers, and not to share information to the outside world, to stay away from the ascetic.
7. To be in secret (to feel God in his being)
8. To be Abraham (to see the Divine Light),
9. To be disciplined (to live within Divine Light)
10. To be one with Divine Light[76]

The most important motive of the Bektashis is 'don't come, do not come, don't turn, do not turn.' As to be understood from this motive, the person to enter the order will be supervised very strictly. Another important cause of the Bektashi Fathers is 'to explain the unseen with the unseen and the unknown with the unknown'.

There are two conical column symbols in Bektashism. These symbols are two triangles on a flat surface based on infinity. In addition to being a symbol of Macrocosmos and Microcosmos, it's surface symbolizes humanity and the summit symbolizes the spirit. It expresses the sermon of humanity from multiplicity to singularity and back to multiplicity once again. With this symbol, Bektashis knows that there is no point in life where the cause of reason and virtue comes to an end. The similarity of this symbol with the universally used infinity sign is striking.

'We know that we are, we are, we are children.

We are plagues, we are bountiful ...'

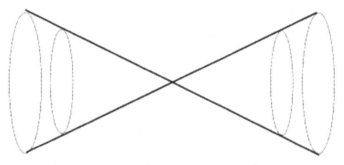

Macrocosmos and Microcosmos are the same
(A Bektashi Symbol)

Only those who have the ability can understand and comprehend the meaning of All is One'. For this, the Bektashi says, 'The body is not two, but one' and adds: The only thing that can be said in this case, Existence' ...

A famous Bektashi Poet Kaygusuz Sultan says:

'The path to Allah is close, but quite precarious. Always give your essence to the essence; then you find God, and treasure the two Cone Symbols Adjacent to Each Other. Be time, your path shall go far. And thus you won't spend your life for nothing.'

For the Bektashis, the Hallac-ı Mansur, an Enel Hak (I am God) sayer, is a very important Kamil Man. Mansur, who is not afraid to sacrifice his life for his rights to say that he is God; The Bektashis tried to pay their debts by naming the very middle of the hall where the ceremonies are held as 'Dar-ı Mansur' (Door of Mansur).

The name of the place of worship of the Bektashis is 'Chamber of Square'. The Chamber of Square is the place for Divine Love Garden, the Paradise of Lovers and of the Divine Secrets. While in Islam, Qibla-oriented worship is fundamental, the disciples in the Bektashi Chamber of Square perform worship facing each other. The reason for this style of worship is that every place where man is, is seen as Kaaba. Within the Kaaba, believers worship at each other's faces, lining up on the edges of the walls, since there is no need of turning to Qibla. Gulbank, the Bektaşi prayer, is 'to remember God with a loud voice'. In education, prayer, the language used is Turkish. As in other anagogic schools, Bektashis use special cues, signs and symbols to recognize each other.

God can not be bound by any limitation, he is both the Creator and is Created. God's Attributes are within the seen world, and he himself is outside the visual world. They can not be separated from each other. Allah is neither an ore nor an attribute. He is both an ore and an attribute. The two are not separate things, but they are not the same. Only the stages are different.

Just because the father is a Bektashi, doesn't mean that the son is a Bektashi too. This is one of the most important differences with Alevism. Bektashism comes by personal choice whereas Alevism is born to with birth from an Alevi mother-father. When an Alevi Dede dies his son replaces him. In the Bektashis, every duty is assigned as a result of election. Among the members of Dergah (lodge), the Father chooses the ones to be raised to become Dervishes with the approval of İhvan (Brethern). However, the one to be chosen as the Father is chosen by the Halifa Father among the Dervishes and asked for approval from the Dede Father. Dede Father than appoints the most eligible as 'Halifa Father'. In the event of the availability of Dede Father's position, the Halifa Fathers choose a Halifa Father among themselves with secret ballot as the new 'Dede Father'.

Haci Bektashi Veli was the symbol of the Janissary from the beginning of the 14th century until the beginning of the 19th century. The Janissary would organize ceremonies and read the so-called "Gulbank" prayer on his name.[77]

Bektashism has managed to resist even to the Ottoman rulers of Sunni Caliphate thanks to the backing of the military power of the Janissary organization and the Sunni Caliphates of the Ottoman Empire until Sultan Mahmut II have hesitated interference with the Bektashi Dervishes.[78]

The Janissaries were a recruited army of children gathered from the Christian lands occupied by the Ottomans. However, the Janissaries were not simply chosen from the children of the Christians who were captured, on the contrary they were chosen among the children of the Christian families who were close to the Bektashi way of life, who were Gnostics. Yet another condition for being elected is to be the only son of the family. According to the Bektashi thought structure, it is right to state that Jesus is God. But God can not be names as Jesus. God can not be transcripts as God, but Jesus can be extended with God. Within this concept, Christians understood Bektashism and became 'Janissaries'. Rather than be connected to strict Sunni beliefs, they accepted the Bektashis' faith free of all kinds of superstitions of Islam. Thanks to this elite force that formed the backbone of the Ottoman army, the Bektashis managed to survive in the period of Yavuz Sultan Selim, despite the fact that the Ottomans had taken over the leadership of the Sunni Muslim world and succeeded in being influential within the state structure.

Bektashism has created a bridge between Christians and Muslims in the Balkans for hundreds of years with its profound tolerance and not denying the symbols of different religions. According to Bektashism, Judaism of the three heavenly religion is the glorious whereas Christianity is the similitude one. Muhammad is beyond his self and similitude his traits.

The excess of the opportunities provided to the Janissaries by the Ottoman administration caused a growing number of unrest and jealousy among some Muslim subjects, and thus Sultan 3rd Murat's decision to withdraw the monopolized right of the elected Christian children to be Janissary, opened the door to various Muslim classes. Sultan Murat promising the firebombers, jugglers, rogues and instrumentalists otherwise known as 'zobu' who he enjoyed watching during the circumcision ceremonies for the princes, to fulfill any of their wishes; and for the demand of wanting to be Janissary, he could not turn back from his word and facing all the resistance from the religious parties, he still granted the right to zobus. The army became increasingly corrupt due to the addition of the zobu who have not received the Bektashi education and the ancient Bektashi laws eventually were destroyed. Later the Janissaries led to various revolts and began to collect tributes under the name of protection from the people. The leader of the Patrona Halil Rebellion, one of the biggest revolts of the Ottoman Empire, Patrona Halil himself was a Zobu. The persecution of the Janissaries had reached such a point that the name attached to the abolition of the Janissaries was the 'good cause'.

But the only reason for the abolition of Janissaries was not the persecution or riots of the people. Sultan Mahmud the 2nd who considered himself a believer, considered this non-Sunni and self centered Bektashi Janissaries as a threat to his ideals. The of Nizam-i Cedit (Regular) army, established as an alternative to the Janissaries, destroyed and the janissaries from the Bektashi origin are killed as the forest is completely burned down. Janissaries who were not of Bektashi origin also immediately changed sides to report to the Sultan. The Bektashis describes this event as "The Sinister Act".

Following the elimination of the Janissaries in 1826 and the killing of the Janissaries with the Bektashi origin, by means of great impacts to the Bektashi quarters, and the sect was almost completely wiped out of Anatolia, and the Bektashi quarters were transferred to the Naqshbandi sect.[79]

This destruction process of the Sunnis could only have been saved by the 'Kaygusuz Sultan Dergah' in Egypt, which could be considered as the continuation of the Temple of Osiris and the Alexandria School. In those years, due to the fact that Egypt received its independence from Istanbul, many historical documents could be stored in the Kaygusuz Sultan Dervery, which had escaped the Ottoman administration's violence campaign. Although Dergah is used as a military facility today, many valuable historical monuments belonging to the Bektashis are still preserved in various Egyptian museums.

Although most of the formations of the Bektashis in the Ottoman lands were devastated, they managed to recover quickly thanks to the presence of an important Alevi mass supporting their good-organization and society, and they continued their activities even under more difficult conditions.

Throughout the history of Bektashi, it is possible to talk about the four main Derveries outside the Hacı Bektash formation. These are the Sayyid Ali Sultan Dervery in Dimekota in Rumelia (today it is located within a Greek military facility and is closed), the Dervery in Karbala (today is in the hands of Shiites), Abdal Musa Sultan Dervery in Alanya (today is visited by the public as a tomb) and Egypt as Kaygusuz Sultan Dervery (today used as a military facility) in Cairo. Later on, the Şahkulu Sultan Dervery in Göztepe was added to them (the Dervery still belongs to an Alevi foundation and is used by the Alevis to worship).

The Bektashis, who have been living under the pressure of the Sunni government for about 700 years, have embraced it as soon as Alevis, together with Mustafa Kemal, had the chance of getting rid of these pressures.

During the War of Independence, Ataturk was supported by Turkish officers, who were the successors of the Committee of Union and Progress, and on the other hand by the Bektashis and Alevis. Just before the start of the national struggle, Atatürk visited Hacı Bektaş Dergah on 25th of December 1919 and demanded the support of Bektashi and Alevis. Bektashi and Alevi group already prone to the secular system in religious terms provided full support to the Nationalists Forces.[80] Beyond this, the leading supporters of Ataturk in the National Assembly were Bektashi and Alevi MPs. Thanks to their favorable votes, it was then possible to remove the Caliphate system.

Presently, there is no official Bektashi dargah in Turkey due to the fact that any kind of cult activity is banned in Turkey. For worship and meetings, Bektashis use various places.

Another interesting information about Bektashism is that in 1953, Recep Ferdi Khalifa founded a Turkey-connected Bektashi convent, in Michigan, USA. The secrecy of the Bektashis is so well known that during World War II, US President Roosevelt stated that the Bektashis were brought to important tasks related to American state secrets.[81]

AHISM

Another institutionalization of the anagogic doctrine in Anatolia came through the Ahi organization. As mentioned before, as the continuation of the ancient Egyptian guilds, the Ismaili Futurvve organization, spread among the Turks in Central Asia and had been called 'Ahi'. With the spread of the organization, Fütüvvetnâmes (Rules of Futurvve) were written covering the principles of the Futurvve organization with the aim to standardize the system within the Islamic world.[82] In this first Fütüvvetnâme, it is clearly stated that the origin of the Futurvve system is the belief of mysticism.

The oldest Turkish Fütüvvetnâme, written by Çobanoğlu, has revealed the rules applied in Ahi zaviyas (schools).[83] According to this Fütüvvetnâme; They were taught history, important people, life stories of scholars, mysticism, Turkish, Arabic, Persian and literature. A person had to have an art, trade or profession before joining the Futurvve. Ahi could not be the one who did not work in any of these efforts. This decision was later changed.

It is seen that in Çobanoğlu Fütüvvetnâme, the meanings are hidden from others, and in this sense, it is said that 'do leave others and turn to us'. In Çobanoğlu Fütüvvetnâme, it is noteworthy that the translation interpreters as the one who enters the path, resemble the Bektashi teachings at the joining of the shed ceremony. In Bektashi, interpretation means prayer. In Turkish interpreters (prayers), it is stated that those who join the way of Ahi's will be servants to the other Ahi lovers, and Shed (generation) is struck by three knots while connecting to the waist of the disciple. In Fütüvvetnâmes, the similarity of Ahism with the teachings of Alevi-Bektashi is quite evident. According to this Fütüvvetnâme, sufism forms the basis of the Futurvve...

Ahis, who came to Anatolia with Yesevi dervishes and Ismaili verses, settled in cities rather than rural areas as they belonged to a vocational organization. Ahism is a vocational organization, as well as an anagogic one with its rituals and secrets for joining and behaviour. Ahi Evren Veli, who was one of the Khorasan Fathers, provided for the Anatolian Ahis to become an organized power.[84] This is his soubriquet. His real name is Nasiruddin Mahmud bin Ahmed (1171-1262). In the 1220s, the Mongols burned down the lands of Turkish Khorezms, and came to Anatolia from there. Ahi Evren came to Konya after coming to Anatolia, where he took lessons of Sufism from Shams Tebrizi a dear friend of Mevlana Celaleddin Rumi and became a Dervish. As a result of the discord between the Konya ulamas and himself, Ahi Evren went to Kayseri and became aggrieved by the Ulamah and the Sultan. But he left behind a very strong organization in Konya, the Seljuk capital. After the murder of Shams Tebrizi, Sadrettin, who was the right-hand man of Mevlana and the right arm of Ahi Evren, and two anagogic schools such as Mevlevism and Ahism have left their mark in Anatolia.[84]

Ahi Evren has established the Ahi organization, taking advantage of the Fütüvvetnâme, which has for centuries served in the field of warfare and in terms has carried out major and important tasks in providing religious-moral information. Ahi Evren, during his life, has brought Ahis which is the harmonious union of art and morality to such reputable level that for centuries it guided the institutions, tradesman and craftsmen in Anatolia and better organized their functioning, and played and along with Haci Bektashi morals and customs played an important role in the establishment of the Janissary organization, and statesmen were honored to enter this organization. The greatest novelty that Ahi Evren brought to the philosophy of Futurvve is that, somewhat like the operative Freemasons who have implemented a system of accepting in the Accepted Masons. While there is an obligation to have a profession to join the other Futurvves and organizations, such an obligation has been removed to be an Ahi. With this decision, teachers, professors, cadres, preachers, commanders, the great and respected people of the region were able to join and thus the efficiency of the organization increased. Since the requirement for acceptance to the community was good morality, charity and generosity, those who entered the organization were moral and kindness lovers.[85] Top executives, doctors, governors, commanders, professors and cadets were nurtured among the Ahis.

Under the sheikdom of Ahi Evren, the organization of Ahism has spread to all Seljuk cities in a short period of time, and during the Babylon Rebellion, Ahism has given all the help to the anagogics. In later years, Ahis saw Alevis, Bektashis and Mevlevis as the people closest to them. Ahis played an important role in the establishment of the Ottoman Empire. Some sources state that Orhan Gazi the son of Osman Gazi, the founder of the state, and the 3rd Sultan Murat the 1st were members of the Ahi organization. However, when the Ottoman Empire started to expand into an empire, the sultans chose the way of their Turkish predecessors and entered the Sunni sects which gave the rulers much more opportunity to manage the masses by providing more power to the administrators. The basic principle in Ahism is the absolute equality of the members within the organization. The members are all brothers of each other. But in terms of progress, there is an eternal respect from young to elderly. Certain qualities are sought for those who wish to join Ahism. For membership, one has to be proposed by one of the members of the organization. Those who are involved in unworthy jobs and are not well-known, and who are thought to bring bad reputation to the organization cannot be Ahi. For example; human killers (murderers), animal killers (butchers), thieves, adulterators can not participate in the organization. For butchers to be considered in the same category as murderers come from anagogic beliefs.

The following results were obtained with the establishment and expansion of the Ahi organization in Anatolia:

1. The transition from nomadic to sedentary live style, meaning the Turkish urbanization has accelerated.
2. Until the second half of the 13th century, the Turks began to enjoy and participate in trade and trading craft and commerce of a large majority of non-Turkish indigenous people.
3. Turkish tradesmen and craftsmen had a privileged position in the region thanks to the mutual solidarity and trust among them and they gradually became influential in the city economy.[86]

Ahism, in Anatolia, has spread the synthesis of ethics and art interdependence, to the villages. The extension of the Ahism in the Anatolian villages is the 'Yaran Rooms'. In Iran and the Arab regions, we do not come across a class like Ahi. There are no aiding institutions similar to the 'Yaran Rooms'. The members of the Ahi professional and craft organizations in the cities resolved all kinds of needs of the poor around them by establishing foundations. These were; nurseries, hospitals, schools etc. The poor people of the fallen villages that have been devastated by epidemics, famine, fires, military service, etc. have managed to survive thanks to the help of 'Yaran Rooms'. Through these foundations, the villagers could receive aid collectively, more quickly and more effectively as needed.[87]

Entry into the organization, like other Anagogic sects, takes place with a special ceremony. In the ceremony a girdle is tied to the west of the candidate and he is advised to be loving and respectful to all people and not to leave the truth and secrecy. Members are asked for absolute commitment, infinite obedience and discretion. The irreligious cannot enter the organization; however, there is no place for Sofus among the Ahis. In Ahism, stages such as knowledge, patience, purity of the soul, loyalty, friendship, tolerance, prohibition of compliance are passing as qualifications. cqualifications, the foremost six principles of Ahism:

1. Be generous
2. Welcome the hungry
3. Be welcoming to your home
4. Keep what you see to yourself
5. Be decent
6. Be discreet

In Ahism, a three-stage and 9-degree initiation system is applied. At the first stage, the Shariah Gate, the students are taught professional knowledge, Quranic knowledge, literacy, Turkish, mathematics and Fütüvvatnâme, which is the constitution of the organization. At the second stage, the Sect Gate, knowledge of Sufism, music, Arabic and Persian are taught. At this stage, the disciple also receives military training. At the third stage, which is the Shaykh level, is the Marifet (Skills) Gate. At this stage, the disciple is asked to believe in God, to kill his individuality, to serve the nations, and to remain silent in the face of ignorance. According to the constitution of Ahism, only after the completion of the realization of the truth, one is able to become Kamil. Like the Fütüvve it pursues, the Ahism is based on a 9-degree system. Each gate contains three degrees. These degrees are as follows:

1. Brave
2. Stooge.
3. Apprentice.
4. Fellowcraft
5. Master.
6. Nakip
7. Khalifa.
8. Shaykh.
9. Shaykh ul Mashah.

Brave and stooge are the preparatory stages before acceptance to the organization. The realization of the Ahi organization starts with the apprenticeship stage. Operative degrees are Apprentice, Fellowcraft and Master degrees. The next degrees of the organizational ones. The transition period between these degrees would last around 1000 days -as close to three years-, but the transition from apprentice to fellowcraft would take two years. Theses transitions would depend on the person's craft and the level of progress in his profession, and could even exceed three years.

The inauguration and degree ceremonies of the Ahi organization are as follows:

Yigit (Brave): Children under 10 years of age are determined from good families and morality, and are nicknamed Yigit.

Yamak (Stooge): To be taken as the help of a shopkeeper, one needed to be least ten years of age, and the continuation to the work must be provided by the father or guardian. At the inauguration ceremony, in one of the nine steps of the Ahism, the person in the step of the Nakip, takes salt in one hand and releases it into the water standing in the middle of the community. Then the other Nakips open the door, remember the past men one by one, pray, present the candidate to be taken to the lodge. After that, they would have a young person in a series of ceremonies. Only professional information before apprenticeship is given to the Yamak.

Apprentice: Works for two years free of charge as a stooge. Then he is promoted to Apprenticeship. This rise is done in a ceremony. The master of this apprentice, his elders, his parents, his boss gather together in the shop of the head of the guild after the morning prayer. The master talks about the work and skill at the workplace. The Nakip (Ceremony Master) of the guild introduces him to everyone of the guild.

The apprentices should be kept under regular control and should be trained under the supervision of reliable persons. As seen in the Fütüvvetnâmes, each apprentice had two brothers, a path guide, a "master", a teacher of art, and a patriarch. Ethics, general morals and education rules, and the religious knowledge were told by the experts to each subject, as a separate subject every night. On the other hand, on a certain day of the week, military information was given for the use of weapons such as horse riding, use of swords, shields, arrows and spears.

Fellowcraft: The young person serving three years as an apprentice would move up and the ceremony would be held at the guild chamber itself. The entire guild board would be at the ceremony. Apart from the tradesmen, the masters who are not in the profession, who are accepted to the guild, are also invited to the ceremony. The most veteran Fellowcraft performs the service and guidance. The young to be promoted that day for the first time wears the tradesman's outfit. Three other masters with their own master testify to their good morals. A preceptor who is there, prays. After that, everyone stands up, the guild master the Sheikh garbs the candidate with a shed and gives him advice about craftsmanship and commerce. The ceremony ends by kissing the hands of the new master, the other masters and the elders.

Master: In order to be risen to mastery, the master had to receive a three-year fellowcraft training, and there would be no complaints about him during this period, and he had to perform the duties assigned to him carefully; in particular, being diligent in raising apprentices, to be on good terms with other fellowcrafts, to be dependent on his craftsmanship, to behave well to customers, to be able to manage a separate store on his own and have enough capital status.

Mastery ceremonies are done in the spring. At least thirty days ago, the candidate is notified by the mastership for promotion and is given time to find himself a shop. He then informs his master that he has found a shop and the date of ceremony is then organized. All masters, all clergymen, the mufti and kadi are invited.

In the Kahya ward, the craftsmen and masters constitute a two-row circle. In the front row the fellowcrafts and the masters sit behind them. In the center of the circle on a round cedar, the oldest and the mufti and the staff sit. Master to be fellowcrafts, enters the court with the fellowcraft on the right, and the master to the left and greets people. Upon the sign of the Mufti, the Imam opens the meeting by reading a prayer. The Mufti reads some verses about trade, craftsmanship and work, and Kadi aslo read a few hadiths and interpret their meanings. The Kahya chairing the meeting, gets up and rests on his wand, calls his new master and takes him in front of himself. After telling which of the prophets, the art of the prophets, and the traditions of the tradesmen, the loyalty and rightness in the trade, respecting the customer, not mixing up the goods, telling the buyer before the sale the defame and defect of his property, in summary, the need to not work for the detriment of anyone. He ends his words with obedience to the Sultan ends his words by respecting the scholars, compassion for the people, loving the young, not grieving anyone, caring for the apprentices and fellocrafts as their children. The Master then informs that he is working sincerely with the intention of raising a new master, and with the help of God, that the new master is satisfied with all things. He bears witness to the new Master, who has acquired the characteristics that he can master, and asks for helal (good prayers). However, the new master, who now has the power to speak at the meetings, mentions his master that he does not have a right, and his master, rubbing the back of his old assistant and says:

"Hold the stone to turn into gold, let God make you a saint in both worlds. Let all your work be beneficial. Let the mercy of God be on you and not show any poverty or cause any trouble to you. Should you not abide to the teachings of your masters and persecute the people and claim the rights of the infidels and orphans and not avoid all God's prohibitions, then let my twenty nails be hooked in your neck hereafter". Then, takes off the shed from the waist of the Fellowcraft, and with his own hands puts on the shed of mastery. And prays after that. The new master kisses the hands of the elders one by one and takes their prayers. After that, the muftis and the kadis make a tour of the city, forming a procession, with two masters hand in hand and one kahya in front of them along with four masters and ten disciples and five apprentices behind them, and the banner of tradesmen in front. After the ceremony is over, fellowcrafts, apprentices and kiss the hand of the new master.[88]

They were becoming complete in art education in the workshop; Turkish tradesmen and craftsmen in Ahi lodges who have been studying, culture and general knowledge, established a solidarity and cooperation between themselves and the ability to compete with members of Collegia of local Byzantine artists. Ahism, has provided the spirit to Anatolian Turks to live honestly self-securing living skills. Ahis, by establishing a strong and effective auto control between themselves, selling standard, robust and cheaper goods to people from all religions and nationalities in a safe environment managed to continue their business.

Ahis considered the following as immoral;

1. A drinker,
2. Fornication,
3. disparity, gossip and defamation,
4. pride and arrogance,
5. unjust,
6. jealousy,
7. hatred
8. untrusting
9. Lying
10. blasphemer
11. not covering ones' shame

12. parsimony

13. Murder

They did not only organize an economic organization, but also a religious-military organization, such as the Knight Sects of medieval Europe. The admitted to the organization was taught the art of using weapons as long as he knew not to defend himself as a professional soldier. This tradition has been going on since the first Fatimid Islamic organization in Egypt.

In the Seljuk period, apart from the regular armies of the sultans, the most powerful armed organization in the country was the Ahi detachment, which consisted of young successors and masters. During the Mongol invasions, when the forces of the sultan defeated and escaped, many cities defended the Ahi detachments. Use of weapons, horse riding, arrows, swords, military use, such as the use of military knowledge, was given by people who knew them well to the soldiers. Those who would give these lessons would have the following experience: 1. See Ahi, 2. See Sheikh, 3. Train a candidate. Those who did not receive this training under the supervision of Ahi and Sheikh, could not have been teachers in this field.[89] This shows how much the Ahis valued education and experience in every field.

Yet another name of Shaykh ul-Mashah, the leader of all sheikhs, was Ahi Baba. Ahi Baba, the chairman of the organization would come to power by means of election. His instructions and warnings were strictly observed. These people would take over the management where there were no sultans or emirs; thus their rules and prohibitions, their behavior, the rules of protocol in their horseback riding were similar to those of the sovereigns. Even the Beys (Lords) and Emirs protected by militia were scared of the Ahis. After the final victory of the Mongols, governors and gentlemen fled from the cities, and Ahis they carried out their duties too. In this period, the powerful vizier of the Seljuks even subservient to the power of the Ahis.

The first person giving collective information on the Ahis was the famous Berber traveler Ibn-i Batuta. Ibn-i Batuta visited many cities, towns and villages of Anatolia during the time of the Ottoman Sultan Orhan (1326-1359) and was a guest of the Ahis. Batuta describes his impressions as follows: "This country, which is known as Bilad-i Rum, is the most beautiful place in the world. God gave all of the beauties that it gives separately to other countries. The faces of the people are very beautiful, the clothes are clean and the food is delicious. It is said that blessing is in Sham, and the Greek. True kindness is among the Turkmen of Anatolia. In this region whichever house or dervish lodge we would be asked as to how we are. Women do not cover themselves here nor do they distant themselves from men. Upon departure they see you off as if you are one of them, a relative as such, women cry. Ahis are found in every city, town and village of the Turkmen region who live in Anatolia. They are one of a kind to help foreigners and feed them, to see all their needs, and to eliminate tyrants who are disturbing.[90]

Ahism; due to its delivery of high esteem and dignity to a person and to his occupation, it has managed to hold together the arts and trade for the Anatolian Turks for almost 630 years until 1860 where all activities were taken away from this organization. According to the rules of Ahi Evren, all kinds of processes, from the division of professions and trades to the sale of goods, are finely tuned. These rules have eliminated the competition between the profession and the producer-consumer friction and the quarrel.

175

As an organization Ahism which directed the Anatolian Turks during the Selchuk and Ottaman periods in their crafts, trade and economy, continued to live on for almost 630 years with its own rules and regulation until the reign of Sultan Ahmet the 3rd. During this period of the Ottoman Sultan, in 1727, a system called "gedik" was introduced. It was until the 17th century that the Ottoman Empire, as the trade of the Ottoman Empire grew and expanded, the art and craftsmen grew up and the branches increased and the Muslim and non-Muslim distinction increased. In the absence of more unsuccessful, non-Muslim subjects, there was a necessity to work together among people of various religions. This is a new organization, which was founded without considering the distinction of religion, and had not lost much of its old quality, and was called "gedik". The word Gedik is Turkish. It means Monopoly and concession (privilege) that the rights of the owners shall be exercised by the government, or by the rights granted in the article, provided that the others cannot work the line of profession.[91]

Gedik; the work done by the owners and others to sell what is sold on the condition that others can not sell by the provisions of the government issued by the government and the implementation of the provisions of this kind of artisanship and artistry continued until 1860. A person couldn't trade by opening a shop unless a person had grown up from an apprenticeship and fellowcraft to a position of mastery. However, people with concession orders could do craft and trade. These edicts include provisions such as not increasing the number of tradesmen, not increasing the old rents of the owners, not giving the art and trade to the non-residents, giving the apprentices to the apprentices and masters of the tradesmen, and not accepting anybody from the outside. When a tradesman gave up his craftsmanship, when he gave up his mastery of the craftsman, he sold a piece of his artwork and/or to one of the shopkeepers, his instruments were transferred to the new master by paying some money to the heirs.

In 1860, when all the citizens of the Ottoman Empire were allowed to do all kinds of arts, trade and professions freely, the Ottoman Empire was annulled all the gedik berat (warrant). After the proclamation of Tanzimat and trade agreements with foreign states, the monopoly rule that has been going on for a long time was harmful in the development of trade with crafts. It was understood that it was necessary to develop the trade and industry, and no longer benefited from the government in maintaining the rule of gedik and monopoly. The distribution of the lonca organization was approved by the Ottoman State during this period. The sale of overhead gedik products were banned in 1860 on the grounds that they were faulty. The state was dealing with Europe, and not dealing with the craftsman situation. The guilds, which had collapsed with this thought, did not go the way to correct the gediks. In 1861, the monopoly procedure was abolished and a new breach was not established. Thus, this historical organization of the craftsman was introduced to non-craftsmen and could not be expanded. The artisans collapsed. There was no longer a working body. Finally, in 1912 with a law, the Ahi institution was completely removed.[92]

The Union of Truth and Progress, has tried to revive the Ahi. As a result of this effort, the Tradesmen Unions emerged.[93] At the beginning of each union had a kahya, these clerics were very close to the Union and Progress. However, they were effective in the political field, not in the economic sphere, and could not have an impact on the resurrection of the Ahi organisation. During the War of Independence, these tradesmen fought for independence by establishing resistance organizations in cities and towns.

MEVLANA

Mevlânâ Celâleddin Rumi was a famous Sufi of the period who owed his existence and reputation to the support and assistance of the Ahi.[94] He migrated to Anatolia. He was born in Horasan in 1207 and died in Konya in 1273. His first lessons were given to him by his father, famous sycamis Bahaeddin Veled. When Celâleddin, who was intertwined with the anagogic doctrine, encountered Shams Tabrizi, who was a companion of Ismaili Dais and also an Ahi, he gradually emerged from his own school.[95]

The best known characteristics of Celaleddin Rumi is that he explains the anagogic doctrine with the use of poems. In his work, he has included such issues as God, human, universe, soul, love, death and immortality.[96]

Mevlânâ, could read are write Greek very well. He read all of Plato's works in his own language. He also held a number of discussions with priests of the Greek Orthodox Church in Konya on Plato's views. Celâleddin, who studied such an in-depth analysis of the Greek origins of Sufism and anagogic belief, reached the climax of mysticism in his poems:

"The brench of Love is at before the begining, the rooth is at after the end.

This supremacy do not suit to this mind and this manners.

Get extinct, abort your existance, your being is murder.

Love is nothing but to find the true path."[97]

According to Celaleddin, the origin of everything that existed was love. A plant can also love, an animal too. However, man is the only being who can love both his body and his consciousness, his thought and his memory. Love is light. Here is the most beautiful of love, this consciousness is reached through the whole world to unite in love, to keep up with its universal return. The fact that one of his hands is pointing towards the sky and the other looking at the earth during Semah (holy dance) is nothing more than presenting the love he receives from God to the whole world. The soul longed for the first source, the return to God. It was there before the body and it will exist after the body. Ney's (an instrument) sound is the sound that expresses the painful, intimate longing of the soul. Death is the dissolution of the elements that make up the body, the salvation of the soul. Religions are contradictions within them and institutions that are incompatible with the divine being.

This is what Mevlânâ says for Hacc;

"Oh Pligrimers, where are you to?

Come back from the deserts, returning,

The Lover you are looking for is here!

Your neighbour right beside your house.

Wait, if you have seen the formless form of him,

You are the Pilgrimate, you are the Quabe, you are the house keeper...."

The universe is God's vast presence. It is love that governs the universe. The person who can see this love with the eyes of the heart knows himself, knows God, "He deserves the rights." With his strings; "O you're the one who called, looking for God" ...

Celaleddin Rumi believed in the brotherhood of all men. his famous call:

"Come, no matter who you are come,

177

Either you are an Atheist or a prayer of Light,
Even if you have reversed your penitence a tousand times,
Our Dervish Lodge is not lodge of despair, come."

"Come, no matter who you are, come" are the best indicator of brotherhood. The world is a place where all people must live in peace. All people are identical. What matters is the evolution of human beings. The effect of Celaleddin's influence on people was seen in his death and at his funeral the Muslims, Christians and Jews from various sects, as well as the Ahis participated.

Mevlana paid great importance to women. In his book "Fihi Ma Fih", while teaching the Muslims on this subject, he has said that 'while you try to cover your women you at the same time whip the idea of everyone else to see her'. If a women's heart is good as a man, no matter what ban you can apply, she will still go to the path of goodness. If she is bad at heart, whatever you do can not affect her in any way. Do not know what jealousy is. It is the ignorant who believe they are superior to women. The ignorant are rude. They do not know what a smile or love is. Only the animal male is superior. And a loving men is equal to women.'

When Mevlânâ Celâleddin Rumi met Shams Tabrizi, it became a turning point in his life. When an Ismaili Dais, Tabrizi, who had left Iran after the Mongol invasion and dissolution of Ismailis, and who was an Ahi comrade to Anatolia, who was a Ahi's companion, could not find anyone to share his vast knowledge between Ahis, he went to Konya to be with Mevlânâ Celâleddin Rumi.[98]

Mevlânâ's love for God and people influenced Tabrizi in the same way, while influencing Mevlânâ to fight wildly against all kinds of clarity and narrow-mindedness in the ideas of anagogic. Two people who were able to find the real secret of the truth, the two Kamil men together, led to the emergence of an anagogic school that would last for centuries. They both found themselves in each other. They saw that the other man was a divine lover. This inseparable pair were interpreted incorrectly. Intense rumors have caused the gathering of hostile clouds over them. Afraid of the people's reaction, Tabrizi left Konya several times, but had to go back because of Mevlânâ's intense insistence. Tabrizi 's fear came true that at the end Mevlana's younger son filled with depraved circles killed him.

This incident shock Mevlana deeply. However, after a while, he met with yet another Kamil man Ahi Sheikh Sadrettin. Sadrettin had reached the Kamil man status at Ahizm. Unlike Tabrizi, he was supported. He was the head of the Ahis in the Seljuk capital of Konya. Even the Seljuk administration was afraid of his power. There were no rumors about him as there were with Tabrizi. Thanks to the close friendship of Celalleddin with Sadrettin, the whole of Ahi organization followed Mevlânâ.

During the Mongol invasions, Mevlânâ: by saying;

"What is faith against all impiety
A fly, who appears before a Phoenix
Whatever a seddle for a horse is, that is what faith is for a religion
But who needs a horse, whose path is Love!"

He meant to say that the real power is not in hands of religion but in the hands the people and thus become a source of morale to the public.

The students of Mevlana were called 'Kitap-el Esrar' (clerks of secrecy). Among these students there were Muslims, Jews, Christians, Greeks, Persians, Arabs, Armenians and Turks. Until that day, there were no other schools admitting such a variety of people from different religions and nations. Mevlânâ's poems and speeches were compiled and submitted to these days by the clerks of secrecy.

The only place where Mevlana found peace apart from his school was the 'Wise Platon Monastry' in Sille. This famous Sufi stayed in this monastery sometimes for weeks.

As Celaleddin prophesied, 'as God is my witness, my poems will travel from east to the west, all over the world, and will be taught in meetings and gatherings'.

Following the death of Celaleddin, his elder son Sultan Veled institutionalized his father's school. The members of the Order were called Mevlevi meaning 'Turner' in Persian. However due to the difficulties of the used language, Mevlevisim remained limited to the intellectual circles and did not become public.

YUNUS EMRE

Yunus Emre was the person who could expalin the anagogic doctrine to the people in their own language and thus was considered to be the true heir of Mevlânâ.[99]

It is no coincidence that Father Elyies, Hacı Bektashi Veli, Ahi Evren, Celaleddin Rumi and Yunus Emre were the people of the same period. As a matter of fact, in the following centuries, despite the fact that the main source did not change, the thought structure changed, so there were not so many effective philosophers among the Turks.

It is known that Haci Bektashi knew Father Elies. Although Haci Bektashi did not meet Mevlânâ face to face, he carefully followed his thoughts. Some sources suggest that Shams Tabrizi stayed with Haci Bektashi for a while before he went to Konya and was a disciple of him. According to these sources, Tabrizi was commissioned by Haci Bektashi to influence Mevlânâ's thoughts and sent to Konya.

Yunus Emre, another anagogic genius of the same period, came to Konya shortly before the death of Mevlâna and received lessons from him. By saying the following, Yunus Emre:

> "During the chat with Mevlana
> There has been a sign with my Saz (instrument)
> The Enlightened submerged into sayings
> That is why it happens."
> Emphises that he has joined his classes.
> Also by saying:
> "His highness Mevlana, after glancing to us,
> His enormous gazing is the mirror of our heart."
> He once again emphasizes his respect to his master.

Yunus Emre was born in Sarıköy, near Ankara in 1245. Yunus Emre was not born in Khorasan, but all of the inhabitants of the village he lived in were from the Yesevi sect who emigrated from Khorasan. Yunus Emre's name was given as his father's name, was given as reference to the Ismaili faith.[100] Yunus, who grew up with Yesevi beliefs even though he is not a hundred percent Ismaili, went to Haiı Bektashi, the most famous of the period, to learn Sufism in his youth. However, Haci Bektashi, who was very old, sent Yunus to a "Yesevi Father" and a Bektashi like Father, Taptuk Emre.

Father (Baba) Taptuk received hands from Haci Bektashi's Caliph, Sarı Saltuk. When Sarı Saltuk migrated to Dobruca with his followers, Barak Father (Baba) and Taptuk Emre were brought to the sheikhdom of the Bektashi tekkes (schools) in Anatolia. Having passed 30 years with Taptuk, Yunus expressed that he had passed through the Gate of Truth in the same dervish lodge as:

"To the countries we went
Welcoming to all hearts
The sayings of Baba Taptuk
We spreaded fo God's sake
At the Tample of Taptuk
We have been a doorman
Yunus myself was raw
Have been cooked for God's sake."

The greatness of Yunus, like the other Bektashi Fathers, is his using Turkish in his poems but he is able to do so with utmost skill, in a language that is simple enough for the people to understand. Yunus Emre, even using the language of poetry, even the most profound philosophical issues to the public, even the most philosophical philosophy of the language throughout the centuries to be loved and said that the language, in this way prevented the disappearance of the mother tongue, Turkish. His poetry is the expression of the anagogic doctrine in core Turkish. His poems were compiled 70 years after his death and they were published under the name of "Divan". There are some contradictions about his death. Some claim that he died naturally, while others claim that he was killed during a religious debate and even an uprising.

Yunus, alongside Taptuk Emre, passed through four gates and became a Kamil man. First he learned the contents of all religions at the Shariah Gate. Yunus refers to this as 'I have read four books'. Logic, philosophy, the works of the Greek philosophers, Arabic and Persian, are the other sciences that he learned in the taptis of Taptuk. Yunus received the best possible education of his time. His, "I read neither the beginin nor the end" saying, emphasizes him not paying attention to the zahiri (apparent) ones next to batıni (anagogic) science.

Love for Yunus, or as he preferres "light" is everything. God is light. Nature is light. Human is light. Life and death, absence and being are always the works of light. [101]

According to him, God, who is the light, reveals the universe as all things, in love, and as beasts. Like all beings, the human self is the reflection of divine love. Existence is nothing but divergent wave propagation and expansion. Indeed, astronomers, the universe is constantly growing, with the technology of today confirms this.

Like other Sufis, Yunus, thanks to true love, suggest that people are increasingly approaching God, and ultimately finding God in itself. Man is evident in seeing God in itself. Yunus, who believes in the immorality of the soul, has stated that he is trying to return to the main source of the soul by which he always comes out:

"Your Işk (Love/Light) has taken my self from me
All I need is just you!
I am on fire till yesterday to today
All I need is just you!

I am neither delighted with wealth
Nor complained for powerty
I'm just consoled with your Love
All I need is you!
Your Love just kills the lovers
Makes them dive into the sea of Light
Fills them with appearange
All I need is you!
Let me drink from the wine of Love
Then I can climb to mountains as a great lover
You are the only worry for me yesterday and today
All I need is you!
If they would kill me
And throw my ashes to the sky
The ground calls me simultaniously
All I need is you!
I am called Yunus
My fire increases everyday
My only goal is to reach you
All I need is you!"

Yunus, who says that there is only God, states that diversity is merely an image, the universe that emerged as the result of the Divine Water, and the identity of man's principles. This thought was expressed in the following verses of Yunus Emre:

"I've become moon, rose to the universe
I've become cloud, rained to the sky
I've become rain and fall to the ground
I've become Light and born to the Sun."

To become Light and borning to the Sun (Love)... That is the real goal of Yunus. There is no death, there is returning to the source. By saying;

"Leave duality
Hang in to Unity
You will find the dearest of the dear one
Inside Unity"

Yunus Emre, according to the teachings of the tekke accepts three degrees in divine faith. The first and the lowest grade is the 'İlm-el Yakin Iman' formed through the mind and science. The second degree of faith is the "Ayn-el Yakin İman'. The place is the heart. The dervishes, who have not yet seen the light of truth, have such faith. The third and highest degree of faith is the" Hakk-el Yakin İman - Faithful of Faithfulness". It is achieved only with spiritual intuition power, only to God, to people who have faith, religion has nothing to do with faith, for Yunus he says:

181

"If you ask about the religion of people
There is no need of religion for lovers
Lover becomes devastated
Love/Light do not know what is religion or devoutness."

For Yunus, religious worships are unnecessary. They are even harmful because they are obstacles for reaching God.

"Fasting, Salaat or Pilgrimage are not necessary for lovers
Lover is free of those, who is in pure eager
Oh lovers, oh lovers, Light sect is religion to me
My eyes have seen the face of Friend, mourning is a wedding feast to me
Feasting, Salaat, Alms, Pilgrimage are all attemps for a murder
The poor one is free of them, who is in pure velleity."

Yunus Emre, argues that reality is not in religion or its rules, but it lies in the self-knowledge of man. By saying:

"Knowledge is to know how to learn
Knowledge is to know your self
If you do not know your self
What is the meaning of knowledge?"

By saying this, he attacked directly to the ones who memorized only Koran as Knowledge.

"The meanings of all four books
I read and memorized
As I came to Love/Light
I saw it is just a long syllable."
"Unbeliever, come to my arms
Call the name of the Friend
I will tear my shroud
And come again from soil, purified."[102]

Yunus said that even if the body disappeared, the soul would come back every time, and if it were on the right way, every time, the souls would be more purified.

In addition to Turkish Language, Turkish poetry art has survived to a great extent with Alevi-Bektashi poets. Besides giants like Yunus and Haci Bektas, because of Karacaoğlan in the nature of their successors, such as the poet of the Pir Sultan Abdal, thanks to tightly wrap the essence in Turkish, has been recognized as the official language of Turkey.

After this brief reminding, let's put a stop to Anatolian Anagogism and its development, and let's examine the reflection of this doctrine in the western world.

References

1   Erentay İbrahim, - Hiram Abif, Irmak Pub., Istanbul 2000
2   Gener Cihangir, - *Different Perspectives on Hiram (Hiram Menkıbesine Farklı Bakışlar),* Barış Pub., Ankara 2001
3   Naudon, Paul - *Origins of Freemasonary (Masonluğun Kökenleri),* Homer Pub., Istanbul 2007, p. 23
4   August Le Plonge - *Origin of Egyptians (Mısırlıların Kökeni),* Ege Meta Pub., Istanbul
5   Dursun Turan, - *This is Religion (Din Bu),* Kaynak Pub., Istanbul, 1991, Vol.2, p. 125
6   Gündüz, Prof. Dr. Şinasi - *Paganism in Anatolia (Anadolu'da Paganizm),* Ankara Okulu Pub., Ankara 2005, p. 31
7   Gündüz, Prof.Dr. Şinasi, r.w., p. 33
8   Sever Erol, - *Yezidism and the Origin of Yezidis (Yezidilik ve Yezidilerin Kökeni),* Berfin Pub., Istanbul 1993, p. 33
9   Gündüz, Prof.Dr. Şinasi, r.w., p.49
10 Gündüz, Prof.Dr. Şinasi, r.w., p. 78
11 Şeşen Prof. Dr. Ramazan, - *History of Harran (Harran Tarihi),* Diyanet Vakfı Pub., Ankara 1996, p. 3
12 Gündüz Şinasi, - *Saab's; The Last Gnostics (Saabiler; Son Gnostikler),* Vadi Pub., Ankara 1995, p. 5.
13 Gündüz, Prof.Dr. Şinasi, r.w., p. 68
14 Şeşen R., r.w., p. 9
15 Özbudun Sibel, - *Transformation Dynamics of a Religious Tradition from Hermes to Idris (Hermes'ten İdris'e Bir Dinsel Geleneğin Dönüşüm Dinamikleri),* Ütopya Pub., Ankara, p. 211
16 De Nerval Gerard, - *Travel to the East (Doğuya Seyahat),* Kültür Bakanlığı Pub., Ankara 1984
17 Şeşen R, r.w., p. 41
18 Sarıkavak Doç. Dr. Kazım, - *Urfa and Harran in the History of Thought (Düşünce Tarihinde Urfa ve Harran),* Diyanet Vakfı Pub., Ankara 1997, p. 27.
19 Gündüz, Prof. Dr. Şinasi, r.w., p. 77
20 Dursun T., r.w., Vol. 2, p. 23
21 Özbudun P., r.w., p. 205
22 Şeşen R., r.w., p. 17
23 Şeşen R, r.w., p. 41
24 Şeşen R, r.w., p. 44
25 Şeşen R, r.w., p. 42
26 Gündüz, Prof.Dr. Şinasi, r.w., p. 40
27 Gündüz, Prof.Dr. Şinasi, r.w., p. 78
28 Şeşen R, r.w., p. 49.
29 Gündüz, Prof.Dr. Şinasi, r.w., p. 52
30 Şeşen R, r.w., p. 10
31 Özbudun P., r.w., p. 246
32 Özbudun P., r.w., p. 207
33 Özbudun P., r.w., p. 342
34 Özbudun P., r.w., p. 165
35 Özbudun P., r.w., p. 225
36 Özbudun P., r.w., p. 227
37 Gündüz, Prof.Dr. Şinasi, r.w., p. 74
38 Özbudun P., r.w., p. 231.
39 Özbudun P., r.w., p. 279
40 Sankavak K, r.w., p. 43
41 Sarıkavak K., r.w., p. 98
42 Eyüboğlu İsmet Zeki, - *Mysticism; Sects; History of Order (Tasavvuf; Tarikatlar; Mezhepler Tarihi),* Der Pub., Istanbul 1990, p. 116

43 Tunaşar Seyhun, - *Rational Arab Thinkers (Akılcı Arap Düşünürleri)*, Piramit Pub., Ankara 2005

44 Eyüboğlu İ.Z., r.w., p. 15

45 Eyüboğlu İ Z, r.w., p. 130

46 Şeşen R., r.w., p. 46

47 Çubukçu Prof. Dr. İbrahim Agah, - *Turkish Islamic Culture (Türk İslam Kültürü)*, Ankara İlahiyat Fak. Pub., Ankara 1987, p. 207

48 Baldick Julian, - *Mystical Islam (Mistik İslam)*, Birey Pub., İst. 2002, p. 125

49 Eyüboğlu Sebahattin, - Hayyam; *All Quatrains (Bütün Dörtlükler)*, Cem Pub., Istanbul 1991, p. 73

50 Dursun T., r.w., Vol. 2, p. 17

51 Uraz Murat, - *Turkish Mythology (Türk Mitolojisi)*, Mitologya Pub., Istanbul 1992, p. 125

52 Ada, Ural, - Cultural *Origin of Turks (Türklerin Kültür Kökeni)*, HKEMBL Pub., Istanbul 2006, p. 117

53 Ayan Tamer, - *Double Headed Eagle (Çift Başlı Kartal)*, İtidal Olgunlaşma Pub., Istanbul 1998, p. 199

54 Uraz M., r.w., p. 298

55 Dursun T., r.w., Vol. 3, p. 101

56 Arsel İlhan, - *Arab Nationalism and Turks (Arap Milliyetçiliği ve Türkler)*, İnkılap Pub., Istanbul 1990, p. 62

57 Köprülü Fuad, - *First Sufis in Turkish Literature (Türk Edebiyatında İlk Mutasavvıflar)*, Diyanet İşleri Başkanlığı Pub., Ankara 1984, p. 13

58 Arsel İ., r.w., p. 64

59 Köprülü F., r.w., p. 6

60 Ocak Mehmet Yaşar, - *Rebellion of Babilonians (Babailer İsyanı)*, Dergah Pub., Istanbul 1980, p. 52

61 Eyüboğlu İ.Z., r.w., p. 277

62 Özbudun P., r.w., p. 324

63 Eyüboğlu İ.Z., r.w., p. 343

64 Dierl Anton Josef, - *Anatolian Alevism (Anadolu Aleviliği)*, Ant Pub., İst. 1991, p. 39

65 Uraz M., r.w., p. 13

66 Çamuroğlu Reha, - *History, Heterodoxy and Babilonians (Tarih, Heterodoksi ve Babailer)*, Metis Pub., Istanbul 1990, p. 153

67 Ocak M.Y., r.w., p. 133

68 Birge John Kingsley, - *History of Bektashism (Bektaşilik Tarihi)*, Ant Pub., Istanbul 1991, p. 48

69 Zelyut Rıza, - *Alevism by Essence (Öz Kaynaklarına Göre Alevilik)*, Yön Pub., Istanbul 1992, p. 27

70 Yıldırım Ali, - *Alevi Doctrine (Alevi Öğretisi)*, Yol Bilim Kütür Araştırma Series, Ankara 2002, p. 20

71 Yörükan, Yusuf Ziya, - *Alevis and Woodmen in Anatolia (Anadolu'da Aleviler ve Tahtacılar)*, Kültür Bakanlığı Pub., Ankara 1998, p. 313

72 Dierl A.J., r.w., p. 83

73 Eyüboğlu İ.Z., r.w., p. 182

74 Birge J.K., r.w., p. 109

75 Ekonomi Politika Dergisi, Vol. 38, August 1993

76 Sezgin Abdülkadir, - *Hacı Bektaş Veli and Bektashism (Hacı Bektaş Veli ve Bektaşilik)*, Sezgin Pub., Istanbul 1991, p. 155

77 Eyüboğlu, İsmet Zeki, r.w., p. 171

78 Birge J.K., r.w., p. 85

79 Birge J.K., r.w., p. 97

80 Şener Cemal, - *The Alevi Case (Alevilik Olayı)*, Yön Pub., Istanbul, 1989, p. 135

81 Ekonomi Politika Journal, r.w.

82 *Tradesmen and Craftsmen in the 50th Anniversary of the Republic (Cumhuriyetin 50. Yılında Esnaf ve Sanatkâr)*, TESK Pub., Ankara 1973, p. 5

83 *Tradesmen and Craftsmen (Esnaf ve Sanatkâr)*, r.w., p. 14

84 Fiş Radi, - *A Sufî, An Ahi Humanist, Celâleddin Rumi Mevlânâ (Bir Mutasavvıf, Bir Ahi Hümanisti, Celâleddin Rumi Mevlânâ)*, Yön Pub., Istanbul 1990, p. 218

85 *Tradesmen and Craftsmen (Esnaf ve Sanatkâr)*, r.w., p. 23.

86   Neşet Çağatay, - *What is Ahisim (Ahilik Nedir?)*, TESK Pub, Ankara 1974, p. 56

87   *Tradesmen and Craftsmen (Esnaf ve Sanatkâr)*, r.w., p. 24

88   Neşet Ç., r.w., p. 68

89   Neşet Ç., r.w., p. 73

90   *Tradesmen and Craftsmen (Esnaf ve Sanatkâr)*, r.w., p. 32

91   *Tradesmen and Craftsmen (Esnaf ve Sanatkâr)*, r.w., p. 49

92   *Tradesmen and Craftsmen (Esnaf ve Sanatkâr)*, r.w., p. 110

93   *Tradesmen and Craftsmen (Esnaf ve Sanatkâr)*, r.w., p. 124

94   Eyüboğlu İ. Z., r.w., p. 240

95   Dierl A. J., r.w., p. 47

96   *Mevlânâ Celâleddin Rumi, - Mesnevi*, Devlet Pub., Istanbul 1973

97   Fiş R., r.w., p. 85

98   Fiş R., r.w., p. 178

99   *Abdülbaki of Gölpınar, - Yunus Emre,* Varlık Pub., Istanbul 1971, p. 8

100 Ergüven Abdullah Rıza, - *Yunus Emre,* Yaba Pub., Ankara, 1982 p. 29

101 Bayrakdar Mehmet, - *Yunus Emre and Philosophy of Love (Yunus Emre ve Aşk Felsefesi),* Türkiye İş Bankası Pub., Ankara 1991, p.21

102 Bayrakdar M., r.w., p. 59

CHAPTER X

THE WESTERN WORLD AND ESOTERISM
THE TEMPLARS

We have already mentioned that there was an intense struggle between the Anagogic and the Sunnis in the Islamic world. While this civil war was going on in the East, a completely different attempt in the West was giving its first fruits. Popes, the spiritual and political leaders of the Christian world, had flagged the holy land for the rescue of the unbelievers.

After the emergence and spread of Islam from the East with the Seljuks to Anatolia and from the West with the Murabites to Spain, the Christian world has led to the emergence of great concern. All trade routes were in the hands of Muslims. The Christians felt imprisoned and overwhelmed. As a matter of fact, because of the intense efforts of the Christians, they had to try different ways because of the failure of the Mediterranean to monopolize the Muslims, because they did not fall into the hands of the trade routes of the east, and they took their ships and realized their famous discoveries that widened the boundaries of the known world and started a new era.

In the 10th century, in Europe, the feudal lords were very powerful and the conflicts between them did not stop. For all these reasons, the Pope had long seen the necessity of organizing an eastward expedition. This kind of voyages would enable the economic life to revive, the riches of the east to be transported to the west, and most importantly, the Christian conflicts in Europe would be channeled in a much more positive direction to the redemption of the holy land.

The first attempt in this direction came from Pope Uranus the 2nd. Urbanus found the excuse he was looking for in Byzantium. Urbanus began its propaganda activities to send aid to the Byzantine Christians who were helpless in the face of the Seljuk forces.[1]

Despite Rome being sceptical of the Eastern Church and because of the intense competition between the Papacy and the Orthodox Church of Constantinople, Urbanus succeeded in gathering many adherents around in a short period of time, promising Heaven to those who had helped the Eastern Christians. However, almost none of them were professional soldiers, they were all idle unemployed, and their biggest dream was to return to their country rich with their plundering from the east.

The Pope had declared that the goal was to free Jerusalem from the hands of Muslims. Christians who swear by being united by the Pope and put their possessions and their relatives under the auspices of the Papacy until they return and put their crosses on their clothes as the mark of their oaths. Thus, these forces were called "The Crusaders".[2]

In the Muslim world, the Sunni-Ismaili conflict continued, the Fatimans were not identified as a dangerous enemy, and the Crusaders, who dared due to the dispersement of the Great Seljuk Empire, began their first voyages in 1095. But the first ones were not even an army. These undisciplined pioneers could not even wait to enter Muslim lands to demonstrate their true intentions. They began to fall within the borders of Byzantium. These early Crusaders arrived fast. As soon as they moved to Anatolia, almost all were destroyed by Turkish forces. Later, more regular troops of 2nd Crusaders re-emerged in Anatolia under the leadership of the Norman count Baumond. They invaded Iznik and won the war against the Turks. The Turkish forces continued the gang war and were constantly wearing down the Crusaders. The Crusaders took Antakya from the Seljuks after a long siege. Beaumont did not give the city to Byzantium and kept it under its sovereignty.

The East-West struggle between Christians, between Constantinople and Roman churches, continued for hundreds of years. For this reason, it was not a secret that the Byzantine forces looked at the crusader forces coming from the west. Constantinopolis preferred not to open its doors to these forces. Cardinal Humbert was the last person to put an end to the Roman struggle. Humbert, the representative of Rome in Constantinople, came to Hagia Sophia in 1054 and gave the Patriarch a fatwa of Pope Leo 9. In this fatwa, the Pope excommunicated the Patriarch Cerularius and the Orthodox dignitaries. The Patriarch also explained that he excommunicated the Pope from Christianity. This disconnection between the two churches would last for 911 years. The biggest difference of the Byzantine church from the Roman church was the beginning of the Hermetic collection. Hermetic texts were passed to the Greek Orthodox historian and philosopher Michael Psellus when the last Saabi Temple was destroyed in Urfa in 1050. Psellus translated these texts into Greek. This Hermetic work, called Picatrix, was translated into Spanish in the 11th century. The Roman church was increasingly seeing the Byzantine church as heretics. Already, many gods of the old Eluisis and Mithra religion were saints in the Orthodox church. When the Byzantine Church came to terms with the doctrine of Hermetism, the Roman Church followed a strategy that enabled the first crusade to be carried out on Byzantium. At the time of the first crusade, the Papal voices had not been heard by the Papal Orthodox church, but rather by encouraging the relocation of many relics and bringing them to Rome. Similar looting took place during the 4th Crusade. In 1204, the Latins captured Constantinopolis and carried many of the manuscripts to Rome. The Orthodox Church carried out its activities underground until Constantinople was restored in 1261.[3]

The Crusaders came to Jerusalem in 1099. At that time, Jerusalem was under the rule of the Fatimids. After a short siege, the Christians who took over the city killed all the Muslims and Jews in the city. In Jerusalem, it was announced that the Latin Kingdom was established. Baudoin went to the kingdom. Beaumont became the Prince of Antioch, under his own prince. But after a short time, Baumond passed into the hands of the Turkish forces, and in Antakya again Turks. All the forces sent to save the prince of Antioch were repelled by the Turks.

The struggle between the Turks and the Crusaders was then limited only to the battles of the Crusaders during their passing through Anatolia.

Crusades continued at intervals until the 1270s. However, after the Selahattin Eyyubi took back Jerusalem and ended the Latin Kingdom in 1187, it was seen that the Crusaders were only able to achieve partial success in the Middle East. The most successful result of the Crusades was to save the Mediterranean trade from the hegemony of Muslims. While the trade in Europe has come alive, the Islamic world has gradually declined.

The later encounters of the Crusaders and the Turks were during the Ottoman Empire. The fact that the Ottomans took permanent lands in Eastern Europe and advanced to Vienna completely abandoned Europe for its holy lands and the Christians acted in a purely Crusader mentality and solidarity against the Ottoman armies to protect their land. The wars against the Ottomans were carried out under the leadership of religious-military knight sects, whose first seeds were laid in the

Latin Kingdom of Jerusalem. Although these temples were distributed in 1312, the Temples of Rhodes in Malta continued to survive until the end of the 18th century with the Ottoman forces.

The Crusaders were taking the members of the monastery associations "Gilde" to carry out various arbitrations on the roads and build bridges on the rivers.[4] The Roman legions would also take the troops of the Collegia construction guilds, the main source of the Gildes, together for the same purpose. Thanks to this system, which increased the army's mobility very much, the priests of Gilde encountered members of the Orthodox College in Byzantium during their difficult travels, and those who were powerful among the Turks, and finally, the members of the Ismaili organization, the Futurist. These encounters enabled Gilders to resemble the East-Western professions. In this analogy, the Templars made the greatest influence on the Gildes with extremely good relations with the Ismailis. The Templars made the Gilde members under their orders to further develop the esoteric doctrine within their body. Gilde members who returned to Europe also caused similar developments in the Confreries, a relatively secular analogue of the same organization in France. First craftsman Gildes, it appeared in England between 1100-1135 A.D. The roots of these unions were based on the artisans' unions established within the Templars in Jerusalem. Gildes had a three-degree study system. These are Disciple (Apprentice); Formuli (Fellow Craftmen) and Magistri (Master) degrees. These units formed the first core of the London Mason community.[5]

The Templar Knights were founded in 1118 by the patronage of St. Bernard[6] and his nephew, Knight Hugs De Payens, under the name of "The Poor Soldiers of Christ". He went to Jerusalem in 1119.[7] Indeed, was this the only purpose? How could this group of nine protect the holy land from the unbelievers? Who were the Templers and what were the facts behind the establishment of the Templar sect? In order to find answers to these questions, the situation of esoteric schools should be examined in the early days of Christianity.

After the change of its structure within Christian Orthodoxy, the first gnostic movement affecting the western world was Manichaeism.[8]

Manichaeism, in Baghdad in AD 214, it claims to be descended from the Persian Royalty, was founded by a man named Mani. Mani called himself the Apostle of Jesus. In 240, Mani dressed in a white gown, like Jesus, and tried to spread his teaching by baptizing his disciples and healing with his hands. His supporters argued that he was born of a virgin mother and was the "New Jesus." Other titles of Mani were the saviour, the apostle, the illuminator, the Lord, the guide, the revival of the dead, and the captain. It is noteworthy that all of these titles are nicknames that describe Jesus. Mani said that Jesus, Zoroaster and Buddha were his predecessors and that they came from the same source. Believing in the universal war of Darkness and Light, Mani worked in the doctrine of esoteric ideas, such as the migration of souls and the entry of souls into new bodies. Defining Jesus as the "Son of the Widow", Mani accepted the initiation ceremony and enlightened the elite. According to Mani, Jesus was a symbolic deity because he was an illuminating guide. He was a mortal, but he did not die on the cross and died at a later date. In 276, he was imprisoned, his skin swollen, and his head cut off. After his death, his teachings quickly spread to the whole Christian world.

Manners are an initiative doctrine that is made special to a small number of people. Mani defines three types of people: chosen, prepared to enter religion and sinners. The first group are the Manic monks. They are moving away from the Earth and constantly turning to light. They will reach eternal life. The second group is the people who have to follow, but have not yet been purified from the pollution of the world and are living with the hope of being born again one day. The final group was doomed to death and to be forgotten.[9] Cathar's ideas were significantly influenced by Maniheism.

Mani's thoughts were the cornerstones of the Cathar philosophy. Manic schools were opened in Italy, Spain, Southern France and Bulgaria. The Albigen Crusade against the Cathars was actually a war between Catholic Christianity and the supporters of the Manichaean philosophy.

Despite the attack of Albigen, Maniheism did not disappear completely. In 318 A.D., Priest Arius of Alexandria was defending almost the same views.[10] According to Arius, Jesus was not divine, but a mortal being, and nothing more than a tutor inspired by him. It was a curse to think that Jesus was a god. Arius said he believed in a Great God who was omnipotent, not embodied in a body, died in the hands of the world he created. Arianism, like Manichaeism, spread in Western Europe. In the face of the increasing worldly power of Catholic Rome, advocacy received wide support from the masses. The accords were condemned in the Council of Nicaea, but their supporters increased. During the reign of his son, who was succeeded by Constantine after his death, Arianism was accepted as a sect. In the centuries in which the Morovenj emerged, a large part of the priests of Christianity was an Agrarian.

According to French folk legends, we have seen that the Holy Grail was brought to Marseille by Magdalena, who had emigrated from Palestine to France at the beginning of the first century. The sacred remains claimed to have belonged to Magdalena still receive great respect in the Christian world. According to the legends, the representatives of the lineage coming from Magdalena were tasked with not revealing the secrets of the saviour and keeping it secret. This chosen community has kept the secret of the Holy Grail to this day. The bowl was called "Sang Real". Sang Real, "Royal Blood", it was used to mean one blood.[11] Magdalena, the wife of Jesus, emigrated to France with the daughter of Jesus, after the crucifixion, and at that time he had mixed with the Jewish community in France. The marriages between the holy family and the Visigoth nobles have taken place and the holy blood has existed for four centuries. Again, the Frank-based Morovenj, which emerged as a result of marriages with Visigoth nobles, carries this blood.[12]

Julius Africanus, one of the first-century historians, writes that the surviving relatives of Jesus complained about the Roman rulers who systematically annihilated the levels of the Jewish aristocrats. A family who would witness first-hand incidents was a serious threat to the formation of the Christian Orthodox doctrine. If possible, it would have to be eliminated, if not, to be disabled. In 180 A.D., the Priest of Lyon, Irenaeus, wrote five books, "Against perversity".[13] According to Irenaeus, all kinds of gnostic thought and current were heresy and should be destroyed immediately. Irenaeus, who insisted in a Catholic (universal) church, saw that there was a need for a fixed and specific law, and uncovered the Ahdi Jadid Law.

One of the movements Irenaeus described as heresy was Catharism, the supporter of the holy family, which became quite widespread in the Christian world. The word Cathar in Greek means pure one's Cath. Catharism is a general name given to different heretic sects.[14] The Bogoms in the Balkans, Patarines in Italy, Albigensians in France, Arinon in Spain, Marcionites and all Manikaens widespread all over Europe are considered as Cathar.

Bogom is a Western school that has migrated from Anatolia to Bulgaria. Bogoms, whose origin is in Anatolia, Nevşehir and Niğde, was influential in the Balkans and then in France and Italy. The reason for the migration from Anatolia is the Byzantine rule during the Byzantine queen Teodora and the intense oppression and massacre of the people of Anatolia who are believed to be Pagan West. With the order of the Orthodox church, more than one hundred thousand people were massacred and many others had to appear Christian to get rid of the massacre. The word Bogomil means Rights Friendly in Bulgarian.[15] New candidates accepted to the community with an initiation ceremony are said to be Christians first, but in the later stages of the teaching, the church and the Orthodox faith are abandoned and the secret is given to the member. Like the Cathars, Bogom does not accept the Cross symbol. The holy book of Bogoms is Liber Sectelum (Book of Secrets). They believe that God is a god of evil. This is not the true God. The true God had a son before Jesus, and this is Ishmael. Ishmael, represent Logos. Mary is not Jesus' mother, but "Jerusalem of the planets". All of the French Cathars are of Bogom origin.[16] It is possible to speak of a belief and origin unity between the Anatolian Alevism and Bogoms.[17] The name of the arm of the Bogoms who migrated to France is the Albigen. Albigen means "Bright Light Man" in Latin.

Cathar preachers were called Parfait. It was believed in a feminine Supreme being. Parafaiters could be men or women. The only religious ceremony of the Cathars was Consolamentum, a purifying ceremony. This ceremony is applied only on the death row of the members.[18]

Cathars, women's rights in religion were defended. The idea of the Catholic Church order being subject to a single church with a certain doctrine was completely rejected since the belief of Catharism was that there could be no clergy in the Cathar faith. For a human being to pass through mystical experiences and to purify himself/herself.[19] Cathars, who defined themselves as the children of light and Rome as the children of dark, saw the knowledge above all else, with the view that knowledge obtained by mystical and religious experiences would bring people closer to God. They were evil with good, dark with light and between the soul and the matter, there was a constant struggle since the formation of the universe.

In Cathar's belief influenced by Manichaeism, Kabbalah and Mithra agnostics, it is argued that the universe is an arena of struggles between good, evil, light, dark, soul-matter. Cosmological dualism is founded on two opposing and equivalent concepts such as beauty and force. Beauty, the divine power, is the God of love and is a pure spiritual principle, far from any material weaknesses, not been created or creates. In contrast, force is the expression of material creation. The evil God is responsible for the creation of the universe, of the world and of matter, and this action is an ominous act. This power, which is at its core, is the world itself. This power that contains the negativity in its structure, the King of the World, was called "Rex Mundi".[20] The purpose of a Cathar, Rex Mundi as far as he can to get away from the matter and to be combined with the Beauty principle. The ultimate goal is to get rid of materialism, restore spirituality and return. Jesus is the evil created in the Trinity, which is the dogma of the Catholic church, and the Father is the master of evil. The figure of the cross and the crusification have no sacredness. Jesus is just a prophet who was executed as a result of his efforts. There is no divine side to the crucifixion. But Jesus is a prophet of love who has fought for beauty, that is AMOR. While Amor symbolizes beauty, ROME symbolizes the force, that is the evil, which is read in reverse order. The Catholic Church is the representative of Rex Mundi.[21]

Sex and childbirth are the continuations of the first material creation and serve the Force. Therefore, birth control and women's miscarriage are acceptable. This situation has been described by the Catholic Church as sinfulness. In the eyes of the Roman church, the Cathars prickled believing that Jesus was dead. The Cathars denied the dogma that Jesus was the son of God and accepted Jesus as a prophet of God. Jesus was the prophet of Amor for his cleansing practices. According to them, the Roman church argued that the dogmas it posed were Jesus' representative to Rex Mundi. Therefore, the cross where Jesus was crucified was accepted as the symbol of Rex Mundi and the cross was rejected. They refused to take the cross, just as the rites of communion, baptism, and wine and bread-eating ceremonies.[22]

According to Rome, heresy Cathar beliefs were a great danger. The ideas that were cursed by the Church spread all over Europe. All these thoughts and practices gave rise to the reaction of the Catholic Church and the elimination of the Cathar beliefs, which were described as heretics. The decision was made in 1165. In 1198, Pope Benedictine Innocent was asked to put an end to Catharism by the 6th Raimond of the city of Toulouse, the centre of the Cathar movement. When Raimond refused this request, he was excommunicated, and a Catholic army was created in 1209 and a military campaign was launched against the Cathars.[23] A 30,000-strong Catholic army attacked southern France on the order of Pope Innocent III, led by Cathar-led Languedoc. All the Cathar towns and cities were destroyed, the sword was passed. The Albigen Crusade, called the war, lasted 40 years. With the order of the pope, hundreds of thousands of Cathar believers were killed in a forty-year period. Against the possibility of "good Christians" among them, the Pope said, "Kill them all. God will separate those who are on his side."

A Spanish Catholic fanatic called Dominick Guzman helped the pope's troops. Guzman was the founder of the Dominican sect, later known under his own name. In 1233, the Inquisition was also the Dominicans.[24]

At the beginning of the 13th century, Languedoc was a non-French principality. In the field of philosophy and intellectual activities, there was a great improvement. The schools in the region were taught in Greek, Arabic and Hebrew, and were given Kabbalah training. In the rest of Europe, the nobles could not even write their names, all of the nobles in the region were studying at the upper level. Information about Islam and Jewish thoughts came through Spain. The Languedoc region had reached a level of culture not seen in Europe until the Renaissance.

By 1243, except for the Montsegur stronghold, all the Cathar cities had been captured by the invaders. A sheltered position, this fortress was besieged for ten months. Although many attacks were pushed back, the last Cathar site fell in 1244 and the appearance of Catharism was apparently discontinued.[25] But their ideas could not be completely destroyed. The Cathar faith was generally accepted and continued to live in and around the Rennes chateau, under the control of the Templar knights, where the holy family existed.

The Cathars were famous for having a treasure, including the Holy Grail. The Cathar treasure, something more than material wealth, was hiding in Montsegur. Three months before the fall of the castle, two Parfait pierced the siege and concealed the treasure they had taken with them in a well-guarded place. Again, just before the castle collapsed, four people escaped from the cliffs with ropes and took with them the last of the treasure. It is believed that these four people were taken with them, they were tried to be kept in the castle until the last minute, but when they realized that the castle would fall, they were abducted and had spiritual values. Among them, it is possible that the Holy Grail of Graal, which is rumoured to be in the Cathars, is also present.

Between the 5th century and the 7th century A.D., the region is known today as France and Germany ruled the Morovenj, which held holy blood through marriage. In the 5th century, during the occupation of Europe by the Huns, the ancestors of the Morovessians, the Cambrian, settled in northern France. This Frank tribe, who adopted Roman customs, after the collapse of the Roman Empire at the end of the 5th century, it established a state compatible with the Roman state tradition.

The name of the Frank kings, Morovenj, comes from Merovee, the first king of Morovenj. In 448, Merovee was proclaimed King of Frank.[26]

In French, Merovve means both Mother and Sea. Merovee's name is that this dynasty is a descendant of the mother and also proves to be related to overseas. Morovenj Kings, known in the esoteric sciences, "known as the kings of the miracle". Because of the spiritual nature of their blood, they were rumoured to be among the people with whom they distributed healing. It was also rumoured that the Morovenj, known as Priest-Kings, carried divine holy blood, that they were God's human manifestations, and that there was a hole drilled in their skulls for religious purposes. This hole is reminiscent of the third eye practice of Tibetan monks in their skulls, and this practice of his descendants is another proof that Jesus was educated in Tibet.

In the Morovenj Kingdom, literacy was promoted, and philosophy and art movements strengthened. Morovenj, since the priests were king, they did not deal with earthly deeds in accordance with their abilities. Government and administrative affairs were left to an administrator, called "the palace head". The management of the Morovenj was governed in a similar way to today's constitutional monarchies through a system that was not found in its age. The kings of the Morovenj believed that their descendants came from Noah. This form of promotion was adopted by Freemasonry in later centuries.

Merovee's son 1. Clovis, came to throne in 481. During his reign, the Franks agreed to be subject to the Roman church. The priest of the Roman Church had declared himself a Pope in 384, but the Roman church had no influence over other churches during this period. Cathar Church, the emergence of the Papacy, in Europe it was much more common and active. An agreement was made in 496 between the 1st Clovis and the Roman church, which was the strongest king of Western Europe.[27] The agreement affirmed the Roman church as the highest religious authority and aimed to eliminate the opponents of the church. Clovis was also given the title of "New Constantine", and the religion of the Moorovenj with the Holy Blood was approved as the political rulers of the Holy Roman Empire. With this agreement, the establishment of a new Christian Roman Empire, whose worldly affairs were led by the Morovenj dynasty and based on the Roman church, was taken, and the status of the Roman church was raised to the same level as the Greek Orthodox church.

With the death of Clovis in 511, the empire was divided among his four sons. A period of constant conflict between these four small kingdoms began. Born in 651 as the heir to the Austrasie Kingdom, Dagobert married in 671 with the sister of the Visigoth king and settled in Rennes.[28] He had gathered the treasures, including the sacred relics of the Cathars. The Treasury also included part of the treasures of the Temple of Solomon in Jerusalem. In 70 AD., Jerusalem was burned by Roman soldiers. The precious treasures in the temple moved to Rome.[29] There is a stone relief that was brought to Rome by the Jews, which is a very sacred and everlasting candlestick, and the Ark of the Covenants. In 410, Rome was invaded by the Visigoths. The treasures of Solomon passed into the Visigoths. The treasure was hiding in Rennes, a castle of Visigoth, and when the castle passed to Dagobert by marriage, the treasure also reached the Morovenj.

3rd. Dagobert, who strengthens his territory by taking the support of the Visigoths and extends his lands, perverted by the church Cathar was closer to their views. His policies prevented the development of the Roman church and drew the reaction of the church. In 679, Dagobert was assassinated by a Roman assassin. The Pope ordered the head of the assassin Pepin, who was closer to the Roman ideology, to be elected as the new King of the Franks. Thus, the agreement signed two and a half centuries between the Morovenj and the Papacy was terminated. As a result of this appointment, the Pope became the highest mediator between God and kings. All kings had become the second man and entered the service of the Pope. Rome was the capital of Western Europe with Pope's approval.[30]

Together with Pepin, the royal has passed from the Morovenj to the Karolenj dynasty. However, an agreement which was considered sacred was ignored and there was a seizure of power. In order to get rid of these extortion charges, starting from Pepin 2, Karolenj rulers made marriages with the Morovenj princesses. Charlemagne granted to him in 800 the title of Holy Roman Emperor, who was put to the Morovenj lineage that gave his name to the dynasty. Charlemagne's wife was also a Morovenj princess. All these efforts, however, failed to end the claims that the royal was the right of the Holy Morovenj. Some groups, such as the Sion Monastery, which would describe the carnivores and others as extortioners, continued to work to bring the Morovenj dynasty to work, with the son of Dagobert II, Sigesbert. As a result of the intrigues of the Papacy, the Morovenjs were destroyed and the Karolenj Dynasty, which did not leave the Pope's orders, was replaced. Unification under one rule was established, but empire He was touched.

The same tradition was preserved in the Holy Roman German Empire. After the Holy Roman Empire, and the imperial coat of arms remained a double-headed eagle. All the European dynasties were related to the bloodshed of the Morovenjs and the double-headed eagle, which became their symbol, reached today and spread to countries and ages. The Russian tsars, the emperors of Austria, the British nobles, have always carried the same emblem, the double-headed eagle, the emblem of the emperors, nobles for thousands of years.[31]

In the 4th century, the Visigoths, which were Christian by adopting Fidelity, seized Rome in 480. Under the supervision of the Visigoth, the apostle became the dominant element in the Christian world. However, the Visigoths declared that they accepted Roman Catholic Christianity in 711 after the collapse of the Morovenj. All Jews in the country of Visigoth were massacred. The Jews, then, took refuge with the Muslims who had occupied Spain in 711. In 758 the Jews made a deal with the Franks, and in Septimania, they established a principality that was dependent on the Karolenj. Aymery, who was the descendant of Sigesbert, who was the head of the prince and who maintained the holy family, got the name of Thierry, a Frank name. Thierry was Guillem de Galone's father. Galone's mother was Charlemagne's aunt Alda. The Godfroi de Bouillon, the conqueror of Jerusalem, descended from Guillem de Galone, the owner of the holy heritage.[32] In other words, Godfroi de Bouillon was also a Marovenj. In 792, Guillem de Galone founded an academy in the city of Galone, bringing scientists from outside to teach. The city soon became the centre of Gnostic studies. The city of Galone was also the first known centre of the Magdalena cult in Europe. In the cult, Magdalena and his womb were consecrated instead of the Virgin Mary. The figures depicting a mother and child in gothic cathedrals were made with the promise of a wife and her child, instead of the mother of Jesus.

According to the Sion monastery, Sigesbert escaped to London, where he was the Duke of Razes, and his uncle's nickname was Plandart.[33] In 363 The Lord of Rennes ruled the land after his uncle. In 790, Guillem de Gellone, of the same lineage, received the Rule of Rennes. According to the same genealogy, the Godfroi de Boullion from the descendant of Plandart was the Earl of Rennes before the Crusades. Godfroi de Boullion was a legal successor who claimed the kingdom of Merovenjs, but the conditions of the day did not permit the creation of this kingdom in Europe. For this reason, Boullion began attempts to create a kingdom in Jerusalem, in the holy land of Muslims.

Godfroi de Bouillon's brother The Duke of Loren, Baudoin, was named the first King of Jerusalem with the name of Baudoin 1. It is understood that Bouillon, one of the preparers of the Crusades, went to Palestine by selling all of his property in Europe and he was determined to settle in Jerusalem. According to the "Secret Documents" belonging to the Sion Monastery, in 1099, after the conquest of Jerusalem, a council of occupation commanders and religious leaders gathered and offered the throne to Bouillon. When Bouillon rejected this offer by claiming his different duties, he was brought to the kingdom by his brother Baudoin.[34]

Jerusalem was taken away by the Christians. But the Fatimids did not see this as a great loss. On the contrary, the most conservative section of Islam, they entered an alliance with the Christians because they were fighting the Sunnis. The fighters of the Crusaders were Sunnis because Jerusalem was a sacred city for them to take back Jerusalem. The Druzes, the successors of the Fatimids today, show examples of the solidarity between the Crusaders and the West Muslims in the rituals of the sect. Some of the Christian beliefs of this denomination are also under the aforementioned cooperation.

Selahattin Eyyubi's end to the Fatimid state in 1171 increased the solidarity of the Ismailis and the Crusaders who were in constant struggle with Sunni power. The most radical branch of the Ismailis, Hasan Sabbah bouncers and Crusaders among the leading knights, a special bond has formed over time.[35] Some documents about the taxpayers of the Fedais (Assassins) have reached today.

After the Knights came to Jerusalem, they were appointed by King Baudoin to protect the Temple of Solomon, and at the place of the temple, in 540 A.D., the "Poor Soldiers of Jesus", which was given to them in the church built by the Byzantine Emperor Justinyanus. They changed their names because of their new duties and took the name of Knights Templar in 540. After a while, these knights and organizations were briefly called the Templars.

The grandfather of Hugues De Payens, the founder of the order, was Tibaut De Payens, whose nickname was Gardielian Magribi. It is understood that grandfather De Payens lived in Andalusia. The Latin word for Payens is Pagano. So Pagan, non-Christian. Hugues De Payens, married with the Scottish noble Catherine de Saint Clair VL is. This name will later be changed to Sinclair and become a family with important roles in history.

Knight De Payens and his retinue to Jerusalem shortly after arriving, they met with Ismailis. Hasan Sabbah, who learned about the knights of Gilde, learned about the knights and learned that they were the most influential and knowledgeable people in the Christian community, wanted to meet with the Knights of the Temples. Under this request, they also had the influence of the Tempers to undertake the task of protecting an ancient West doctrine temple and to reveal some of the lost secrets in the temple. Some researchers argue that Saint Bernard, De Payens' uncle, learned of the places of the esoteric secrets and treasures that were buried in the temple, and founded the sect to find them and sent them to Jerusalem. According to some allegations, most of the secrets, including the stone slab, where a sacred word was lost among them, were revealed by the knights between the foundations of the temple.

The most noteworthy information about the bumper was written by Frank historian Guillaume de Tire between 1175-1185.[36] Tire says that the knights did not take new members of the denomination for 9 years. De Paynes, and eight of his friends, King Baudoin was written in the ruins of the Temple of Solomon, the royal historian Fulk de Chartres, the first nine knights did not provide any information about, rather than Papacy after the approval, the 50-year history of the sect has been written.

In the mid-12th century, Johan Van Würtzburg, who visited the holy land to become a pilgrim, wrote that he had visited the stables that were just under the ruins of the Temple of Solomon. At the beginning of the 20th century, the British royal engineer Charles Wilson, who was studying in the ruins of Herod Shrine in Jerusalem, excavated under the temples of the temples revealing a great number of finds that could be described as belonging to the knights, which they have done.[37] In the inscriptions of the Dead Sea in 1956, 24 different treasures are found in the Temple of Solomon. It is understood from the excavations that the knights of the temple were assigned to find the remains of these treasures. The temple knights kept a secret as to what the treasure in the Temple of Solomon contained and where it was preserved.

According to Tire, the order was established in 1118 and no new members were elected for 9 years. However, there is evidence that the Lord of Anjoun of Western France had joined the Order in 1120 and Lord of Champion in 1124.[38] If the Lord of Anjoun became a member in 1120 and the order was not actually taken for 9 years, the first foundation date of the Templars is not 1118 but 1111. In fact, in 1114, in a letter to the Champagne Lord of the Chartes priest, he said, "We have heard that before you go to Jerusalem, you are involved in Jesus' Misilar". This statement is known as the name given to the sect by Saint Bernard and other religious officials. It is clear from the priest's letter that the Knights Templar was present at that time. It is known that at least three of the nine knights who founded the sect were related to the Champagne Lord. In 1070, the Lord of Champagne, who opened a school of Kabbalistic in his own territory, in 1115, part of his territory was allocated to Saint Bernard, and the monastery of Clairvaux was built here. The Champagne Lord and his followers held a special meeting in 1104. Among those at the meeting were Saint Bernard's uncle, Audre de Montbard. Right after this meeting, Champagne His lord went to Jerusalem as an officer. He stayed in Jerusalem for 4 years and returned to his motherlaned in 1108, finishing his studies. These events show that the group is knowledgeable about temple supplies. Jesus was a descendant of Solomon, and he had knowledge about the treasures in his family through inheritance. The holy family who continued the descendants of Jesus had this information and they started to be discovered by Godfroi de Bouillon and his followers.

In a short period of ten years, the fame of the Knights spread throughout Europe. The religious authorities in Europe praised the Temperians because of their supreme duty, which was not explained. Until 1128, no one but the priest of Clarvaux, St. Bernard, mentioned the merit of the knights. In his treatise "Praise of the New Chivalry," Bernard showed the Knights Templar to the highest of Christianity. In 1127, nine knights returned to Europe and were greeted splendidly by St. Bernard. In 1128, the Church Council gathered in Trayes. At this council, the Knights Templar was recognized as a religious-military sect. Hugues De Payens was given the title of "Grand Master". In the same year, by Pope Honarius 2, this title was approved. In 1139, a second papal edict by the Pope Nicholas II was published. According to the decree, the knights were not responsible for any other religious or political authority other than the Papan.[39] In the charter of the Order, written in Latin, many changes in the content of the Papacy, translated into French. In the Latin charter, the expression non-apostle knights are found, while in the French charter, carefully abducted and concealed by the eyes of those who are not members of the religious order, such as the gathering of anodized knights, the Cathars declared by the Papacy as perverse there were expressions showing that they were between them.[40]

De Payens returned to Jerusalem in 1130. Hugues De Payens and other knights visited Hasan Sabbah on the invitation of Alamut Castle. Here, they also received first-hand information about the Knights of the Sabbah system, the organization of bouncers and the doctrine of the West. After acquainting the teachings of Ismaili, from the acquaintance of Templars, Hasan Sabbah and his Dailar, their loyalty to Esoteric doctrine increased. In 1194, a summit of the Count of Henry of Champagne between the Sheikh of the period and the Sheikh Shabel of Kehf.[41]

In 1102 AD, the Grand Master of Ismaili sent an apostle to the king of Jerusalem, Baudoin. The close relations between the Tempers and Ismailis, which lasted eighty years, have thus begun. As a result of this close relationship, the Grand Master of the temple came into play and in 1129 AD, an agreement was signed between the Crusaders and Ismailis, and it was accepted that the Tyre was given to the Ismailis against Damascus. As a result of this interaction, the Templars adopted the form of organization of the Ismailis, their rituals and symbols and their secrets. The concepts of the ascension system connected to the degrees, the unconditional obedience to the orders of the upper rankers and the commitment to the life of the Grand Master were taken from the Ismailis. The bond has been so strong that there have been attendances from the Templars to the Ismailis and from the Ismailis to the Templars. White and red colours are at the forefront of the clothing of both organizations. White, Light; Red is the symbol of Fire.[42]

Thanks to the strong organization they have established as a model of the Ismaili organization, esoterism is spreading all over Europe, this development is gradually weakening of the Catholic church led the test. The relationship between the Ismailis and the Temperians also included the accusation that ended the organization. While searching for an excuse to destroy the Templars, the Papal sect was accused of "engaging with Muslims and even becoming Muslims".

The Templars learned from Hasan Sabbah, besides the organization, another thing; to keep their true beliefs and to continue to look like good Christians. So much so that in 1128 the Papacy allowed the branches of the cult to be opened in the entire Christian world because of their usefulness. The Papacy, in 1139, explained that the Temperians could not be subject to any kind of worldly and religious authority and that only the Pope was responsible to him. With this permission, all kinds of suspicions and religious pressure over the Tempers have been lifted.

The Knights chose the St. John Gospel, which had an esoteric structure to swear on it to hold the necessity of a Christian appearance and esoteric beliefs. This choice of Templars also affected other knight organizations. In all attempts, other knight organizations that took the Tempers as a model started to swear on the same Bible. Another famous representative of the knighthood organization, and because of their help for those injured in wars, they were called "Hospel" knights, another name was "You Jan Knights".

De Payens was awarded the "Great Pay" by King Henry I of England. When De Payens returned to Palestine, a knight group of 300 men were left behind to train apprentices on European soil. In the twenty years that followed the Council of Troyes, the organization developed at an extraordinary pace. In 1146, the white dress, it was decided to use the red Templar Cross. During the next century, the knights became an international event. The high-level diplomacy between the dynasties and the nobles was led by the knights. In England, the Master of the Temple was a permanent member of the king's parliament and the leader of all sects. The knights assumed the role of an arbitrator when there was disagreement between the religious authority and the royal. Magna Carta was the product of this kind of arbitration. In England, the Tempers mediated between the two sides in the signing of the Magna Carta Libertatum (the Great Edict of Freedoms), which was signed in 1215 as the first democratic constitution, as a result of the friction between the land barons and King John. A good example of Templar diplomacy, this agreement carried a title that was extremely diplomatic and did not offend both sides, as "the Barons hoped to obtain and their masters the subjects that the King granted them".[43]

According to one claim, the Templar organization is not a spontaneous structure. Behind the tempers, there is the Sion Monastery Sect, which is another organization that established the Knights Templar as a military organization.[44] The Sion Monastery, like the Templars, is ruled by the Grand Masters. Solve the Tempers between 1307-1314 Sion monastery has existed for centuries. Sion is still active today and is very influential in European affairs and in international affairs. The aim of the Sion monastery is to ensure that the Morovenj dynasty is back to work and that these members of the dynasty are governed by blood ties not only in France but all over Europe.[45]

Sion monastery, the year of Sion Sect is given as 1090 years. Its founder is Godfroi de Bouillon. The centre was the Notre Dam Monastery in Jerusalem, which was conquered in 1099. The Notre Dam Monastery was built on the ruins of a Byzantine church dating back to the 4th century on the orders of Bouillon. The official name of the order is the Order of the Holy Sepulcher. The Knights were also called "the Knights of the Order of Notre Dam Sion". In 1125, the name of Hugues De Payens is referred to as the Grand Master of this order. In other words, De Payens is the Grand Master of both Tempers and Sion, and there is an organic bond between the two orders. In the Sion Monastic Documents (Prieur Documents), among the founders of the order, De Payens, as well as Comte De Champagne and Andre de Montbard, are included. According to the same documents, Templars was established as the administrative and military branch of the Sion sect. Andre de Montbard also joined the Tempers for a while, and then, his nephew St. Bernard, put the priests, members of the Cistercian cult which were attached to him, at the disposal of the Tempers.

At the end of the Crusades, the knight of the 95 Sion members returned to France with the King of France, Louis VI, and in Saint Jean Le Blanc, they formed the Sion Mountain Small Monastery. 7th Louis, the Sion sent to the sect, a berate has survived. In 1178, Pope Alexander III officially endorsed the assets of the Sion sect.[46]

From 1118 until 1188, it is seen that the Tempers and Sion members act together and the task of Grand Master is carried out by the same people. But in 1187, the hands of the Muslims of Jerusalem. As a result, the monastery on the mountain of Sion was passed on to the Muslims and the members of the sect were forced to seek refuge in France as a refugee. These developments and perhaps the fact that they kept each other accountable from the fall of Jerusalem caused the breakup of the two sects, and in 1188, a formal departure took place. The Tempers have become an independent organization, not an administrative and military wing of Sion. After the separation in 1188, the first Grand Master of Sion was Jean de Gissors. The Sion Order also changed its name to "Sion Monastery-Ormus".

Ormus was a scholar of the Alexandria school, living in the 1st century. Ormus and six of his friends accepted Christianity, under the influence of Mark, but by interpreting the teachings of Jesus under the light of his Hermetic knowledge, they gave birth to a new sect it is given.[47] This is the secret school that the creator of the Gnostic Gospels mentioned by the Priest Clemens. These Bibles, along with hermetic documents, were unearthed in Nag Hammadi. His teachings, in addition to the sayings of Jesus, are based on Hermetism, Pythagoreanism, Mythology and Neo-Platonism, and the name, the Order of Apprentices, is the symbol of this sect, the Red Rose Cross. It is interesting to note that Rose Croix has his own roots in the Ormus organization, and another name that Sion has chosen for him is his showing the "L'Ordre de la Rose Croix Veritas", showing the organic bond between Sion and Rose Croix.

The allegations concerning the Sion Monastery and the following to return to activities in the future, let's continue to examine the Tempers.

The Tempers, who carried out their organizations by taking the Ismaili organization as an example, continued their Ismaili practices such as discipline, hierarchy, absolute devotion and obedience to the Grand Master who was the head of the order. They built a three-degree initiation system. In the masses called the Massleri, the bread they regarded as the symbol of the Holy Spirit was made of clay, wearing aprons, and gloves, not to touch their dirty hands.[48] The temples were all white, not only their aprons and gloves. The Tempers, who received this tradition from the Ismailis, had erected a Red Cross on their breasts, the only difference being the symbol of the Crusaders. The members of the Templar Order were taken by the oath of the Sacrifice, and those who broke their oath paid with their lives. The knights called each other "Brother". In three-tier organization structures, the first-degree holders were called "Serving Brothers" because of the obligation to serve higher-ranking members. Second degree, the members of the tariqa, were called "Chapleini". "Knight" title, was the highest degree he could have.

The ceremony of entering the Templar order begins with the introduction of a candidate in the entrance of the temple with a Knight.[49] His neck was tied up with a rope, representing Tau symbol. The last letter of the Hebrew alphabet is symbolized to have died in a previous life with these Tau signs. Then the candidate shroud Templar Cross at the end of the ceremony and the ceremony, it is removed from its shroud and given to it. Now he is born to a better life. The secrets of the Templar order are explained to him and he is sworn in for poverty, chastity and obedience. White cloak and cape given to him are required to carry continuously. The charter of the Templar Knights prohibited members of other sects from dressing in white clothes. Thus, only the Knights of Templars were intended to offer a pure and spotless life to their Gods. Iniciation, who is a knight, because of the poverty vow, all his assets donate to the sect. It was Hugues De Payens who first started this application. When the knights die, their only property consists of an unnamed rectangular stone with a sword pattern on it.

The Templar's flags consisted of black and white colours to symbolize the coexistence of good and evil in the universe. In the Tempers, the teachers believed that a great existence, such as the Ismailis, was a part of that being. The most important principle of the knights was to free everyone from their beliefs and not to force their beliefs to anyone. This has become one of the most important differences between the Priest and the Catholic Church. Skulls and crossbones are etched into history as a symbol of the Tempers. The skull and crossbones symbolizing the tomb of Master Hiram, the temple maker of Solomon, were used in the 17th and 18th centuries as a sign of each master Mason's tomb.

Like the Ismailis, the tempers used secret signs, passwords and symbols to recognize each other. This secrecy also worked to get rid of the oppression of the Papacy in later years. The Templars claimed Jesus was a mortal. To them, what rose to the sky was the evolved spirit of Jesus. So, it was the Divine Word that united with God.

There are different classes in the Templar order. The leading knights must be noble and European. While the Sergeants, who were the deputies of the knights, were non-noble Europeans. Another class, called Turkopol, which consisted of Muslim Turks and Arabs, fought under the command of the knights. Mercenary light cavalry regiments were formed from the Turkopolies.[50] The knight's clothing, the Templar cross on white, the sergeants on the brown and the Turkopoly on the green are the Templar cross. In addition, there are also Chaplains (priests) of the Gilde, who conduct the correspondence of the knights, who make their accounts and use them as interpreters. Their managers are called the Prier or the Presenter. The brothers in the priest class, like knights, use white gloves in the Eucharist rite to avoid sacred bread and wine. It is known that the Chaplains who keep the records of the tempers and know the different languages, use the mixed codes in the correspondence between them and thus prevent the emergence of the secrets of the order.[51]

All the noble members of the sect had to wear a white priest's suit and a cape on the armour. Nobody except the Templars could wear these clothes. If a knight was taken captive in battle, he could not wish for mercy. He would never pay a ransom. They had to fight until they died, unless they were more than three times the enemy. The most disciplined military power of the time was the Tempers. The most outstanding military their technology was in their hands. They had their own ports, military naval fleets. In their own hospitals, surgeons with their orders were operated, antibiotics and other drugs were used for treatment methods. Unlike other Christians, cleanliness and sanitation were strictly adhered to.

The Tempers built their own fortresses and complexes using their own masonry masters. The architecture of these structures is usually a Byzantine style. In today's Israeli city of Athlit, two Templar masonry graves known as the oldest Mason tombs in the world were found. In addition to the masonry masters, it is seen that masters and gilds from different crafts are also patronized by the Templars and over time these masters have been initiated into Templar membership. Thanks to these masters, it is understood that the Temperians had a deep knowledge of the secrets of sacred geometry and architecture, in the direction of belonging to the same organization, they learned professional secrets. Most of the Gothic Cathedrals in Europe, by Templar architects, was built.

Apart from the Great Masters in Jerusalem, it is known that the Tempers chose one Grand Master for each country of operation and another Grand Master who was also responsible for all of Europe. It is imperative that the Grand Master of Jerusalem, who is the leader of the entire order, resides in Jerusalem and is elected by the general priest's communion.[52]

The Tempers began a kind of bankerage after Papal received permission to organize all over Europe. Coins of soldiers or pilgrims who set out to go to the holy land for holy war or pilgrimage, he was taken by the Templar organization and in return received a document stating the amount of money received. When the soldier or the pilgrim showed this document to the Templar organization in his country, he was taking his money. The good working of the system at the hands of the honest knights have increased the trust in the Templars over time. After a while, the Tempers started to operate significant amounts of money. The business has led to the accumulation of tremendous wealth and, in the meantime, the Freemasonry with the members of the masonry and other professional organizations, all under the orders of the knights.

When Selahattin Eyyubi captured Jerusalem in 1187 and put an end to the Latin kingdom, the Templars were forced to leave Jerusalem together with the other Order of the Knights. The Tempers first moved to Akka and then to Cyprus. In 1187, all Palestinian lands, except for Akka, were captured by Muslims. In 1291 Akka also fell and the Templar centre moved to Cyprus. When the activities in the Middle East diminished, in the 13th century the Templars turned their attention to Europe. To the east of the Baltic Sea, the Teutonic Knights, under the name of "Ordensland", established an independent and secular principality far from the repression of Rome. The Temperians took this principle as an example and attempted to create the same structure in the Languedoc.[53] The Templars converged with the Cathars had taken most of their saints into the Order. At least one of the founding members of the organization was Cathar. Bertrand de Blancheford, the fourth Grand Master of the order, was known as Cathar. Blancheford, who was the Grand Master in 1153, was also the owner of the Rennes castle. During the attack of Albigen, although Templar acted as neutral, many Cathars were listed as asylum seekers. they allowed them to participate. Most of the Cathars, who survived the massacre, joined the Templars. Many of the top executives of the Knights became Cathars. Most of the Knights Templar knew Arabic and Hebrew and maintained relations with Arab and Jewish scholars. The level of esoteric discourse increased with the participation of the Cathars. Cathar was the believer of Blancheford, who made the knightly knights into a well-organized, multidisciplinary hierarchical institution.[54]

After Cyprus, the Temperians chose London as the centre. Although the majority of the managers were in London, the organization's Paris branch was extremely strong. One-third of the city was under the control of the Tempers and was outside the jurisdiction of King Philip. Again, all the craftsmen of the institution were free artisans in accordance with the rights given to them by the Papacy and they were bereft of all obligations of the kingdoms.

Strong organizational structure and tremendous wealth brought along anxiety and jealousy with great power. At the end of the 13th century, the Grand Master of the Order was Jacques De Molay, who came from a noble French family. At that time, the French King of the time "Beautiful Philip" lived on the power days. He had borrowed large amounts of money from the Tempers to overcome his financial troubles and had trouble repaying them. The fact that he was a very financially strong organization spreading throughout Europe prevented King Philip from taking action alone. As noted earlier, the Papacy had also realized that the Temperians were increasingly weakening the Catholic church and was waiting for an opportunity to destroy the organization. King Philip, who wants to put an end to this situation and intends to get rid of his debt to the Tempers, as a result of intense backstage activity, he chose 5th Clement to be a Papal. Pope Clement, who knew well what the secular system of the Temparians meant for the Papacy, and who wanted to pay the debt to King Philip, issued an order requesting the abolition of the community throughout Europe. The Baptists, who fought and died for Jesus in the holy land of thousands, were accused of rejecting Jesus two centuries later and taking the cross under their feet. Just before the Pope published this order, King Philip invited the Great Master of the Tempers De Molay and other leading figures from Britain to France on the pretext that a new Crusade would be organized.

De Molay and 60 Templar knights went to Paris in October 1307, following Philip's call. During a meal in honour of Philip, De Molay and his knights were arrested, while the Papacy was simultaneously impeached, against all the churches in order to provoke the people against them.[55] In all Europe, a large Templar hunt began. While the assets and lands of the organization were seized by kingdoms, some of the portable treasures moved with 18 ships from the port of Rochelle, along with some of the Knights. The fate of this treasure was never learned. There have been many speculations about the lost treasure. Some claimed that the treasure had been moved to a base formed in the American continent before Christopher Columbus, while some claimed that they were taken to the North African continent and hid in Algeria. As a basis for these claims, the Algerian pirates under the command of Barbarossa Hayrettin Pasha, who later declared their allegiance to the Ottomans, attacked the Catholic forces, and on the crossbones over the black flag, which was a Templar symbol.

They showed the dry head to choose them as flags. This flag in the future, all the pirates of the common symbol of the attacks of Barbarossa's Catholics was caused.

According to the other allegation, in Jerusalem or Alexandria, an old map of the United States found the Templierler, the 12th century knew the existence of the continent. The Tempers, who went to America with ships, built a secret military base here and brought various riches to Europe. In Portugal, the Knights Templar changed their names to the Knights of the Messiah and survived the inquisition. For three hundred years the Knights of Christ, operating in Portugal, formed one of the best navies in the world and realized the discoveries that changed the face of the western world. The sailor Prince Henry is the Grand Master of this order. The famous explorer Vasco de Gama is also among the members. The crest is a red cross on a white background, just like Templars. Christopher Columbus was also a member of the Order.[56] Christopher Columbus, who was a member of the Knights of Jesus organization, was a continuation of the Templars, and had the same map of Alexandria and Columbus, knowing that he was going, was on his way. On the ships of Columbus, the familiar cross of the Tempers was used as a symbol. Here is the treasure, the United States this secret base of the Templar was abducted.[57]

Famous novelist Wolfram Von Eschenbach of the Middle Ages wrote in his famous novel, Parzival that the Tempers preserved the Holy Grail, the Grail Castle, and the Grail Family. Beyond the material treasures that have been abducted by ships, it is claimed that the treasure, which has spiritual values and among them the Holy Grail, is hiding in the Blatchford family in Rennes.

The attitude of the Papacy, together with the Tempers, brought the end of another organization, Guilds, who had a close relationship with them. The church began to work at the beginning of the 12th century from the architect, Mason and labour professional groups organized outside its control. In 1189, it was decided to close Guilds, a professional priests' associations.[58] The monks of Guilds were faced with the obligation to continue the profession of the priesthood or to choose construction. Guilds were also buried in the dark pages of history, while those who chose to build were among the Freemasons. A similar prohibition was published in Paris in 1306, this time for Mason lodges. The reason was that the lodges had political activities. In the Council of Avignon dated 1326, professional fraternity organizations were condemned for their activities with special signs, clothing, a special language and secret writings.

Philip and the pope put pressure on Edward King, the son-in-law of Philip, to follow the cult. But Edward just apparently fulfilled these requests. A small number of knights were arrested, and many were allowed to flee the country. Captured people were sentenced to very slight punishment.[59] The knights who fled from England took refuge in Scotland. Scotland was at war with England. The papal decisions were never enacted in Scotland, and the knights from England and France were accepted as refugees. In the battle of 1314, the Templar knights fought against the British alongside the Scottish Robert Bruce.

In Germany, the Principality of Lorrain, part of the country, supported the Tempers. The German Templar knights also received great recognition alongside Hospitaliers and Teutonic Knights. Teutonic Knights, 1522 they explained that they had severed all ties with Rome and were openly involved with the Protestant forces of Martin Luther. In Spain, while the Templars sought shelter in other sects and organizations, in Portugal, with a small name change, they continued under the name of "Knights of Jesus".

The knights who took refuge in Scotland were aware that they could no longer be active as an organization. For that reason, they joined the Freemasons, the most popular Esoteric organization. Not only in Scotland, but all over Europe, Mason lodges opened their doors to the Templar knights.[60] Freemasonry, a professional organization as well as the esoteric doctrine, he became the most powerful practitioner and emitter in Europe. In the meantime, as a result of the participation of the knights and the clergymen of Guilds, intellectual works started to come to the fore as well as professional studies in lodges.

The Knights, captured by King Philip and the Papacy, were tried by a clergy council. They were charged with violent rituals, insulting the Cross and putting Cross under their feet, denying the Godhead of Jesus, cooperating with Muslims and getting closer to Islam, deviating from religious laws and doing magic. All of them were subjected to inquisition torture and their confessions were forcibly taken. The organization was officially abolished in 1312. The immovable properties and all their concessions were granted to the Sen Jan Hospitalier Knights, who were closer to the Catholic church. Founded in Jerusalem in 1048 under the name of Knights Hospitaller, in the process, the Knights of St. John, the Knights of Rhodes and finally took the name of the Knights of Malta. In 1530 these knights, named after the Maltese Knights, have kept the Tempers' goods to this day without adding to their own assets. The Maltese knights now exist as two different groups. One of them is the Catholic Maltese knights in the Vatican, and the other is the Protestant Maltese knights in London. Both groups do not recognize one another. The Catholic Maltese knights are the Papal militias connected with an oath to the Pope's death. Templar property assets are also in the hands of this group.[61]

De Moley and other prisoners were burned to poles in 1314 after seven years in prison. Thus, the doctrines of the Esoteric-West have sacrificed their followers in the Muslim world, even after centuries of Hallac-i Mansur, despite the fact that centuries had passed. When the last Templar Grand Master Jacques De Molay was burned alive, he condemned the Pope and the King of France and invited them both to account for the court in the presence of God. Indeed, both died a year later. Despite this, their desire to avenge the Tempiers continued, and after the French Revolution of 1789, a revolutionist who jumped into the guillotine table after the incarceration of Louis III, "Jacques De Molay, was taken from revenge."[62]

The warriors were immortalized by Dante under the name of "Divine Comedy". Behind the relief of a Dante in the Vienna Museum, the phrase Brother of the Imperial Prince of the Holy Kadesh Priest indicates that the Templar organization, even though it has been for a long time, is still present in other organizations.

A brief look at the esoteric interpretation of Dante's famous work will also give some insight into the beliefs of the Tempers.[63]

It is no coincidence that Dante came out of Italy. Italy is home to the Papacy and the Catholic Church, the Pythagorean Institute, Rome's Colleges, the Comanians, the Gilds. Considering that the main source of Freemasonry is the students, the birthplace of this organization in Europe can be accepted as Italy. The fact that Dante received the title of Templar Knight within the Freemasonry shows that the existence of esoteric doctrine and sect continued in Freemasonry. Born in 1265, Dante became a member of a chamber of doctors and alchemists in 1295 when he was 30 years old. Dante, like all Esoteric believers before him, was a fan of secularism and devoted his entire life to the separation of religion and state affairs. According to Dante, the Papacy is spiritual power, and the empire is the owner of worldly power, and both are literally equal. The church should not interfere with state affairs and the emperor should not be involved in religious affairs.

Dante seems to use a symbolic language in Divine Comedy. For example, Hell is just under Jerusalem. From this point, the Earth is extended to the centre of the Earth, but Purgatory is in line with Hell but not underground, but on the contrary, there is Paradise on top of a mountain. If the same line continues in the sky, God is reached.

Dante's most frequently used symbols are numerical symbols. 3, which expresses the divine eloquence, 9, and 9, the remainder of the doctrine of the Pythagorean, uses the 10 counts of excellence. Divine realm is divided into three as Heaven, Purgatory and Hell. Comedy, these three consists of parts. There are 33 sections in each section. The book consists of 100 sections with the initial introduction. Dante sees perfection, God in Chapter 100, which is the square of 10.

In the Paradise section, Dante tells a wolf who's hungry. This wolf reminds the Catholic church. The Master qualifies Pope 5. Clement, a shepherd, as a hungry wolf, causing the Tempers to die.

Dante merged with the Divine Light, which is impossible to describe when human souls approach God, gradually transforming them into the light writes. This style of expression is nothing but the expression of the esoteric doctrine, which says that the only goal of the soul is to reach God.

According to Dante, the Trinity in God, which exists in the divine power, describes the Christian trinity and Jesus, both man and God. Dante connects God's creation of man in His image to the divinity of man, for the esoteric secrets, in the Hell chapter he writes: "You have a healthy mind. Grasp the doctrine stored between these strange verses" ...

At this point, it is necessary to express that; Dante was also a member of the literary movement "Fedeli D'amore" (Friends of Love), which was very common among intellectuals during his lifetime. This esoteric content has a secret language that cannot be understood by others, like other similar organizations.

Dante seeks truth in his Divine Comedy. It makes three trips for it. The first journey is Hell and is full of great obstacles. The second trip, Araf journey, is easier and hopeful. The third journey, heavenly journey, is a journey with music, dance and light. These journeys Dante, Virgil (Mind), Beatris (Beauty), and Divine Will (God) symbolize you by Bernard. At the end of their journey, Dante regains Divine Nura, the Divine Truth.

Dante expresses his thoughts as follows:

"The divine power that makes me is the supreme mind, wisdom and first love" ...

Dante sees the Divine Spirit as a triangle. In other words, he has seen the Lightning Delta. In the middle of the delta, Dante's own reflection, the human being, stands. Man is a part of God and God is in man. If a person investigates himself well enough, develops the qualities in him, he will understand the secrets that exist within him and find the truth in which he is seeking.

There are various information and documents that Templar organization exists within Freemasonry. In Scotland, the town of Roslin, south of Edinburgh, is famous for its chapel built by the Templar. In the chapel, there are plenty of symbols and motifs used by Freemasonry today. The construction started in 1446 and lasted for 40 years.[64] It was built under the patronage of the Sinclair family. Sir William Sinclair brought stone masters and craftsmen from Continental Europe for the construction of the chapel. William Sinclair was appointed as Magistri and patron of the Scottish Freemasonry by King James II of Scotland in 1441, and he remained in the same family for a long time. Santa Clair means "Holy Bright Light." Roslin, in Celtic, means "ancient knowledge transmitted through generations".[65]

In the Operative Freemasonry, the head of the Masons who undertake the construction is the "Master of Business". Sinclair, the Roslin Chapel during the construction, it appears that he directed the construction as Master of Business. The fact that Sinclair undertook this task was not the only reason why he was appointed as the patron of the Freemasons, and that his technical knowledge was sufficient and that he was approved by the Templar/Mason Masters. Marie de Guise from the Guise dynasty, in a letter to Willam Sinclair, said, "We will become real masters depending on the Council and we will keep the secrets given to us secret."

It is known that the craftsmen who built the chapel were united under a Guild, and they got patents under the name of Mary Chapel Hall. In 1583, in the earliest recordings of the Mary Chapel Lodge at Edinburgh today, James James I, William Schaw, was given the title of "Master of Business and the General Minister of Masons". In another document called Saint Clair Patent, it is confirmed that William Sinclair and his heirs were the Masters of Art, Grand Master of the Scottish Freemasonry, 1437.

In 1460, he was given to the Sinclair family by King James the King of England. One of the first written records about Freemasonry, which remains from 1601, is called Sinclair's "Hereditary Grand Masters of Scottish Freemasonry ".[66]

In ancient Masonic manuscripts, the temple knights held various rituals at their main headquarters in Scotland; The "Holy Master of the Ninth" was created by referring to the nine Templar knights excavating in the temple; In the inner room where the twin columns of the temple support the arch of the double door, there is a treasure buried at three cubic depths facing east; in one test there are manuscripts and under him six hundred talent gold coins are written. In these manuscripts, it is stated that Moses formed the degree of the Prince of Tabernacle, and when the bright star reappeared, Moses' new princes held the ritual for acceptance, which was practised until the Temple was destroyed. Again, in 1118, a new Masonic organization under the name of "Prince of Jerusalem" was formed, and later they formed the East-West Knights degree, and in 1140 some sacred documents are also described in Scotland.[67]

In Scotland, where the Templar tradition was maintained, the most influential Scottish Guards Regiment of Neo Templar organizations emerged. The Scottish Guards Regiment is one of the institutions that have ensured the strengthening of the esoteric disciplines in continental Europe. In 1560, the Scottish parliament passed an end to the Pope's authority over the country and announced that it supported the Protestant reform. In 1564; James Sandusu, the High Priest of the Church of St. John, has made it clear that he was not tied to any religious organization and monastery except for the Knights of Solomon and the Knights of Jerusalem.[68]

As a result of the barriers to France, the Tempers, who acted with them, led to the birth of a pro-Stuart French Jacobite Freemasonry. The most popular unit of the French army, rebuilt by King Charles I of France, was based on Scottish nobility with the Boards. The title of the commander of the Scottish contingent was "First Master of the Army of the French Knights". The Union, which was known as the Scottish Guards and was the most elite class of the army, consisted of 33 people. In the future the regimented Scottish Guards Union elected its officers from Scotland's most respected families, such as Sinclair, Stuart, Montgomery, as well as their selection of noblemen from among them. A transitional rhythm was created for Scottish nobles, and the young nobles were elected to the regiment in a special ceremony after being subjected to all forms of education. It is known that this semi-Masonic, semi-Chivalry ritual, which is called the Organization of the Sanctuary, is a variety of ritual practices which are kept very secretive.[69]

After the massacre of France, the members of the Tempers survived the Mason lodges, but the Papacy did not touch Freemasonry for a long time. He did not remove the privileges given to them, for the Christian world needed people who built churches and cathedrals. The masons had maintained the secrets of building construction with great care, and these secrets were the real reason for the maintenance of their existence. As Guilds were distributed, Freemasonry was another reason to live. Brickworkers were always free because they were the kind of work that required their work to go on. The first privileges granted by the Papacy to the unity of troops, it lasts up to 614. This privilege diploma was given to the Builders of Benedicten by Boniface. Pope Nicholas I in 1277, Pope Benoit I, in 1334, empowered the Masonic lodges to become the only power in the field of construction on all Christian lands and left the monopoly of the construction of religious structures in the Masonic lodges.[70] Thanks to the advantages of being free to roam and organizing, many esoterical ideas have spread across Europe with the Freemasons. In 1315, the first painting in Strasbourg, France Mason meeting was held. The Masons who came from all over Europe for the first time used the title of Council of Free Masons for the first time.[71] One hundred years later a second meeting was held in the city of Ragensbourg in Bavaria, the first Masonic Federation was established and the statutes and rituals of the federation were established.[72]

Thanks to the influence of the Tempelans and Guilds, the Mason lodges, whose organizations were based on the Ismaili craftsman organization, were not only a union of builders but also a training hearth where philosophical subjects were also handled. These qualities were further strengthened by the inclusion of the Knights and Guild members. The Masons who obtained their first knowledge about the science of alchemy by means of the Tempelans who received this information from the Ismailis were also in contact with the Kabbalists. As a result of the relationship established with the Kabbalah school members, Alchemy came to the fore among the Masons. After the disintegration of the Tempers, it is estimated that there were approximately 9,000 masonry lodges in all European countries when Freemasonry was the most powerful esoteric organization in Europe. The masonry of the lodges, the new identity, attracted the attention of the nobles and the intellectual environment. For example, in 1442, many of the nobles in the king of England, Henry and the court were members of the brotherhood.

Metaphysics, theology and philosophy were spoken in the lodges. But the Medieval Freemasons, according to their teachings, were far away from the Roman church. The intense religious pressures of the period prevented the Masons from revealing their true beliefs. Essentially, the masonry masters are careful not to fall under the domination of the Papacy, even in the time of the Guilds, the closest they are to the church, they avoid. The only place where the Medieval Freemasons could reveal their true thoughts was their creation. Freemasons always used Esoteric symbols in their works. Along with his greatest works, the cathedrals and churches, the symbols of alchemy as well as his own symbols they did not hesitate to use the alchemical symbols. They even went a little further, filling the cathedrals with sculptures that could be called racy, ridiculing the Papacy's official attitude.

As an example of the Alchemical symbols used by the Freemasons in the cathedrals, we can give the word "VİTRİOL". Vitriol is a word which is the combination of the initials of the words "Visita Interiora Tellus Rectifacando İnveniens Occultam Lapidem" in Latin. Visit the centre of the earth.

The esoteric opening of this word, which means you will find the secret stone (Philosopher's Stone) there, where every human being will find the truth in itself. The word is used as a symbol of modern Freemasonry.

In addition to great architects and stone masters, the philosophers of the time were also very useful for the Freemasonry. Possibility to accommodate in the houses called 'Inn of Mother' on the road, meeting in the lodges in these halls, borrowing money when needed, travelling to the next lodge, finding solutions to any health-related problems, were the blessings that could not be found for that period. The presence of a chest to help older and sick siblings, the widows of the masons, shows the strength of the social aspect of the association and how it plays an active role in the emergence of the Humanism movement.

Another organization, such as Freemasonry, is the Compagnons that emerged in France. Compagnon organization, the form is very similar to the Masonic order. Therefore, historians argue that both organizations are actually identical to each other. In the 14th century, Compagnons emerged during the construction of the great cathedrals. In the 14th century, state-led official professional organizations distribute the "Master" rating, which allows workers to work on their own behalf. Craftsmen, who were members of the guilds that emerged at a time when the degree of Master was almost never given by these official channels, refused to receive this degree in the monopoly of the organizations they criticized and formed their own independent organizations. Three professional associations, including stone workers, joinery and locksmiths, were established and called "Compagnon", which means "sharing bread". The members of the Compagnons, who took the Mason guild structure as their example, were also called "Fraternite" members in French, meaning "Fraternity".

The candidate who wants to participate in Compagnon is undergoing a trial period of several months. At the subsequent ceremony, the candidate is asked to prove the virtue of professional commitment and to make a moral commitment. The candidate is asked to create a real masterpiece to prove his mastery of the art. This masterpiece is itself. At the reception ceremony, the candidate is invited to die to be born again. After the rebirth ceremony is carried out, the name of the candidate is changed and "Big-Hearted Perigord"; A pseudonym like "Virtual of Avignon" is given. It has now become a ring of the Compagnons' unbreakable chain. For the chain called the Chain of Unity, which symbolizes a union to be killed by death, each member holds the arms of his brother next to him, crossing his arms. The new member, the Tower of Babel and the maze symbols are printed. He is asked to order this gigantic work during his tour of France. He is then accepted as a member by taking a ribbon and a wand in the colour of his professional guild from the hands of an experienced Compagnon.

The most important symbol of the Compagnons is the mitre and the calliper. These symbols represent morality, use of correct scales, love of work, creativity and similar virtues. Compagnon oaths are on the "Pride of the Famous Architect of the Universe". Compagnons' clothes consist of a black suit, a spring cylinder hat, ribbon and a cane given to him during the ceremony. After the ceremony, the new member begins a tour of France where he will prove his moral virtues and increase his knowledge. In this tour called "İn Initum" (On the Road), the new member develops himself and his professional skills by visiting different cities of France. The journey is done clockwise. The young member identifies himself and lives in non-Compost places. Compagnons recognize each other with pre-determined hand touches and ritual words. In particular, these signs and words on the tour of

France are very important for the new member to introduce himself. The Compagnon spouses of the Compagnon are the women of the Compagnon spouses. Each city has a new member. During the day, Compagnon's training continues during the night and after hours of work, speculative works called Cayenne Comp are carried out in meeting rooms. Teaching is done orally and the member is asked to keep what they have learned as secrets. A tour of France takes years to complete. At the end of this round, however, the member is generally accepted as a true Compagnon.

For the "ceremony of surrender", which is the transition to the second degree, it must take a few years to complete the round with this ceremony, Compagnon is presented with new symbols. These are the symbols of the Pyramid, Temple, Grave and Cathedral. These symbols have different meanings depending on the profession guild where the craftsman is a member. With the "Completion" ceremony held a few years later, the member obtains the title "Full Compagnon". The symbol of this degree is a pentagram with a man holding a mitre and compasses inside. This symbol defines the "Universal Human" whose quest has been completed.

Following the religious wars in the 16th century, the Compagnons were divided into two branches. The gap between the Roman Catholic Compagnons and the pro-reform Protestant Compagnons was evident in the 17th-century Nantes Edict. In 1655, the University of Paris Faculty of Theology convicted the Protestant guilds, called "Gavot", as "professional associations based on sin, sinful and superstition". This decision led to a different effect than expected, while the Protestant guilds strengthened and the Catholics gradually weakened. The Compagnon secrets were better protected, and many young craftsmen became members of Protestant Gavots. In 1791, despite the prohibition of any kind of unity with the Le Chapelier Act, the Gavots passed the French revolution without any problems. In the 19th century, two great rites came together once again.

Devoir and Catholic Devoir de Liberte workers often started to clash with Catholicism. Among the members of the Devoir, de Liberte are many Mason. Devoir de Liberte (Free) The guild claims that Jacques the master and Father Soubise left two of the masters of Hiram, who had left Jerusalem after the construction of the Jerusalem temple. While Jacques masters the guild of stone sculptors, Father Soubise becomes the grand master of the journey. In a few ways, Jacques master, Father Soubise, is killed by his disciples. In this symbolic narrative, Jacques represents the Protestants and Father Soubise represents the Catholics. According to another rumour, the Jacques master is Jacques de Molay, the last great master of the Knights Templar. In 1940, during the Nazi invasion, a secret organization was adopted and banned by law. On the other hand, the organization has been reorganized with the efforts of Marshal Petain himself and has continued to exist until today.[73]

In the 15th century, kings and emperors established a certain superiority against the feudal lords. They began to make attempts to be more independent against Papacy, who had become accustomed to seeing the Christian world as its own deed. However, the Papacy had a very powerful weapon, "Curse" threat. Whoever, no matter who the Pope, when he excommunicated a person or institution, that person or institution was completely isolated from society. After being Cursed, Charlemagne waited barefoot in front of the church for days to pardon him. However, the use of this weapon would cause a backlash. Increasingly, in response to the popes, national feelings began to gain strength. As a result, national churches came out with some claims against the Papacy. The confusion has reached those dimensions, in which there have been three popes that have become outraged. At this point, the Sion Monastery, who claimed the Holy it will be appropriate to examine the historical development and its effects on events.

THE SION

In 1956, a series of books were published in France about the Cathars, Templieres, Movorenjian, Rose Croix and Rennes. These books are the "Secret Documents" of the monastery of the Sion.[74]

According to these documents, the first four Grand Masters of Sion in 1188, after their departure from the Tempils, were Jean de Gissors, Marie de Saint Clair, Guillame de Gissor and Eduardo de Bar. According to the documents of the Sion monastery, Sion Grand Masters include the famous names of Leonardo Da Vinci, Robert Fludd, Robert Boyle, Isaac Newton, Charles Radclyffe, Charles de Loraine, Charles Nodier, Victor Hugo and Claude Debussy. In addition, Boticelli, Dante, Shakespeare and Goethe are also members of Sion. A significant part of these names is also a member of Freemasonry.

It can be seen that Sion's great mastery changed hands between two different groups. The first of these is the important personalities of Esoteric philosophy, fine arts and science which have important effects on western tradition, history and culture. The second groups are the nobles and members of the royal families who have blood relations with the Morovenj Dynasty. Jean de Gissors is said to be a Morovenj. Again, Charles de Lorraine is the brother-in-law of Empress Maria Teresa who is the blood of the same dynasty. Most of the names in the list, blood ties or friendship it is observed that they are connected to the Lorrain mansion and to the Rennes castle in some way. The church in the castle of Rennes is the church of Magdala. Mary Magdalene, as previously stated, medieval men according to the Qibla, France is the Saint that brought the Holy Grail.

The Sion Great Master Rene D'Anjou's titles (1418-1480) are the Count of Anjou, the Duke of Lorein, and the King of Jerusalem.[75] Although the title of the King of Jerusalem is a symbolic title, it appears that the title shows blood ties with Godfroi de Bouillon. Christopher Columbus worked with D'Anjoun. It is said that the Holy Grail is in the hands of D'Anjou and that he came to inherit from Mary Magdalene on his own. D'Anjou, who is interested in Jewish astrology and Kabbalah, lived in Italy for many years. In Florence, he established a close relationship with the Meddici family, one of the pioneers of the Renaissance, and paved the way for the Journalists to collect works of historical significance from all over the world and to translate them into European languages. As a result of these developments, Pythagoreanism, Neo-Platonism, Hermetism and other Gnostic sciences were first taught in Florence and the Renaissance emerged through the institutes and academies established all over Italy.[76]

In 1461, "Brotherhood Protocols" was drafted, and through D'Anjou these protocols were spread in France, Germany and the United Kingdom. The protocols are thought to have been written by theologian Johann Valentin Andrea, a specialist in Hermetic and esoterism. Andrea's name is also on the Sion Grand Masters list.

In 1613, the German nobleman Frederik married Elizabeth Stuart, daughter of King James I of England. With this marriage, through the Stuart dynasty, Lorraine passed blood to the Frederik lineage. Frederik founded an esoteric philosophy school in Heidelberg on his own soil.[77] He was a Freemason and, at the helm of German Freemasonry, Frederik was elected king in 1618 by the Bohemian nobles. The election of Frederik was angered by the Papacy and the Holy Roman Empire. 30 years' wars began. Protestant "Christian Unions" were created under the leadership of the German Rose Croix organization in order to protect and support the scientific developments that were described by the Roman church as heresy. Through these troops that have become refugees for many philosophers, scientists, and Mason escaping the inquisition, many of the brothers from various European countries have been smuggled to England and have gathered in the Masonic lodges in England.

Elias Ashmole, a member of the Rose Croix, an expert on the Order of the Knights, joined the British Freemasonry in 1646, while Robert Boyle became a member of the Sion monastery. European and British intellectuals formed an institution that Boyle called the "Invisible School". In 1660, as a result of the revision of the British Monarchy, this institution was transformed into the Royal Society under the protection of King Charles II of the Stuart dynasty. Meanwhile, Isaac Newton, who was a member of the Royal Society and then Mason, became the next Grand Master of Sion. According to the monastery documents, Newton was commissioned by Charles Radclyffe. Radclyffe joined the Scottish uprising in 1715 when he was tied by the blood to her mother with the Stuart dynasty. Radclyffe imprisoned by Britain, escaping from prison and joining the Jacobins in France, in 1725, he founded the first Scottish Mason lodge in France. He was the Grand Master of Sion Monastery after Newton. Returning to Scotland in 1745, he began a battle for the rebuilding of the Stuart dynasty. After the defeat of the Scottish army in 1746, Radclyffe was executed.

In 1735, the Duke of Loren Francois married the Austrian Emperor Maria Teresa of the Habsburg-Loren dynasty and took the title of Holy Roman Emperor. Francois, the first European prince to declare that he is Mason, has made The Hague city of the Netherlands the centre of the Masonic activities.[78] After the proclamation of the Empire, Vienna has reached the same position. After the death of the last representative of the Medicis, Francois, who received the Duke of Juscany, prevented the inquisition of the Inquisition in Florence. According to the monastery documents, the person who brought Radclyffe to the Great Masters of Sion was Francois's brother, Charles de Lorraine. Lorraine was the Grand Master of the Sion after Radclyffe.

Another Sion Grand Master, Charles Nodier, was appointed the director of the French Arsenal Library in 1824. After the French Revolution, the monasteries in the country were looted, all the books and manuscripts were gathered in Paris. Again, Napoleon had brought all the archives of the Vatican to Paris in order to create a world library. Among these archives, there were also Templar vesicles forming 3 thousand bales. Some of the passports were returned later to the Vatican, but most remained in France. All of these books and manuscripts in the Arsenal library were made by a team led by Nodier, who was identified as a Pythagorean, was classified. In this way, a large number of esoteric information and documents remain hidden in the light of the day. Balzac, Gerard de Nerval, Musset, Dumas Pere and the next Great Master of Sion Victor Hugo, near Nodier friendly and working together. These names, Hermetic and Esoteric produced a large number of works.

In a paper called "Protocols of the Sion Almighties" published in a newspaper in Tsarist Russia in 1903, "The New World Order' is mentioned in these protocols. A king from the blood of Sion will emerge and the kingdom of King David of the new kingdom will be established." According to the Gospels, Jesus is a descendant of David, and described as the "King of the Jews", and the new king will be a descendant of Jesus. In an article in the French daily Midi Libre published in 1973, the true heir to the French throne was Alain Poter from the Movorenjnesian. In another magazine, a person who was thought to be a member of the Sion and whose name was not described, would not have been Sion, unless he had the motives. In 1981, it was announced in the French press that the Sion Assembly convened in January and Pierre Plantard de Saint Clair was elected to the Grand Master.[79]

According to the Sion Documentaries, which were published in limited edition special edition books and whose examples are still in the French National Library, the Order worked with a 7-degree system until 1956. The seventh highest grade only belonged to the Grand Master, whose title was "Seaman". As it is to be remembered, the Ismailis had the highest degree of grade 7, and this degree only had the president of the religious order. In Sion, the sixth grade was named "Noashid Notre Dam Prince". Noashite means Noah's believers, and it is a sign that all three heavenly religions are accepted. 5. The names of the 9 brothers in the "Sen Jan Crusaders" is. The Grand Master and his 12 assistants, who hold the highest three degrees, form the ruling staff of the cult. The board of directors of Sion is the "Rose Cross (Rose Croix) Council". It can be concluded that there is an organic connection between Rose Croix and Sion.

According to the documents, after 1956, the number of degrees was increased to 9. It has a total of 9.841 members and operates in 729 provinces and 27 influence areas. Sion grades are as follows:

1-Apprentices;
2-Crusaders;
3-Heroes;
4-Knightworkers;
5- Knights;
6- Deputy Commanders;
7- Commanders;
8- Judges;
9- Seaman.

According to the Laws of the Sion Monastery signed by the Grand Master Jean Cocteau, members are accepted regardless of their gender, race, philosophical, religious or political considerations. A member must determine the person to be a member of the organization after that. The new member of the admission is sworn to work for the peace of humanity and to serve the order under all circumstances. All acceptances are made with the approval of the Rose Croix Council. Appointments and assignments are carried out by the Grand Master and a life-time assignment is made for each task. The membership of the organization shall be inherited as a right to the children of their choice if the members propose. But this child has right to waive. There is no waiver in favour of another. The duties and titles of the Grand Master of the Sion Monastery are passed on to the next successor with the same privileges. The treasure, defined as the Heritage of the Order, can only be used when it is very necessary or if the monastery members are in danger.

The Grand Master of Sion has survived to the present day through the families who have been in contact with one of the Morovenj descendants for centuries. In the event that a candidate is not an eligible candidate or if the applicant is rejected the offer, it may be possible for a person outside the family to be appointed to this post according to the rules of the monastery's law. The names such as Leorando, Hugo, Newton, Noudier were Grand Master in this direction.

In 1973, a French magazine published a telephone conversation with Sion's last Grand Master, Plandart.[80] Plandart, while refusing to explain Sion's goals in this meeting, said, "I have a long tradition in the community. I am only one point in the series. "We are the guards of some things, and we do this without publicizing." Plandart was invited to the country by the Swiss government before the Grand Master was elected in 1947. Switzerland was the country where Sion delegates from all over the world gathered. The Swiss Alpina Grand Lodge is known to be the seat of some of the Sion passages. This Great Lodge is not regarded as a regular lodge by the general Freemasonry. An official of the lodge told Sion that today he is living as a modern organization, a British journalist working for the BBC. In an interview with the authors of the book "Holy Grail of the loss of the temple of the Sion monastery", Plandart said that this treasure is a spiritual treasure, despite the insistence of the contents did not explain the content and said that a secret.

In an article in the 4th issue of Ciurcuit, which was published in France since 1959 and apparently became the publication organ of the Sion Monastery, he wrote, "Today, we are the power that wants to rebuild a clean and new France, we declare that we will continue the philosophy "found to be found. In this article, it is understood that the target is the re-establishment of a folk monarchy governed by the Morovenj dynasty lineage. In this article, the secret Sion Monastery, whose aim is to establish a folk monarchy from the Morovenj canal, has the secret line of the Morovenj, and the monastery has strong contacts in Switzerland and France.

Sion Monastery today suggests a union between the church and the state. According to Sion, there will be kings of the Morove lineage at the beginning of the state, but these kings will not have control over the administration just like the Morovenj. In other words, the King will be a symbolic priest-king, the administration will be carried out by other hands. This new empire would be a kind of theocratic European United States, ruled by the radical revised and reformed church.[81]

From Sion's connection with the Temperi, there were claims that the "Sion Nation" was an organic bond between Sion and Freemasonry because of the fact that they were also Masonic and the esoteric views were defended, and that the goals of both organizations were the same. Under the orders of Freemasonry, Sionism these assumptions are rooted in the claims. The Sionism expressed here is not the Zionist movement, that envisions the establishment and protection of the state of Israel, but the policies of a different organization, suggesting the throne demand of the Movements. But in Freemasonry, the purpose of bringing the dynasty with sacred blood to work is never put forward. Freemasonry, whose aims we will deal with later, even banned any kind of religious and political dogma, not a goal, to be discussed. Again in Freemasonry, there are no applications such as life-long assignment to any task, taking individuals into membership due to blood bond. As a matter of fact, the fact that Sion had a limited and dogmatic aim, such as bringing the Movorenj Dynasty to work, caused this organization to be limited to certain members in certain countries and the number of members, while the Freemasonry, which explained its ultimate goal as Establishing the National Temple for Humanity or, became widespread all over the world have been effective in the countries. At this point, it is necessary to go back one more time in history and study Rose Croix, another school that is influential in the development of esoteric philosophy in the western world.

ROSE CROIX

In England, the Union of Astronomers was founded in 1510 by alchemist scientists in line with the Masonic ideals. This association, which took its origin from the Kabbalists and the Knights and Tempers who fled Jerusalem, led to the founding of the "Rose Croix (Rose and Cross) Brothers" in Germany in 1570.[82]

The Fama Fraternitatis manifesto of the Rose Croix Brotherhood, published in 1614, it appears to be under the influence of the Ihwan-i Safa brotherhood. It proposes a universal reform. It was attributed to Christian Rosecroix, who was said to have been born in Germany in 1378. According to these documents, Rosecroix studied Alchemy in Yemen and Morocco and returned to Germany and established a religious and high moral order. It is said that Rosecroix grew up with a Teutonic knight and went to Jerusalem with him. Rosecroix went to Damascus and Damcar. Rosecroix studied alchemy and occultism, then moved to Morocco and Spain. Then he moved to his native Germany and trained countless students there. Rosecroix's book called "Liber Mundi" was written in Arabic. In this book, God describes how He created the universe and humanity through magic and symbols.[83] The manifesto proclaims that Rose Croix is the continuation of Renaissance esoterism. Rose Croix invites people to join fraternity organizations and opens their doors to anyone who wishes to be initiated to build the castle of truth. Those who want to provide interest are definitely not taken into the organization. There is confidential information in the hands of the brothers to start a new age. Those who will start the new age will be enlightened initiates by the light of Hermetic wisdom. The journeys of Christian Rosecroix trips in the east, and then the passage through Spain symbolizes the journey of the esoteric doctrine and the transfer from east to west.[84] A document confirming that Rose Croix was founded as the side branch of the Union of Meritists, a manus from Michel Maier. It is currently located in the Leipzig library.

One of the most prominent figures of alchemy in the 16th century, Paracelsus, Rose and Cross Brother historical leader is known as. Born in Switzerland in 1493, Paracellus is a contemporary of Martin Luther. According to Paracelsus, if we can get something from God, the reason is not religious ceremonies, but our heart, alchemy is an art in which real knowledge is acquired. True knowledge is the way of recognizing Nature. Human microcosmos, nature is macrocosm and both are identical. What is important for alchemy is the variability of matter and its properties. There are no static items that will not change, because each being is part of the Mysterium Magnum. Decomposition is the birth of matter from Mysterium Magnum. The Alchemist is the one who can pull nature's fire and light out of the Mysterium Magnum. Thus, the pure one is separated from the non-existent and through the alchemy perfected the things that nature leaves without perfecting. Alchemy, by changing the properties of simple structures, brings them to higher points of existence. For alchemy, every kind of substance is metal-alive, and each has its own secrets. The new Europe is Paracelsus, who first worked out the idea of new science. He was the first to put forward the idea of Europe unifying under new science. The Manifesto of the First Rose and Cross handed out to all the administrators and intellectuals of Europe in 1614, is titled "The Principles of the Fraternity of the Roses and Crosses are brought to the attention of all the Governors and intellectuals of Europe". In 1710, after Paracelsus's manifestation in Europe, a book entitled "Preparing the Philosopher's Stone According to the Roses and Cross Brotherhood" was published. This was followed in 1785 by a book called "The Secret Symbols of the Rose and the Cross Brotherhood". Thus, it was possible to obtain information about the structure and activities of the organization.[85]

The first leader of the Fraternity of Roses and the Cross is Johan Valentin Andrea. The emblem Andrea chooses for the organization and the emblem Martin Luter chooses for Protestantism are very similar to each other. The five-walled red rose is placed in the centre of a black cross in the emblem of the Fraternity of the Rose and the Cross, while Luter's emblem features a heart in the middle of the same rose and a black cross in it.[86] German Rose Croix brothers spread the organization throughout the country under Andrea's leadership led many esoteric doctrines to escape to England. After the administration of the Protestants in England, Rose Croix increased its activities there and supported the establishment of the Invisible School and the Royal Society.

The Union of English Expatriates turned into a "Royal Society", covering all branches of science, with the participation of Robert Boyle's "School of the Invisibles". This organization, which was a member of many British scientists and under the auspices of the royal, was renowned for keeping members in the forefront of rationality. However, the members also managed to combine science with an intuitive approach.

In addition to being a member of the Royal Society, John Dury, one of the people of Rose Croix, wrote that similar works were written by Francois Bacon, one of the founders of experimental Physics, and by Robert Boyle, who is known as the father of all modern sciences, while he wrote that light is in man. Isaac Newton developed the theory of gravity within this community. Bacon, in his famous work "Nova Atlantis", plans to establish a new world in which the esoteric doctrine is at the forefront and Boyle had created the School of Invisibles, which he hoped would accomplish.

The Rose Croixes were in constant contact with the Freemasons, who were advocates of the esoteric doctrine. Most of them were members of the Mason Lodge. For example, Christoper Waren, the great master of London lodges, was both Rose Croix and Mason. Also, Robert Moray, a chemist and mathematician, who was a member of both organizations, was the first president of the Royal Society. The principles of Rose Croix and Freemasonry became the same with Elias Ashmole, who was nicknamed "Hermes". Ashmole, who established an association which aimed to make the House of Suleiman the Magnificent, also made Sion the great mastery, ensured that this association was gathered at the mason houses. Over time, this relationship has reached the point where Freemasonry shares the same goal, and the association has melted in Freemasonry.

Founded as a synthesis of Hermes, Kabbalah, Pythagoras, and all the Esoteric schools, Rose Croix, with the influence of Plato, brought to mind the rationalism of the Esoteric doctrine. With the works of philosophers like Valentin Andreae, Michael Maier, Francois Bacon, Jacob Boehme and Robert Fluud, Rose Croix has become an influential organization all over Europe, especially in Germany, England and France. Rose Croix, however, reached the peak of the world's destiny with Martin Luther.[87] The intertwining of the symbols of rose and cross in Luther's coat of arms is the expression that Rose Croix is an integral supporter of Luther's reformist views. Rose Croix is a totally Protestant movement that aims at state and church reform.[88]

In 1505, Martin Luther, a member of Rose Croix's German organization, received the title of Theological theoretician in 1512 and defended the German church against the Roman church. started his battle. In Christianity, Luther wanted to return to the days of Jesus, where there was no dogma, and to find God with the intuition of every Christian. Luther, angry with the Roman church and the Papacy's ability to exorcise sins and forgiveness of sins, especially documents showing that human sins were forgiven as a result of the financial donations, described the giving of keys to heaven as comedy. Luther was excommunicated by Pope Leo 10 in 1520 because of his thoughts which he did not hesitate to state clearly. This excommunication became a whip that allowed Luther to more aggressively attack Rome and its blessing theory. Describing faith as an invisible and human feeling, Luther accelerated his attempts against the Papacy. However, the excommunication of the Papacy by the German rulers was of great importance, and Luther was expelled from Germany. Luther took refuge in the chalet of Frederik. The German theologian translated the Bible in German in 1522, which was published only in Latin so far. Luther thus earned his first major work in German literature. The translation of the Bible into German allowed the German people to better understand the holy book and support Luther's teaching. Lutheranism spread all over Europe in time. With the Lutheran view that received the name of Protestantism, the Catholic Church's absolute domination over societies was broken.[89]

With the signing of the French decree in 1598, Protestants were accepted in France as well as Catholics. On the other hand, the geography of the vast majority of the world population with large discoveries Christian turned out not to be. This fact weakened the public's belief in the Papacy. At the same time, scientific progress did not stop. The Polish scholar, Copernic, proved that the world revolves around the sun and around itself. Contrary to what Catholics claim, the world was not the centre of the universe. In the Catholic Bible, however, the sun was revolving around the earth.

Another organization, which paved the way for the emergence of Luther in Germany, is the reformist Bohemian Fellowship, the first of its existence in the 1400s. Luhter's rebellion in 1517 reached its peak with the 30-year wars between Catholics and Protestants in 1618.[90] In the meantime, all religious institutions, especially the Jesuits, began to attack the Crocuses, especially in continental Europe. These attacks lasted until 1630, and the Council of Malins issued an order to close the sect and arrest its members, accusing Rose Croix of magic and religious heresy.[91] It is clear from the following verses written by Henry Adamson in the mid-17th century that the two organizations act together:

We're the Rose Croix brothers.

We have a Mason password and intuition."

In addition, the "Secret History of Masons", published in 1724, is also called "Rose Croixes and Masons, the siblings of the same faith."

Today Rose Croix is active in the US rather than Europe. In the US, there are two organizations, the Old and Mysterious Rose Croix Sect (AMORC) and the other, the Fraternity of the Rosicrucian. Rose Croix's Emblem, side R.C.[92] Rose Croix's official establishment date is the late 19th century. The founding date of the Rose Croix Brotherhood of the Republic of America is 1880. AMORC, the most powerful Rose Croix organization in America, was founded in 1915. This organization has 250,000 members worldwide. The most famous member of Rose Croix on the new continent is Albert Einstein.[93]

ILLUMINATI

The most operative esoteric organization of western origin is the Illuminati. Illuminati, a Latin word, means "Enlightenment". Although it is said that the organization first appeared in the 11th century, there is no reliable data in this direction. All the founders and their representatives are representatives of the Enlightenment Thought, which started with the Renaissance and Reformation movements in Europe. It is anti-papal. The sole aim of the organization is to weaken the power of the Papacy and to fight in all areas with Catholic bigotry.

When the Vatican vigorously opposed scientific developments in the 1500s, the first Illuminati organization was revealed in Rome, all of whom were very well educated, by experts in their fields. The Church immediately opposed this formation and subjected the Illuminati members to inquisition investigations and torture. Some members are caught, first branded with a cross before the names of other siblings were taken from their mouths. Later on, the captured people were killed and left to the dogs on the streets of the Vatican in order to be a sign.

In order to show that they were Christians and to get rid of church oppression, the members tried to establish a church called "Enlightenment Church", but this church was declared "Satanist" by the Vatican immediately. The most famous name of the Italian Illuminati is Galilee Galileo. As it is known, in 1633, Galilean was sentenced to life imprisonment by the Vatican because he defended scientific facts against religion. Illuminati's life in Italy has not been very long due to intense inquisition pressure. Illuminati in a process similar to the Spanish word "Alumbrados" in the name of Spain is trying to institutionalize. The founder is a Spanish writer named Menenez Pealyo. It was founded in 1492 in Madrid and operated until 1623. The Papacy published an inquisition in 1623, declaring all members of the Illuminati illegally and excommunicating Christianity. With the decision of this excommunication, the organization was drawn underground in both Italy and Spain.

The re-institutionalization of the Illuminati was carried out by Adam Weishaupt in Bavaria in Germany in 1776 after the Reform movement.[94] After the failure of the organization in Catholic countries, it was easier to develop in a Protestant controlled country. In 1759, the Bavarian prince Maksimilian Joseph, who had favoured the Enlightenment, founded a science academy. The aim of the Academy was to break the Jesuit monopoly in the field of education and to open the way for enlightenment.[95] In 1765, Emperor Joseph II was chosen as the Emperor. Joseph carried out reforms, such as the abolition of serfdom, the establishment of religious freedom and civil marriage, and the secularization of public employees. Thus, law professor Adam Weishaupt opened the way for the formation of the Illuminati.

The Illuminati organization, which has an esoteric structure, is based on three degrees. The first degree is called Minerval (Student), the second degree is Minerval İlluminaties (Enlightened Students), and the third degree is Illuminated (Enlightened Person). The symbol of the organization is the eye in the triangle. There is an internal organization, which is kept very secretive, above the first three degrees of the Illuminati. The existence of this internal organization called Areopagites does not even know the first three degrees. Those who managed to rise to Areopagites, the organization's real goals and secrets are explained.[96]

In 1777, Weishaupt entered Freemasonry, another organization that thought and struggled in parallel with him. Thus, he had the opportunity to disseminate his ideas within the Freemasonry community in all European countries. Within a short period of 3 thousand people from the Freemasons became members of the Illuminati. One of these Masons is Baron Adolf Von Knigge. Knigge, he added three more degrees to Illuminati. These are "Illuminatis Major"; "Illuminati Drigens" and "Magnus Rex" grades given only to the administrators of the organization.[97]

The Illuminati is an organization of 54 people at first, most of them young nobles, philosophers and scientists. In the city of Bavaria, there are handles. The most famous German Illuminati members are the counties of Saxony and Weimar, Goethe, Schiller, Harder and Hegel.

However, it is not possible to say that all the German Freemasons share the ideas of the Illuminati against Christianity. In Germany, the friction between Illuminati and Rose Croix came to the surface. Rose Croix blatantly criticizes Weishaupt for establishing an anti-Christian organization that he does not believe in Jesus Christ and in the end. The Illuminati also accused Rose Croix of being under the influence of the Jesuits.[98] The Rose Croix Mason lodge in Berlin has therefore decided to combat the Illuminati. According to this lodge, Illuminati wants to completely destroy the Christian religion and transforms Freemasonry into a political system. Frederick Wilhelm of Germany, himself a Mason, strongly opposed the Illuminati because of his anti-Christian, Atheist ideas. Under his orders, the Prince of Bavaria, Karl Theodore, announced that the Illuminati was declared illegal and that those who insisted on membership would be arrested. Upon this development, the Illuminati concealed itself in Germany in 1782, turning into a higher degree of Freemasonry. This degree, founded under the leadership of the Duke of Bruswick, is called the Illuminated Free Masons degree.[99] The president of the Illuminati lodge is called Areopagites. The headquarters of the lodge is located in Frankfurt, and the founders include representatives of the Rothschild family. This is famous the banker family has a branch in both Germany and England, and this family has had important implications for the acceptance of the degree in England. The revival of the organization in Germany took place in the early 19th century with the participation of the famous German philosopher Hegel in the Illuminati. Hegel, theses-antithesis theories and the Illuminati, it has made it a community in which the idea of the New World Order develops. The biggest supporter is the Rothschild family.

In 1787, the Illuminati member, Johacim Christoph Bode, decided to seek refuge in France due to the pressure in Germany and established a branch of the organization under the name of "Illuminants". In this deeply rooted country, the organization grew up and turned into the French Revolution Club. There are also many Mason members among them. Behind the French Revolution in 1789, this club is known to have worked. Robespierre, the leading figure of the revolution, is the head of the organization. The symbol of the eye of the Illuminati, which has seen everything, has emerged as a symbol of the French revolution.

In 1798, the Scottish scientist John Robinson stated, "The goal of the Illuminati is to dominate the economies and the countries of the country. To achieve this goal, they are trying to destroy all the institutions of the established order, especially Christianity. They will overthrow all the European Royal administrations and then they will spread their secret goals to the whole world."

Again in France, the power was united between the Illuminati and the powerful French Deist or Atheist philosophers, and the Jacobin party was born of this unity. French Grand Orient Freemasonry, the politics of the movement resulted in the removal of the obligation to swear on the "Great Architect of the Universe". Among these Freemasons, there are names like Voltaire, Diderot and Montesquieu.

In 1860, the French Catholic church bishops strongly opposed the proposition of accepting Freemasonry in France. The Deist philosophers, who were members of the French Grand Orient, took action and in 1865 they made a decision in the Grand Orient Grand Conan to make everyone considered a member regardless of his religious conviction. Thus, in France, Freemasonry and the Catholic Church came to a complete rupture point. In the Grand Orient's 1877 Grand Conan, the necessity of believing in God and Spirit is abolished and the first article of the Masonic Constitution was changed as "Freemasonry, in principle, adopts absolute freedom of conscience and human freedom." In 1878, the Grand Orient announced that they accepted those who did not believe in God and those who did not believe in it.

The Jacobins played an important role in the French Revolution. Its founders are the Duke of Orleans, the Grand Master of the Grand Orient, and French members of the Illuminati. The Jacobin name comes from the "Jakob", the Latin of the name of King James II of the 17th century. 2. James is a Catholic Stuart deposed by the Protestant son-in-law William. When James was dethroned, he escaped to France with some British Masons who were his followers and continued his claim on the throne.[100]

217

Sir Francis Bacon, who is considered to be the founder of modern Freemasonry in England, is mentioned for the first time in his book Nova Atlantis, "The New World Order". This utopia portrayed by Bacon in his mind ultimately inspired the founding of the United States. It is known that Bacon made the Great Command of the British Rose Croix Society at the end of the 16th century.

During the immigration to the American continent, as well as a large number of British Mason, the French Mason also set foot in the new world. These include the members of the "Illuminated Free Masons" and "Illumines". The most familiar names are Thomas Jefferson and Benjamin Franklin. The branch of the organization established in America is called the "White Illuminati Lodge" or "White Brotherhood". Jean Jacques Rousseaus, a member of the Illuminates, is known to have been a revolutionary ally in America before the war of independence. Edmont Genet, a French ambassador in America, was also a Jacobin and Mason, and it is said that he played an important role in organizing the Illuminati here. Among the organizations that started the colonial wars, Illuminati was the leader.[101]

After the war of independence, the United States seems to be founded on three esoteric organizations. These are, in particular, Freemasonry, Illuminati and Rose Croix. It is known that 28 out of 40 people who signed the Declaration of Independence announcing the establishment of the state were Mason. The number of Illuminati or Rose Croix members is unknown. General George Washington, the first President of the state, is Mason. The groundbreaking ceremony of the White House was carried out in a Masonic ceremony as a result of the participation of all the brothers. On September 18, 1793, George Washington, as the Grand Master of the Great Lodge of Maryland, laid the foundation stone of the Capitol building and a large number of Masonic symbols on the foundations. First Many institutions and organizations, including the constitution of the new state, are organized according to the Masonic rules. It can be said that the US is a Republic of Masonic order.

The Great Seal of the United States was formed by the combination of the Esoteric symbols. The Great Seal we know from the one dollar banknotes in 1776 by Benjamin Franklin, Thomas Jefferson and John Adams has been made. On the one-dollar bill, there is an incomplete pyramid with an eye in a triangle. The eye symbol in the triangle is one of the oldest symbols of the Great Architect of the Seeing Universe and has been used by the esoteric schools for thousands of years since the sunken Mu civilization. In addition to Freemasonry, the Illuminati adopted the same symbol. Latin, just below the pyramid, says "Novos Ordo Seclorum". Meaning is the New Secular Order. This discourse is the goal of Illuminati. Thus, the US announced that its national policy and religious rules were applied within the framework of this new secular order. The secular order was one of the most important demands of Freemasonry as well as the Illuminati. Just below Novos Ordo Seclorum is 1776. This date, in addition to declaring independence, is the founding date of the Illuminati in the United States.[102]

Under these symbols, Latin also writes "Annuit Coeptis". It can be translated as "Plan will be achieved". The plan is the establishment of the Illuminati's "New World Order". Another Latin sentence on the money is "E Pluribus Umum". This expression can also be translated as "Single among many". The US is the first and only state in the world to be established in line with the Illuminati goals. When all these symbols and sentences are combined, it means that there is a big plan and this plan is not just for the US. The "New Secular World Order" is the name of this international plan and it is explained by the founding fathers two hundred years ago. The goal of the Illuminati is that the Republican system of administration prevails in every country.

The first step of the realization of this plan at the international level outside the US was in 1877. The "Round Table" was founded in 1877 by five businessmen from the United States and the United Kingdom, referring to the legendary King Arthur's Knights of the Round Table, which united the United Kingdom. The goal is to bring the English-speaking countries together under the umbrella of a federation. This union will constitute the main core of the future World Federation. These five business men, recognized as the richest men in the world in those days, were John Rockefeller, John Morgan, Andrew Carnegie of the United States, and Mayer Rotschild and Cecil Rhodes from England. They are all members of İlluminati and 33rd Degree Mason. The Round Table group is a dual entity, internal and external groups. The inner group is called the White Brotherhood Initiatives or the Exquisite, while the external group is called the Union of Helpers. The British Lord Milner Rhodes and Lord Victor Rothschild are the initiates. In addition to the Rhodes Fund, Charnegie Thrust, J.P. Morgan, Rockefeller and Rothschild provided financial support to the group.[103]

In 1910, this time on the Jekyll Island of the United States, the head of the National Monetary Commission, John Rockefeller, the head of the National City of New York, Frank Vanderlip, First National Bank's chairman Charles Norton, US Deputy Finance Minister Abraham Andrew, John Morgan's representative Henry Davison, Morgan another assistant of Benjamin Strong and Nelson Aldrich and German Warburg Bank representative Paul Moritz Warbrug held a closed-door meeting. Banker Mayer Rothschild was not able to attend this meeting but was known to support the formation with all his power.[104] The outward announced agenda was the formation of the US Central Bank, but the main agenda was the implementation of a secret world government projected by the Illuminati. It is highly probable that there will be a struggle against the European Aristocracy behind the closed doors. As a matter of fact, the first world war broke out after a short while, with the intervention of America, Europe was finally isolated from the royal administrations. American General Albert Pike, a 33-member member of Mason and Illuminati, is also known as the theoreticians of the "New World Order". The project, which Pike had been working on between 1859 and 1871 for the formation of this new order, seems to have been put into effect with the First World War.

On May 30, 1919, just after the First World War, a Round Table meeting was held at the Majezik hotel in Paris. It was time to draw a new direction to the world. At this meeting, the participants decided to establish the Institute of International Relations. In addition, the establishment of new think-thank organizations for the creation of new world order was decided at the same meeting. The branch of the International Relations Institute, which was decided to be established in the USA, was called "Council on Foreign Relations" (CFR). The name of this organization's twin in England was determined as "Royal Institute of International Relations". Enlightened Free Masons of the Institute had direct relations with the organization. Lord Milner Rhodes and Lord Victor Rothschild were initiated. In addition to the Rhodes Fund, United Kingdom Charnegie Thrust, J.P. Morgan, Rockefeller and Rothschild provided financial support.[105] The purpose was to serve world peace. The International Relations Institute, which was a continuation of the Round Table group, held its meetings at Chatham House in London.

The League of Nations, which was established after the First World War, is another organization formed by the Institute of International Relations. However, the opinion of various national economic enterprises and companies contradicting each other, this initiative has remained idle and the second world war has emerged. As national companies grew in international platforms, the fact that their interests did not coincide and the environment of compromise diminished gradually became a big lesson, and the necessity of establishing mechanisms to provide control at international level has emerged. After the Second World War, the organizations were designed according to this need.

The Council on Foreign Relations, the central committee of the New World Order, was founded in 1921 in New York. The Rockefeller family, the Carnegie Institute and the Wall Street bankers have provided financial support to the CFR. From the date of establishment, the organization regulating US foreign relations was always CFR. Especially in the aftermath of the Second World War, all kinds of foreign policy were conducted under the guidance of this organization. Today, the international strategies of the USA are determined by CFR and are carried out by Presidents and Foreign Ministers. Since 1945, all US Presidents have been CFR members.[106]

CFR has completed its institutionalization in the United States in the period of Roosevelt. Since then, almost all of the members of the US governments have been members of the CFR. Today there are 1500 CFR members in the USA and 3300 worldwide. All of these members are high-grade Masons or Mason wives. There are currently more than 5 million Mason in the United States. CFR members can also be members of Bilderberg or the Trilateral Commission, which we will examine later. However, it has been observed that the members of all three organizations are only US citizens.

The organization chart of the Council on Foreign Relations consists of two intertwined circles. The Inner Circle consists of 40 members and is chaired by David Rockefeller. The decisions of the inner circle called the Central Committee are final. All members of the Central Committee are the 33-degree Mason. All members of the CFR's external committee have the right to make suggestions and participate in the voting. However, recommendations and decisions are not binding, but recommendations. Only inner circle decisions are binding. All members of the Ministry are also natural members of the Central Committee.

After the organization of the Round Table, it was decided to limit the number of the members of the Illuminati, which is the foundation of the pyramid, to 10 people, and to organize all kinds of organizations through the formations under the order of this structure. This is another name for the 10th Illuminati organization, the "Council of Emperors". Members of the Illuminati come from 10 families who now control the global economy. Judging by the money, they have reached their current position. All generations, especially the first founders of the organization in the United States, are investors and bankers. It is not even possible to calculate and even estimate how much money these 10 families have today ruled. For over 200 years, they have been controlling almost all the world's traffic in the world, with companies, banks, monopolies and other financial structures. It is not a general acceptance that all of the Illuminati members will come from only ten distinguished families. For example, Bill Gates, the owner of the Microsoft company, the most prominent member of the electronic world, who is considered to be the last member of the organization, is not one of these families. However, it is a fact that most of the members of the organization are members of these ten families.

There is no religion of money. Illuminati does not have any religious preference. However, there is no religious hostility. The only goal is that the New World Order is Secular. Religion will not be allowed to be decisive on politics. Religion will only be left as a matter of conscience and ritual for believers. All religions and all nationalities, including Christianity, will remain secondary, and all will be regarded as cultural differences.

The slogan of the Illuminati is Ordo Ab Chao. This sentence, which means the order of chaos, is also the motto of Freemasonry, of 33 degrees, and it should be remembered that all the members of the Illuminati are 33-degree Masons. The unfolding of its philosophy was conceived as the chaos in the world today seems to prevail, but it will eventually turn into a universal order.

The most famous of the Illuminati families are Rockefellers from the United States and Rothschilds from England. British banking trust Rothschilds and American oil giant Rockefellers are in the world economic arena, arrow has a number of partnerships. This partnership has turned into strategic cooperation over the years. Thanks to their power over the economies, these two families had the chance to determine world politics significantly from the beginning of the 20th century. First of all, they destroyed the aristocratic and royal families of Europe, the most powerful enemies of the first world war, and ensured that they were replaced by secular governments and democracies. Then, with the second world war, the biggest opposing force, nationalism, was struck and the front of the nationalist platforms was opened. Other families that support both families are Ford, Morgan, Rhodes, Oppenheimer, Carnegies, Sinclairs and Bofmanns.

In the United States, the Rockefellers captured the CFR and the Rothschilds in England took control of Chatham House and became the most effective foreign policy-making mechanism in their country. They have gathered the brightest brains in their countries within the same organizations and thus have taken control of all political constructive mechanisms in this way. Since then, it has not been possible to take any international political decisions without the knowledge of these families.

CFR has a decisive role in international decisions. In the United States, the programs of political parties are made by CFR members and the candidates for the parties are elected by CFR members. The United States decides to enter the Second World War near England by. The CIA and the FBI, under the control of the CFR, have always been in the hands of the organization that led the international economy, such as the post-war IMF and the World Bank.

It is stated in the regulation of the CFR that any member of the Council involved in the discussion of the activities of the Council shall be immediately removed from membership. The CFR's headquarters are in New York, and the building known as Harold Pratt House was donated to the CFR by the Rockefeller family. In 1950, David Rockefeller was elected as vice president and then president of CFR. The financial resources of CFR are known to be provided by companies such as Xerox, Bristol Mayers Squibb, General Motors, Ford Foundation, Andrew Mellon Foundation and Rockefeller Brothers Fund.[107]

In an interview with the International Newsweek Magazine in 1999, David Rockefeller said, 'government in the New World Order, we must give up our independence and adopt World Citizenship for the benefit of the international community. It is a market economy and no boundaries should be left to achieve this."

Bohemian Grove is the name of a California-based camp, where American businessmen, politicians and publishers meet once a year, and a closed-door meeting of US and world issues and solutions is addressed. The issues and conclusions discussed in the Bohemian theme are never leaked out. The names of George W. Bush, Henry Kissinger and James Baker are regularly attended by David Rockefeller.[108]

The role of CFR in making strategic decisions that determine the future of the world is enormous. The goal is to bring world politics to a certain route, to unite economies and to create a World Confederation. In order to achieve this objective, which will prevent and control the conflicts of interest of international monopolies, a United Nations organization has been established and financial structures such as the World Bank and the International Monetary Fund have been established.

However, despite the support of all these organizations, it is not possible to achieve this success only with CFR structuring around the world. In other parts of the world, there will be functional and CFR-like structures are needed.

The new World Confederation is expected to consist of three different Federated States. These are the European Union states that will cover the entire American continent, the American Union, the Pacific Union and the European countries that will cover the countries of Asia and the Pacific. In order to achieve this goal, we needed two more organizations to be organized and worked just like the CFR. The first "Bilderberg" meeting was held in 1954 under the leadership of Catham House. The founders of Bilderberg are the Dutch Prince Benard, the president of the Unilever company Paul Rijkens and the Polish sociologist Hieronim Rotinger. The first meeting was held in Osterberg, the Netherlands. The name of the hotel where the meeting was held was Bilderberg, and the meetings were later given the same name. Some of Bilderberg's members are members of European royal families. Members include aristocrats from the royal families of England, Sweden, Spain and the Netherlands. These aristocrats, with the Sion organization or the Vatican, who has no connection, is peace with the Illuminati, is the most Protestant. The Bilderberg group is headed by Lord Peter Carrington, who is also chairman of the Royal Institute for International Relations.[109]

The first proposal for the adaptation of the CFR organization for the whole of Europe was carried out by the European Movement Secretariat in 1952. European countries have just emerged from the war, and there is a strong threat to Communism. For this reason, the European liberal countries, under the leadership of Britain, wanted to unite their forces and attract the United States. Bilderberg meetings were held every year since the first year in 1954. Meetings are held annually in different European countries. The agendas and results of the meetings are never included in the press. The prerequisite for participation is a tight mouth.

Bilderberg is a CFR project and a European sequel. The establishment of the Trilateral Commission, the Pacific leg of the same organization, was also decided at a Bilderberg meeting. All three organizations have organic ties with the Illuminati. The present European Union is a manifestation of the Bilderberg meetings. The aim is to expand this structure to the whole world. The majority of the participants in Bilderberg meetings are businessmen and bankers. However, there are many politicians and government officials at various levels. Bilderberg meetings are held behind closed doors and no official statement is made. In these meetings, political, social, industrial and commercial structures of countries are discussed, guided and shaped. With the adoption of the Euro as the only currency following the formation of the European Union, an important step seems to have been taken. The European Common Market, formed following the Treaty of Rome, is rapidly evolving into a new state formation.

Following Bilderberg, in 1973 a Trilateral Commission was formed. The fathers of this formation are David Rockefeller and Zbigniev Brzezinski. The idea of the establishment of the Trilateral Commission was first mentioned by Brzezinski in 1970. Brzezinski presented this idea to the members at the Bilderberg meeting in Belgium in 1972 and the proposal was accepted. Thus, in 1973, the Trinity Commission was founded under the direction of David Rockefeller. The Trilateral Commission, which is designed to organize all of the Asia-Pacific countries in a new structure, is managed by a board of thirty-five members. Financial resources for the Commission's activities are provided by the Rockefeller Brothers Fund, the Ford Foundation, Time-Warner, Exxon, General Motors, Wells Fargo, and Texas Instruments.[110] The members of the Trilateral Commission are typically American, European and Japanese businessmen. However, just like Bilderberg, businessmen, politicians and officials of many liberal Asian-Pacific countries are among the members of the organization. Following the collapse of the Soviet Union, the Russian businessmen and the Chinese decision to integrate China into the capitalist system, the Chinese businessmen were accepted as members of the organization. It is thought that Michael Gorbacov, who is the architect of the collapse of the communist system, is one of the supporters of the Trilateral Commission behind the scenes.[111]

The first meeting of the organization was held in Tokyo in 1973, and the Asian Tigers were created to form the cores of the Pacific Union. Trilateral Commission There are three centres. These are Tokyo, New York and Paris. The meetings of the organization are held in these cities, in turn, each year. Following each Bilderberg or Trilateral Commission meeting, a CFR meeting is held in Washington and the decisions are taken are communicated to the Illuminati through this organization. Following the approval of the CFR inner circle and the Illuminati, the final application is started.

Candidates from all three organizations are selected from young and bright brains, even during their student years. Especially in the USA and England, this system has been successfully operated for many years. In the United States, Carnegie and in England, Rhodes scholarships are used to support successful students from around the world and are encouraged to come to certain points after training. The most famous example of this system is US President Bill Clington, who graduated from the University of Oxford with a Rhodes scholarship.

In addition to the scholarships, another method of involving young minds in the organization is the student associations established within the famous universities. The most famous of these is Skull & Bones which was founded in 1883 at Yale University. The organization was founded by General William Russel. Alphonso Taft, the father of US President Hower Taft, is another founder of the organization.[112]

The name of the organization comes from the symbols of the Tempeles' dry heads and bones. Admission to the membership of the Skull and Bones organization is the first step of participation in CFR and even Illuminati. Skull & Bones was created as a youth organization of the Illuminati. Skull & Bones to be a member of the nines in the penultimate student at Yale University is mandatory. Every year only 15 members are taken.[113] The new members are knighted and the old ones are given the title Patriarch. In its 150-year history, 2,500 people became members of this organization. The administration building of the organization is located on the university campus in Connecticut. Numerous American presidents have been members of the Skull and Bones organization. The most famous of these are the father and son Bush. All members are WASP. So White, Anglo-Saxon and Protestant. After Yale, the organization was expanded to eight US universities. With this construction, all the important universities under the name of "Ivy Union" are directly connected to Illuminati. According to Ivy Law, each member is bound to another member with indestructible ties and is obliged to help him whatever the circumstances.

Starting from the beginning of the 20th century, economic activities have been moved from national to supranational and increasingly international. Meanwhile, international organizations under the control of the forces controlling the economy have emerged and had further strengthened the structure in this direction. All these formations motivated the economic, political, social, religious and cultural structures in line with the final plan. Thus, a new Neo-Platonist management style is rapidly moving. This structure is moving towards a world-class elite democracy. As a result, a community system will be created under the control of a group of Kamil men and the administration will be left in the hands of the New World Elite.[113]

There will be no national state or border, and the goal of transnational universal brotherhood unity will be achieved. One State, Single Money, Single Law will be valid all over the world. All decisions will be taken by the central parliament.

It will be applied. Since the whole world is gathered under the umbrella of universal brotherhood, there will not be any conflict or war, the radioactive danger will be eliminated, and solutions to hunger and environmental problems will be brought. In the absence of third world war so far, it should be kept in mind that the various actors of the new order of the world play a big role in the wars of the world.

The New World State has no preference for religion. Its aim is secularism. Although Christianity did not have a direct demand for state administration and was not essentially interested in state affairs, the Papacy, the Orthodox practice tool of the Christian religion, was able to claim directly in this area. Illuminati gave the greatest struggle for the renunciation of this claim of the Papacy. The secular and Liberal order can only be achieved at the expense of the Renaissance, the Reformation, the wars of 30 years, the wars of 100 years, two great world wars and the blood of thousands of people. The Illuminati never intends to give up this secular and liberal order. Most of the Masonic organizations engage in speculative activities in line with this goal. However, the Illuminati and the other international organizations that it directs carry out the purpose-oriented operative activities. In the 1930s, the Illuminati, which had intense activity for the general acceptance of the United States as a secular state, recognized and declared in 1970 the new religion of secularism as the new religion.[114]

Given what has been said to this point, the intention of the Illuminati and its affiliates, which appear to have made great distances on the way to their plans, is not to establish a world dictatorship, a fascist repression regime. Yes, management will be the elite management. But which government is not elite management? Even the election to a national parliament has certain rules. Anybody who desires cannot go into management. Each power is, in its broadest sense, "elite" power in one way or another. Therefore, this projection of the Illuminati cannot be directed as an accusation to organizational policies. The proposition of extending Western-type democracy to the whole world coincides entirely with the narrative of esoterism, which has continued for thousands of years, to establish an ideal temple for humanity.

References

1 Naudon Paul, - *Freemasonry in History and Today (Tarihte ve Günümüzde Masonluk),* Varlık Pub., Istanbul 1968, p. 36

2 Altındal, Aytunç, - *Which Jesus? (Hangi Isa?)* Destek Pub., Ankara 2006, p. 39

3 Altındal, Aytunç, r.w., p. 45

4 Michael Baigent, Leigh Richard, - *Temple and Lodge (Mabet ve Loca) (1)*, Emre Pub., Istanbul 2000, p. 160

5 Naudon, Paul, - *The Roots of Freemasonary (Masonluğun Kökenleri)* Homer Pub., Istanbul 2007, p. 74

6 Baigent Michael/Leigh Richard, - *Holy Grail, Holy Blood (Kutsal Kâse, Kutsal Kan) (2),* Emre Pub., Istanbul 1996, p. 71

7 Baigent M. Leigh R., r.w. (2), p. 117

8 Baigent M. Leigh R, İe (2), p. 386

9 Signer. w.r, Jean Francois Thomazo, Renaud - *Secret Organizations (Gizli Örgütler)* Larousse Oğlak Güzel Kitaplar, Istanbul 2006, p. 37

10 Baigent M. Leigh R, r.w. (2), p. 387

11 Baigent M. Leigh R., r.w. (2), p. 303

12 Baigent M. Leigh R, r.w. (2), p. 388

13 Baigent M. Leigh R, r.w. (2), p. 359

14 Baigent M. Leigh R., r.w. (2), p. 56

15 Altındal, Aytunç - *Brotherhood of Rose and Cross (Gül ve Haç Kardeşliği) (2)*- Alfa Pub., Istanbul, 2004, p. 118

16 Altındal, Aytunç, r.w. (2), p. 101

17 Çınar, Erdoğan - *The Lost Thousand Years of Alevism (Aleviliğin Kayıp Bin Yılı)* Kalkedon Pub., Istanbul 2007, p. 83

18 Benson, Michael - Secret Communitites Glossary (Gizli Topluluklar Sözlüğü) - Neden Kitap- Istanbul 2005, p. 41

19 Baigent M. Leigh R, r.w. (2), p. 58

20 Baigent M. Leigh R, r.w. (2), p. 59

21 Baigent M. Leigh R, r.w. (2), p. 60

22 Baigent M. Leigh R, r.w. (2), p. 61

23 Baigent M. Leigh R, r.w. (2), p. 53

24 Baigent M. Leigh R, r.w. (2), p. 60.

25 Baigent M. Leigh R, r.w. (2), p. 62.

26 Baigent M. Leigh R, r.w. (2), p. 232

27 Baigent M. Leigh R, r.w. (2), p. 238

28 Baigent M. Leigh R, r.w. (2), p. 267

29 Baigent M. Leigh R, r.w. (2), p. 47

30 Baigent M. Leigh R, r.w. (2), p. 241

31 Ayan Tamer, - *Double Headed Eagle (Çift Başlı Kartal)*, İtidal Olgunlaşma Pub., Istanbul 1998, p. 282.

32 Baigent M. Leigh R, r.w. (2), p. 267

33 Baigent M. Leigh R, r.w. (2), p. 259

34 Baigent M. Leigh R, r.w. (2), p. 98

35 Boucher Jules, Naudon Paul, - *This Unknown Masonry (Masonluk Bu Meçhul),* Okat Pub., Istanbul 1966, p. 15

36 Baigent M. Leigh R, r.w. (2), p. 68

37 Erentay İbrahim, - Hıram Abif, Irmak Pub., Istanbul 2000, p. 34

38 Baigent M. Leigh R, r.w. (2), p. 90

39 Baigent M. Leigh R, r.w. (2), p. 70

40 Erentay İ., r.w., p. 38.

41 Daftary Farhad, - *Ismailis; History and Theory (İsmaililer; Tarih ve Kuram),* Rastlantı Pub., Ankara 2001, p. 30

42 Naudon, Paul - *The Roots of Freemasonary (Masonluğun Kökenleri)* Homer Pub., Istanbul 2007, p. 89

43 Baigent M. Leigh R, r.w. (2), p. 65

44 Baigent M. Leigh R, r.w. (2), p. 97

45 Baigent M. Leigh R, r.w. (2), p. 228

46 Baigent M. Leigh R, r.w. (2), p. 112

47 Baigent M. Leigh R, r.w. (2), p. 122

48 Baigent M. Leigh R, r.w. (2), p. 82

49 Ünal Tahsin, - Ante Anne Caedo, Gün Pub., Istanbul 1999, p. 41

50 Baigent M. Leigh R, r.w. (2), p. 74

51 Erentay İ., r.w., p. 40

52 Baigent M. Leigh R, r.w. (2), p. 128

53 Baigent M. Leigh R, r.w. (2), p. 75

54 Baigent M. Leigh R, r.w. (2), p. 94

55 Baigent M. Leigh R, r.w. (2), p. 67

56 Benson, Michael - Secret Communities Glossary (Gizli Topluluklar Sözlüğü)- Neden Kitap- Istanbul 2005, p. 164

57 Baigent M. Leigh R, r.w. (2), p. 103

58 Altındal, Aytunç - *Brotherhood of Rose and Cross (Gül ve Haç Kardeşliği) (2)* Alfa Pub., Istanbul, 2004, p. 217

59 Baigent M. Leigh R, r.w. (2), p. 79

60 Boucher J. Noudon P., r.w., p. 20

61 Benson, Michael, r.w., p. 160

62 Baigent M. Leigh R, r.w. (2), p. 113

63 Erman Sahir, - *Esoteric Interpretation of Dante and Divine Comedy (Dante ve İlahi Komedyanın Ezoterik Yorumu)*, Yenilik Pub., Istanbul 1977, p. 5

64 Baigent M. Leigh R, r.w. (1), p. 138

65 Knight, Christopher; Lomas, Robert - *The Hiram Book (Hiramın Kitabı)*, Bilge Karınca Pub., Istanbul 2008, p. 85

66 Baigent M. Leigh R, r.w. (1), p. 140

67 Knight, Christopher; Lomas, Robert, r.w., p. 70

68 Baigent M. Leigh R, r.w. (1), p. 122

69 Baigent M. Leigh R, r.w. (1), p. 128

70 Naudon, Paul - *The Roots of Freemasonry (Masonluğun Kökenleri) (2)*, Homer Pub., Istanbul 2007, p. 226

71 Naudon Paul, r.w., p. 34

72 Akin Asım, - *Freemasonry Throughout History (Tarih Boyunca Masonluk)*, Hacettepe Pub., Ankara 1998, p. 134

73 Signier, Jean Francois Thomazo, Renaud - *Secret Organizations (Gizli Örgütler)* Larousse Oğlak Güzel Kitaplar, Istanbul 2006, p. 101

74 Baigent M. Leigh R, r.w. (2), p. 98

75 Baigent M. Leigh R, r.w. (2), p. 134

76 Baigent M. Leigh R, r.w. (2), p. 161

77 Baigent M. Leigh R, r.w. (2), p. 140

78 Baigent M. Leigh R, r.w. (2), p. 154

79 Baigent M. Leigh R, r.w. (2), p. 213

80 Baigent M. Leigh R, r.w. (2), p. 219

81 Baigent M. Leigh R, r.w. (2), p. 402

82 Naudon Paul, r.w., p. 35

83 Altındal, Aytunç - *Brotherhood of Rose and Cross (Gül ve Haç Kardeşliği) (2)* Alfa Pub., Istanbul 2004, p. 68

84 Tecimer, Ömer - *Rose and Cross (Gül ve Haç)* Plan B Pub., Istanbul 2004, p. 165

85 Altındal, Aytunç, r.w., p. 54

86 Altındal, Aytunç, r.w., p. 97

87 Boucher J. Naudon P., r.w., p. 31

88 Tecimer, Ömer, r.w., p. 19

89 Bayet Albert, - *History of Thought Against Religion (Dine Karşı Düşünce Tarihi)*, Broy Pub., Istanbul 1991, p. 55.

90 Tecimer, Ömer, r.w., p. 97

91 Baigent M. Leigh R, r.w. (1), p. 142

92 Benson, Michael - *Secret Communities Glossary (Gizli Topluluklar Sözlüğü)* Neden Pub., Istanbul 2005, p. 94

93 Tecimer, Ömer, r.w., p. 422

94 Signier, Jean-Francois, - *Secret Organizations* (Gizli Örgütler)- Oğlak Güzel Kitaplar, Istanbul 2006, p. 143

95 Tecimer, Ömer, r.w., p. 309

96 Tecimer, Ömer, r.w., p. 308

97 Signier, Jean-Francois, r.w., p. 145

98 Tecimer, Ömer, r.w., p. 309

99 Benson, Michael - *Secret Communities Glossary (Gizli Topluluklar Sözlüğü)* Neden Pub., Istanbul 2005, p. 108

100 Porter, Lindsay – *Illuminati, The Secret Organization That Rules the World (Dünyayı Yöneten Gizli Örgüt İlluminati)* Neden Pub., Istanbul 2006, p. 49

101 Benson, Michael, r.w., p. 113

102 Akar, Atilla - Deep *World State (Derin Dünya Devleti)* Timaş Pub., Istanbul 2004, p. 157

103 Marrs Texe - *Illuminati Intrigue Circle (İlluminati Entrika Çemberi)*, Timaş Pub., Istanbul 2002, p. 81

104 Benson, Michael, r.w., p. 114

105 Benson, Michael, r.w., p. 318

106 Akar, Atilla, r.w. p. 97

107 Benson, Michael, r.w., p. 52

108 Benson, Michael, r.w., p. 37

109 Çimen, Ali. Yılmaz, Hakan - *Who Has Control (İpler Kimin Elinde)*, Timaş Pub., Istanbul 2002, p. 165

110 Benson, Michael, r.w., p. 284

111 Marrs, Texe - Dark Majesty, Timaş Pub., Istanbul 2003, p. 183

112 Akar, Atilla r.w., p. 244

113 Benson, Michael, r.w., p. 127

114 Altındal, Aytunç - *Brotherhood of Rose and Cross (Gül ve Haç Kardeşliği)* Alfa Pub., Istanbul, 2004, p. 210

CHAPTER XI

VICTORY OF ESOTERISM; HUMANISM AND RENAISSANCE

In 1453, by the Turks recent invention of Byzantine Empire's Istanbul, many Byzantines emigrated to Italy. Immigrants included Orthodox Collegia brothers, as well as scientists and philosophers. These new brothers who joined the Freemasons in Italy caused the momentum of the events to climb. In addition, the discovery of new continents resulted an increase in the prosperity in Europe. With increasing prosperity, abstract concepts such as human rights came up.

Shortly after the conquest of Istanbul by the Turks, in 1460, "Plato Academy" was founded in Florence, Italy.[1] In this academy founded by Marcile Ficin, the views of Christian philosophy and esoteric doctrine were tried to be reconciled. The same qualified work spread in cities such as Venice, Genoa and Rome. As a result of the research of these academies, in the dusty archives of the Byzantine monasteries, ancient Greek artefacts have been unearthed after centuries.

Academics led by the Plato Academy in Italy brought to light the Greek classics which brought a new breakthrough in science and art, and especially in life. Esoteric doctrines, which were included in various works, started a new era. This period even took its name from the esoteric doctrine: Renaissance. The greatest aim of the thinkers of Renaissance, which means "Rebirth", was to establish a relationship between Greek-Roman civilization and Christianity, and to create a new world by dissolving two civilizations in the same pot.[2]

During the Renaissance enlightenment, the texts of Hermes, Plato, Astrology, Alchemy, Kabbalah, Sacred Geometry which were collected in Byzantine libraries for thousands of years, were transferred to the west, and the works hidden in Byzantine libraries such as the Corpus Hermeticum were translated into various languages. Hermeticum's, French edition of 1549 is seen to have been printed. As a result of the oppression of the Spanish kingdom in Spain after the expulsion of Muslims from the peninsula, the esoteric information here has flowed north. This intense bombardment has changed the structure of western civilization and rendered Renaissance inevitable. The source of esoteric information is now of Italy. Many Italian nobles, such as Cosimo de Medici, were closely involved with the Byzantine esotericism.[3] Academies were created with Byzantine and Spanish materials, translations were made and publications were published. A wave of esotericism, and has spread for a century and examples of architecture and art movements began to be seen in Europe.

The Renaissance scientists discovered the existence of an important concept during their study of the works of Plato; "The Architect of the Universe." Plato, in his book Timaeus, refers to the Supreme Lord as "Tekton", which means artisan or constructive. According to Plato, Arche Tekton, the Master Producer, created the universe through geometry.[4]

The Greek works brought with the immigrants from Byzantium to Italy and the translation of the Roman works in the monasteries of Italy into an understandable language led to the emergence of a national understanding of literature and history. In the same period, the Latin Bible was translated into Italian and it was tried to prove that there was continuity between ancient civilizations and

Christianity. Meanwhile, the invention of the printing press allowed the books to be printed in a greater number and more people read them. Thus, new ideas began to be discussed in many contexts, and new ideas were created as a result of these discussions. The individual came to the forefront rather than the society and the human values were kept above all other values.

This philosophical movement, which includes the views that esoteric doctrine has been arguing for thousands of years, was called "Humanism". Esoteric thinkers such as Petrarca and Boccacio have written that the human being is at the centre of the universe, that the world is a tool to develop the human spirit, that the goal of the soul is to reach God, in short, the works that cover the content of the esoteric teaching. The same subjects, some of the Plato Academy, some of the other brothers also worked with thinkers such as Manetti, Erasmus, Mirandola, Monteign. These philosophers, who put forth various works on the supremacy and dignity of human beings, did not refrain from saying that the only thing that will determine the destiny of man on earth and in later life is divine love and that there is no unity between man and God.

Such a clear expression of esoteric doctrine has allowed the imagination that created Renaissance poetry and artworks to find its way freely. Boccacio argued that the biblical book was dealt with a poetic language, claiming that poetry and religion complemented each other. He argued that it was. As a result of these and similar initiatives, the poets and writers who worked on non-religious subjects gained sacred respect because of their creativity and they had the opportunity to work more easily on the subjects they wanted.

Humanism was taught to be proud of human beings by the flow of humanism. This way of thinking has spread all over Europe in a short time with Freemasonry, which incorporates esoteric teaching. The search for the beauty of the teaching has spread to all branches of art, and hundreds of works have been born, whose perfection cannot be reached even today. With the masters such as Leonardo da Vinci, Michelangelo and Rafaello, Renaissance reached its peak.

As a result of all these developments, the static system of the Middle Ages was destroyed. Instead, positive thinking came to the forefront of rationality. Renaissance, in a philosophical way, reconciles belief with reason.

The effects of Humanism and Renaissance continued to expand from the 15th century until the 18th century. The Papacy saw that these currents gradually damaged their interests and imposed a blow to the established order.

From now on, it has waged war against free thought. Big blows to science, Galilean Galileo was excommunicated and imprisoned on the Inquisition for "writing a book carrying very effective evidence on teaching contrary to written provisions."

In France, the Nantes Edict, which envisions the Protestants living in peace with Catholics, was abolished. It was announced that all writers and publishers who attacked the religion with a royal decree published in 1757 would face the death penalty.[5]

A decade after this decision, Marmontel defended only religious tolerance, and was sentenced to death on the grounds of "suppressing all kinds of offences such as deism and atheism, as well as all kinds of incidents that could undermine the foundations of the Catholic church." It was a decision to condemn the esoteric doctrine. However, medieval times were now over, and there were giant thinkers in the face of the church, not the silent masses. After the Protestant leaders, Calas and Sirven were sentenced to Papacy, Voltaire launched a major campaign against the injustice of the church. As a result of the campaign that had a profound repercussion in the society, the Catholic Church released the Protestant leaders and reinstated Protestants.

On the other hand, the Papacy decided to burn Denis Diderot's Encyclopedia of Esoteric, which is looking for justice in good, good and good terms. Voltaire was closed to the Bastille. About his arrest, Rousseau found an escape. Holbach's "L'esprit" (spirit) and the Dictionary of Philosophy were among the works burned. The Italian clergyman and thinker Geordano Bruno was put on trial in 1600 as a Chief Infidel and burned to death because of his esoteric thoughts.[6]

The Inquisition often resorted to violence to intimidate the philosophers against them. Like Bruno, not to greet the mockery of La Barre and condemn him to death by reading objections such as the Philosophical Dictionary, his tongue was decapitated and his body burned, on the contrary, the philosophers showed their reactions by unity. Voltaire, the "terrain of the Pope" for the Montequieu, even a man famous for his self-indulgence, "the Pope, customary to break the neck of the neck is an outdated obsession," he could not get himself.[7]

The attitude of Freemasonry against the Papacy caused the Roman church to condemn members of the Brotherhood. The first orders that condemned Freemasonry, Pope 12. Published by Clemens in 1738. 13 different popes from this date, until 1884, the Emperor and the oppression of the Freemasons issued an order to prohibit. On April 28, 1738, Pope Clemens 12 commanded no-one to be a member of Freemasonry or a similar organization and announced that the members would be excommunicated. The following popes continued to publish their orders up to the 13th Leo, who condemned the Freemasonry and repeated the anathema over the members.[8]

As Pope Clemens Freemasonry was convicted, this accusation, as well as meaningless accusations that would bring evils all over the world, had accusations that the unification of the people of different religions and sects would pose unimaginable dangers but be the products of a bigoted mindset. The most important reason for Clemens was "the right and reasonable reasons for themselves"!

The edict of the Freedom of Freemasonry, even in Catholic countries, it didn't work much. The Catholic Australian King Franchois was a fervent defender of Freemasonry, even in Italy and Spain, the castles of the Roman church, the Masonic organization could not be prevented.[9] This decree of the Papacy had no meaning beyond the transformation of the Masonic lodges into a gathering place for their opponents. Over time, Freemasonry has become a focus of revolutionary ideas and actions against the official church and priest class in all of Europe.

The Kings of the Popes and the Catholic States were concerned that they were connected and that their meetings were secret. It revealed historical concerns that these concerns were not unwarranted. In France, the Masons played the most important role in the realization of the great revolution and the secularization of the system, in Italy, the end of the papacy, the national unity and the secularization of the system.

England played important roles in the Western world after the Reformation in the context of the victory of the esoterism. In 1531, the king of England, Henry 8, declared himself head of the Church of England. When the Pope did not approve of his marriage and excommunicated the king of England, the British Bishop announced in 1535 that they had withdrawn from the Pope's authority, and the Anglican Church was established[10] and the Catholic traditions were wiped out of the Freemasonry.[11] One of the milestones in the expulsion of the state administration, the Papacy and the Catholic church was taken in England in 1714. A law is issued and any Catholic monarch the UK was banned from the throne. Thus, England was able to get rid of the intense repression of

Rome.[12] This free environment emerged by the new law made the Masons feel safe and they opened their doors to the outside world. At this time, the members of the Templars and other Knight organizations, Rose Croix, the followers of the Royal Society, were members of the Mason lodges. These were called "Accepted Mason" because their original profession was not a masonry and later joined the organization.

After the Papacy excommunicated the Masons in 1738, Voltaire entered the Freemasonry with the title "Accepted" to support these people, even though he was 80 years old, who provided him with great support in the anti-church campaigns and shared the same beliefs with him. In defending the human rights and the right to plea as its extension, Voltaire argued that everyone is free in their beliefs and that all people are brothers, regardless of their religion. "Is a Turk, a Chinese, a Jew, a brother?" Voltaire asked, to his question, he was answering; "Of course, aren't we all the same father, the children of God?"

Like Voltaire, Diderot, Montesquieu, Lafayette, Boucher, Danton and Pastoren were also famous French Freemasons. The fact that such a famous philosopher and scientist came together under one roof is an indication of how Freemasonry supports the secularist movement against religion.

Another famous Accepted Mason, the British philosopher and scientist, John Dee, led Britain to become the central centre of the esoteric studies in the 17th century. Dee, known for his studies on astrology, alchemy, Kabbalah and mathematics, refers to Jesus as Our Grand Master of God ad in his preface to Euclid's English translation.[13] According to him, architecture is extremely important in all other arts because of this science is. It is important, the architect must be a master who can do every job and understand everything. In the former gospels in England, God is portrayed as Architect. Accepted Masons like Francis Bacon and Robert Fludd are students of John Dee. As a result of the unification of England and Scotland, Templier doctrines began to spread in England and Ireland. The new King James 1 is the patron and member of the Operative Freemasons. Thus, the connection between Freemasonry and the throne of England was also strengthened.

In the 10th century, during the reign of King Athelstan; Edwyn, brought by Amphibal, takes over the patronage of the king's son Edwyn in the city of York, in 925, and takes part in the work of the history of Staffordshire, published by Robert Plot in 1686, in which he collected the Masonic obligations based on the old rolls and parchments.[14] According to this document, Edwyn was given the title of "Great Architect" at the meeting. In 1150, another Masonic meeting took place in Kilwinning, and in 1180, King Henry I issued a decree stating that various privileges were granted to the British Masons and initiated the continuous development of the land of Freemasonry. In England, working hours and wages of stonemasons were determined by the "Workers' Law" in the 14th century. The founder of modern Freemasonry is Sir Francis Bacon. Bacon's Nova Atlantis in his book New it is mentioned for the first time from a World Order. This utopia, inspired by Bacon's mind, ultimately inspired the founding of the United States.[15]

On the other hand, technological developments in the world adversely affected the operative branch of Freemasonry. Information previously stored as a secret on the construction of construction, the secrets of the school and taught in schools they become their hands. This situation led to the names of the construction craftsmen, who were later called "Operative Mason", and the emergence of new competitors who were not school members and members of the organization. Over time, these masters became hard to find work. The last and most impressive work of the Operative British Freemasonry is the city of London. The last major activities of the Operators were the reconstruction of London. After 80 per cent of the city was burned with a fire in 1666, the British Masons rebuilt the city with the help of Operative Freemasons from Europe. Thanks to the extraordinary architecture of these buildings, including numerous cathedrals and palaces, Freemasonry has gained great respect in the eyes of society.[16] The organization, which has become a unifying force, has become an effective institution even in the Anglican Church. The foundations of democracy were laid in the Lodge where aristocrats and artisans, intellectuals and artisans could come together.

But after London's reconstruction, Operative Freemasons did not have to be done again, and the manual labour-based operative arm of Freemasonry began to disappear. At this stage, commissioned Masons entered. These Freemasons, who participated in the intellectual works of the lodges, gradually increased in number even if they were minorities. His work, not craftsmanship, head work, ie to work on the idea of because of its relevance, the Accepted Masons, who considered themselves "Speculative Masons", declared in a decree in 1703 that the privileges of Freemasonry would no longer be unique to the construction workers.

After the outbreak of Protestantism in England and the destruction of the Catholic Church, the Anglican Freemasons decided to establish a high authority that could decide on the regularity of the lodges and open new chambers. Thus, in 1717, four London lodges established the Great Lodge of England.[17] The Great Lodge, which was intended to collect the Mason Laires in England under one roof, was founded on June 24, 1717, on the day of the memorial of John the Blessed. The number of lodges increased rapidly and reached 52 in 1723. Considering the fact that 26 of them existed before 1717, the number of lodges doubled in a short period of time and the favour of the British to Freemasonry arises.[18]

The new law of the Great Lodge has been written by a Protestant priest, James Anderson. Another Protestant priest, Desagulier, helped write this law. He was a close fellow of the famous scholar Newton, a member of the Royal Society. In the first part of this law, which is called the Anderson Laws, "A Mason has to obey the code of ethics because of his attributes and he can never be a Deist or Atheist."

While British Freemasonry was a three-degree Freemasonry consisting of apprentices, fellowcrafts and masters, the Scottish Freemasonry was working at 25 degrees. Called high degrees this practice began to be recognized by the British Freemasonry, but after 1745, when the Standards were completely out of danger for the throne, the Great Lodge of the United Kingdom began to be recognized, and in 1813, the United Grand Lodge, which adopted both methods of practice, was born.[19]

As a result of the recognition of Scottish Freemasonry by the Great Lodge of England, the Scottish Freemasonry began to spread in America in 1761. In this continent, eight more degrees were added to the Scottish Rite, and the Scottish Rite Freemasonry was adopted at 33 degrees with the acceptance of the whole world.[20]

In 1815, a new Great Lodge Act was published in England and the first chapter on God and religion was changed as follows; "Because of his or her character, a Mason is obliged to abide by the code of ethics. If he has a good understanding of the profession, he will never be a God or a Godless. He has to understand better than anyone that God sees everything otherwise than man. A person, regardless of his religious temple style, will not be taken out of the sect. Just as he believes in heaven and earth by the Supreme Architect and fulfil the sacred duties of morality.[21] Thus, the prerequisite for being a Mason evolved from being a Christian to Nassithi. In addition to the Christians, it was possible for Jews and Muslims to join the organization. In this way, Freemasonry showed the existence of free thought in every country where it sprouted and spread all over the world.

In the 17th century, Freemasonry was extremely weak in continental Europe, France, Italy, Spain and Germany, due to the intense pressure of the Catholic church and the unemployment caused by technological progress. Britain and in Scotland, the situation was different. In both countries, the excess of Accepted Masons had ensured the existence and strength of the organization. In 1649, after the dismissal of King Charles I of England from the Stuart Dynasty, Charles V, had been dismissed, his widow, Queen Henrietta, returned to her native country of France. Short after a while, many Scottish aristocillus followed him. The majority of these aristocrats accepted Masonry.[22] They carried out their activities in the Freemasons lodges, which they established in France, for the Stuart dynasty to regain the throne of England. Some of these chambers were of a military character, and when they had no chance to return to the British throne, they joined the French army. Thus, in the French Army Freemasonry began to spread. In addition to the military Scottish lodges, the civil lodges combined with the pre-existing lodges in France enabled the profession to spread throughout the country. This Freemasonry, based on ancient traditions and the rituals that have been practised for hundreds of years, was referred to the new emitters in the European continent as the "Scottish Freemasonry". The British Freemasonry lodges were built in order by acquiring the Great Lodge of England, while the Scottish chalets were built on their own, in accordance with the old traditions, without relying on any authority.

These self-established Scottish niches were connected to the National High Councils, which were established as superintendents. The Ripening Rit, established in 1762, was operating over 22 high degrees. In 1786, the Prussian Emperor Frederic approved the double-headed eagle, which we had previously seen as an emblem of the empire, as the special coat of arms of the first international convent of the Scottish Rite in Berlin. 10 degrees Sefirot and 1 final "En-Soph", described in Kabbalah Ezothism with the addition of degrees, the total number of Rites has been increased to 33.[23]

Scottish Rite Double Headed Eagle

The French lodges, in response to the Great Lodge of England, formed a supreme organization called the merc Grand Orient Loc in the French Grand Lodge setting in 1736, in order to obtain the same status. In France, in addition to this independent French establishment, a French Grand Lodge, set up by the Great Lodge of England, was established.

At that time, the most important speech about the origins of Freemasonry was performed by Knight Ramsay. Ramsay, who was a Scottish aristocrat and passed to France with the Standards, gave an enlightening talk about the past of Freemasonry in the Grand Orient in 1737.[24] Ramsay, who said that Freemasonry was based on the Tempers and that their brotherhood was spread all over Europe, said, "The roots of our sect, Jerusalem You are in the knights of Jan. That day our lodges, are called Jan Localis." Ramsay, during his famous speech, reminded that the Freemasonry, which had regressed in many European countries, remained alive in Scotland thanks to the Tempers.

According to Ramsay, Masons were not only great architects who had conveyed their talents and beauties to great temples, but also princesses illuminating the living shrines of God. Ramsay, who claimed that masonry had started between the Crusaders in the Holy Land, Christians who formed a unity in a fraternity, Jerusalem he said that he had merged with the Jan knights, and over time, the organization had established many lodges in Scotland, Germany, Italy, Spain and France. Ramsay, stating that the Scottish nobleman, James Steward, was the Grand Master of a chapel in Kilwinning in 1286, stated that Freemasonry survived in Scotland during the ages and that the Scottish Guards, who ensured the protection of the kings of France, had improved again in this country.

Freemasonry before the French Revolution was very widespread in this country. In addition to many aristocrats, bourgeois leaders and intellectuals continued to the locales. Thanks to the intellectual work carried out in the lodges, ideas such as the freedom, brotherhood and equality of people, which are the basic principles of Freemasonry, became the flag of the French Revolution. The revolutionaries of the revolution were Bailly, Talleyrand, Brissot, La Fayette, Mirabeau, Condor and Masculine. Some sources argue that Danton and Robinson are also Mason. In the 1789 revolution, even if there was no activity of Freemasonry as an organization, even the main cadres were prepared in the lodges for the formation of the revolution.[25] The revolutionaries came together in the secrecy of the chambers and formed the infrastructure of the revolution. In addition, the continuous spread of secularism in the lodges prepared the people to carry out all kinds of religious reforms. As a matter of fact, in 1793 all the churches and temples in the country were closed, and all religious beliefs were prevented. It was foreseen that those who wanted the church to be opened, and that priests would be banned from all kinds of public duties and rights, but Danton and Robespierre's attempts to abandon these hard measures. All forms of violence against freedom of belief and he were contented with the prohibition of oppression. In 1794, the revolution conquered the state and the church. One year later, the freedom of belief was enacted, which allowed those who wanted to benefit from churches and who wished to live away from any religious worship.

In 1860, the French Catholic church bishops decided to propose the legal acceptance of Freemasonry in France. The Deist philosophers, who were members of the French Grand Orient, took action and in 1865 they made a decision in the Grand Orient to accept everyone as a member regardless of their religious conviction. Thus, in France, Freemasonry and the Catholic Church came to a complete rupture point. In the Grand Orient's 1877 Grand Column, the necessity of believing in God and Spirit's inability has been abolished and the first article of the Masonic Constitution has been changed to "Freemasonry, in principle, adopts absolute freedom of conscience and human freedom".[26] The number of Catholics in the French Masonic lodges gradually decreased. Grand Orient, the "Grand Master of the Universe" to remove the obligation to study the lodgings in the UK

Grand Lodge, the French Grand Orient immediately interrupted all relations with the organization and announced that the world does not regularly recognize this organization. French Freemasonry thus fell apart with the universal Freemasonry community.[27]

In France, the powerful lobby against the Catholic Church continued its activity during the period of directing following the revolution. During this period, the Jacobins were seen to dominate the church. With Napoleon's arrival, the situation is reversed. Catholics, weight during the Empire they made them feel. In the aftermath of the Empire, the struggle between the parties continued without a definite advantage of anybody. Nevertheless, the lodges were revived in the empire. Napoleon had never been initiated, but his brother Joseph Bonaparte became Grand Master to the Grand Orient.[28]

In the 1877 judgment of the French Freemasonry, the 1848 revolution had a great influence. In the third republic established after Napoleon's fall, the majority of the rulers of the country are Masons and are tired of the pressure of the Catholic church. In France, freedom of the press is possible thanks to Masons. Victor Hugo, in his famous speech at the republic parliament, is buried in the clergy with all his might, and they are the ones who beat Prinelli for saying that the stars do not fall, who tortured Harvey for proving that blood is circulating in the body. They are those who excommunicate Montaigne, Moliere, for the sake of religion and ethics. The great light that France has emitted for three hundred years harasses them. That light is composed of mind.

In this state of mind, the French Freemasons endorsed a decision to strengthen the Catholic church, to remove the necessity of believing in the Great Architect of the Universe, and to contradict the esoteric doctrine, in order to ensure that those in the Deist and even Atheist faith were included. Esoteric doctrine argues that there is a Supreme Being, albeit different from the orthodox discourses of the divine religions. The elimination of the necessity of believing in this Supreme Being is equivalent to the fundamental disappearance of the doctrine.

In spite of all these efforts, the secularization of primary education in France was only possible in 1879. Church's teaching, he was banned in 1904, and the state and religious affairs were separated in 1905. Finally, in 1907, the immunity of secular laws was guaranteed by law. In France in the 19th century, three of the four senators of the Radical Party and half of the French ambassadors were Masons. In 1922, the Communist Party forbade its members to be Mason. During the Nazi occupation, the Vichy regime launched an anti-Mason campaign and in 1940 the Mason lodges were closed, reopened after the Second World War.

Freemasonry in Italy followed a path similar to that of France. In Italy, Bruno, Dante, Boccacio and other euphoric doctrine thinkers, the doctrine of secrets was a traditional heritage since Pythagoras. However, because of the Romanity of the Catholic church, the intense pressure of the Papacy made itself felt most in Italy. In this country, which was the cradle of the Renaissance, when the 17th century, Freemasonry was almost completely erased. The revival of Freemasonry began in Italy with the supporters of the Stuart dynasty, as in France. The first chamber connected to the Scottish Rite was founded in the second half of this century. Freemasonry, whose traditional infrastructure was ready, spread rapidly in Italy and took its natural place against the Catholic church.[29]

The Spanish sovereignty of Italy, which lasted until 1713, led to the strengthening of the Catholic Church, the institutionalization of the Inquisition and the loss of the Renaissance. After the overthrow of Napoleon in 1814, after the rule of Austria and France, the Italian states re-emerged. The kingdom of Naples, the kingdom of Sardinia and the Pope became independent. However, the Hellenistic bound to Toscana, Parma and Modena, Austria. The Lombardia-Venetian kingdom was ruled directly by Austria. Italian lands such as Trentino, Istria and Trieste were officially included in the territory of the Austrian Empire.

Profit from the Austrian invasion and intervention The Masarians, which have been strengthened in the country with the Carbonari organization established by the Italian intellectuals, formed an alliance and began to struggle for the unity and independence of Italy. This struggle lasted until 1848. The Italian Carbonari associations were established for the first time at the beginning of the 19th century under the protection of Italian troops in connection with the non-imperialist anti-Papist brotherhood associations in France. Initiatives vow to sacrifice their lives for freedom, equality and unity. The slogan is National Unity. However, when we are unity, they are free. In 1817, the project of revolt against the church institutions in Macerata is put into effect. Giacomo Papis was the Grand Master of the Carbonari. The first Carbonari organization was born in the Kingdom of Naples. Then it spread to Genoa and from here to Italy. The locales where members came together were called Vendite. The red, blue and black stripes were the symbol of the Carbonari organization. He represented the desire to reach the blue God, his belief in the transformation into the red fire, and the pain and mourning over the loss of immaturity. At the ceremony of participation of various degrees, scenes of national independence struggles were displayed. Each member was attending meetings with weapons equipped with symbolic colours of the organization. In 1820, a partisan army invaded Naples. However, with the intervention of Austria, many Carbonarians were thrown into the dungeons.[30] Papacy, free of charge he was opposed to the idea of the Italian Union, with the awareness that they were thoughtful and secular, and would never listen to their orders. The greatest fear of the popes was that the last lands under their sovereignty were out of their hands. In addition to the intense oppression of the Papacy, as a result of the wars waged by the Austrian armies, the organization was gradually weakened and in 1831 the organization disappeared. The survivors of the organization joined the Freemasons, their fellow mates, and from now on, the Masons gave the struggle against the church to unity.

The February revolution in Paris in 1848 led to the March revolution in Italy and the national unity revolution in Italy in the same year. Wars for the Union continued until 1861. At that time, all the Italian states, except the Roman-Pope state territory, were united and the Kingdom of Italy was born.

The leaders who fought for unity like Garibaldi, Cavour, Emanuel I, Mazzini were always Mason. These intellectuals, against the unification of the church against the principles of Freemasonry, came out. In 1786, with the support of the Pope, the Austrian queen, Maria Teresa, tried to ban the Freemasonry in Italy. But in this country, the foundations of the Freemasonry tradition were very deep. The Academy of Pythagoras, the Romans of Rome, the Comanige Freemasons, the Gilde, the Plato Academy, the Renaissance were always born in this land. For this reason, Freemasonry, despite the intensity of the Catholics, was greeted with sympathy among the people and was also receiving great support because of their appeal to national feelings. With the help of the French Freemasons, the Austrian queen's attempt failed.

In 1848, when Pope Pius No. 9 refused to declare war on Austria for the independence of Italy, Masons, they started a riot in Rome. The Pope had to flee from Rome. But after the French forces took over Rome, Pope Pius returned to the city. When France entered the war with Germany in 1870, the French forces withdrew from Rome. The units of the Italian kingdom that were founded at that time entered the city. Upon the reception of Rome by the royal troops, the Pope retreated behind the city walls of the Vatican City, but failed to absorb the defeat and continued the campaign of the curse of Freemasonry. Leo 10, who came to the Papacy after Pius, banned the Catholics of Italy from participating in royal parliamentary elections in order to show that he did not approve the new regime. However, as a result of this decision, the Catholics had no influence on political grounds.

The Masons, who provided the Italian unity and took power in their hands, practised Masonic beliefs in many areas, particularly in a secular state system. For example, Zanardelli who prepared the Italian Penal Code, which was accepted as the first democratic penal code, was a Mason and the law he enacted included many Masonic principles. Zanardelli envisaged that this law would punish those who would oppose this freedom as well as accepting freedom of religion by making no distinction between religions.

Papacy and Freemasonry were able to recover not only in the 20th century but also to be a Rose Croix. Pope John the 13th published a decree in 1960 that Catholics could become Mason.[31]

Masonic discourses and ideas have also become the banner of the war of independence among American colonists. Freemasons, Freedom, Brotherhood and it has ensured the spread of supreme concepts such as Human Rights in all colonies. Britain the war of independence, which was initiated by the end of 1783, was signed with the Paris agreement and was born in the United States.

The first 13 colonies of the Confederation were based on the organization of the Masonic federal system. During the Constitutional Congress convened in 1787, Freemasonry was the only institution operating in every region of independent colonies. At the Constitutional Congress, two important principles were institutionalized. The first one is the principle that power is not in individuals, but it is in individuals and the individuals are elected by voting at regular intervals. The principles of the Masonic organization were prioritized in the creation of this principle.[32] In fact, in Freemasonry, lodges and Grand Masters are elected to the authorities for a certain period of time by their equal. The second principle is the audit and balancing system. According to this system, power is divided equally between two different governing bodies. The executive duty was given to the President and the legislative task to Congress. Because of their autonomy, both organs can prevent the concentration of powers in the hands of another. In addition, the separation of the person with the authority, as in the lodge system, is guaranteed by mandatory and regular legal choices.

It has been possible to transform the weak Confederation, which has gained its independence but has not yet achieved integration, into a strong nation with the system of the Federated States. The US Constitution, in a way, can be called a Masonic document. The three names behind the constitution are Washington, Franklin, and Randolph, whose orientation is entirely shaped by Freemasonry.[33] Washington was elected President in 1789, later, he appointed John Marshall, another Mason, to serve as Judge. Marshall is the name that makes the judiciary equal to the executive and legislative bodies. Thus, the basis of contemporary democratic systems was taken into consideration with the Masonic organization.

The sworn-in of Washington, the first President of the United States, was led by the Grand Master of the Grand Lodge of New York, Robert Livingston. Over the US dollar, the Great Seal of the Lodge was printed; On the pyramid, see the eye in the triangle. Washington, as well as many US presidents, are known to be Mason.

Freemasonry in the United States has been effective since its inception. There are still 50 Grand Lodges and 4 million Mason in each state. Freemasonry is so widespread in America that the name of a city in the state of Iowa is even "Mason City". Another interesting Masonic information about this country is that the astronaut Edwin Aldrin, the second person walking on the Moon, placed a Masonic plaque on the Moon. In 1969, Aldrin, a symbol of the universality of Freemasonry, was drafted by the Great Lodge of Texas, stating that the Moon had been included in the Jurisdiction of this lodge and a flag bearing the double-headed eagle symbol.[34]

Mason also played an important role in the establishment of the Republic of Turkey. The date of the establishment of the first masonry lodge in the territory of the Ottoman Empire is 1738. From this date, it is known that until the establishment of the first National Supreme Council in 1909, 23 lodges connected to foreign Great Lords or Supreme Councils have been operating in various periods in Ottoman lands. In these chambers connected to foreign objects, in particular, the Sultan Murat 5, prince Nurettin and Kemalettin masters, Namık Kemal, Mithat Pasha, Fuat Pasha, Talat Pasha, Ahmet Vefik Pasha, such as the famous people and grand viziers have participated in Freemasonry.[35] In 1876, the Meşruti (Constitutional) administration was established. But two years later, in 1878, Sultan Abdülhamit rescinded the constitution from the constitution and annihilated the prominent leaders and the elders of Mason.

The intellectuals, who opposed the absolute sovereignty of the sultan, were organized in Turkey and abroad since 1899 and started to oppose the Young Turks. Abdülhamit, who came to the throne by taking the power of the Masons behind him, immediately after he had taken all the power, a complete anti-Masonic enemy was interrupted. Abdülhamit, who was identified with the Catholic church in charge of the Freemasons, the irreligion and the inadmissibility of God, nevertheless did not make it sound for the Masonic lodges to operate. Two reasons were the reason for this. First of all, Sultan Abdülhamit had a very sceptical and cunning personality and calculated that if all Mason were to shut down their lodges, all the Masons could be drawn underground, and they could use more intense efforts against him. Instead, they kept the chambers open and were constantly under control through their braces. This method of Abdülhamit was extremely influential, especially in Istanbul, and the Freemasons of Istanbul showed no presence throughout the period of despotism. Secondly, the Ottoman administration became totally dependent on the economy from the outside. Abdülhamit, Mason lodges in the case of foreign countries, the great pressures of Freemasons had calculated that it would remain, which would affect the economic benefits to be taken.[36]

Despite the passivity of the Freemasons of Istanbul, the mason lodges in the Balkan peninsula, and especially in Macedonia, were extremely effective. Due to the mixed situation in the Balkans and the national uprisings, the Sultan's rule was not in Macedonia. The Young Turks, who came together in Macedonia under the name of Union and Progress Society, took the example of French revolutionaries and Italian unionists and found their meeting in Mason lodges to be more appropriate to protect their privacy. The fact that there was a degree of harmony between the program cited by the Committee of Union and Progress and the Masonic principles made it easier to unite. The leaders of the Committee of Union and Progress were organized in lodges, especially Talat Pasha, and they determined the strategy they would pursue against the administration.[37]

The lodge where they were the most intense member of the Committee of Union and Progress, was the Rizorta (Reborn Macedonia) lodge of the Macedonian Obedience, which was working in Thessaloniki. His founder was Baruh Kohen, a Voltaire, a free-thinking Jew. The Jews, unlike other Balkan nations, were working together with the Turkish intellectuals because they found it more appropriate to stay in Ottoman nationality. For this reason, there were many Jews in the Rizorta lodge of Macedonia, as well as members of the Committee of Union and Progress.

The fact that the Jewish Masons were so close to the Unionist Progressors led to the reaction of the religious circles and allegedly serious claims that Freemasonry served Jewish purposes. The fact that some symbols used in Jewish religion were used in Freemasonry because they were taken from the same origin was enough evidence for these circles. Thus, the Sunni arm of Islam and Christian Catholics came to the same point in the campaign to blame the Freemasonry.

Among the Bektashis, another defender of the Ottoman Masons and Western doctrines, there was considerable solidarity during the reign of Abdülhamit. The Tanzimat (Reform) Edict published by the Grand Vizier Mustafa Reşit Pasha, who was himself a Mason, and the Masons gained a strong position in the Ottoman Empire, and there was a strong interaction between Bektashism and Freemasonry, and it was seen that the important names were brought into both schools. While the Masons in Thessaloniki benefited from the Bektashi dervish lodges for their meetings, a Bektashi Father, like Tevfik Bey, participated in the Freemasonry.[38]

Union and Progress was rapidly spreading among army officers. It is thought that Mustafa Kemal, who was in close contact with the Unionists, also joined a Masonic lodge in Thessaloniki, but he was no longer a member due to his absenteeism. As a result of the intensive efforts of the Committee of Union and Progress, Sultan Abdulhamid was forced to re-declare the Constitutional Monarchy in 1908. In the elections held in the same year, the League provided a large majority in parliament. On the other hand, after a year, the religious began an uprising in Istanbul in 1909. In order to suppress the insurgency, the troops of the Movement Army of Thessaloniki entered Istanbul and Abdülhamit, who was in close contact with the religious circles, was dethroned. Meanwhile, in the same year, the first National Mason High Council was established and all the chambers in the country were connected to this Supreme Council.[39]

After the First World War, in the process of disintegration of the empire was initiated by Mustafa Kemal Pasha in the War of Independence there were no important functions. However, the leading forces at the beginning of the war were people who grew up in the Union and Mason quarries and shared the same belief: Freedom.

First Grand National Assembly of Turkey the first Prime Minister Rauf Orbay, however, Ali Fethi the first prime minister of the Republic of Turkey Okyar, General Kazim Karabekir, General Kazim Ozalp, Republican People's Party general secretary Şükrü Kaya, the first government of the Minister of Interior General Rafet Bele, still Atatürk era foreign minister Tevfik Rüştü Aras, another Interior minister Mehmet Cemil did Uyba, Turkey's first ambassador to Washington, Mukhtar Tahsin and Atatürk's the closest colleagues, MP Jawad Abbas proud to be a Mason, Masonic beliefs, War of Independence established in and after what the Republic of Turkey show that it is effective.[40] Atatürk and his staff, renaissance and enlightenment held in the Christian world as a result of the reform, a Muslim country, performing secular system in Turkey and became the first team are successfully implementing. Sultanate and Caliphate abolished, Turkey has reached only a Muslim country in modern civilization and the ability to capture real democracy. Freemasonry today, as in other democracies based on free thought, to protect the secular and democratic system in Turkey, serves falling over.

References

1   Boucher Jules, Naudon Paul, - *This Unknown Masonry (Masonluk Bu Meçhul)*, Okat Pub., Istanbul 1966, p 33.

2   Bayet Albert, - *History of Thought Against Religion (Dine Karşı Düşünce Tarihi)*, Broy Pub., Istanbul 1991, p. 45.

3   Michael Baigent, Leigh Richard, - *Temple and Lodge (Mabet ve Loca)*, Emre Pub., Istanbul 2000, p. 160

4   Michael B., Leigh R., r.w., p. 161

5   Bayet A., r.w., p. 74

6   Michael B., Leigh R., r.w., p. 164

7   Bayet A., r.w., p. 65

8   Ülke Faruk. Yazıcıoğlu A. Semih, - *Freemasonry in the world and Turkey (Dünyada ve Türkiye'de Masonluk)*, Başak Pub., Istanbul 1965, p. 55

9   Michael Baigent. Leigh Richard, - *Holy Grail; Holy Blood (Kutsal Kâse; Kutsal Kan)*, Emre Pub., Istanbul 1996, p. 154

10 Tecimer, Ömer - *Rose and Cross (Gül ve Haç)* Plan B Pub., Istanbul 2004, p. 100

11 Naudon, Paul - *The Roots of Freemasonry (Masonluğun Kökenleri)*, Homer Pub., Istanbul 2007, p. 257

12 Michael B., Leigh R., r.w., p. 168

13 Michael B., Leigh R., r.w., p. 165

14 Michael B., Leigh R., r.w., p. 184

15 Michael B., Leigh R., r.w., p. 183

16 Naudon Paul, - *Freemasonry in History and Today (Tarihte ve Günümüzde Masonluk)*, Varlık Pub., Istanbul Istanbul 1968, p. 50.

17 Benson, Michael - *Secret Communities Glossary (Gizli Topluluklar Sözlüğü)* Neden Pub., Istanbul 2005, p. 64

18 Michael B., Leigh R., r.w., p. 199

19 Michael B., Leigh R., r.w., p. 201

20 Naudon P., r.w., p. 76

21 Naudon P., r.w., p. 52

22 Boucher J. Naudon P., r.w., p. 21

23 Ayan Tamer, - *Double Headed Eagle (Çift Başlı Kartal)*, İtidal Olgunlaşma Pub., Istanbul 1998, p. 299

24 Michael B., Leigh R., r.w., p. 211

25 Ülkü F. Yazıcıoğlu A.P., r.w., p. 47

26 Naudon P., r.w., p. 95

27 Ülkü F. Yazıcıoğlu A.P., r.w., p. 43

28 Altındal, Aytunç - *Brotherhood of Rose and Cross (Gül ve Haç Kardeşliği)* Alfa Pub., Istanbul, 2004, p. 220

29 Michael B. Leigh R., - *Holy Grail, Holy Blood (Kutsal Kâse, Kutsal Kan)* Emre Pub., Istanbul, p. 164.

30 Signier, Jean Francois Thomazo, Renaud - *Secret Organizations (Gizli Örgütler)* Larousse Oğlak Güzel Kitaplar, Istanbul 2006, p. 148

31 Signier, Jean Francois. Thomazo, Renaud - r.w., p. 111

32 Michael B., Leigh R., r.w., p. 235

33 Michael B., Leigh R., r.w., p. 238

34 Benson, Michael, r.w., p. 75

35 Soysal İlhami, - *Masonry and Masons in the World and Turkey (Türkiye'de ve Dünyada Masonluk ve Masonlar)*, Der Pub., Istanbul 1978, p. 382

36 Koloğlu Orhan, - *Unionists and Masons (İttihatçılar ve Masonlar)*, Gür Pub., Istanbul 1991, p. 72

37 Koloğlu O., r.w., p. 26

38 Koloğlu O., r.w., p. 41

39 Ülkü F. Yazıcıoğlu A.P., r.w., p. 294

40 Tunaşar Seyhun, - *Our brothers who left their mark on the Republic (Cumhuriyete Damgasını Vuran Kardeşlerimiz)*, Mimar Sinan Journal, 2002, Vol. 126, p. 1352

CHAPTER XII

MASONARY AND ESOTERISM

The esoteric doctrine begins to be given to the initiates in the Freemasonry, at the degree of apprentice, which is only the first degree. Opening a Worshipful Master, director of the lodge, "A Mason should occasionally move away from the concerns of daily life and begin to contemplate. That is when our thoughts begin to rise towards the Supreme Being we call the Great Architect of the Universe, our work gives us new forces, "he says. As can be seen from this statement, the goal is to reach the true truth in Freemasonry, to reach the Supreme Being.

To the east of the lodge, there is a Sun, a Moon and an Eye symbol in the Triangle behind in the middle of the Worshipful Master's chair. As we see in the teachings of Naacal and Hermes, the Sun is the masculine symbol of God, the Moon is the feminine symbol. The eye in the triangle reminds that God's eye is always on human beings. As with other esoteric schools, in the Freemasonry, the president, the Worshipful Master, is the expression of the divine will within the chamber. Therefore, absolute obedience to itself is essential. Worshipful Master sits in the east, referring to the sunrise. A lodge begins to work symbolically when the first lights of the sun emerge, that is when divine enlightenment exists.

Masons work to make an ideal temple for all mankind. This task of Freemasonry will only come to an end when all people reach perfection. According to the Freemasons, the greatest quality God has given to humans is Reason. People are responsible for searching for Good, Truth and Beauty by using their minds. The Mason sanctuary stands on three pillars. These are Mind, Force and Beauty. Brotherhood's greatest wish is to spread the love of Brotherhood all over the world.

The opening ceremony of Freemasonry is also a synthesis of the methods used by the supporters of an esoteric doctrine in their organizations. The candidate is first taken to a closed cell and is left with his thoughts. In this room, the word in Vitriol is used by the old Alchemists and Knights is remarkable.[1]

The candidate is then blindfolded and taken to the sanctuary where three symbolic journeys are made, as Dante described in the Divine Comedy.[2] Before the journey begins, the island is asked if he believes in God. If the candidate confirms his belief in God, the ceremony may continue. Otherwise, it will be rejected. In fact, the candidate's belief in God was also investigated in his request form. Upon being seen that he is a man who believes in God, he is invited to the ceremony.

The first journey in the temple is quite difficult and in the end, the candidate is subject to the Water exam. At the end of the second journey, which is easier, there is the Fire exam, and the third exam, which is very easy, is the Soil exam. These exams, which were extremely arduous in the old ages, gradually became easier in the direction of the development of civilization and now they have become symbolic. After the voyages, the island is reminded that it is up to him to go beyond extinction or death. The diet oath is repeated in every degree. The oath is made by remembering the name of the Great Architect of the Universe and seizing upon the Holy Books. Then, the bond in the eyes of the candidate opens and sees the Divine Light of Truth. He is now an Apprentice Hall.

At the centre of the temple, at least one of the three divine religions, Judaism, Christianity, and the Holy Scriptures of Islam is located on the seat of the oath. In accordance with the beliefs of the members of a lodge, one of the holy books may be open, and if there are members of all three religions, they are all open. The adoption of all three books shows that for Masonry the secondary differences between religions do not matter, the only truth is to believe in the existence of God. The Bible is kept open during the studies. This is an expression of the tolerance of Freemasonry against all religions. The Worshipful Master, states that, as the work begins, the Truth of Divine illuminates the work. The existence of holy books, regardless of their religion, shows that the Freemasons believe in One God.[3]

In the Turkish Freemasonry where there are brothers from all three religions, the need to keep three books on the oath, even in meetings where there was no one other than a different religion, the practice of keeping three of the holy books open was continued.

Preacher, told the new apprentice that his mission was to get rid of all imperfections and that Freemasonry would help him to achieve that. The individual must always control himself and thus, must constantly evolve by turning towards the right, the good and the beautiful. In all buildings, the foundation stone is placed in the north-east of the building. Therefore, the new apprentice representing the cornerstone of Lodge.[4]

The aim of the initiation ceremony is to awaken the internal intuition and to make an effort to inform the new member. As A. Makey points out, Freemasonry aims to reveal the light that exists in the minds of its members. For this reason, the Masons also qualify themselves as "Children of Light."

Step by step, the new apprenticeship uses the Symbols Language. Thanks to this very old and universal teaching method, the esoteric doctrine has never moved away from modernity and rationality by the fact that the symbols can be loaded into the symbols of the age in every age.[5]

The initiation ceremony is the first step in which the Mason reaches God. The goal of Freemasonry is to evolve its members. This evolution, however, is limited to each individual's own capacity. The old words are a sea of Freemasonry, but every Mason can take water from him, up to the greatness of the container in his hands.[6]

Jan says, "God is in you." As a matter of fact, the Christian Freemasons vow, You do on the Jan Bible. In the Christian world, the first three degree lodges are also called "Jan Janis". In a book published in 1742, a foreign Mason asked to know the "Where do you come from?" The answer to the question, "Sen Jan Lodge" seems to be in the form. As mentioned earlier, Yoanna embodies the Gospel, the Esoteric aspect of Jesus' teaching.[6] Freemasonry also believes that God is in humanity, as stated in each school of esotericism. Freemasonry, defending the identity of the man to God, believes in God, the Universe, and the Human Unity, and it is stated that Freemasonry is universal in the light of this belief. The fusion of the individual with the entire humanity and the universe enables the common bond between them, the bond of love, and this love is the only way to reach the Great Architect of the Universe. Goethe, who is also a Mason, expresses this feeling:

> "No matter how big the heart,
> Fill it with the invisible object.
> Give him the name you want;
> Happiness, Love, Heart, God ...
> The name is nothing but noise.
> A magnet that hides the glory of the heavens from us ...[7]

It is the supremacy of God's supremacy in Freemasonry. Therefore, there is no difference in religion between people. Believing in the Supreme Being, but staying away from all kinds of dogma within the religion, is a condition to be a Mason.

In 1924, in a Great Lodge meeting held in New York, the uniqueness of God and the God of all people, the sacred books were only light for the Freemasons is explained. In this statement, which emphasizes the belief of soullessness, it is stated that the most important task of a Mason is to love God and man. Freemasonry advocates the belief that the body is dead and the soul is alive, and those who want to become Mason are also asked whether they believe in the Immortality of Spirit, just like their belief in God. Those who are not in this belief are not included in the association.[8]

In a meeting held in Lausanne in 1875, it was announced that the Masonic doctrine included recognition of the existence of a superior force, that this being was declared under the name of The Great Architect of the Universe and that Freemasonry was a Brotherhood Organization.

The name Grand Architect of the Universe is the Master of the Great Geometry. This style of expression is in harmony with the character of the "Divine Geometry Masters", which Esoteric doctrine has been using for thousands of years.

In the ceremony of transition from apprenticeship to fellowcraft the candidate is asked to create a complete and perfect work. The Worshipful Master, says: "This is such a work that it should be a symbol of justice and love. This work is taught to the student who is astonished. This expression is nothing but the expression that God exists in man. One of the most important symbols of Freemasonry is the five-pointed star. The symbol, which we see that Hermes and Pythagoras have used since the Nacals, is also human. But Freemasonry added a letter "G" to the middle of this star. The star is the man himself, the letter "G" symbolizes the divine principle, God. In other words, God is in man. The word "G" placed in the United States for the first time in the US means God in English, it is thought to be derived from "God", or "Master of the Supreme Geometry".

Masonic Blazing Star

Another symbol in the middle with the letter "G" is perhaps the most well-known Masonic symbol in the world, Square and Compass. The square symbolizes the divine justice, and the compass symbolizes the universe with the ability to comprehend the infinity. The coexistence of the two at the same time remembers the Man of Man.

Square and Compass

The third degree of ascension into the Master is divided into faith in the immortality of the soul. In this ceremony Hiram, the great architect who built the Temple of Solomon was used as a symbol. Hiram is not a Jew. That is, it is far from the dogmatic aspect of religion. However, he also believes in a Supreme Being and builds a temple in his name. Hiram prefers death to avoid secrets of mastery to be known. In this ceremony, the symbolic death and rebirth of the candidate are revived and attention is drawn to the fact that individual works are limited to human life, and that the common effort of all human beings is immortality. At this level, the expression of God is "the Supreme of the Supreme". He argued that there were many Almighty people who used this expression as a remembrance of God, and therefore God could only be called the "Supreme of the Highest". This way of expression proves the close connection between the esoteric doctrine of Pythagoras and the Masonic Esoteric doctrine.

According to Freemasonry, the journey from birth to death must be the purpose of evolution. It is also emphasized that science supports reason and wisdom in the path of evolution and that Freemasonry is always in favour of rationality and science.

At higher degrees, the esoteric teaching continues to be given to the initiating step by step. The famous Mason writer Paul Naudon classifies Masonic degrees as follows:

In the first three degrees, the esoteric first steps are taken to the initiates and they are also taught to master them. From degrees 4 to 18 degrees, the members recognize the universe, and through love, the goal of universalization is shown to them. From the 19th to the 30th degrees, the ways in which human beings first identify with the universe and with God are taught. The next three degrees are only administrative degrees.[7] Whether to continue to the higher degrees above the first three degrees, called evolution or maturation degrees, depends on each Freemason's free will. Since the first three levels are given an overview of the doctrine, the Masons who want to get to know the doctrine better are going on their evolution.

Freemasonry rejects supernatural forces and miracles. He argues that under reasonable conditions, the mind will evolve despite all sorts of obstacles outside. The reason is the primary means of evolution. The purpose of evolution is to seek the truth. The last truth that man can find is the existence of the universe and the opening of the secrets of life. However, to reach these secrets, the only reason is not enough. The mind can mature to a point. From this point onwards, intuition starts because the reason is insufficient. Thus, we can say that the true evolution of the soul and the most important means of reaching God is the Intuition power under the guidance of the Mind. Man hides the spark that can turn into a great flame on his way to God, in his own being. The important thing is to reveal this spark. This is only possible with the education of intuition power as well as an education in the proper direction.

Freemasonry, since ancient times, against all kinds of religious and political, idols, and all kinds of dogmas against demolition are among the most important duties. Small-minded big people are convinced that only God has universal intelligence. They cannot understand that this intelligence is actually produced by combining the intelligence of all human beings throughout human history. The most powerful weapons used by Masonry to oppose dogma are rationality, freedom of opinion and belief, and tolerance through the guidance of science. While Freemasonry was tolerant of all religions, it prohibited religious and political debates in the lodges in order to avoid restricting their members' freedom of opinion and belief and to avoid unnecessary discussions.

According to Masonic thought, nothing in the universe has an end or beginning. Everything is in constant development and change. This can be explained by the laws of evolution and movement that dominate the universe. The universe is in constant motion and growth within the framework of these laws. Man is part of the universe, and only in him is the ability to grasp the truth. Freemasonry does not accept the idea of God from anything. God is Divine Light/Love, Spirit is Khaki, Justice, Work, and Love. God is forbidden and infinite. It is the centre of truth and the source of attraction for all souls that have come out of it. All souls are immortal and are constantly striving to reach God. The eternity of space, time and life and the eternity of God are the same things.

The ritual of the construction of the Temple of Solomon is the most common ritual practice of medieval Masons. In this esoteric ritual, the Temple symbolizes the Macrocosm, while the human symbolizes the Microcosm. The temple of Solomon is a symbol.

The true temple of God is Man. The testimonies of the greatest miracle, God is man, and Man is God, are found in the Masonic Dumfries Manuscripts of 1710.[8] The universe is identical to God. In the microcosm, there is also Macrocosm. Man always sees him in the smallest reach he can reach. Non-living beings are transformed into living beings by a combination of certain conditions. Microorganisms reach simple animals, these animals are more developed and mammals, as the final stages, the ape species, and finally the human being, the last link in the chain. Inteligence, the most distinctive feature of life, appears even in the simplest animals, reaches the highest level of human expression. Man is the only creature that can think and reach certain results and convey these results to the next generation. The person who thinks that the extraordinary order around him cannot be a coincidence, with the help of his mind and intuition, he can comprehend the existence of God.

However, the concept of God is often corrupted, God's love is forgotten, it has been taught to approach with fear. By those who claim to have exchanged with God, He has been turned into a being to be feared. The doctrines in this direction have led to the formation of many dogmas, wisdom and replaced them with bigotry and darkness. For this reason, one of the important tasks of the Masons is to examine the history of philosophy and religions and to reveal the true truth against those who claim to be in the truth. Freemasonry argues that the history of religions is, in fact, the history of mankind, that every religion is influenced by its predecessors, and all are based on a common basis.[9]

Like all Esoteric schools before him, Freemasonry adopts the view that the four basic elements of the universe are Fire, Water, Air and Earth. For Freemasonry, the force over time is the proof of God outside time. The matter is transformed into force, ie energy, as the matter is born in the universe at any moment. Nature tends to mature and mature.

The number seven has a special significance in Freemasonry. As in the Pythagorean school and Sabism, this number reminds the seven planets or seven basic elements of the universe. Freemasonry has a symbolic meaning for each of the seven planets. Each of the planets is a symbol of God's faith, hope, compassion, will, prudence, honour and justice. It is also stated that the number 7 is the expression of seven natural colours and seven notes and divine will.

Another Masonic symbol, number 3 and trilogy. Everything in Freemasonry is almost as if it were built on the number three and trilogy. The Master degree, which is the third degree for Freemasonry, is the most important degree and all the secrets of the doctrine are so hidden. Therefore, a Mason who has reached mastery has also reached maturity. As mentioned earlier, only those who want to do a more detailed examination and learn more deeply the doctrines can continue to the higher degrees. This is not a must.

A lodge rises above three basic columns. These are the columns of Beauty, Force and Mind. The Miter on the oath table forms a trilogy of compasses and holy books. The manor, the Worshipful Master, and his two assistantsthe Wardens, namely the three men. The master symbol of the Worshipful Master, representing the absolute will, is the triple light behind it. In the East, Moon, Sun and Triangle Eye symbols make up another trilogy. According to a Masonic myth, Hermes engraved the secret name of God on a triangular gold plate with its tip down. This gold triangle was then made of a chamber with nine arch domes, which was engraved on the gate, and this gold plate containing the secret of Hermes was hidden under the bottom dome. Then a temple was built on them.[10]

In Pythagoras' teachings, the number 10 is the symbol of perfection, the Kamil Man identified with God. In the Freemasonry, the highest level secrets of the doctrine, which leads the initiate to perfection, are given at the 30th degree, which is ten times the three. In addition, Freemasonry, the highest degree is 33 degrees, and in every Supreme Council, only 33 people are given this degree. 33 degree symbolizes the head above the spine.[11]

The number 3 and the trilogy are used in many places in Freemasonry. As an example, we can give the Masonic Alphabet. The alphabet and key are as follows:[12]

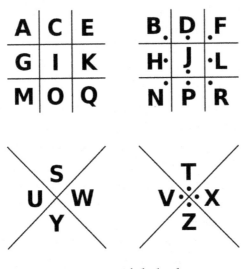

Masonic Alphabeth

"The whole argument of Freemasonry is that the soul has a spark to the eternal God's existence and that therefore is immortal. In the human, it can be said that the divine object is united with the human object. What follows is as above. The universe is a large scale. Isn't that the miracle of unity?"

References

1   Boucher Jules, Naudon Paul, - *This Unknown Masonary (Masonluk Bu Meçhul)*, Okat Pub., Istanbul 1966, p. 123

2   Erman Sahir, - *Esoteric Interpretation of Dante and Divine Comedy (Dante ve İlahi Komedyanın Ezoterik Yorumu)*, Yenilik Pub., Istanbul 1977, p. 11

3   Ülke Faruk. Yazıcıoğlu A. Semih, - *Freemasonary in the world and Turkey (Dünyada ve Türkiye'de Masonluk)*, Başak Pub., Istanbul 1965, p. 129

4   Knight, Christopher; Lomas, Robert - *The Hiram Book (Hiramın Kitabı)*, Bilge Karınca Pub., Istanbul 2008, p. 27

5   Naudon Paul, - *Freemasonary in History and Today (Tarihte ve Günümüzde Masonluk)*, Varlık Pub., Istanbul Istanbul 1968, p. 139

6   Naudon P., r.w., p. 121

7   Ülke F. Yazıcıoğlu A.P., r.w., p. 190

8   Naudon, Paul - *The Roots of Freemasoanry (Masonluğun Kökenleri)*, Homer Pub., Istanbul Istanbul 2007, p. 238

9   Naudon P., r.w., p. 150

10 Tecimer, Ömer - *Rose and Cross (Gül ve Haç)* Plan B Pub., Istanbul 2004, p. 31

11 Giz Benson, Michael - *Secret Communities Glossary (Gizli Topluluklar Sözlüğü)* Neden Pub., Istanbul 2005, p. 58

12 Boucher J. Naudon P., r.w., p. 17

LAST WORD

Like all other Esoteric schools, Freemasonry also claims to be universal. This universality is the result of being identical with all humanity and the universe. For the initiate to the secret of the doctrine, this secret is essential for the individual to identify with humanity and the universal being. The Freemasonry, which has reached the position of the most prominent advocate and practitioner of the esoteric doctrine by passing through the filters of the ages, is the teaching of how this identification can be achieved in a certain harmony. Many institutions such as Sion, Alevism, Druze and Ismailism still continue to practice the esoteric doctrine, but these institutions have not been able to renew themselves in line with the requirements of the era and their teachings have lagged behind the age at some point. In order to maintain their existence, they have to accept some religious discourses have turned into dogmas in time and have led to the elimination of the rationalism of esoterism.

Although Freemasonry, for a short period of time, gave the impression that it was under the influence of Christianity, he knew how to get out of this situation quickly, and in accordance with the structure of the esoteric doctrine, Mind and Wisdom succeeded in making him a leader. The Masons, who succeeded in using the symbolic language of the esoteric doctrine, made it possible to adapt the symbols to the realities of today and to adopt new meanings in the light of progressive science. Thus, in transferring the teaching to the next generations, Freemasonry was a Key Stone.

Freemasonry, the practitioner of esoterism, has played a very active role in achieving the world at a contemporary level in the fields of art, literature, philosophy, religion and society. Especially in the 18th century, Freemasonry, which was able to combine mysticism with reason, managed to maintain Creative Consciousness, which is the only conception of the Absolute.

The science tells us that the universe is in constant development. In other words, the universe is in constant growth, and evolution. The existence of evolution has been proved by the development of world life. Evolution is dynamic and creative. Esoteric doctrine is the most vivid and accurate evidence of the rise towards perfection. Evolution is an expression of a rise to the Great Architect of the Universe.

Some thinkers claim that Freemasonry is Deist. Freemasonry does not accept anyone entering between God and man. In all the heavenly religions, the purpose of life is to be rewarded in the other world. Monotheistic religions say that if they become good people, they will go to heaven, otherwise they will go to hell. In Freemasonry, the goal is very different, like the other schools of Esoteric beliefs. He leads his Masonic professors to strive to achieve excellence. However, he argues that good people can reach the stage of Kamil Man and approach God.

In theism, God is the owner of every living thing. However, none of the celestial religions does make sense of the fact that God, who has such a saving on human beings, is the only desire, that each one is good, but why, by using his power, he does not create them all as well. On the other hand, in esotericism, they have the freedom to determine their future with their will, and as a result, they have access to perfection.

In addition, the miracles and dogmas within the religions are the cases that Freemasonry rejects. Freemasonry and other esoteric organizations have been struggling with orthodox beliefs of religions for thousands of years. For these reasons, Freemasonry is certainly not of theism.

On the other hand, Freemasonry is not Deism. Because, according to the Deist belief, God is only the first reason. It's a creature and it's done with creation. Freemasonry is a school of Esoteric Teach, which argues that God exists not from the wound but from himself. Deism denies that there is an ongoing relationship between God and the universe, while Freemasonry advocates the unity of God-universe-human and the idea that the universe constantly flows towards God. Deism does not clarify what God has done with the creation, what it does or what it is. Freemasonry says that God will continue to exist forever. Rationalism is at the forefront of Deism. The most important reason for defining Freemasonry as Deism is that rationalism is kept superior in both beliefs. But while Freemasonry attaches great importance to rationalism as well as Creative Intuition, Deism definitely rejects it.

Deism, like intuition, does not accept the existence of the soul because it has no scientific explanation. In Freemasonry, the unfaithfulness of Spirit is one of the most important beliefs. In addition, every Mason, the oath in all of the great architect of the Universe wishes to help him. This wish is proof that God's work for the Freemasons is not yet over and that he is not drawn to a corner.

This is why Freemasonry, nor Theism, nor Deism, to be expressed in a philosophical way; Freemasonry is Pantheism.

"Comments never claim to be a" Final Word "or "to be "... ... to write the foreword of this book. Dr this statement by Sahir Erman is a warning for both the theses in this book and the Freemasonry itself.

Just as many other Esoteric schools have disappeared in history, Freemasonry can also be buried one day in the dusty pages of history. However, by using human intelligence and intuition, there will surely be someone who will pass the esoteric doctrine to the next generation.

Cihangir Gener